Yale Agrarian Studies Series
James C. Scott, Series Editor

The Agrarian Studies Series at Yale University Press seeks to publish outstanding and original interdisciplinary work on agriculture and rural society—for any period, in any location. Works of daring that question existing paradigms and fill abstract categories with the lived experience of rural people are especially encouraged.

—*James C. Scott, Series Editor*

For a complete list of titles in the Yale Agrarian Studies Series, visit yalebooks.com/agrarian.

Collecting Food, Cultivating People

Subsistence and Society
in Central Africa

Kathryn M. de Luna

Foreword by Elizabeth Colson

Yale
UNIVERSITY PRESS
NEW HAVEN AND LONDON

Published with assistance from the Louis Stern Memorial Fund.

Yale University Press books may be purchased in quantity for educational, business, or promotional use. For information, please e-mail sales.press@yale.edu (U.S. office) or sales@yaleup.co.uk (U.K. office).

Set in Fournier type by Westchester Book Group.
Printed in the United States of America.

Library of Congress Control Number: 2016935621
ISBN: 978-0-300-21853-4 (hardcover : alk. paper)

A catalogue record for this book is available from the British Library.

This paper meets the requirements of ANSI/NISO Z39.48-1992 (Permanence of Paper).

10 9 8 7 6 5 4 3 2 1

For Sean, Mialoh, and Torin, with love and gratitude

There was a certain man, who used to hunt animals
continually every day, until he was gazed at every day.

—"Chief of the Fishes," a Tonga folktale (J. R. Fell,
Folk Tales of the BaTonga and Other Sayings)

Contents

Foreword

> It could be argued that biased historical anecdotes, ill-understood
> patterns of early language development, and hard archaeological "facts"
> —the artefacts, Ecofacts, and structures of the past recovered through
> excavation—should not, and indeed cannot, be brought together to create
> a coherent picture of the past. This position is firmly taken by some and
> energetically argued; it is not one with which I have much sympathy.
> —Barry Cunliffe, *The Ancient Celts*

I too have little sympathy for a position that recognizes no possibility of learning about the past of those for whom there is only recent written evidence. You have to be a skilled detective to find historical traces of people like Bantu Botatwe speakers. The earliest published accounts that mention them date, I believe, to about 1850. Their own traditions take one little further back. Anyone looking for earlier traces of them must depend on other kinds of clues: those provided by language, ethnography, archaeological artifacts, genetic maps, or the study of past climates and related shifts in the distribution of plants and animals.

Kathryn de Luna has exercised great ingenuity and imagination in combining her skills as a historian with the findings of linguists, archaeologists, anthropologists, and climatologists to produce the first history of the million or more people in south central Africa who today speak dialects of Bantu Botatwe, a branch of Bantu that seems to have emerged about 1000 BCE. The territory they occupied by 1850 now comprises much of Central, Lusaka, and Southern Provinces in Zambia, spilling across the Zambezi River into Namibia, Botswana, and Zimbabwe. Those living within Zambia have begun to think of themselves as having a common political identity vis-à-vis other peoples of that country despite the different names under which they are officially recognized. Increasingly they want to be recognized as people with a history though their legends and recorded historical memories do not carry one much beyond the beginning of the nineteenth century.

Over the last half century and more I have carried out ethnographic research among Botatwe speakers, specifically the Plateau and Gwembe Tonga in Southern Province, Zambia. In the 1940s and 1950s, when I asked about their history, they talked about what had happened in their own lifetimes and about events experienced by their parents and grandparents. Genealogies were shallow. Of more far-reaching events, they had experienced or knew of raids by Lozi, Chikunda, and Ndebele bands that devastated Gwembe and Plateau Tonga villages in the last half of the nineteenth century, and the arrival of Europeans, first as explorers and then as colonial rulers. When archaeologists began exploring Iron Age sites in Zambia in the late 1940s and 1950s, the history of these people shot backwards almost a thousand years, to the early years of the second millennium. This meant, they were told, that their ancestors were among the first, if they were not the first, Bantu speakers to arrive in Zambia. It has become a proud claim among many who now see themselves as descendants of the "first settlers," an important status over much of Africa. Therefore, they say, they have a special relationship to the land that ought to be recognized by later comers.

Kathryn de Luna, the first scholar to collect linguistic information from speakers of most of the dialects of Bantu Botatwe, has now provided them with a history beginning early in the first millennium before the present era when pro-Bantu Botatwe differentiated from other Bantu languages. In this book she describes how subsequent population movements led to the occupation of diverse ecological environments and encounters with non-Botatwe speakers. From such experiences, together with normal linguistic drift, emerged the Botatwe dialects spoken today. Linguistic clues provide evidence of encounters with non-Botatwe speakers, archaeological evidence provides a means of dating the borrowing or invention of new technologies (including new crops and domesticated animals), and evidence from the study of past climates date and explain periods of population expansion and retreat. These, in turn, date the emergence of vocabularies linked to new experiences and so provide dates for the emergence of present-day Botatwe dialects.

This is an imaginative and lively reconstruction. De Luna never forgets that what happened was the result of the choices and actions of men, women, and children whose ingenuity was sparked by curiosity and a desire to impress others. Her reconstruction also challenges earlier ideas about the routes that Botatwe people traveled to reach their present destinations. She shows the importance of the Kafue River and its floodplains in their early history and as a refuge area to which those colonizing other ecological zones withdrew when dryer climatic conditions made the new areas less hospitable. Another surprise is the evidence for an early colonization of the wetlands, to the south and east of the Kafue hook, that border on the eastern Zambezi floodplain well before the Botatwe occupation of the Tonga Plateau and Gwembe Valley. Perhaps less surprising is the linguistic evidence that most Botatwe speakers throughout the centuries have clung to the egalitarian ethic and lack of respect for authority vested in hierarchical organization structures that have characterized them throughout the nineteenth and twentieth centuries.

De Luna has made a major contribution to the history of south central Africa and demonstrated once again the rich possibilities for probing the past afforded by a multiple disciplinary approach. Her work should stimulate new research, which will in turn challenge her reconstruction. Here new archaeological and linguistic studies and genetic mapping will be important. The last will lead to a new understanding of the complexity of the biological heritage of Botatwe speakers. But new research will now build on the foundation provided by de Luna. Subsequent workers will be indebted to her.

Elizabeth Colson
Professor Emeritus,
University of California, Berkeley

Acknowledgments

Behind the words on the following pages stands a supportive network of colleagues, teachers, friends, and family. This book could not have been written without the hospitality of families and friends in Zambia, Botswana, and Namibia, who endured grueling hours of questioning with a deep well of patience and the warmest hospitality in 2004, 2005–6, 2010, 2011, and 2014. The knowledge in this book belongs to the men and women who agreed to walk me through the bush and to share their meals and homes, naming objects, actions, and concepts every step of the way. This list of interlocutors is partial; not everyone wanted their name associated with a research project that asked people to talk about activities of which some are illegal. But I appreciate equally the help of both the named and the anonymous, listed here as they wished to be known: Elina Cabbage; Milliam Chasa; Samson Ntaulu Chibiya; Frederick Chikuta and wives; Maria Chikuta; Evans Chimwaya; Catherine Matafela Dambe; Charles Disho; Sharon Dobe; Alice Habanyama and family and neighbors; Anges Hamelumbe; John Hanamaila; Elizabeth Kaffi; Liyuba Kahundu; Robin Kajiko; Nsefwe Kalundu; Reverend Ozias Kamwi; Dismoni Kamwi; Edith Mbaliki Kasale; Kasalu Kasanda; Lambi Kashikwa; Beatrice Kashinka; Tommy Kazoka; Patson Kero and colleagues of the Mukuni woodshop; Kenneth Masiala Kufwa,; Patricia Kuzibuka; Regina Lilanda; Jonathan Mumani Liteta; Regina Lwambi; Noreen Majanga; Dolika Makole; Beatrice Makole; James Makole; Bruno Makole; Georgina Makondo; the hunter Patrick Malaya; Edina Mangala; Petrona Masaka and neighbors and friends; Josephine Masiziani; Catherine Maswabi with family, neighbors, and colleagues in the market; Ruben Matambo; Agnes Matimba; Mackson Mayungono; Claris Miyoba; Joshua Moonga; Raphael Moonga; Mbiyana Morongwe; Edie Motho; Moses Mowa; Josephine Nanzala Msiiwa and other market women; Catherine Mudenda and friends; Bors Mugwanda; Timothy Mukanda and wives and neighbors; Andrew Dixon Mukutu with family, neighbors, and friends; Peter Mulonga and family; Francis Mungu and neighbors and friends; Kasaila Munihango; Felicitas Munkomba; Christina Munshindu; Benson Sitongo Muroto; Brave Mushabati; Zinnia Musole; Samuel Muswolomoki; Charles Iluba Mutumba; Muzingili Muwanei; Savior Muzeta; Theresa Mwangala; Mercy Mwashalenga; Philmour John Mwashalenga; Shadrick M. Mwayisithiya; Mr. Rabson Mwemba; Justin Mwiinga; Maria Namwemba; Estnat Nasilele; Zindoga Ncube; Jackie Ng'andu; Kelezo Njekwa; Martha Nkamu; Lillian Ntalasha; Malita Njambe Nukamapulanga; Kerrister Matakala Numwa; Tubalike Numwa; Richard Nzundamo; Mapayi Rularo; the healer Masene Samunzala; "Joyce" Mulike Seta; Godfrid Levi Makankila Shamulenge and neighbors and friends; Ian Shamulenge; Jennifer Shimbabo; Eunice Shimbabo; Shedrick Shashembengo; Wilson Chidi Siachinga; Victor Siamani; Phillimon Siamisindo; John Sianene; Martin Sibwidu; Ellen Sikalumbu and family; Senior Headman Naluchele Golias Sikombe; Jennifer Sikusibwidu; Goliath Sikwelukuba; Her Highness Bedyango Siloka I; Alfred Simanungu; Patrice Sisoowe; Victor M. Sitongo; Mapenzi Tubalike with daughters, grandchildren, male neighbors, and an unnamed village hunter; Godwin Tuhemwe; and Fabian Tutavuke.

On many trips to Africa, I enjoyed the help, hospitality, and company of Sue Hancock, Kim Phippen, Remmy Chibiya, Reggie and Mbiyana Morongwe, Jacky Ng'andu, Brave Mushabati, Beatrice Makole, and Elizabeth Colson. Elizabeth's generosity and fireside conversations sparked many a reassessment of my ideas, even those with which she might beg to differ! Other colleagues in Africa provided assistance at key moments in research: Neil Parsons, Wilfred Haacke, Peter Manchishi, Yizenge Chondoka, the late Father Vincent, Father Wafer, Vincent Katanekwa, Collins Kabyema, and Nicholas Katanekwa. Financial support and time to write were generously provided by Fulbright-Hays, various departments and institutions at Northwestern University, the History Department and Humanities Research Center at Rice University, and the College at Georgetown University.

Portions of this book were previously published as articles: "Hunting Reputations: Talent, Individuals, and Communities in Precolonial South Central Africa," *Journal of African History* 53, no. 3 (2012): 279–99 and "Affect and Society in Precolonial Africa," *International Journal of African Historical Studies* 46, no. 1 (2013): 123–50. This material is reprinted with permission from Cambridge University Press and the editor of the *International Journal of African Historical Studies*, respectively. Further material is reproduced with kind permission from Springer Science+Business Media: "Surveying the Boundaries of Historical Linguistics and Archaeology: Early Settlement in South Central Africa," *African Archaeological Review* 29, no. 2/3 (2012): 209–51. For help with illustrations, I thank Ellen Feingold, David Hagen, Mr. Lungu, Ms. Emmah Nakapizye, Prof. Macwang'i, Mr. Siulapwa, Mr. Bwalya, and Stephanie Kitchen. The beautiful maps must be credited to Jean Aroom of the GIS/Data Center, Fondren Library, Rice University. Jean Thomson Black at Yale University Press gave the project unwavering support from its earliest form as a "shot in the dark" book proposal. The Yale team, especially Samantha Ostrowski and Ann-Marie Imbornoni, ensured that the process was enjoyable. Eliza Childs's keen eye saved me from many an error during a time of great transition.

If books come at the end of long journeys, this one began in Ron Atkinson's classroom. Without his inspiring teaching, I would never have become a historian, much less one of precolonial Africa. If Ron set me down a path, it was a path carved out by the small but lively group of scholars who write histories from singular words. More than most historical fields, these practitioners depend on each other to share attestations, field notes, and hunches; I've learned from each of them. I am most indebted to David Schoenbrun for introducing me to this world. David mastered the delicate dance of a good mentor: pushing me forward and backing off, taming my flights of fancy and encouraging me when I elected to explore topics like "subsistence" that were staid, dry, and even tired or topics like "reputations" that were rather unconventional in precolonial historiography. Somehow David still manages to find time to read, comment, and encourage; I am grateful to remain his student. During my time at Northwestern, I had the pleasure to learn from a community of scholars at that institution and beyond, including Timothy Earle, Jon Glassman, Jane Guyer, Bill Murphy, Chap Kusimba, and Andrew Reid.

I've benefited from the generosity of time and spirit shared by a host of colleagues, especially Susan McIntosh, Kairn Klieman, Kerry Ward, Becky Goetz, Aysha Pollnitz, Lora Wildenthal, John McNeill, John Tutino, and Carol Benedict. Jeffrey Fleisher and Meredith McKittrick are in a class of their own as close collaborators, role models, and, most important, friends. Jeff has taught me everything I don't know about being a scholar of early Africa and he has done so with a kindness I can only hope to emulate. Andreana Prichard,

Rhiannon Stephens, Neil Kodesh, and Emily Callaci also populate this distinct class of supporters. Neil has shared unwavering encouragement at key moments in my career and, although he may not know it, has clarified many a muddled argument through his thoughtful conversations. Rhiannon produced insightful comments from a scattered draft in the urgent weeks before peer review. Andreana and Emily have read every word across multiple revisions. Despite my best attempts, I was unable to wear out their patience. This book would not have seen the light of day without Andreana's and Emily's encouragement. Thank you.

My debts extend further. Emily Hughes, Grace Apfeld, and Adwoa Hinson helped me pour through the voluminous published ethnographic and archaeological records in Houston. The manuscript benefited tremendously from the thoughtful reviewers pressed into service by Yale and Cambridge University Presses and readers of the journal articles from which parts of this manuscript were drawn. For reading all or parts of the book draft, I also thank members of the faculty reading groups of the Southern Connecticut State University and Rice University History Departments in spring 2009 and 2011 and, in the fall of 2014, members of the Africa Seminar at Johns Hopkins, the Georgetown African History Seminar, and David Schoenbrun's HIST 465 course at Northwestern University. William Fitzsimons, who was tasked with presenting an unfinished manuscript to that class, provided comments that influenced my revisions to chapter 4.

If most journeys for this book oriented me toward loved ones in south central Africa, I was welcomed home at the end of my travels by a growing family of LaPlatneys and de Lunas. Sean, you let me upend the house, create a growlery to prowl in each of our successive residences, and make demands on your career that no spouse should entertain. Thank you for helping me live in Africa when I was at home and feel I was at home when I was in Africa. Mia and Torin: you add complexity to the picture, questioning and dispersing the authority of our household as only plucky young children can! Thank you for enduring my absences. What humanity is captured in the pages that follow stem from the lessons I could only have learned from Sean, Mialoh, and Torin.

A Note on Spelling and Reconstructed Forms

The story told in this book relates the history of speakers of languages belonging to a subgroup of the Bantu family known as Botatwe. Therefore, the book includes evidence in the form of words reconstructed to protolanguages spoken in the distant past. I have used the following orthography to represent the Bantu seven-vowel system in word reconstructions: i ɩ e a o ʊ u. Each reconstructed word, recognizable by its preceding asterisk, appears in an appendix at the end of the book in the form it exhibited in the earliest Botatwe protolanguage to which it can be reconstructed. Rarely, the reader will encounter a term preceded by a degree symbol, following the conventions of another author. To facilitate cross-referencing, numbers referring to the reconstruction's position in the appendix appear in brackets after its first mention in each chapter. In some cases, I have subsequently used modern-day attestations of reconstructed words to facilitate reading, often when I am using descriptions from the recent ethnographic record or when I conjure up historical imaginings from that record. Thus, the reader will encounter both the reconstructed word *-ámí, a term for a wealthy or respected person written out in the format for a word reconstruction, and also *mwami*, which represents the way the word is written today in most eastern Botatwe languages. Where appropriate, I apply the noun class prefix for language (ci-), place (bu-), and person or people (mu-, ba-) to proper names delineating the languages, speakers, and territories discussed. However, I also use such roots as adjectives, without a prefix. For example, the reader will learn of Tonga kinship systems described by anthropologists working in Butonga and conducting interviews in Citonga with elderly batonga.

Introduction

This is a story about collection—the collection of food and the collections of individuals and communities, both living and dead, who undertook this work. Although histories of farming communities are not usually told from this perspective, farmers' investment in food collection propelled the spread of cereal agriculture across the savannas of central Africa, as it did in many other parts of the ancient world. Therefore, this is also a story about cultivation—the cultivation of food and the cultivation of forms of individual distinction and group association among the living and dead, who saw that their experiments in food procurement opened novel paths for good living. In order to better understand the contribution of wild resource use to historical change, this book traces the ways in which hunting, fishing, and foraging were practiced and valued across nearly three millennia by farming communities speaking Botatwe languages in south central Africa.

This book began as a project to address a common but largely unelaborated observation in histories and archaeologies of precolonial Africa: that hunting, fishing, and gathering remained important even after the transition to agriculture. I wanted to understand how and why food collection articulated with food production and with what changes over time. South central Africa is a compelling place to try to understand the relationship between the variety of strategies people use to secure food and the means by which they give those practices social and political meaning. The poor soils, uncertain rains, and distribution of human and animal disease vectors of the wooded grasslands of south central Africa have long required a diversified subsistence regime to support any use of domesticates, all of which were introductions to the region. Today, speakers of Botatwe languages living in central and southern Zambia, northern Zimbabwe and Botswana, and the Caprivi Strip of Namibia combine cereal agriculture with fishing in streams and pools, hunting in the bush, and trapping nearer the homestead; the care of fowl, goats, some sheep, and cattle; and the collection of wild vegetable relishes, mushrooms, and fruits gathered from gardens and along paths connecting homesteads and villages.

By following the meanings that Botatwe speakers layered upon the words they invented to describe their food systems, what began as a simple series of questions about the subsistence economy developed into a complicated history of ideas about celebrity, the landscape, and how one went about "doing things" successfully. The words that are used by speakers of Botatwe languages today carry the interconnected histories of collecting and cultivating in their multiple meanings and derivational markers. Botatwe speakers today cultivate (*kulima*) the wild greens sprouting among legumes and gourd vines, and they plant traps (*kuteya*) between sorghum, millet, and maize stalks, transforming fields into hunting grounds and harvests into bait. However, vocabulary for some kinds of food procurement, particularly some forms of hunting and fishing, also speak of leadership and social aspiration, linking food collection to the politics of farming communities. Botatwe speakers hunt (*kuweʐa*) game, fish, and honey, but they also hunt wealth and social status. They esteem their most successful hunters (*mwaalu*) as friends and elders capable of great generosity, a characteristic of true leadership. These words are products of the history told in this book about the process by which some kinds of subsistence activities came to be understood as distinct from others and to be associated with a gendered politics of reputation and social mobility. By reconstructing the histories of such words we can trace the coproduction of forms of food collection and cultivation and the forms of personal distinction and community association that sustained them.

This book is concerned with the *longue durée* history of bushcraft— particular forms of hunting and fishing—as an economic and a social strategy employed by farmers speaking Botatwe languages in south central Africa from the tenth century BCE through the seventeenth century CE. The spread and intensification of farming and trade are often considered axiomatic to political change in the premodern world. Yet transformations in farming, trade, and political change in south central Africa were actually contingent on developments in hunting, fishing, and foraging—the very activities farming supposedly replaced. If the earliest Botatwe farmers cultivated weeds and planted traps alongside sorghum stalks, confounding the familiar distinction between collecting and producing food, their descendants participated in a wider, regional revolution around the technologies of spear hunting, rapid-current fishing, and metallurgy to invent a new category of landscape: the bush. The difference between food collection and cultivation was not a foregone conclusion to the practitioners who worked hard to distinguish their activities from agriculture by inventing a novel path to singularity, fame, friendship, and ancestorhood based on their knowledge of the bush. Subsequent generations of Botatwe farmers further developed the social and political significance of bushcraft, revealing the dynamism of subsistence strategies usually assumed to be static and peripheral to the agricultural economy. Indeed, for Botatwe speakers farming the savannas of central Africa over the last three millennia, the activities of food procurement categorized by scholars as either "collecting" or "cultivating" were only sometimes understood as distinct work, and only for particular kinds of people. A central argument of the book is that the ability to redefine the categories of hunter, forager, fisher, and farmer in different historical eras, annual seasons, and geographic spaces was at the heart of the development of the distinctly decentralized political culture for which Botatwe societies became famous in twentieth-century anthropology.

Botatwe speakers' inventive history of subsistence was part of a wider regional story in which celebrated technicians—hunters, fishers, smelters—across the central African savannas drew on the powers associated with the bush to ensure the success of activities undertaken in its shadows, albeit with significant local differences. Botatwe speakers manipulated their location within the changing geography of settlement and technological innovation in central and southern Africa. By the end of the first millennium, those who could safely travel through the bush participated in the expansion of trade networks connecting important industrial districts like Tsodilo Hills and the Copperbelt to regional centers and the Indian Ocean. Eventually, such networks linked the capitals of regional kingdoms and states and extended west, to the Atlantic Ocean, even as the influence of older centers of industry and wealth diminished. The persistently acephalous Botatwe communities occupied a central frontier zone for over a millennium as a sequence of kingdoms, states, and trading networks—the Luba-Lunda constellation, Great Zimbabwe, Mutapa, the Bemba chieftaincies, the Lozi kingdom, and others among them—were forged and dissolved on its distant periphery, offering mobile Botatwe hunters, in particular, the opportunity to broaden personal networks and cultivate a worldly sensibility. The history of Botatwe speakers is a history of the central and southern African savannas from the perspective of those who lived not within the orbits of its famous precolonial kingdoms and districts of great wealth and industry, but within a central frontier encircled by such waxing and waning centers. The history of Botatwe subsistence reveals the interrelated, contingent histories of fame, talent, political authority, landscape, and personhood (both in life and in death) across the watershed events of central and southern African history, from the transition to food production to the invention of matrilineality, the centralization of political authority in some neighboring societies, and the intensification of long distance trade.

Subsistence in Theory and in Practice

Subsistence is not simply about securing food. Rather, it is about the tools, skills, labor, landscapes, travels, exchanges, and relationships used to provision a community. Subsistence links the material world to the range of social practices and beliefs that exist beyond the domain of food but, like food, are bound up with existential concerns in the broadest sense. For this reason, the invocation of distinct subsistence strategies like "pastorialist" or "hunter-gatherer" has been a powerful tool for articulating cultural difference. Even the idea that some societies are "beyond" a subsistence lifestyle is a way to articulate a set of values about how labor, food procurement, and exchange should be organized in a "modern" society: around the generation of subsistence surplus to sustain economic specialization and, thereby, commerce. In ancient south central Africa, subsistence connected smelters crafting bloom and smiths hammering blades to ancestral spirits alert to the dangers faced by descendants out hunting. It linked nimble-fingered basket weavers to children trapping fish by damming the standing pools of last season's rains. Women's work was linked to men's with each hoe dug through the ashen dirt left after male relatives cut out new fields, perhaps converting some of the wood to charcoal to feed the fire of a smith forging new hoe blades. Subsistence practice in Botatwe communities included cohorts of technicians who might be labeled "craftsmen" or "specialists." But such designations obscure more than they reveal because, in Botatwe communities, these technicians spent most of their time laboring at the same subsistence practices as their neighbors, relatives, and friends. They were not professionals, guilded specialists, or even full-time craftsmen but, rather, men and women who farmed and also hunted, fished, trapped, potted, smelted, wove, and forged. For the very best of these, new words like *mwaalu* had to be invented to describe their degree of artistry in forms of labor available to all and practiced by most. To be sure, the idea that laboring to secure food should be divided from crafting and exchanging objects used to undertake such work is a legacy of a particular understanding of subsistence. Specifically, it is an idea tied to the model of the Neolithic Revolution, which supposes that the invention of food production led to surplus, freeing some people to lay down their hoes and develop technical and ritual specialties that stood outside the main activities of food production. In contrast, the multiple meanings of Botatwe words for subsistence activities require us to study food procurement alongside the technologies, materials, exchanges, and social ties that sustained them.

The interconnected history of food and politics embedded in Botatwe vocabulary is a story worthy of our attention because it challenges an assumption that has shaped popular and scholarly understandings of subsistence since antiquity: pithily, that mode of subsistence (hunter-gatherer, agriculturalist, pastoralist) is a category of identity that functions much like race, gender, or ethnicity. This assumption has graver implications for our understanding of subsistence in other historical contexts than we might expect from its simplicity. The methods by which communities feed themselves have long been used to articulate difference, distinguishing the civilized from the barbarians, modern societies from those that lag behind, and even humans from animals. Indeed, our own impoverished vocabulary of subsistence belies the primary political value we attach to the way people provision themselves. The compound term "mixed farmer" probably best describes the diversified system of cereal agriculture, animal husbandry, hunting, fishing, and gathering that characterizes subsistence in the Botatwe region today. It also demonstrates the imprecision of our categories, which emphasize one method of securing food to the exclusion of others. Scholars rely on convoluted compound words like "agro-pastroforagers" because our vocabulary reflects the cultural ideal that every society should depend on one primary mode of subsistence.[1] The inadequacy of our subsistence vocabulary begs the question: how did subsistence categories acquire their exclusionary quality and what purpose did it serve those who deployed them?

Histories of subsistence demonstrate that, in practice, the ways people fed themselves muddy the waters of our tidy classifications: farmers have long collected famine foods after poor harvests or in the hungry season; hunter-gatherers tended small stock; pastoralists and farmers hunted; and, as studies of domestication reveal, hunter-gatherers weeded, cultivated, and selectively harvested stands of ancient grains, eventually domesticating them. Yet *intellectual* histories of subsistence have followed the categories of its classification. Historians and anthropologists usually don't explore how categories like "farmer" and "pastoralist" are coproduced within a political ideology of subsistence.[2] Instead, studies painstakingly reconstruct from antiquity to the twentieth century the political significance of cultural ideas about a particular kind of subsistence, such as the transition to agriculture, or specific kinds of practitioners, such as hunter-gatherers or pastoralists.

Botatwe speakers, too, found that fashioning distinctions between related subsistence activities was a powerful political tool. The intellectual histories of subsistence categories in central Africa and Europe are coeval, complimentary stories with much in common. But as the study of African societies was incorporated into Western academic traditions, terms like "farmer" and "hunter-gatherer" were applied as universal, naturalized categories to describe and explain African ethnicities, social organization, political culture, and economies, creating a paradigm in which there could be no intellectual history of vernacular subsistence categories and their social and political powers.[3] What is original about how Botatwe-speaking communities invented and refashioned categories of subsistence comes into sharpest relief when set alongside the story of how subsistence categories were transformed from a political abstraction into a scholarly heuristic in a Western intellectual tradition.

As was the case in central Africa, both intellectuals and laypeople contributed to how different categories of subsistence were made meaningful in particular historical contexts across several millennia of European history. Many—and often contradictory—strands of thought contributed to the flexible ways in which communities and individuals could think with subsistence categories, but three chapters in this complex history are particularly important for this story. Our first concern is how Enlightenment thinkers invented the subsistence category "hunter-gatherer." This concept played a key role in Enlightenment theories of political economy, which were developed, in part, to explain the emergence of modern forms of commerce and statecraft.

Our second interest focuses on how scholars conceptualized the activities defining subsistence categories as evolutionary "adaptations" in the nineteenth and twentieth centuries. Following in the Enlightenment tradition, they used subsistence categories to define stages in social evolutionary models and to explain development through those stages and the forms of political and social organization attributed to them. Finally, since the late twentieth century, scholars working in all world regions and time periods, including Africa, have dismantled such social evolutionary models while recognizing the value of key insights like the economic significance of subsistence surplus and the relationship between subsistence activities and political power. A key contribution of Africanist scholarship has been describing the range of subsistence activities undertaken within a single, integrated economy, an approach taken in this book, albeit following the subsistence categories developed by Botatwe speakers.

Subsistence and Political Economy

The intellectual foundations for the distinction between food production and food collection reach deep into classical antiquity and appear in the writings of Thucydides, Aristotle, Diodorus Siculus, Lucretius, Tacitus, Strabo, and others. In some classical texts, the subsistence-based classification was a dichotomy of farmers against non-farmers, a dichotomy that hinged on the importance of sedentism, the affiliated trappings of civilization, and the ideal of the agrarian life as superior for its self-sufficiency.[4] Through this binary, explanations for the origins of society converged with explanations for the origins of agriculture and progress from a state of nature to a state of culture. Property ownership was (and would remain) fundamental to both civilized society and agriculture.[5] Other classical thinkers articulated the value of the agricultural lifestyle and its distinction from other subsistence strategies through stadial schemes meant to explain change in human history.[6] Of course, the juxtaposition of nomadic, barbaric non-farmers and civilized, sedentary farmers developed in particular historical contexts. These ideas performed political work in periods of conquest and colonization, much as similar ideas did in seventeenth- and eighteenth-century Europe, often consciously drawing on classical models. For example, as the boundaries of the Roman Empire expanded under Augustus, Strabo explained the "more simple and barbaric" nature of the Brits as compared to the Celts—both groups laying just beyond the empire's boundary—by the fact that the Brits "have no

experience in gardening or other agricultural pursuits."[7] The antique practice of recognizing and explaining difference through subsistence practices
proved to be a persistent, if not an unchanging, root metaphor in which food
production stood in for qualities like "progressive" and "civilized" and invoked cultural ideals, such as sedentism and property ownership, that shaped
how later intellectuals understood the relationship between subsistence and
a civilized, moral politics.[8]

Ties between subsistence and politics lay at the core of some of the most
important concepts developed during the Enlightenment, including political
economy. Working under the assumption that social progress was a law of
nature, Enlightenment thinkers explored the relationships between land ten-
ure, labor, subsistence, and sociopolitical organization, eventually inventing
the subsistence category "hunter-gatherer."[9] Popular antique texts associating farming with civilized life were combined with new ideas about the relationship between man and animals, allowing intellectuals to attach a particular
moral value to farming. As worked land came to be understood as an "improvement," progress was understood to be directly associated with cultivation
and private property, both essential to the work of building a just society. The
morality of hunting, in contrast, was suddenly in question in light of the
possibility that animals, in their likeness to man, also held rights. Importantly,
questions about the morality of hunting emerged at the same time that the
first "scientific" ethnographic observations of societies in the New World circulated among European intellectuals. It was a small step in the seventeenth
century to move from the observation that "primitives" encountered in distant lands relied on hunting and foraging to describing them as a "natural"
state of man and their hunting as the "primordial human enterprise," one so
"morally objectionable" that it was identified by Lord Monboddo at the end
of the eighteenth century as the root of human depravity.[10] Indeed, Rousseau
could opine "the savage is a hunter, the barbarian a herdsman, the civil man
a plowman" and expect his audience to agree.[11] Ideas about the morality and
relative productivity of different subsistence practices as measured in surplus
and land improvement justified both the colonization of distant lands and the
forced removal of native peoples, especially hunter-gatherers.

For the eighteenth-century economists, lawyers, landowners, and "im-
provers" involved in the rapid growth of agrarian and mercantile capitalism
and penning conjectural histories, subsistence practice was a shorthand for
political organization and a key factor in understanding difference both his-

torically and in the contemporary world.[12] Scottish Enlightenment thinkers assumed that subsistence practices determined key attributes of societies. For example, Adam Smith outlined four ages of human society: hunting, pastoralism, farming, and commerce. Smith's contemporaries used the distinction between hunting and gathering, pastoralism, and agriculture to explain the origins of private property; gendered and social hierarchies; and human language, sociality, and depravity.[13] For our purposes, Smith's assertion that the age of hunting was "prior to" government is particularly important. In Smith's understanding, the origins of government lay in the transition from hunting to pastoralism, when land was first appropriated, thereby initiating property ownership and social inequality.[14]

Enlightenment theories of political economy insisted that subsistence practices were fundamental to understanding the origins of inequality, class, the accumulation of capital, social and political organization, the gendered division of labor, and many other problems that came to be foundational to the social sciences. The idea that economies defined by subsistence determined property rights and that systems of property rights determined social organization and politics had a profound influence on scholarly thought. Smith's work, for example, echoes through Marx. Lewis Henry Morgan read Kames. Evans-Prichard and Radcliffe-Brown cited the conjectural historians of the Scottish Enlightenment as inspirational fodder theoretically, if not methodologically.[15] The conceptual links forged between property ownership, social inequality, and productivity sustained the distinction between hunting and gathering, pastoralism, and farming and the discrete political and social capacities associated with each. This typology was an enduring Rubicon whose course shaped generations of scholarship, including, paradoxically, later work challenging the very distinctions between hunter-gatherers, herders, and farmers. It could be so precisely because the relationship between social inequality and control over resources like property, labor, and surplus have shaped political and social complexity in many historical contexts. In persistently acephelous political traditions, like the one defining Botatwe political history, the social and economic value of subsistence activities, surpluses, and differentiation are harder to discern.

Subsistence as Evolutionary Adaptation

As assumptions about universal laws of social progress were carried into the nineteenth century, they were connected to evolutionary theory. However, scholars like Spencer, Darwin, Galton, Lamarck, Lubbock, Morgan, and Engels decoupled narratives of universal progress from economic explanations of change. They replaced their predecessors' emphasis on property rights and static subsistence categories with the idea of evolutionary adaptation, for adaptation was understood to be a pivotal force of change and differentiation. For example, using the idea that subsistence strategies developed as evolutionary adaptations, scholars in the emerging field of hunter-gatherer studies argued in the late nineteenth and early twentieth centuries that hunter-gatherers represented a primordial state of humanity.[16] Thus, the study of contemporary hunter-gatherer populations could answer questions about early human history.[17] Antievolutionists also saved an important place for hunter-gatherers in their understandings of difference and historical change. For example, the noble savage idea built on an older trope of degeneration common to universal human histories and the popularization of environmental conservation to critique the societies at the apex of the social Darwinist hierarchy.[18] The evolutionary paradigm—whether you were for or against it—was merely another way to articulate the theoretical value of the distinction between hunter-gatherers and farmers.

The notion that subsistence technologies were, themselves, human adaptations was a central problem for early twentieth-century scholars, who pondered the origins and significance of such adaptations. Tracing the history of social evolutionary theories lies well beyond the scope of this book, but two models reveal key ideas that developed from this body of scholarship: the familiar Neolithic Revolution and the Killer Ape theory and related Hunting Hypothesis.[19] Both the Killer Ape theory and the Neolithic Revolution followed the long-established idea that subsistence could explain difference. Although each has far earlier roots, these ideas became particularly significant in both scholarly and popular thought in the aftermath of World War II. The idea that changes in subsistence practices were evolutionary adaptations with the power to produce new sociopolitical configurations—even new species!—permeated mid-century anthropology. Shifts from one subsistence strategy to another seemed to show remarkable similarity across cultures and periods and, therefore, underscored the importance of adaptation, rather than race, in explanations of human variability. Thus, study of transformations in subsistence practices played an important role in recovering social evolutionary theory from its nineteenth-century racial trappings.

V. Gordon Childe's masterful reformulation of the nationalist archaeologies of Europe purposefully equated all transformations to human lifestyles that resulted from techno-economic innovation: the Neolithic represented the introduction of farming; the Bronze Age marked the establishment of regular trade and craft specialization; and the Iron Age drastically altered the demography of Europe, facilitating land clearance and population expansion.[20] To Childe, these revolutions separated Lewis H. Morgan's cultural stages of savagery, barbarism, and civilization and marked moments of punctuated development in early human history that were as transformative as the more recent Industrial Revolution. For Childe and his contemporaries, agriculture and sedentism not only facilitated but, inevitably, created the accumulation of property and surplus production. Childe redefined the moral superiority attributed to farming by Enlightenment thinkers into an economic superiority. In Childe's model, farming created the possibility to store surplus food that might then be used to support a series of related innovations Childe described as the "Urban Revolution": first, a class of nonproducers who specialized in governance, ritual life, trade, and crafts like metallurgy; second, a new settlement pattern that brought diverse specialists into contact in cities; and, third, the birth of statecraft and commerce from the contact urban centers facilitated between specialists, including professional traders.

Childe's earliest musings on the significance of the advent of farming were contemporary with a parallel, related interest among physical anthropologists in the significance of the advent of hunting. The Killer Ape theory suggested that the invention of hunting was an adaptation that allowed humans to evolve into a new branch of the primate tree and, recalling Lord Monboddo, that human depravity was rooted in a primate propensity for predation. By the middle of the century, scholars' perspectives on the earliest human subsistence strategies had changed considerably. Scholars debated the relative productivity of different hunter-gatherer food systems and their benefits as a form of subsistence, building up the field of hunter-gatherer studies. Marshall Sahlins famously claimed that hunter-gatherers were the "original affluent society" if time and labor, rather than property, were placed at the center of definitions of poverty. That Sahlins's observation was remarkable in 1966 speaks to the persistence of Enlightenment ideas asserting private property and farming as definitive of productive labor. Mid-century scholars of hunter-gatherers puzzled over why so many foragers became farmers if farming was neither a better way of life nor a certain evolutionary destination. Indeed, this question suggested that the Killer Ape theory had the hunting hypothesis backward. While humans may have evolved from apes because they developed hunting, this adaptation was not the source of human depravity but an achievement in the universal narrative of human history. This "Man the Hunter" hypothesis inspired the "Woman the Gatherer" thesis, which asserted the significant contributions of women to the prehistoric larder, in part, by gendering "female" the subsistence identity of "gatherer." The explanatory power assigned to changes in subsistence in early human history continued to justify the study of contemporary hunter-gatherer societies to produce analogous data from which to reconstruct early human history, a point to which we will return.[21]

Together, several centuries, perhaps even millennia, of inquiry and practice produced a distinction in Western thought between farmers and non-farmers, juxtaposing most frequently the subsistence categories of "farmer" and "hunter-gatherer." For intellectuals from the Enlightenment through the twentieth century, the differences between farmers and hunter-gatherers explained the origins of key attributes of the modern world: commerce, social inequality, and political centralization. Enlightenment thinkers imagined that subsistence defined the degree of social and political complexity and framed farming as the pinnacle of preindustrial productivity, in terms of both land improvement and the generation of surplus to sustain trade. Social evolutionary models claimed that changes in subsistence, governance, and exchange moved in lockstep, propelling societies from one stage to another. Arguments about the relative social, political, and economic benefits of one or another form of subsistence turned on the idea of "surplus," whether the surplus leisure time of affluent hunter-gatherers or the surplus food of farmers feeding the urban revolution. Although scholars had developed more sophisticated categories of and meanings for subsistence than the dichotomized worldview of antiquity, the terms of the debate had changed very little: subsistence defined societies and changes to subsistence transformed society.[22]

Integrated Approaches to Subsistence

Social evolutionary models that had dominated scholarship since the 1950s—in some cases with far earlier antecedents—were beginning to unravel by the 1970s. The hunting hypothesis was largely rejected after nearly two decades in textbooks. The ennobling "affluent society" theory was critiqued by work

on "complex" hunter-gatherer communities that exhibited great social stratification and were often sedentary. Indeed, the very categories of "farmer" and
"hunter-gatherer" were vulnerable to attack as calls mounted for a better
understanding of the range of subsistence activities to which farming and
foraging belonged.[23]

The study of African communities was at the center of critiques of
social evolutionary models because such models were so often a poor fit for
evidence from the continent.[24] In conversation with scholarship from other
regions, Africanists contributed to undermining the social evolutionary
paradigm by foregrounding the interaction between and contemporaneity of
practitioners of different kinds of subsistence. The wide body of research on
the histories of African subsistence systems can be divided into two general
approaches. One focuses on the range of subsistence activities undertaken by
members of a single political or social group. In the other approach, scholars
foreground interactions between distinct communities practicing different
kinds of subsistence within a shared regional economy. In each case, the interconnectedness of a variety of subsistence activities belies the complicated
relationship between food procurement activities, exchange, and identity
politics and demonstrates that subsistence and political and social organization don't change in lockstep.

Within Africanist scholarship, the Kalahari Debate is probably the most
widely known engagement with social evolutionary models. Researchers interested in the earliest human past had long studied modern Kalahari communities that were defined by anthropologists as "hunter-gatherers" in order
to better understand the livelihoods of our earliest ancestors. The path-
breaking work by Ed Wilmsen and others demonstrated that this approach
removed modern hunter-gatherers from history and elided the contingencies
of their own subsistence histories. The hunter-gatherer lifestyle of San communities of the Kalahari was, in fact, a far more recent development of a particular history of interaction with and exclusion from the regional political
economy. Africanists studying hunter-gatherer communities in the Kalahari
and the equatorial forests have disproved many of the assumptions about the
politics, economics, and historiocity that had adhered to hunter-gatherer
societies since the Enlightenment, including the notion that hunter-gatherers
were unchanging remnants from humankind's ancient past and that such communities were universally egalitarian. Importantly, studies of hunter-gatherers'
histories demonstrate that the pasts of farmers and hunter-foragers were

intertwined and that both farming and foraging economies were products of historical interactions. By recognizing that practitioners of both kinds of subsistence strategy shared common exchange networks, studies of hunter-gatherers in the Kalahari and equatorial forests have shown that both farmers and hunter-gatherers contributed to the development of economic specialization, long-distance trade networks, and regional political cultures.[25]

In a similar move, archaeologists have developed the concept of a "mosaic" to demonstrate how farmers, pastoralists, and hunter-gatherers who lived in the same region but exploited different microenvironments collaborated to create integrated regional economies in which all groups had a stake.[26] Using the mosaic metaphor, archaeologists have been able to account for interaction between practitioners of different subsistence strategies, that is, practitioners who are usually understood to belong to different social or political communities because of their different material cultures. Yet thinking through "mosaics" shifts the relationships of subsistence difference from the chronological framework of progress (and regression) central to theories of social evolution to a spatial framework emphasizing the coeval but interconnectedness of difference. With this concept, geography has replaced chronology as the mechanism of separation.[27]

The legacy of the subsistence-based criteria used to identify ethnic groups in colonial Africa may well still shape Africanist scholarship. Many scholars continue to study hunter-foragers as linguistically, ethnically, economically, geographically, and even racially discrete groups, even as they demonstrate the historical contingency of their identities as foragers and the porous boundaries of their communities within larger regional economic mosaics. The trend is to recognize hunting, fishing, and foraging activities as definitive of an ethnic, specialist, or caste-like group, even when they are practices developed with farming in an integrated economy.[28] Be that as it may, the achievements of studies tracing the contingent histories of hunter-gatherers and the regional ties between their communities and those of other subsistence practitioners are substantial. Because such studies have demonstrated the complementary, coeval status of farming, herding, and hunting and gathering, we are in a better position to study those individuals and communities who, like Botatwe-speaking societies, have simultaneously pursued multiple subsistence strategies.

If studies of hunter-gatherers in the Kalahari and equatorial forests revealed the important contributions of communities taken out of history by

evolutionary approaches to subsistence, the study of the adoption of agriculture in the wooded savannas that lie between them—a region of uncertain
rains and often poor soils—has taught us much about farmers' own efforts
in hunting, fishing, and foraging. Jan Vansina was among the first to observe
in the African context the essential role of food collection to the precarious
work of adopting and elaborating on the technology of cereal agriculture.
Vansina pointedly called the transition to cereal farming in central and southern
Africa a "slow revolution," directly contradicting the notion that worldwide
Neolithics were as immediately transformative as once thought. Vansina traced
out the incremental process by which generations slowly integrated cereals
into preexisting subsistence strategies, only eventually making cereals the
center of the diet. For Vansina, once agriculture provided the "main" source
of food, other subsistence pursuits like hunting, foraging, and fishing served
as either supplemental activities, a form of insurance against seasonal
shortages, poor rains, and natural disasters, or, in the direst of circumstances,
strategies to which farmers could "revert." With the larder secured by cereals,
communities could further elaborate on non-farming subsistence activities,
like hunting and metallugy, eventually reaching an "optimal" balance between
labor, food needs, and the local environment.[29] Vansina's accomplishment
was nothing shy of recasting the Neolithic Revolution in Africa by reversing
the relationship between food collection and food production in the slow
process by which Africans established integrated, resilient subsistence economies. In the end of this new story, however, farming remains triumphant. In
this regard, Vansina's approach is not alone.

Most scholarship assumes a complete distinction between the activities
of farmers and those of hunter-gatherers, but even in studies that unite efforts in farming with efforts in hunting, fishing, and foraging, the latter are
treated as activities that lie on the fringes of daily life in agriculturalist communities. Scholars marginalize the food collection of farmers in one of two
ways. Sometimes, forms of food collection, particularly gathering, are treated
as the undertakings of the poor, as strategies for seasons of general vulner-
ability, or as activities that contribute only modestly to the overall calories
consumed by households. At other times, forms of food collection, particularly hunting and fishing, are treated as marginal compared to food production because they are liminal endeavors, imbued with danger and great ritual
potency; in this treatment, hunting and fishing are often seen as symbolic of
other kinds of social and political concerns. Hunting in central Africa, as we

will learn in chapter 3, has long been recognized as significant for its symbolic role in regional political culture. The marginalization of food collection activities in studies of communities that produce food reflects the ideal that societies should be identifiable with one, core subsistence strategy. In the Western intellectual tradition, this ideal was central to the manipulation of categories of subsistence in identity politics. It was also central to identity politics in Africa, as we learn from Kairn Klieman's *longue durée* study of the identity "Batwa" in west central African history.[30] But in the Western intellectual tradition, this ideal was also central to explanations of differences in social and political organization across time and space, with, as we have seen, important implications for the study of African societies.

At the root of the problem is the relationship between subsistence surplus and occupational specialization in social evolutionary models, like Childe's Neolithic and Urban Revolutions. Each of these concepts was thought to play an important role in the origins of large-scale exchange networks and political complexity. Social evolutionary models suggest that when subsistence practices like fishing and hunting are not the source of subsistence surplus, they are marginal to the subsistence economy and, therefore, to the practice of power. When such endeavors do supply the surplus to finance political complexity, we identify an example of political complexity among foragers. If subsistence activities, such as elephant hunting, contribute essential products, like ivory, circulated within the local and long-distance trade networks of farming communities, they are treated as the domain of specialists and professionals. Even individuals must be identified with primarily one or another kind of strategy within the broader work of provisioning communities. In contrast, Botatwe societies emphasized the importance of demonstrating skill in a seasonal or part-time economic activity pursued by most community members (rather than full-time specialization or guilded professionalization) when they invented the new subsistence category of bushcraft in the late first millennium. The significance of talent alerts us to the contribution of nonmaterial products of marginal subsistence activities, such as knowledge and renown, to the kinds of exchanges and circulations that engendered some people with higher status than their peers. Food collectors and food producers have remained reified heuristic categories even in studies attempting to conjoin them precisely because they lay at the heart of political economic theory and long-standing ideas about how leaders secure authority. As we will see, scholars of Africa's past have thought very differently about how leader-

ship, authority, and power worked within early African societies, which requires different thinking about the contribution of subsistence practices to
political life.

Taken together, the many challenges Africanist scholarship has leveled
at the ubiquitous dichotomy between food collection and food production in-
vite the question: did central Africans develop their own subsistence categories in the past and, if so, for what social and political ends? This book traces
how Botatwe societies developed changing categories subsistence over the
course of nearly three millennia and imbued them with social and political
meaning. The communities involved in this conceptual work debated the various labor relations, distribution networks, and mechanisms of material access and ritual oversight for each of the different subsistence categories they
invented. Feeding families was both a social and a political enterprise, but not
always in ways that neatly match how historians of early Africa have studied
the social and political lives of communities living centuries and millennia ago.

Power, Politics, Subsistence, and Affect

Political change and, particularly, the development of more complex forms
of political organization—"political complexity"—has long been an important focus for historians and archaeologists studying early African societies.
Recent scholarship on early political cultures of Africa has complicated our
understanding of increasing political complexity to include both a building
up through hierarchical layers of authority as well as a building out into multiple, overlapping, heterarchical nodes of authority that form a web of cooperation and competition.[31] This work helps us rethink the development of both
statecraft and authority in population, industry, and trade centers. Although
the study of acephalous societies always existed alongside the study of kingdoms, much of the literature on the development of political complexity
through heterarchy has, surprisingly, focused on the histories of states, cities, and their precursors. The contribution of small-scale societies already
recognized for their decentralized politics had been largely left out of conversations about heterarchical politics, with the outstanding exception of Jan
Vansina's work on the durable political tradition of equatorial African Bantu
societies, *Paths in the Rainforests.*[32]

When scholars discuss the political organization of acephelous societies
in early African history, they often identify leaders as either Big Men or the
ritual heads of small kinship groups. Indeed, the ubiquity of the two archetypes

is captured in a debate over which kind of leader best describes the meaning of *mfumu*, one of the oldest Bantu words for a political figure.[33] The authority of ritual leaders depended on their status as senior members of a family group, a status that conferred proximity to ancestor spirits and, hopefully, the ability to serve as an intercessor between the needs of the residential family group and the demands of the spirits to ensure the fertility of the land and the fecundity of the family. In the history of decentralized Botatwe societies, however, kinship was a far more flexible idiom with which to claim or deny association. As described in chapter 4, in some periods, such as the early second millennium, kinship was a fairly precarious anchor for claims to authority over others. The definition of who could be counted among family and how family groups related to one another had the potential to change in the face of population movement and demographic change. We learn from Jan Vansina's pioneering work that the authority of Big Men in early central African societies was decidedly ephemeral because it was tied to the lifespan of a single incumbent, even though the values of the political tradition underpinning Big Man politics were durable across millennia. Big Men competed for followers, so both the redistribution of wealth and the composition of knowledgeable community members were key aspects of their politicking.[34] Wealthy, influential Big Men figured in the political history of Botatwe speakers as well. Yet the story told in the following pages also insists on the contribution to the politics of dependency and knowledge made by middling figures, skilled community members whose achievements were also celebrated, even if their social influence did not translate into a more durable, formalized, or institutionalized political authority.

The models generated by scholars of Africa's diverse political cultures have revealed many paths by which power was diffused within early African societies, whether in the self-organizing landscape of cities in the middle Niger, the multiplicity of small-scale leaders of neighborhoods of residential kin groups, or the Houses of Big Men in equatorial Africa. Such heterarchical configurations of institutions and offices—whatever the scale of the society in which they are found—are thought to "resist or at least restrain" the concentration of power in the hands of a few, producing a "balance" between the aspirations of leaders and the ideal of egalitarianism.[35] This polarized understanding of power—between hierarchy and heterarchy, between leaders and followers, between royal institutions balancing corporate associations—has been a long-standing heuristic. But it depends on two universalizing assumptions. The first is that power is limited, driving competition. There are two approaches to the second assumption. Either power universally possesses a self-animated drive toward centralization, requiring restraint and balance, or ambition for power is universal among leaders seeking to "enlarge and perpetuate their power," creating the need to curb leaders' relentless push toward centralization.[36]

Another approach to politics in early African societies investigates how Africans themselves understood power to work in the deep past.[37] Two studies have been particularly helpful in the analysis undergirding this book. Eugenia Herbert's influential comparative study of ironworking reveals how a "procreational paradigm"—"an imposition of the human model of fertility on the world"—created a particular understanding of creative forces associated with transformative processes like smelting, hunting, and investiture. Here, political authority and social status derive from the capacity to direct such "transformative" power toward socially productive ends.[38] David Schoenbrun's study of Great Lakes Bantu lexicons of power traces the boundaries and overlaps of "instrumental" and "creative" powers, building on Arens's and Karp's influential *Creativity of Power*. While instrumental power secures desired outcomes by forcing or compelling the actions of others, creative power involves manipulating and inventing forms of meaning that resonate with shared but changeable understandings of how the world works and how best to secure a good life. As Schoenbrun observes, the potential proliferation of ideas renders creative power a decidedly difficult force to superintend. To be sure, the creation of meanings may be marshaled toward a variety of ends, from securing community well-being through efficacious interventions in the spirit world to legitimizing instrumental power. "In practice," Schoenbrun reminds us, "the two forms are not divided" because they are "facets of how people work on and in their world."[39]

Thinking with the concept of "creative" power has allowed historians to reject the idea that power is limited, drawing out the many ways in which creative forms of power, in particular, could be invented, amplified, and extinguished. Other recent work complicates the assumed ambition for power on the part of would-be leaders by questioning who might seek it. We are now attentive to the agency spirits, which changes how we think about the relationship between ambition, power, and the human lifespan. The distinction between leaders and followers in ancient Africa has been blurred by evidence that in some historical contexts they jointly experienced the honors of some forms of authority. Even the existential integrity of the material concerns binding people to one another and to those who can muster the instrumental and creative means to meet and control them may well dissolve in the face of the complicated ways in which people become objects and objects stand in for people in central Africa.[40]

Speakers of Botatwe languages today are famous for their flexible forms of social organization and dispersed sources of political authority; this decentralized, informal political culture obtained in the deep past as well. In a context with few ancient, formal, wide-reaching institutions beyond kinship, it is difficult to study even the kinds of "alternative" sites of authority illuminated by studies of heterarchy and creative power, for these tend to highlight social, political, and ritual institutions like professional guilds, healing cults, and the Houses and Districts that collected around charismatic Big Men. Like John Iliffe's appreciation of householders' honor, the histories of Botatwe words demonstrate the value of scaling down to better understand the political history of acephelous societies.[41] In Botatwe history, personal networks and novel forms of individual distinction that were rooted in the celebration of talent demonstrate the political power of inter-peer valuation, which served as a source of authority and influence that diffused power. For the early African past, it remains difficult to draw out individuals' experience of power; indeed, such stories are simply inaccessible for many periods and places. Foregrounding the affective, atmospheric, and emotional dimensions of forms of ephemeral influence like celebrity and honor garnered through an informal recognition by peers gives us purchase on both the significance of social structures and political institutions, however informal, even as it insists on the relevance of individuals' experience within them. This project was not developed to address gaps in our knowledge of the nature of authority or social influence in precolonial Africa. But Botatwe speakers' words about subsistence tell a story in which their ancestors figure as local notables; as rivals, gossips, and lovers; as longstanding friends well known in neighborly lore; as objects of attention, respect, and celebration some seasons but admirers in other seasons; as folks with significantly ordinary lives that unfolded alongside, within, and beyond the reach of those institutions that dominate early African histories. This alternative history of the politics of notability exists because, in the way they invented their words, Botatwe speakers insisted it be the framework for the story told about the relationship between food collection and cultivation, between subsistence and society.

Structure and Arguments of the Book

This story of Botatwe bushcraft and acephelous politics emerges from word histories produced through the methodology of comparative historical linguistics. This primary form of evidence is supplemented with published archaeological, paleoclimatological, and ethnographic data. Chapter 1 introduces each of these very different forms of historical evidence and describes what such information can and cannot tell us about the history of subsistence in central Africa over the last three millennia. The narrative framework for the story told in this book arises from the historical development of the Botatwe language family, also described in chapter 1. The stories told in chapters 2, 3, and 4 drill down into progressively narrower geographical and chronological contexts. Finally, chapter 5 significantly broadens our purview, integrating the stories of the preceding chapters into the larger histories of southern and central Africa.

From about the tenth century BCE to the first century of the Common Era, speakers of the ancestral proto-Botatwe language reproduced the older diversified central African food system they inherited from their Bantu-speaking predecessors. They combined the propagation of root crops with the collection of wild foods through fishing, trapping, hunting, and collecting. As they took up the challenge of growing cereal crops in the first centuries of the Common Era, these early Botatwe cereal farmers revealed the promise of a new agricultural regime based on sowing seeds to contribute a multitude of wild produce to the larder. Chapter 2 explores how, for well over a fifteen hundred years, proto-Botatwe communities and their linguistic descendants, Greater Eastern Botatwe speakers, did not necessarily distinguish between farming and living off wild resources, even as they adopted new technologies like metallurgy and cattle keeping, which sometimes made farming more productive.

Between the mid-eighth and mid-thirteenth centuries, Central Eastern Botatwe communities and their linguistic descendants, speakers of proto-Kafue, participated in a regional revolution in the technologies of spear hunting, rapid-current fishing, and metallurgy and invented a new category of landscape: *isokwe,* the bush. The invention of "the bush" illuminates how technological innovation and cultural ideas about gender, fame, and the politics of knowledge drew on older ideas about landscapes, the transformative power of fertility, the agency of spirits, and the means by which individuals could safely direct the powers of each to secure success in the bush and in village, in life and in death. Chapter 3 tells this story. Bushcraft, this new category of subsistence practice, allowed communities to create a distinction between food procurement undertaken near the villages and some forms of food collection and craft technologies that were now undertaken in the bush, even though these latter activities had been part of the generalized subsistence economy for centuries. This distinction was transformative because it created a novel path to celebrity, friendship, and ancestorhood based on knowledge of the bush, a gendered politics of talent and technology that resisted the centralization of political and ritual authority around the agricultural economy.

The invention of a new category of subsistence practice articulated with both established strategies of food procurement and those ideals of dependency, obligation, and social association that sustained them. Chapter 4 significantly narrows our focus to explore how bushcraft changed and was changed by innovations in how Kafue speakers identified and valued ties to kith and kin between the mid-tenth and mid-thirteenth centuries, as Kafue speakers expanded into lands beyond their middle Kafue homeland. Evidence from both the archaeological and linguistic records independently describe a process by which immigrants from the Kafue region settled among preexisting populations on the Batoka Plateau and absorbed them into their own communities. Through three core innovations—in the scale and sociality of hunting; the development of networks of bond friendship exploiting and leveling the uneven distribution of talent and expertise; and the value of lateral kinship ties of clanship, cousinhood, and marriage—Kafue homesteaders and their Kusi-speaking neighbors dissolved in a few short centuries the linguistic and cultural frontiers that had once divided them on the Batoka Plateau.

Although the histories of precolonial central and southern Africa are usually treated in isolation, the location of Botatwe lands in the most distant frontiers of these two well-studied zones of political, technological, and economic innovation placed Botatwe speakers at the center of the history of the links between them. Chapter 5 places the Botatwe story in a transregional perspective. The inhabitants of this central frontier contributed to the development of the technologies, trade routes, cultural values, and even affectations that sustained the better-known centers of first-millennium industry and wealth and the second-millennium kingdoms, states, and federations of the central African savannas and southern velds. Inhabitants of the central frontier passed objects, foods, emblems, and even lingo between the central and southern African worlds and hosted travelers moving between them. Some ideas, things, and their names were kept on the central frontier and put to local use, sustaining a decentralized political culture of inventive alliance making among peers with varied talents and between such notorious figures and their dependents. The central frontier was a product of its residents, its neighbors, and passers-through; its boundaries and even the character of life within its limits changed over time. Chapter 5 reconstructs this history, tying the story of Botatwe speakers to more familiar narratives about the Zimbabwe Plateau, long-distance trade in Zambezia, and Luba, Lunda, and other famous polities of the central African savannas.

The story told in this book ends at the close of the seventeenth century, around the period when most precolonial histories of this region begin. Such histories teach us that the central frontier collapsed during the eighteen and nineteenth centuries in the face of the violence and political uncertainty wrought by expanding intercontinental trade in slaves, ivory, beeswax, rubber, and other extractable commodities. In the late nineteenth century and into the early decades of the twentieth century, as British missionaries traveled through south central Africa, as colonial officials negotiated treaties with actual and spontaneously appointed chiefs, and as anthropologists rushed to document the "traditional" cultures of Africa before they were lost to the "modernizing" influence of colonialism, they created a historical archive in which Botatwe communities were insignificant players. Indeed, this literature even led to debates about whether some Botatwe societies had a history, so peripheral were they to the obvious sites and mechanisms of contemporary (and future) political power. This historical snapshot, while accurate with respect to the marginalization of Botatwe communities in the eighteenth, nineteenth, and early twentieth centuries, has obscured our understanding of the dynamic savanna culture and the contingencies of decentralized forms of association that preceded the emergence of those states, kingdoms, and trade centers that attracted the attention of missionaries, colonial officers, anthropologists, and, later, historians and archaeologists. This book serves as a rejoinder to the persistent legacy of such colonial scholarship, which has not only obscured Botatwe speakers' past but has also erased ephemeral, affective forms of influence, singularity, and notoriety from our understanding of precolonial African political repertoires. It is a story best told in Botatwe speakers' own words.

1. The Sources and Settings
of Botatwe History

Speakers of Botatwe languages have lived in the southern savannas for the last three millennia and have left us with a rich record of the objects, spaces, relationships, and beliefs they used to provide for their children, their elders, and the dead. This record appears in no archive, for Botatwe societies have, through most of their three thousand year history, been oral societies. They preserved their past for future generations by teaching their children how to craft and decorate pottery, pronounce words, cultivate a cereal field, honor an ancestor, and recount the legends of heroes. Historians of precolonial Africa have been particularly successful in applying innovative methodologies to such diverse historical records. This book follows in this well-established interdisciplinary tradition, using three forms of historical evidence: the histories of words reconstructed to the ancestral languages that gave rise to the Botatwe languages spoken in south central Africa today, the region's material cultural record recovered layer by meticulous layer from the soil, and the changing distribution of flora and fauna that followed shifting weather patterns. When used together, these forms of evidence elucidate the history of Botatwe communities over the last three millennia. The purpose of this chapter is to explain how to use such sources to reconstruct a history of subsistence and society in precolonial south central Africa. The first part of the chapter describes the topography, climate, flora, and fauna of the Botatwe region, setting the landscape into historical motion through an analysis of regional paleoclimatological data. The second half of the chapter introduces the different frameworks of time, place, and subject produced through archaeology and comparative historical linguistics.

The Great Southern Plateau

From the wooded savannas separating the Congo and Zambezi watersheds in southern Democratic Republic of Congo to the southerly fringe of the Kalahari Sands sheet in northern South Africa, the continental landmass forms an elevated, basin-shaped plateau. High escarpments ring this elevated basin, reaching 8,000 to 11,000 feet above sea level and sitting 30 to 150 miles inland from the Atlantic and Indian Oceans. The center of the basin slopes down from these walls but remains about 2,000 to 3,000 feet above sea level. The expansive Kalahari Sands system covers most of the bowl-shaped plateau. These acidic, nutrient-poor soils are made up of 95 percent sand and extend from the equator in the north to Northern Cape Province in South Africa and from the western escarpment to the twenty-eighth parallel, which runs through Ndola, Lusaka, Bulawayo, and Pretoria. From south to north, rainfall, soil moisture, surface water, plant cover and height, and the levels of organic material in the topsoil all increase as the sand sheet grows less dense, having been subject to further weathering and deposition events since the breakup of Gondwanaland. Yet the soils remain relatively poor. Similarly, in a gradient from west to east, rainfall increases across the plateau. Today, rainfall averages within the northern basin range from 500 to over 1,800 mm a year, but they vary seasonally with the annual latitudinal migration of the Intertropical Convergence Zone (ITCZ) to produce three seasons: a warm rainy season that begins between November and January and ends around April or May, a cold, dry season that begins after the rains and continues until around August or September, when the winds pick up and temperatures rise significantly for the hot, dry season. Within these broad patterns, localized variations in soil fertility and moisture retention support unique clusters of plants, microenvironments that have long been exploited by the region's inhabitants.[1]

Speakers of Botatwe languages have lived in the north central area of the great southern plateau for the last three millennia. Their story unfolds in a region that stretches from the upper reaches of the Kafue watershed in the north to the northern fringes of the Kalahari Desert in the south, and from the hook of the Zambezi in the west to the foot of the Machinga Escarpment in the east (fig. 1.1). The mighty Zambezi River and its tributaries dominate

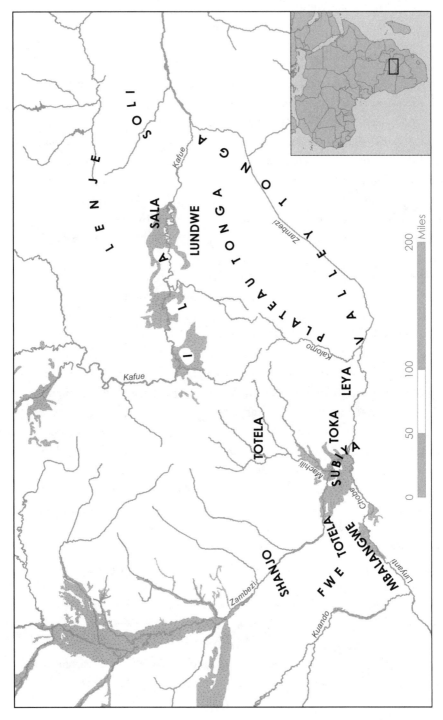

Figure 1.1. Location of Botatwe languages c. 1900.

the geography of the region, and a journey along the Zambezi and her tributaries is a lesson in the physical and human geographies of the Botatwe region. Following the channels of this watershed, we survey the environments typical of the lands once inhabited by the people whose histories we seek.

As the Zambezi reconstitutes itself south of its vast floodplain, it collects water draining from the central Angolan plateau to the west, the iron-rich *miombo* savannas of west central Zambia, and the dense, evergreen *mukwe* forests closer to the floodplain. The Zambezi courses over the Ngonye Falls and through a series of rapids before it hooks eastward, entering the territory where modern Botatwe languages are spoken. Today, the river's hook is the territory of Shanjo and Fwe speakers, the latter having extended into the Caprivi Strip and the former reaching near the border with Angola during episodes of engagement with and retreat from the demands of successive Zambezi floodplain states.[2] Yet this countryside around the hook boasts a very long history of settlement, including some of Zambia's oldest Iron Age sites: small, semi-permanent villages and hamlets dating to the last centuries before the Common Era.[3]

Beyond the hook, as the Zambezi continues its eastward course, it cuts through the driest, sandiest soil in the Botatwe region. Sand-loving teak forests claim both banks and extend northward, spreading into the upper reaches of the tributaries of the Machili River and into the Mulobezi Hills, a region famous in the nineteenth century for the skill of local Totela-speaking ironworkers. A mere twenty-five miles downstream, at the confluence of the Zambezi and Chobe Rivers, the teak forests give way to flooded grassland and swamp, a major dry season habitat for large game and vast antelope herds, which attract their own herds of tourists to local parks protecting this unique environment. Broadening our vista to locate the source of the Chobe, we see that it collects water from the Kuando, which flows from the southern Angolan plateau, past the Caprivian territory of Mbukushu rainmakers, whose influence was known far and wide in the nineteenth century, and stops at the northern Kalahari sand ridge. Here the Kuando shifts its name to "Linyanti" and its direction to the northeast, passing near the homes of Mbalangwe speakers and curving around the southern tip of the Caprivi Strip, slowing through the lowland Linyanti swamps and Lake Liambezi, and emerging as the Chobe River.

Beyond its confluence with the Chobe, the Zambezi River continues east, flowing by southern miombo grasslands and stands of *mopane*, the leaves of which feed both wild game and domestic goats that wander beyond the grass fences, *lilapa*, enveloping households. Today, fishers, many of whom speak Subiya, cast nets along this stretch of the river to feed the distant, growing cities of Zambia, Botswana, and Namibia. The Zambezi broadens as it approaches the lip of the Victoria Falls (Mosi-oa-Tunya), the traditional boundary of the upper and middle Zambezi zones. Suddenly, the river drops 360 feet, sending up a spectacular spray visible in Leya and Toka villages over twenty miles away. The waterfall has long attracted supplicants, who still build their shrines on the steep paths running from the top of the cliffs to the rocky outcroppings below. After this dramatic drop, the river cuts through the sheer, 600- to 800-foot-high basalt walls of the Batoka Gorge, speeding through cataracts and whirlpools to drop another 800 feet over the next 150 miles. From the falls to its confluence with the Kafue River, the Zambezi runs through 2,000-foot-high escarpments and forms a narrow floodplain, an important seasonal resource for Gwembe Tonga homesteaders, who plant gardens in its rich, black, alluvial soils. Up, over the rim of the northern escarpment, mounded villages built up by Iron Age farmers between the mid-first and early second millennium stud the fields and pastures of contemporary Plateau Tonga villages, farms, and cattle ranches, filling the landscape between the twentieth-century railway towns of the Batoka Plateau. On the southern bank of the Zambezi, Tonga speakers build homes alongside people whose ancestors had ties to the many ambitious trade and cattle states of precolonial Zimbabwe as subjects or as suppliers of copper.

The Kafue River is the next major tributary of the Zambezi, draining west central Zambia and the Copperbelt; it is a key environmental feature of the story told in the chapters that follow. The Kafue rises in the copper-rich hills dotting the boundary of the Democratic Republic of the Congo and Zambia and tours through the Zambian Copperbelt before hooking to the southwest, passing through the miombo wooded grasslands east of the Kanyamba Hills. The Kafue then turns southward, between two large flooded grasslands: the Basanga plains and swamps to the west and, to the east, the Lukanga swamp, the traditional homeland of Lenje speakers. The Kafue changes course just north of the rich Basanga salt deposits, flowing eastwards through its own floodplain, the Kafue flats, forming a labyrinth of grassy islands, termite mounds, and water-logged, marshy *dambos* that can reach one to two kilometers wide. These are the dry season pasturelands of Ila-speaking cattlemen, described by the eminent anthropologist Melville Herskovits as exemplars of his Central Cattle Complex.[4] On the northern bank, beyond the flats, lie the Blue Lagoon wetlands, a territory now occupied predominantly by Sala speakers. Together, the Blue Lagoon, Basanga, Lukanga, and Kafue wetlands rival the size of Zambia's better-known wetlands: the extensive Zambezi floodplain to the west and famous Bangweulu swamp to the northeast. The wetlands of the Kafue host an important habitat of grasses and sedges and sustain a variety of species through the dry season, including vast herds of antelope, buffalo, and other gregarious species, like the endemic Kafue lechwe (*Kobus lechwe kafuensis*). Inhabitants of the region have long exploited the diverse mineral deposits cradled in the lands enveloping the Kafue hook: iron, salt, and copper deposits, the latter including abandoned copper workings up to forty feet deep and fifty feet wide and dating to the nineteenth or twentieth century.[5] Earthen dams and long weirs punctured by conical *moono* fish traps announced to twentieth-century ethnographers one of many forms of human dependence on the Kafue and her tributaries.[6] As the river's multiple channels merge east of the central floodplain, between Sala villages and the Blue Lagoon to the north and the famous Gwisho hot springs near Lundwe-speaking communities to the south, the landscape retains its characteristic grasslands and seasonal swamps on the southern bank. The northern riverbank, however, transforms into a series of ridged crests and deep ravines running perpendicular to the riverbed, with mopane trees securing soils against erosion. The river courses through the deep, narrow channel of the Kafue Gorge, east of the Batoka Plateau, and finally drains into the Zambezi, at a point just northeast of the important salt deposits at Lusitu and the famous fifteenth-century trade emporium of Ingombe Ilede. Northwest of the confluence, gold, iron, and copper workings variegate the soils between Lusaka and the Zambezi, an area that was inhabited by Soli speakers as early as 1,500 years ago. At its confluence with the Kafue, the Zambezi turns eastward to meet the Luangwa River, which drains the Muchinga Escarpment and Luangwa Rift Valley to the north. After the dangerous Cahora Bassa rapids, a famous impediment to Livingstone's trade ambitions for the region, the lower Zambezi runs as a navigable river to the Indian Ocean.

Tracing the paths of the major regional rivers foregrounds typical environments of the area inhabited by speakers of modern Botatwe languages. Just as the languages spoken today resemble but are not the same as the languages spoken in the deep past, so, too, have the environments just distributed changed over time. A reconstruction of the changing landscape provides the first narrative framework for our story.

Paleoclimatology and the Historical Framework
of Physical Geography

The region described above, currently and historically inhabited by speakers of Botatwe languages, can be broadly described as a wooded savanna. Here, trees and scrub bushes grow within a thick mat of tall grasses, which reach from three feet to over six feet high. The variety of vegetation communities that form this wooded savanna today reveal important ecological relationships between the characteristics of the natural environment—soil, rainfall, elevation—and living organisms, including people. The distribution of ecosystems observed in the twenty-first century is surely different than the distribution that characterized the landscape exploited by Botatwe speakers living centuries and millennia ago. However, the relationships between the physical, organic, and climatological features of the current south central African landscape are more stable over time than their spatial distributions. For example, the rain and soil needs of miombo forests mirror those of most cereal crops and indicate good sites for future fields; similarly, mopane is a preferred environment for tsetse fly in the wet season. By carefully combining observations of ecological relationships that exist today with evidence for past climatological conditions, particularly rainfall and temperature, we can approximate how the physical geography of the region has changed over the last three thousand years and with what impact on Botatwe speakers' efforts to secure their well-being.

Soils, rainfall, elevation, and temperature determine which of four communities of vegetation, each named for a dominant tree species, flourishes in a particular part of the Botatwe region: miombo (*Brachystegia sp.*), mopane (*Colophospermum mopane*), mukwe (*Cryptosepalum sp.*), or Zambezi teak (*Baikiaea plurijuga*). Over the last three thousand years, the open, two-storied miombo savanna woodland has been the most common form of vegetation throughout the area of this study, thriving on nutrient-poor, shallow, slightly acidic soils that lie in a thin veil over dense laterite deposits. Today, miombo extends from the northernmost reaches of the region historically inhabited by speakers of Botatwe languages in southern Democratic Republic of the Congo to the lands just north of the middle Zambezi River. Miombo vegetation generally indicates 600 to 1,400 mm of rainfall annually and an elevation below 1,800 meters (fig. 1.2). With rejuvenation by occasional burning, it is a favored environment for swidden agriculture. A southern variant of miombo

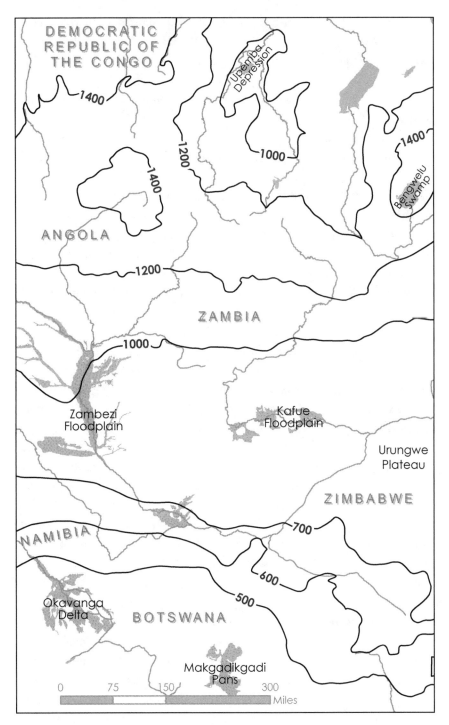

Figure 1.2. Contemporary rainfall averages (mm per year) in south central Africa.

savanna, supporting fewer trees and more scrub than its northern counterpart, grows today in the region to the south and west of the middle Kafue, where rainfall averages tend toward the lower end of the miombo range. In contrast, the vegetation community dominated by the classic southern savanna mopane tree is a more open, grassy wooded savanna indicating a warmer, drier climate averaging 500 to 600 mm annual rainfall. Mopane, a tree in the legume family, is often associated with poorly drained and slightly alkaline clay soils—indeed, it is common in the major river valleys of southern Africa, including the Limpopo, Okavango, Kafue, and Zambezi—and is a preferred habitat for tsetse fly and malaria-infected mosquitoes in the summer months. On the western edge of the Botatwe region, denser forests canopy grasses and undergrowth. Evergreen mukwe, also a tree in the legume family, dominates this three-storied, closed-canopied forest, which flourishes on the dry sandy soils stretching between the Kafue hook and the Zambezi floodplain. To the southwest, closer to the hook of the Zambezi and up through the catchment of the Machili, the deep, well-drained, acidic sands support thick deciduous Zambezi teak forests and their dense understory of thicket. Baobabs (*Adansonia digitata*), more common in mopane zones, are scattered throughout the region and often mark earlier human settlements. Similarly, termite mounds, papyrus, and waterlogged dambos stipple the dominant wooded grasslands and support specialized plant, insect, and animal communities, including riparian and swamp forests.

The distribution of the plants and animals that thrived in particular climate regimes shifted over the centuries as south central Africa experienced warmer and wetter or cooler and drier conditions. As Jan Vansina has observed for west central Africa, the most important impact of changing climate regimes in the southern savannas was the north-south migration of the crucial isohyetal lines of 1,200 mm and 700 mm annual average rainfall. The 1,200 mm isohyetal line currently runs through the northern half of the vast southern savanna region and is significant because it marks the limits of the central African yam-based horticultural system; south of this isohyetal line, farmers must grow cereals. The line marking 700 mm average annual rainfall is currently located along the southernmost limits of the modern-day Botatwe speech area and delineates the limits of predictable rain-fed cereal agriculture.[7] The historical distributions of two vegetation communities, miombo and mopane, are important to this story of subsistence in south central Africa because the transition between them runs along the crucial 700 mm isohyetal line. They literally render visible the boundary of stable rain-fed cereal agriculture.

Tracing out major shifts in regional rainfall patterns and temperatures over the last three millennia in comparison to current averages allows us to approximate the past distributions of miombo and mopane during particular periods of Botatwe history. While there has been no research on the past climate of the Botatwe area itself, a number of studies in palynology, dendrochronology, and geomorphology from the wider region delineate broad patterns of change in the climate regimes and physical geography of the region. Pollen core samples for this region of Africa are rare and of poor quality because cores need to be lifted from moist, still waters. There are few such swamps and lakes in south central Africa; most surface water is swift moving. However, cores have been taken from northern Angola, the Inyanga Mountains of Zimbabwe, the swamps around Lake Bangweulu in the southern regions of Northern Province of Zambia, and Lake Ishiba Ngandu on the Nyika Plateau in Northern Province.[8] These palynological studies shed light on changes in vegetation distribution resulting from climate change and human intervention through deforestation and burning. A second source of climate history is dendrochronology, or the examination of tree growth. For central and southern Africa, we can use results from Natal and Malawi.[9] However, dendrochronology is limited by the relatively short lifespan of most trees—usually a few hundred years—and the degree to which years of greater or lesser rainfall are reflected in the size of the tree rings that mark the annual rate of growth over the several hundred year lifespan of a tree. Changes in the surface of the earth provide a third source of data for climate history. For central and southern Africa, geomorphologists' research along the shores of Lakes Chilwa and Malawi, in the Kalahari Sands, and along the margins of paleolake Makgadikgadi have yielded the best evidence of regional climate history.[10]

The diverse sources of south central Africa's climate history provide the first narrative framework for the region's history over the *longue durée*. From the beginning of the last millennium BCE, a gradual warming trend and increased rainfall transformed the landscape of the northern Botatwe region, north of the Kafue floodplain. The climate shift toward warmer, wetter conditions slowly extended south, reaching the northern Kalahari by the first centuries of the Common Era.[11] This long period of warm, wet conditions reached its peak by the middle of the first millennium and then shifted fairly dramatically to cooler temperatures and lower annual average rainfalls.[12] The cooler, drier climate prevailed until the last century of the first millennium. Warmer, wetter weather returned from the close of the first millennium through the first few centuries of the second, corresponding to the Medieval Warm Epoch. By contrast, cooler and drier conditions characterized the fourteenth and fifteenth centuries, corresponding to the Little Ice Age. These local instantiations of the global Medieval Warm Epoch and Little Ice Age marked the beginning of a new climate regime characterized by an accelerating degree of unpredictability, with a warmer, moister period from the sixteenth to the eighteenth century followed by a widespread dry event from the mid-eighteenth to late nineteenth century, from which there has been limited recovery to present conditions.

In south central Africa, both today and in the past, shifts in temperatures and rain regimes between seasons, across years, and over longer periods of cyclical and episodic time have determined the success of a particular year's harvest or the size and distribution of antelope herds, facilitated the adoption of new crops, and undermined the sustainability of long-standing settlement patterns. Armed with a long-term history of south central Africa's climate, we can explore in the chapters that follow the dynamic relationship between the climate, environment, Botatwe speakers' understanding of different landscapes, their activities in and on them, and the human relationships that gave meaning to and were nourished by such labors. Methods for studying the changing climate and environments of south central Africa have the potential to reveal some human activities when they had a long-lasting impact on the landscape, such as burning vegetation for agriculture, hunting, and tsetse fly control. However, the lack of direct evidence for the regions of Botatwe speech requires us to look to the historical records of material culture and language to better understand how Botatwe speakers lived in and with their changing environments. Theirs was a creative engagement: Botatwe speakers adopted cereal agriculture only to further elaborate on food collection and participate in regional economic and technological networks that inspired the invention of entirely new categories of landscape and personhood.

Archaeology and Material Cultural Evidence

Archaeologists have contributed significantly to our understanding of the early economic and social lives of communities living in south central Africa over the last three millennia. Their research elucidates local iterations of broader transformations common across sub-Saharan Africa (and beyond), such as the adoption of cereals, cattle, and metallurgy; the development of extensive regional and intercontinental trade networks; and changing patterns of settlement and social stratification. Unfortunately, however, there has been little recent archaeological work in south central Africa. Indeed, most archaeological evidence for the Botatwe region was excavated and interpreted between the 1950s and 1980s. This research was part of the post–World War II intellectual project of producing a universal human prehistory by identifying common patterns of technological change that linked Africa, Latin America, and Asia to models of change developed for Europe and the Middle East.[13] In the southern half of the continent, the problem of the Bantu Expansion—a historical process by which one language family, Bantu, diverged into several hundred languages and spread across central, eastern, and southern Africa— dominated the post–World War II research agenda in archaeology. It was just the kind of sweeping narrative that could match contemporary studies of the peopling of Eurasia, the Americas, and the Pacific. Indeed, scholars of the Bantu Expansion even applied similar explanations to these diverse demographic events, emphasizing parallel technological changes. In the case of the Bantu Expansion, hunter-gatherers using stone tools were supposedly replaced by immigrant agriculturalists thought to speak Bantu languages and use iron tools.[14] Mid-twentieth-century archaeology in eastern, central, and southern Africa focused on culture history as a way to trace the Bantu Expansion: connections between regional material cultural traditions were thought to explain the direction and pacing of Bantu speakers' migration. Archaeologists of south central Africa played an important role in archaeologists' engagement with the Bantu Expansion, which may explain why research in the area diminished as the discipline turned its attention from diffusion toward in situ and regional Iron Age developments.[15] Although the questions that once drove archaeology in south central Africa rarely set the research agenda now, the findings of these early studies still offer valuable insights into regional and local human histories.

Archaeologists' periodization of south central African history alerts us to major transformations in subsistence, settlement, technology, and trade over the last three millennia. Late Stone Age sites, such as Gwisho near the Kafue River and Kalambo Falls in northeastern Zambia, evince hunter-gatherer lifestyles with home bases and activities sites (often seasonal), well-developed lithic industries, and small-scale social groups. Late Stone Age sites often contain ceramics, burnt daga, and bones from domesticates, perhaps acquired though trade or as a result of seasonal occupation by communities who had begun to produce food.[16]

The Early Iron Age brings a fairly marked change to the archaeological record of most parts of south central Africa. It is in Early Iron Age sites dating to the centuries before and after the turn to the Common Era that we see the first evidence for cereal agriculture and greater evidence for animal husbandry at sites like M'teteshi and Salumano (fig. 1.3).[17] Modest experimentation with metallurgy—both iron and copper in this region—begins in the first half of the first millennium in regions with rich ore deposits like the Copperbelt of northern Zambia and the iron-rich hills around Lusaka. Dabbling in food production required some degree of sedentism; small villages of fairly impermanent houses might have been occupied only during the agricultural season in the first half of the Early Iron Age, but by the middle of the first millennium, Early Iron Age sites grew in size and in permanence.[18] Kalomo, Isamu Pati, Mwanamaimpa, and other mound sites of the Batoka Plateau and the grasslands of the Kafue hook date to the mid-first millennium and are examples of the shift to larger, more permanent settlements (fig. 1.4).

In eastern, central, and southern Africa, the Late Iron Age generally dates from the eleventh century and is characterized by the elaboration of ceramic styles, greater investment in cereal agriculture, the development of intensive pastoralism in suitable environments, and the emergence of long-distance trade connecting more sedentary and perhaps larger populations.[19] By the tenth century, the forms of material wealth pioneered in the first millennium were intensively accumulated and exchanged. Differences in forms of material wealth have led scholars to distinguish two major cultural zones in central and southern Africa: the cattle-keeping and gold-mining societies of southeastern Africa and communities exploiting iron and copper objects and currencies in the savannas south of the equatorial forests.[20] Though a simplification, these zones are an important part of the story told here, for the Botatwe-speaking region of south central Africa lie at the frontier of these two cultural zones.

The dates and general characteristics distinguishing the Early and Later Iron Ages work well for the archaeological record of the Zambezi Valley and Batoka Plateau but are a poor fit for the middle Kafue, the central stage of this study. Archaeologist Robin Derricourt identified a tripartite Iron Age

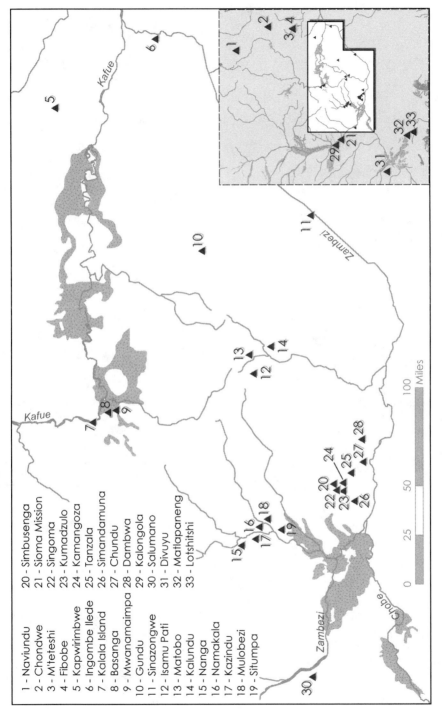

1 - Naviundu
2 - Chondwe
3 - M'teteshi
4 - Fibobe
5 - Kapwirimbwe
6 - Ingombe Ilede
7 - Kalala Island
8 - Basanga
9 - Mwanamaimpa
10 - Gundu
11 - Sinazongwe
12 - Isamu Pati
13 - Matobo
14 - Kalundu
15 - Nanga
16 - Namakala
17 - Kazindu
18 - Mulobezi
19 - Situmpa
20 - Simbusenga
21 - Sioma Mission
22 - Singoma
23 - Kumadzulo
24 - Kamangoza
25 - Tanzala
26 - Simandamuna
27 - Chundu
28 - Dambwa
29 - Kalongola
30 - Salumano
31 - Divuyu
32 - Matlapaneng
33 - Lotshitshi

Figure 1.3. Major archaeological sites of south central Africa before 800.

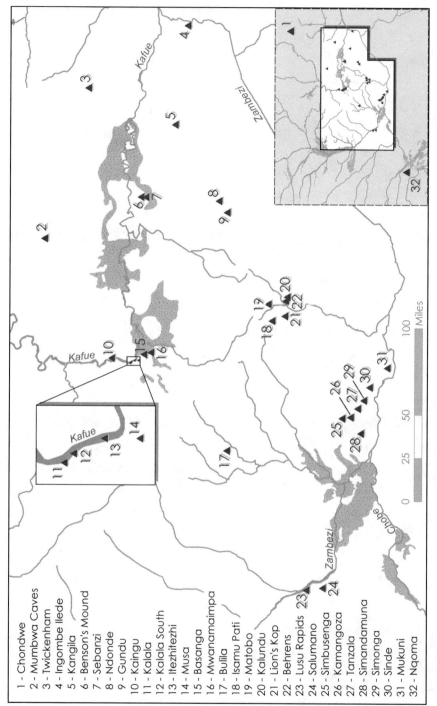

1 - Chondwe
2 - Mumbwa Caves
3 - Twickenham
4 - Ingombe Ilede
5 - Kangila
6 - Benson's Mound
7 - Sebanzi
8 - Ndonde
9 - Gundu
10 - Kaingu
11 - Kalala
12 - Kalala South
13 - Itezhitezhi
14 - Musa
15 - Basanga
16 - Mwanamaimpa
17 - Bulila
18 - Isamu Pati
19 - Matobo
20 - Kalundu
21 - Lion's Kop
22 - Behrens
23 - Lusu Rapids
24 - Salumano
25 - Simbusenga
26 - Kamangoza
27 - Tanzala
28 - Simandamuna
29 - Simonga
30 - Sinde
31 - Mukuni
32 - Nqoma

Figure 1.4. Major archaeological sites of south central Africa after 800.

chronology on the basis of radiocarbon dates and a cluster analysis of pottery samples: an Early Iron Age that followed broader regional trends and began in the early first millennium and then transitioned in the eighth century to the Middle Iron Age, itself followed by a Recent Iron Age dating from between the fourteenth and sixteenth centuries. Derricourt's Middle Iron Age is particularly important for Botatwe history because it spans a period of rapid linguistic divergence, discussed below. With the beginning of the Middle Iron Age, settlements of the middle Kafue region became more centralized and permanent and shifted from an Early Iron Age preference for settlement in the grasslands to settlement in multiple environmental zones.[21] Significantly, the extension of middle Kafue settlements into a greater diversity of microenvironments during the Middle Iron Age is a pattern that repeats itself in the Zambezi Valley with the transition from the Early to Later Iron Age. Archaeologist Joseph Vogel conducted extensive surveys along the Zambezi and concluded that an immigrant population represented by the emergence of Early Tonga pottery, a ceramic tradition with likely origins in the middle Kafue region, taught indigenous Zambezi Valley farmers how to cultivate areas beyond dambo margins in the early centuries of the second millennium. Nearly fifteen years later, Derricourt's surveys of the middle Kafue revealed that the settlement shift identified by Vogel in the Zambezi Valley had a historical precedent in the experiments of Middle Iron Age Kafue communities half a millennium earlier. Descendants of the Middle Iron Age Kafue communities who extended their settlements across multiple ecological zones likely introduced this subsistence and settlement strategy to the early second-millennium inhabitants of the Zambezi Valley studied by Vogel because this contact is also reflected in the ceramic record (discussed below).[22] As the Kafue Middle Iron Age transitioned to the Recent Iron Age between the fourteenth and sixteenth centuries, communities in the middle Kafue returned to smaller, more dispersed settlements, but continued to build those settlements across a variety of environments.

Although shifts in settlement patterns and subsistence strategies are among the most significant changes distinguishing periods of the Iron Age, pottery is actually the conventional material cultural trait used to develop Iron Age chronologies. While the classification of pottery in south central Africa is still a matter of some debate, the overall pattern that emerges from regional studies is an underlying diversity in the Early Iron Age across the broader region, including Kalundu on the Batoka, Kapwirimbwe near Lusaka, and

Dambwa in the Zambezi Valley, among many others surrounding the Botatwe-speaking region. These diverse forms of Early Iron Age pottery were slowly replaced by new, intrusive wares: in the middle Kafue, Early Iron Age wares were replaced in the eighth century by Middle Iron Age pottery; on the Batoka Plateau, Kalomo replaced Kalundu in the tenth or eleventh century and briefly coexisted with but was finally replaced by Kangila around the twelfth or thirteenth century; in the Zambezi Valley, a sequence related to Gokomere (Shongwe followed by Kalomo) was replaced by Early Tonga, a Kafue tradition pottery, by the twelfth or thirteenth century. The ceramic sequences have rarely been studied on the regional level, but the published archaeological record is clear that the introduction of new, intrusive wares replacing the diverse Early Iron Age ceramic profile with a more homogenous decorative repertoire first occurred in the middle Kafue before continuing south onto the Batoka Plateau, and finally reaching the Zambezi Valley by the twelfth or thirteenth century.[23] Significantly, the north-to-south direction of changes in the ceramic records of regional sites parallels the proposed direction for the spread of Botatwe languages and patterns of contact and absorption demonstrated in the linguistic record, discussed below.

In addition to the chronological and spatial frameworks developed from regional material cultural traditions, the archaeological record also sheds light on local narratives glossed over by the imprecise framework of "traditions" and "ages." Even as archaeologists identify broad patterns, their data also attest to localized deviations and the uneven adoption of novel technologies. These subtle differences allow us to tease out the contingencies of the much broader processes scholars use to distinguish material cultural traditions and delineate the boundaries of long chronological periods. For example, most archaeologists would date the beginning of intensive cattle keeping to the second half of the first millennium and would suggest that pastoralism was well established in many parts of southern Africa by the early centuries of the second millennium. Generally, this is true. Sites in southwestern Zambia show a slow intensification in cattle keeping as early as the mid-first millennium and sites with large herds of cattle are common on the Batoka Plateau by the early centuries of the second millennium. Yet this wide-ranging economic transformation was actually very uneven in the Botatwe-speaking region. Indeed, local excavations suggest that villagers living near the Kafue floodplain, an area known today for its consummate cattlemen, took up intensive cattle keeping only in the second half of the second millennium, perhaps as late as the seventeenth century. These localized differences in broader regional transformations offer us the opportunity to better connect the linguistic and archaeological records, a point to which we'll return. When brought into conversation, linguistic and archaeological evidence allow us to create more detailed human stories, which breathe life into monolithic processes like the adoption of metallurgy or intensive cattle keeping. It is to the production of linguistic evidence that we now turn.

Comparative Historical Linguistics and Language Evidence

Following a growing trend in early African histories, reconstructed words are the principal form of historical evidence for this story.[24] The words with which a person communicates his or her personal experiences are given meaning through social interaction. Therefore, speakers transform words' meanings over time as they use words to discuss novel life experiences with others. Individual instances of metaphor making, translation, explanation, or debate over what constitutes meaningful speech regarding concerns like elderhood, land clearance, or respectability accumulate over long spans of time as innovations in words' meanings. Reconstructing the histories of words illuminates the ideas developed by speakers as they described, organized, and transformed their physical and social worlds by talking to one another. Although we have no sources that capture discrete conversations that unfolded millennia ago around our hypothetical topics of elderhood, land clearance, and the politics of respectability, words' histories contain an astonishing amount of information about the past. This evidence is embedded in words' morphological markers, derivational paths, and multiple meanings. Word histories, however, can only speak to the scales of time and space that govern transformations within language families. Those scales are large, spanning huge regions—even continents—and unfolding over centuries or millennia. We might lament the fact that linguistic evidence cannot capture the inventive culinary practices that staved off the miseries of the failed harvest of a particular year or conjure up the conversation between a lineage elder and his nephew, now ready for marriage. After all, these are the familiar scales of individual experience from which social historians, using other kinds of evidence, attempt generalize. Yet reconstructed histories of words already reveal generalized patterns of change because they illuminate the cumulative trends embedded in the utterances of generations of speakers, who, together, constitute the speech community of a language. Words are a particularly democratic form of historical evidence, encompassing the experiences of elites and commoners, political insiders and upstarts, men and women, children and the elderly.[25] Histories organized around the social unit of the speech community challenge conventional understandings of matters of great concern to historians, including agency, subjectivity, individualism, and causation. These histories require us to explore such concerns in the large scales of time and space inherent to the social unit of the speech community and the collective experiences of its members. To begin, we need to define the boundaries of those speech communities, if only to better understand the actions of those who could cross them.

Developing the Linguistic Framework of Botatwe History

Two steps guide the production of historical evidence from spoken language: the development of a genetic classification, which serves as the framework for the history of language change, and the reconstruction of words' histories within that framework.[26] Though a variety of processes can produce similarities between modern languages, a classification focuses on similarities that arise from inheritance—from modern languages' status as genetic relatives that share a linguistic ancestor, or protolanguage.[27] Of course, that protolanguage is, itself, the product of the divergence of an even earlier protolanguage. Thus, the genetic classification of a language group is akin to a family tree. Genetic relationships between languages may be identified and measured in a number of ways, from comparing rates of shared cognates in basic, culturally neutral vocabulary (lexicostatistics) to the distribution of grammatical, phonological, and lexical innovations. In fact, the comparative historical linguistic method requires that we confirm genetic relations within and between subgroups of language families by identifying as many shared linguistic features as possible. When these methods are applied to the Botatwe languages of south central Africa, they produce the classification illustrated in table 1.1.[28]

The relative chronology inherent to the genetic classification can be situated in absolute time and geographic space. This process locates the communities that spoke the protolanguages identified in the classification and establishes the pacing and geographic scope of the stories word histories can elucidate. Glottochronology allows us to convert cognation rates in basic vocabulary into very approximate estimates of the date ranges within which a

Table 1.1. CLASSIFICATION OF THE BOTATWE LANGUAGES

Proto-Botatwe (57–71% [100–900]; 64% median [500])

    I. Greater Eastern Botatwe (63–74% [500–1000]; 68.5% median [750])

        a. Central Eastern Botatwe (70–77% [800–1100]; 73.5% median [950]

            i. Kafue (78–81% [1200–1300]; 79.5% median [1250])

                1. *Ila*

                2. *Tonga*

                3. *Sala*

                4. *Lenje*

            ii. Falls (91% [1700])

                1. *Toka*

                2. *Leya*

            iii. *Lundwe*

        b. *Soli*

    II. Western Botatwe (76–81% [1100–1300]; 78.5% median [1200])

        a. Zambezi Hook (83% [1400])

            i. *Shanjo*

            ii. *Fwe*

        b. Machili (84–85% [1400–1450]; 84.5% median [1425])

            i. *Mbalangwe*

            ii. *Subiya*

            iii. *Totela*

Note: Extant languages are italicized. Cognation rates, both the range of the normal distribution curve and its median, are provided in parentheses. Calendar years for the ranges and medians are provided in brackets.

Source: Adapted from de Luna, "Classifying Botatwe."

protolanguage gradually diverged into new languages. This method assumes that the random, unpredictable replacement of basic, culturally neutral vocabulary accumulates into predictable patterns of change over very long periods of time. Glottochronology, however, remains a contested method for dating linguistic histories and is best applied in tandem with direct associations between the words reconstructed to particular protolanguages and the material cultural remains excavated and dated by archaeologists.[29]

    To locate the speech communities of particular protolanguages in space, linguistic migration theory assumes a homeland in the area with the greatest linguistic diversity and for which the minimal number of moves would bring speakers of the languages that diverged from the protolanguage in question back to a common nucleus, to a homeland. This very approximate means of locating speech communities has rightly been criticized for ignoring local topography, disease vectors, and other conditions impacting settlement.[30] Once a protolanguage is located in approximate time and space, however, direct associations with the regional archaeological record can bring greater precision to our understanding of the places in which speakers of a protolanguage settled. Though archaeologists can recover material evidence for many human activities, we cannot, of course, know the language spoken by people who favored settlement in a particular microenvironment, made and used a particular style of pot, or hunted a favored kind of animal. We can, however, reconstruct words for such preferences. When words for specific human activities are reconstructed to a protolanguage and when the approximate chronological and spatial setting of that protolanguage corresponds with the location and dating of archaeological evidence for the same preferences, we can posit direct associations between the two discrete historical records, an approach taken in this book.[31] By identifying the chronological and geographic setting for ancestral speech communities through linguistic methodologies— however approximate they may be—the language classification itself becomes an historical framework. We may then reconstruct words to the protolanguages of the classification to learn about the lives of the people who spoke them.

Developing the Linguistic Content of Botatwe History

The second step of the comparative historical linguistic method redirects our efforts from reconstructing successive generations of linguistic differentiation across time and space to reconstructing the words speakers used to describe their world. When a word can be reconstructed to the vocabulary of a particular protolanguage through the application of the comparative method, historical linguists assume the idea, practice, or object to which the word refers was part of its speakers' world. The distribution and phonological form of a word within modern-day languages reveals when in the history of the language family the word was invented and into which protolanguages it was subsequently inherited. Distribution and phonology also determine whether an invention was an internal innovation developed within a community of speakers or a loanword borrowed into the speech community from another language; in the case of such word borrowings, distribution and phonology may also reveal the direction of transfer.[32]

Meanings adhere to random collections of sounds (e.g., words). Therefore, historians frequently find words of great historical interest whose age cannot be determined through sound change. To be clear: some words cannot be reconstructed because they do not contain any of the sounds that underwent change in a particular group of related languages. Historians try to draw conclusions about the antiquity of these unreconstructable, common roots by historicizing their distribution, but such efforts are provisional at best. We cannot be as certain of the age of common roots as we can of those words that follow or skew from expected patterns of sound change.[33] Reconstructing lexicons, rather than individual words, allows us to link common roots for which we have only historicized distributions to those with secure histories based on sound shifts. This move can support provisional arguments about such common roots' antiquity but does not replace phonological support for their time depth.

Reconstructed words indicate developments during the spans of mutual intelligibility between protolanguage divergences. The processes that determine a word's status in any node of the classification—inheritance, internal innovation, and borrowing—provide evidence for different aspects of the social history of the speech communities using them. Inherited words attest to the bodies of knowledge that speech communities continued to value as they diverged from their ancestral language. They provide a history of continuity in thought and practice across broad time periods and geographic regions, continuities deserving of historical explanation. Innovated words imply the simultaneous, related innovation of the idea or thing they signify. Innovations may take place within the speech community—an internal innovation—or take the form of a word borrowed from another speech community. Internal innovations often build on older ideas. Speakers derive new terms from familiar vocabulary either by compounding inherited words, transforming roots into new parts of speech (e.g., a new noun from a known verb), or simply layering new meanings onto an older term. Borrowed words attest to historical contacts between distinct speech communities and simultaneously demonstrate the porous nature of those boundaries. Such loanwords make visible processes of linguistic convergence to balance the narrative of divergence inherent to the genetic classification. Convergence is common in Bantu languages generally, but such contact is a particularly pronounced feature of the linguistic and human history of south central Africa, long a crossroads of populations, languages, technologies, and material cultural traditions.[34]

Speakers often borrow a number of words at once, such as the lexicon describing the cultivation of a new crop or the appeasement of a foreign spirit. Speakers borrowing words acknowledge the prestige, superior knowledge, or technical skill of the donor community in that domain of life, especially when the new words refer to an already familiar concept. When borrowed words occur in contiguous, regional distributions, they are called "areal" forms. Areals may be innovations developed within a geographic area by speakers of multiple, adjacent speech communities. Some areals also diffuse from centers of innovation, spreading out across broad expanses of territory, first through the networks of the people who invented the word, then through the networks of the first borrowers and so forth, often demonstrating only slight skews in pronunciation or morphology or showing very little phonological change. Areal forms reveal regional cultures of trade, spiritual practice, or social affiliation that cut across the patterns of linguistic difference emphasized in linguistic classification. To be sure, speech is only one of many ways to reckon belonging and probably was of minor importance in the context of great multilingualism that characterized most of Botatwe history.

Historians trace the development of individual words from their invention, through subsequent processes of borrowing, inheritance, and further innovation. They seek to build up the densest possible lexicon of related reconstructed terms in order to produce evidence of change and continuity over time in a particular domain of life, such as subsistence or political practice. Significantly, changing meanings and derivations might connect semantic domains like subsistence and political practice, offering historians important evidence about agency and causation.

If the distribution and phonological form of a word determine when and where speakers used it, its polysemy and derivation carry historical information about how and why speakers invented it, refining or elaborating its meaning to reflect—or even produce—the changing context of its practical use. In Bantu languages, reconstructed words usually follow four common paths of derivation: noun from verb, verb from noun, noun from noun by shifting noun classes or compounding, and verb from verb by adding common affixes. These processes tell the historian something of the creative, conceptual leaps Bantu speakers made between actions (verbs), objects and people (nouns), and, less often, qualities of being (adjectives as well as verbs and nouns of quality).

Derivation reveals the process by which a speaker proposed to extend the meaning of a known word through an act of association and convinced others to accept the value of that association by adopting the new word. Derivations reveal Africans' own conceptual categories, often in resistance to our best attempts at glossing them.

As an example, we can look to debates about the meanings of one of the best-known Bantu reconstructions: *-kúmú [1], an old word for a position of leadership. There is much historical information embedded in the etymology of *-kúmú, for the word's form reveals its process of creation and, therefore, the understandings of leadership and sociality available to the speakers who invented it. These understandings are conspicuously absent from dictionary translations of the word.[35]

In many parts of the Bantu world, nineteenth- and twentieth-century dictionary writers (European and African, scholarly and amateur) glossed this word as "chief," a translation burdened by the historical baggage of both Indirect Rule and the earlier circulation of new ideas about leadership that spread with eighteenth- and nineteenth-century slave and ivory trade networks alongside traders' political ambitions.[36] The reconstruction *-kúmú was first proposed by Malcolm Guthrie, who accepted the gloss "chief." Guthrie identified additional terms that shared the root, reconstructing the verb roots *-kúm- and *-kúman- with the meaning "to be honored; (become rich)," the noun *-kúmò with the meaning "fame," and the noun *-kúmù, with the meaning "medicine man" and a distribution restricted to the Great Lakes region. Scholars have debated the original meaning of *-kúmú in the earliest Bantu societies, largely drawing from the diverse meanings distributed across the particular subgroups of Bantu that inherited the word. For example, Jan Vansina argues that *-kúmú was a political leader, a Big Man with an achieved rather than inherited position, in keeping with equatorial ethnographic evidence.[37] On the other hand, Christopher Ehret explains that the person addressed by the proto-Mashariki Bantu word *-kúmò is best described as "a ritual leader of a defined kin group or set of related kin groups" because eastern Bantu speakers and members of the wider Niger-Congo-speaking world used their attestations of the root to talk about "kin-connected ritual leadership" and a "lineage level of kin authority" more often than political leadership in the twentieth century.[38]

Yet debates over whether early Bantu speakers used ritual knowledge or wealth to justify authority and power has obscured what ties these interpretations together and inspired the invention of the noun of quality, *-kúmú, and the verb, *-kùm-, in the first place. Underlying each definition is an association between emotively powerful feelings of honor, fame, and respect, on the one hand, and authority over communities, on the other. Indeed, the morphology of the noun *-kúmú, "honored person," and the verb *-kúm-, "to be honored," provide insight about what political work the earliest Bantu speakers thought the kind of honor described by the root *-kúm- actually accomplished. First, the noun *-kúmú is a noun of quality. Its final /-u/ tells us that it was once an adjective before it was transformed into a noun of quality. It was—and is—applied to speakers as a judgment of the person addressed by the noun, implying a sociality by its very use. Second, the verb form *-kúm- is an intransitive verb, a verb requiring no direct object, and this was a feature (or "aspect") of the original verb root. As an intransitive verb requiring no object, we cannot identify the object of the action of honoring; indeed, transitive verbs are those used to maximally distinguish between participants involved in the action of a verb, while intransitivity collapses all such distinctions.[39] Thus, intransitivity disperses any directionality—any *object*—of the verb *-kúm-, emphasizing the widespread, collective experience of being honored at the expense of the atomized agent that currently dominates understandings of the early Bantu *-kúmú and her or his authority. To be more direct: the aspect and morphology of the root demonstrate that the earliest Bantu speakers understood honor as something granted, ascribed through the use of a noun of quality but dispersed across the community, rather than directed at the titled individual. While later Bantu speech communities in the east and west elaborated on the ritual and material underpinnings of *-kúmú's authority, for the earliest Bantu speakers, the root composed a sociality by its use, activating a collective emotional subjectivity of honor with the power to actualize the political community led by *-kúmú. The etymologies of words like *-kúmú expose not only the changing meanings and associations of forms of leadership and affective experience, they also communicate Africans' own conceptualizations of affect, community, and power, in spite of translations like "chief," "ritual lineage leader" or "wealthy man" that force words into the categories of political and ritual authority that so often interest historians of early Africa.

Just as words' characteristics, like their morphology and aspect, illuminate the experiences speakers described as they innovated words, such as the affective experience of political authority revealed in the root *-kúmú, the ways in which words are associated with each other can also teach us about the past. Documents like travelogues, dictionaries, collections of folktales, and ethnographies add rich detail to the stories we can write about early pasts because they help us understand the social and material contexts in which the words we seek to reconstruct were spoken and given meaning, albeit in the recent past. Comparing descriptions of rainmaking practices, hunting tools, or political offices from the ethnographic record of all the communities speaking Botatwe languages and even neighboring languages illuminates patterns of broad similarity that could have resulted from a shared cultural and linguistic history. This hypothesis can be tested by determining the antiquity of the words for those aspects of ritual, technological, and political life that are common in the ethnographic record. Indeed, identifying redundant examples of associations between particular objects, actions, and practitioners through a comparative analysis of the regional ethnographic record is a vital step for developing arguments about associations between such activities, objects, and people in the deep past.[40] These arguments are all the more convincing when the associations are also visible in the derivations that produced vocabulary for those actions, objects, and actors we hypothesize were connected in the deep past. Establishing the antiquity of associations between distinct words and concepts helps the historical linguist make arguments about the contexts and causes of the historical changes that brought new complexes of words and practice into being.

Uncertainties

After a detailed consideration of what the sources employed in this study are able to reveal about the experiences of early central Africans, it is equally appropriate to ponder their limitations. Like any history, different parts of a narrative developed from linguistic, archaeological, ethnographic, and climatic evidence carry differing degrees of certainty, often related to the vicissitudes of preservation. In the archaeological record, the challenges to preservation are quite physical. For example, the organic construction materials of temporary hunting and fishing camps and early hamlets and villages are poorly preserved in the moist, acidic soils of central Africa and difficult to find archaeologically. Similarly, archaeologists struggle to find evidence of cultivated cereals or the many types of collected fruits and vegetables. Other materials, like daga for building more permanent huts, iron, and bone, have better survival rates. As a result, archaeologists can say far more about technological change in house construction, metallurgy, and cattle keeping than about the collection of wild greens, to give one example. Similarly, they can say more about village life than activities undertaken in ephemeral bush camps. Unfortunately, we cannot make strong connections between the linguistic evidence for the earliest periods of Botatwe history and the archaeological record because there has been little archaeology undertaken in the proposed regions of early Botatwe settlement and the material culture of this period (and of early Botatwe economies as attested in the linguistic record) largely consisted of materials that are poorly preserved in the archaeological record.

Similarly, the uneven history of change and continuity in the linguistic record of Botatwe languages compounds the problem of recovering the earliest chapters of Botatwe history. While the settlement narrative inherent to the linguistic classification (outlined below) surely provides a cogent historical framework for our story, it masks the unevenness of the historical account that can be produced from word histories. In the Botatwe language group, the phonological conservatism and poor documentation of western Botatwe languages poses a severe challenge to tracing the history of speakers of these languages. Indeed, the western Botatwe languages share only one solitary sound shift defining the western Botatwe branch, a stunning level of linguistic conservatism. As a result, we can only reconstruct words to proto-Western Botatwe that contain /h/, the voiceless glottal fricative, for *p, the inherited voiceless bilabial plosive.[41] Subsequent branches of western Botatwe were similarly conservative.

The lack of both linguistic and ethnographic documentation and the stunning phonological conservatism of western Botatwe languages impacts the story told in this book in two ways. First, the narrative focuses on the historical experience of speakers of eastern Botatwe languages because the more numerous sound innovations in these languages allow us to trace the histories of a greater number of words. Second, the conservatism of western Botatwe languages makes it more challenging to detect words that were innovations in proto-Botatwe; without phonological change to determine a word's antiquity, an innovation in proto-Greater Eastern Botatwe that was borrowed into proto-Western Botatwe could easily be mistaken for a proto-Botatwe innovation. Our understanding of the earliest histories of speakers of Botatwe languages is severely diminished as a result of the uneven character of phonological change, the lack of documentation in the western Botatwe languages, and the dearth of archaeological research between the middle Kafue and the Copperbelt. The story told here follows the richest data available, focusing on the histories of speakers of eastern Botatwe languages.

Just as sounds in some languages stay constant over time, so, too, do some words' meanings, a problem that also impacts the scope of any study based on word histories. Conservation of words' meanings brings a particular challenge to historians' stories, for we usually seek to identify and understand change over time. Semantic conservatism requires a careful consideration of the contingencies of continuity without necessarily supplying explanatory evidence for it. We see this linguistic conservatism in the vocabulary describing gathering, where the simple technology and labor organization changed very little, sustaining words' unchanging meanings over very long periods of time. We might expect that the vast number of wild plants exploited by the region's inhabitants would provide a source to trace changing practices of collection over time, but here the variety is often too wide.[42] Communities had—and have—local preferences that are reflected in highly localized plant names, even nicknames. Therefore, the word histories developed through the comparative linguistic method give us a history of change over time in the domains of hunting, fishing, honey collection, cereal agriculture, and cattle keeping and of relative continuity in the equally important work of collecting wild fruits, nuts, vegetables, and medicines.

The unique challenges of conservation in the linguistic and archaeological record produce an archive of uneven detail. Like many studies tracing history over long periods of time, the story told here gains precision as we move forward in time and, with the phonological conservatism of western Botatwe languages, as we move southward from the proto-Botatwe homeland and into the eastern Botatwe region. Unlike histories developed from a rich documentary record, however, the primary archive of this story, word histories, creates a gap between the last major divergence—of proto-Kafue at the close of the first quarter of the second millennium—and the beginning of the documentary historical record, which is poor until the nineteenth century. This gap can be bridged by the archaeological record, by the oral historical record of Botatwe speakers and neighboring societies, and by recent patterns of word borrowing that can be linked to datable events from documentary, archaeological, and oral historical sources, such as the immigration of Kalolo and Ndebele in the 1830s.

The Narrative Framework of Speech and Settlement

Weaving together the three forms of evidence described in this chapter—paleoclimatological, archaeological, and linguistic data—produces an integrated historical framework for the region. This framework determines the chronological and geographical scope of the chapters that follow.[43] It also alerts us to historical problems worthy of explanation, such as the changing pace of linguistic differentiation or the cohabitation of a region by makers of distinct material cultural traditions. These were grave matters for the children whose grandparents' speech would have been a different language and for the relatives of a young woman pondering whether to negotiate her marriage with a man whose family constructed its homestead, filled its cooking pot, and reckoned kinship in a different way.

Botatwe languages were not the only languages spoken in the area and Botatwe speakers did not settle in unoccupied lands (fig. 1.5). At each stage in the diffusion of Botatwe languages, their speakers settled alongside or near speakers of other Bantu languages. Contact with speakers of eastern Bantu languages in the Kaskazi and Kusi clusters, central Savanna languages, especially the Luban and Sabi branches, and southwest Bantu languages played a significant role in the history of Botatwe communities, particularly from the middle of the first millennium. Surprisingly, western Botatwe languages show very little evidence of contact with speakers of Khoisan languages, such as the Khwe group. I found no such evidence of contact in the eastern Botatwe languages. This does not mean that speakers of Botatwe languages were not in contact with communities that could be described as practicing a hunter-gatherer lifestyle, as many speakers of Khoisan languages have at different times in the past.[44] To be sure, hunter-gatherer communities, such as those described by Francis Musonda for central Zambia, would already have been living alongside speakers of other Bantu languages and had the opportunity to shift to those pioneering Bantu languages long before they were in contact with speakers of Botatwe languages.[45] The history of speakers of Botatwe languages, then, is a story of consequential settlement, of succeeding the avant-garde of the Bantu expansion.

According to cognation rates between Botatwe and other Bantu languages, proto-Botatwe, the ancestral language of all modern Botatwe languages, diverged from its own ancestral protolanguage some three millennia ago, in the frontier between the great Congo and Zambezi river basins, probably at the headwaters of the Luapula, Lualaba, and Kafue Rivers (fig. 1.6). The

Figure 1.5. Approximate location of major Bantu-language communities of south central Africa before c. 1000.

remarkable longevity of this protolanguage, spanning fifteen centuries from the beginning of the last millennium BCE to the middle of the first millennium CE, attests to the success of its speakers' settlements. Throughout this period, proto-Botatwe speakers innovated slight differences in pronunciation, lexis, and grammar as they mastered additional languages, slowly moved away from their natal villages to establish new settlements, and shared their language, villages, and children with people who did not speak proto-Botatwe. The increasingly warm, wet climate likely supported the extension of proto-Botatwe speakers' settlements southward up to the early first millennium, encouraging communities to live farther and farther away from the heartland of proto-Botatwe speech.

The middle of the first millennium marks the beginning of a period of stunningly rapid language divergence, during which protolanguages diverged nearly every two hundred years. The historical explanation of this remarkable rate of linguistic and cultural innovation in the eastern Botatwe languages is a central theme of this study. By the middle of the first millennium, the expansion of proto-Botatwe speech, resulting from extending settlements into lands populated by speakers of other Bantu languages and from the adoption of Botatwe speech by non-Botatwe communities, produced a linguistic landscape in which the descendants of speakers of proto-Botatwe living at the eastern and western frontiers of their speech community could no longer understand

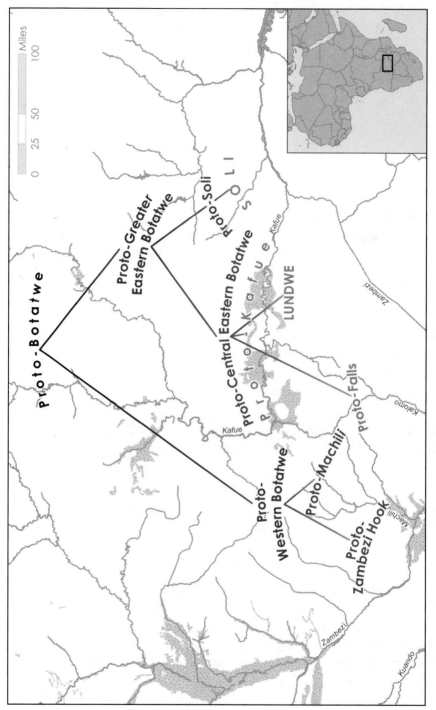

Figure 1.6. Historical geography of Botatwe language divergences before 1250.

each other. Proto-Botatwe had diverged into proto-Western Botatwe, probably located to the west of the upper Kafue River near the Basanga swamps,
and proto-Greater Eastern Botatwe, which was probably spoken in the lands
cradled by the Kafue hook. The rich wetlands of the middle Kafue and Basanga
swamps would have been a welcome refuge for these new speech communities
as the climate abruptly shifted to cooler, drier conditions at the middle of the
first millennium. To be sure, the concentration of populations around these
wetlands as a strategy to mitigate climate change may have sped up the divergence of proto-Botatwe into two distinct speech communities.

Quickly, after only two or three centuries of intelligibility, proto-
Greater Eastern Botatwe diverged by the last quarter of the first millennium
to produce proto-Central Eastern Botatwe and proto-Soli, the former remaining in the greater middle Kafue River region and the latter extending to the
southeast, toward the modern city of Lusaka, perhaps attracted by the prospects of ironworking ateliers established in the region in the mid to late first
millennium. At this point, the archaeological and linguistic evidence becomes
more reliable. For example, the density of direct associations between archaeological and linguistic evidence of localized shifts in subsistence and species
with restricted, specialized habitats supports the proposed linguistic homeland of Central Eastern Botatwe in the middle Kafue River region. These associations, laid out in detail elsewhere, demonstrate a clear link between
proto-Central Eastern Botatwe and proto-Kafue and the Middle Iron Age
(MIA) of the middle Kafue region, lasting from about the eighth through at
least the thirteenth century.[46] They suggest that Botatwe speakers developed
the new settlement patterns of the Middle Iron Age, as modest mounded villages in the grasslands along the Kafue River gave way to small, centralized
villages scattered within both the grasslands and the surrounding woodlands.
Based on stratigraphy and the cluster analysis of pottery, the Kafue MIA can
be divided into early (eighth century), transitional (ninth century), and late
(tenth through thirteenth century) phases. Direct associations connect the
early and transitional Kafue MIA periods to Central Eastern Botatwe communities and the late phases of the Kafue MIA to proto-Kafue speakers.

Linguistic evidence supports the mid-millennium shift to drier, cooler
conditions attested in the climate record. As dry conditions intensified from
the sixth century to the end of the millennium, proto-Central Eastern Botatwe
speakers found the well-watered middle Kafue to be a hospitable environment. However, borrowed words for species such as hare, hartebeest, sable

antelope, and wildebeest suggest that Central Eastern peoples had much to learn about living in such drier conditions from neighbors speaking eastern Bantu languages and living beyond the middle Kafue region.[47]

Near the close of the first millennium, only about two centuries after the divergence of proto-Greater Eastern Botatwe, proto-Central Eastern Botatwe diverged into three new speech communities. Proto-Kafue speakers continued the long settlement of lands adjacent to the Kafue, while proto-Lundwe-speaking communities expanded into lands south of the main portion of the Kafue floodplain, and proto-Falls speakers extended their communities southwest, onto the western Batoka Plateau. The more complicated divergence of Central Eastern Botatwe at the end of the first millennium and the extension of its daughter languages into drier lands to the south was likely possible because rainfall increased from the tenth century. This local instantiation of the Medieval Warm Epoch probably pushed the critical 700 mm isohyetal line southward, extending viable cereal agriculture far to the south—the direction in which languages were spreading.

Linguistic evidence supports two major developments during the proto-Kafue period. First, proto-Kafue speakers extended the limits of their speech community to lands located to the northeast and south of the middle Kafue homeland, a process that would facilitate the divergence of proto-Kafue by the thirteenth century and continued well into the second millennium among speakers of languages that emerged from proto-Kafue. Related to this linguistic process, proto-Kafue speakers continued to have contact with speakers of eastern Bantu languages belonging to the Kaskazi and Kusi clusters. In these exchanges, proto-Kafue speakers often sought to learn more about the local environments into which they were extending their settlements. This is particularly clear in borrowed terms characteristic of the drier environments of the Batoka Plateau and Zambezi Valley. The expansion of both languages and human settlements southward led to intense contact with Kusi speakers and, eventually, the absorption of some Kusi speakers into Kafue communities. Much of the evidence for each of these related historical processes relates to the natural environment. Terms for animal species are particularly illuminating.

Proto-Kafue speakers innovated a cluster of new terms for antelope species with strict preferences for wetland margins. For example, they borrowed Kaskazi term, *-jóbé [2] for the Zambezi sitatunga, a species whose only habitats in the Botatwe-speaking region are the Kafue floodplain and

Lukanga swamps. This borrowing supports the proposed location of Proto-Kafue around the greater Kafue floodplain region in the early centuries of the second millennium. In contrast, a complicated history of multiple episodes of borrowing from two sub-branches of Kusi characterizes the Botatwe words for ostrich [3]. Ostrich terms illustrate the acquisition of knowledge about semi-arid environments, for only in exceptionally dry periods does their range extend much beyond the Zambezi River. They also provide evidence of contact with different communities participating in a trade network south of the Zambezi River, which connected communities residing in the Kafue and Batoka regions to the societies of the Tsodilo Hills, eastern Botswana, and Zimbabwean Plateau, a historical link explored in chapter 5.[48] In addition to the terms for sitatunga and ostrich, proto-Kafue speakers borrowed a Kusi term for wild dog [4] (*Lycaon pictus*), whose preferred habitat of dry grassland and open woodland environment suggests that this borrowing occurred as some proto-Kafue speakers began to extend their speech southward, onto the Batoka Plateau, during the early second millennium. Similarly, proto-Kafue speakers borrowed an old proto-Mashariki root for lion, *-siumba, in the form *sıʊmbwa [5]. Whereas Central Eastern and even Greater Eastern Botatwe societies had borrowed words and knowledge from many different eastern Bantu groups, their proto-Kafue descendants interacted far more intensely with Kusi speakers, who likely inhabited the Batoka Plateau but were eventually absorbed into communities speaking proto-Kafue and its descendant languages. This intense interaction is an important part of the social history of proto-Kafue speakers explored in chapter 4.[49]

Linguistic evidence for contact between proto-Kafue and Kusi speakers and the eventual absorption of the latter into communities of the former corresponds with archaeological evidence from the Batoka Plateau and Zambezi Valley. In the first few centuries of the second millennium, makers of two distinct ceramic traditions lived side-by-side on the Batoka Plateau. One group crafted an intrusive style of pottery with roots in the Kafue and lands farther north. The other continued to fabricate a preexisting tradition, Kalomo, with roots in the Zambezi Valley and lands farther south.[50] Though archaeologists disagree on the appropriate typological definitions and, therefore, terminology, they have all recognized similar intrusions in the material cultural record and posited that such breaks represent the immigration of new communities mixing with and finally replacing or absorbing makers of Kalomo pottery.[51]

By the middle of the thirteenth century, proto-Kafue diverged into the ancestral forms of extant eastern Botatwe languages, the speakers of which continued the long-term trend of spreading Botatwe speech out from its Kafue homeland. Tonga speakers filled in the Batoka Plateau and Zambezi Valley. Sala speakers came to dominate the Blue Lagoon region northeast of the main Kafue floodplain. Lenje-speaking communities stretched Botatwe speech still farther to the northeast, to the Lukanga swamps. Ila speakers remained in the Botatwe heartland (fig. 1.7).

Our knowledge of the history of communities living to the west of the middle Kafue is far less detailed. Proto-Western Botatwe was a long-lived speech community that persisted for some seven centuries in the drier *mukusi* (Zambezi teak) and mopane savanna woodlands west and southwest of the Kafue hook. As the first quarter of the second millennium came to a close, however, proto-Western Botatwe diverged into proto-Machili, spoken along the upper reaches of the Machili River and its tributaries, and proto-Zambezi hook, which was spoken farther to the southwest, between the Zambezi floodplain and the confluence of the Machili and Zambezi Rivers. Some two centuries later, both proto-Machili and proto-Zambezi hook diverged into the ancestral forms of extant western Botatwe languages: Totela located in the upper reaches of the Machili River system; Subiya located along the shores of the Zambezi, downstream from the Machili-Zambezi confluence; Mbalangwe located upstream from Subiya speakers; Fwe on the western shores of the Zambezi, upstream of the hook; and Shanjo across the river from Fwe (figs. 1.6 and 1.7).

By the last quarter of the second millennium, the last Botatwe protolanguage, proto-Falls, diverged into Toka and Leya. During the eighteenth and nineteenth centuries, the political and territorial aspirations of Luyana and Lozi speakers in the Zambezi floodplain and caravan traders encroaching from both the east and the west shaped the settlement of all Botatwe speakers. The upheavals of these centuries were particularly felt by speakers of western Botatwe languages, a history we know from documentary and oral historical sources.[52] Many speakers of Totela, Subiya, Mbalangwe, Fwe, and Shanjo fled southward, across the Zambezi and into the swamps of the Chobe and Linyanti during the expansionist campaigns of the Lozi state. Botatwe speakers in the east generally remained on the frontier, but within the raiding zones of new regional political upstarts and the reconfigured Lozi state.

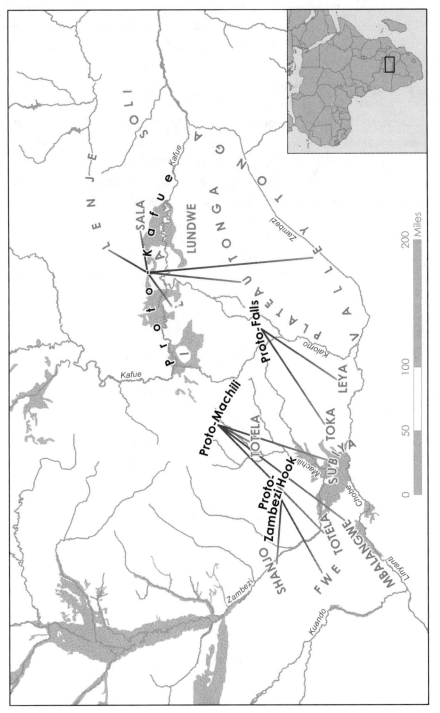

Figure 1.7. Historical geography of Botatwe language divergences after 1250.

The narrative framework outlined above was developed from units invented by academics: protolanguages and speech communities in the case of historical linguists and material cultural traditions and settlement patterns in the case of archaeologists. The leap from such heuristic devices to stories of human agency is a crucial interpretative step that foregrounds the *historical* significance of the evidence. This leap involves reframing changes in pot form, pronunciation, and words' meanings, to give a few examples, as both deliberate and unintentional outcomes of human actions. Armed with the mechanics of time and space delineated by the narrative frameworks of each methodology, we are able to use this technical apparatus to recognize instances of human effort in the deep past of oral societies. For proto-Botatwe speakers living on the frontier between the Congo and Zambezi watersheds, one such domain of effort was the incorporation of cereal agriculture as a novel technology within a well-established, diversified food system.

2. Planting Settlements, Forging the Savanna

Subsistence on the Central Frontier, 1000 BCE to 750 CE

The earliest Botatwe communities combined hunting, trapping, fishing, gathering, horticulture and, later still, cereal cultivation and cattle keeping to form a diverse but integrated subsistence system. From the early first millennium BCE to the middle of the first millennium CE, Botatwe speakers deployed all these strategies in a context of great mobility. Proto-Botatwe farmers participated in networks of movement, contact, and exchange that circulated new subsistence technologies across long distances and across linguistic and cultural boundaries. They and their linguistic descendants acquired the subsistence technologies that would serve as the core of the diet by the middle of the first millennium from neighbors speaking other Bantu languages and already living in the lands into which Botatwe languages were carried. Polygot members of the different linguistic groups inhabiting south central Africa facilitated the exchange of such subsistence techniques and the words that named them.

Cereal agriculture and crafting metal tools were two among many subsistence technologies exchanged across linguistic boundaries. While the adoption of cereals, ironworking, and, later, limited numbers of cattle would undoubtedly sustain great innovation in the lifestyles of later generations of Botatwe speakers, these technological shifts were gradual and uncertain experiments to those who first undertook them. In contrast to later eras of Botatwe history, the earliest two Botatwe speech communities, proto-Botatwe and proto-Greater Eastern Botatwe, did not distinguish between food production and the many other strategies of procuring food. Even later, as the next generations of Botatwe speech communities invented their own categories of subsistence, their distinction did not turn on the familiar divide between collecting and cultivating food. Rather, those innovations we usually assume to be the most transformative in histories of the ancient world—the shift to cereal production and the adoption of metallurgy—were transformative in unexpected ways. As we will see in the coming chapters, they facilitated Botatwe speakers' innovations in political culture not through the control of agricultural surplus but by securing the diet for experimentation with practices we might label food collection, which led to a novel politics of reputation based on knowledge about the bush.

As Jan Vansina observed over two decades ago, the adoption of cereal agriculture and metallurgy were slow revolutions.[1] Proto-Botatwe speakers, who began to sow seeds in addition to planting tubers and to forge iron into implements kept alongside stone tools, incorporated these technologies without committing exclusively to them. Several centuries later, cereals and metals did become more important than other subsistence technologies in terms of calories and utility, but this outcome had less to do with the inherent superiority of these technologies than with the conjunction of a particular set of circumstances relating to the efficiency of smelting, changing climate conditions, and novels ideas about who could achieve the prosperity that made cereals and metals a more attractive investment for some Botatwe communities than they had been before. Moreover, Botatwe speakers continued to undertake and reconfigure the activities of food collection.

Although we can easily rationalize Botatwe speakers' encompassing tradition of diverse subsistence strategies as necessary to their environment, climate, and technology, this encompassing tradition was also a product of the social concerns of Botatwe speakers and their Bantu-speaking ancestors. Matters like obtaining food were connected to the social and material context in which they were undertaken, contexts shaped by and around the ways in which Botatwe speakers believed the world worked. The social and political consequences of changes to subsistence described in the coming chapters come into relief against longer-standing ideas about how communities ensured their future. Like many of their Bantu-speaking neighbors, the earliest Botatwe speakers mobilized very old ideas about the relationship between the living and the dead, the nature of abundance and fertility, and the lands in which Botatwe speakers built villages and raised families. For Botatwe speakers, those who could appropriately engage with the forces of the world were able to meet material needs in ways that sustained both the living and the dead, ways that met the standards of good living. The technologies of subsistence, the character of communities, the nature of authority, and even the landscape itself would change substantially over the coming centuries and millennia— and change differently among related, neighboring Bantu-speaking communities. But the innovations developed by successive Botatwe speech communities over those centuries and millennia took shape within a cosmology in which ancestors were the lynchpin in the complicated calculus connecting subsistence, landscape, communities, and the leaders who took responsibility for ensuring communities' well-being. Spirits were an essential aspect of subsistence, both as recipients and instruments of bounty.

The Social World of Early Botatwe Speakers

Early in the last millennium before the Common Era, in the northern miombo savanna woodlands that lie at the headwaters of the Luapula, Lualaba, and Kafue Rivers on the frontier between the great Congo and Zambezi river basins, speakers developed a new form of Bantu language, proto-Botatwe.[2] This new form of Bantu speech diverged from its ancestral Bantu language as a result of the choices its speakers made about where to live, to whom to speak, and what new words to borrow into their common vocabulary. The generations of speakers who slowly adopted the changes in vocabulary, pronunciation, and morphology that would make proto-Botatwe unintelligible from its ancestral Bantu language created a resilient culture that flourished in the northern miombo environment. The remarkable longevity of this protolanguage, spanning fifteen centuries from the beginning of the last millennium BCE to the middle of the first millennium CE, attests to the success of its speakers' settlements. This success was practical, for families had mastered strategies that secured the food, shelter, and other necessities required to bring children to maturity. This success was also social and cosmological. Proto-Botatwe speakers' vocabulary for family, community, and spirits shows great continuity both during the period of proto-Botatwe speech and with periods that precede it. This continuity tells us that proto-Botatwe speakers had great confidence in the efficacy of their efforts to make lands productive by developing knowledge about how best to produce and collect food, improve soils, secure rains, and engage relevant spirits.

Although it is difficult to reconstruct words to proto-Botatwe because western Botatwe languages were so conservative in their phonologies, continuities in the words used by speakers of Botatwe languages today and those that have been reconstructed to periods of Bantu language history that predate proto-Botatwe reveal the social ideals inherited, if not innovated, by proto-Botatwe speakers. Among the most important of these was the relationship between territories and their inhabitants. Like their linguistic ancestors, proto-Botatwe speakers lived in territories they called *-sí [6], "country, village, neighborhood." They used the same root to speak about the people living in that space, "community, inhabitants of, a body of people and the locality where they live," and, with still another noun class prefix, ritual authority over that territory and those inhabitants. Relatedness was situational and relative. Social identity was rooted in both kinship and neighborhood, for being relatives was as much about the proximity that opened the opportunity for participating in each other's lives as it was about blood ties. These meanings speak to an ancient association between authority and socialized space or, conversely, territorialized groups. Indeed, this connection begs the question of whether human resources were, in fact, understood as distinct from the spiritual and natural resources of the landscape over which a leader claimed or earned authority. The conflation of claims to people, territories, and resources may have been encompassed in the old Bantu word for a kind of leader named *-éné [7], "owner of, master," derived from the proto-Bantu for "self." Although this term may have been used by proto-Botatwe speakers, *-éné dropped out of use among proto-Greater Eastern Botatwe speakers who faced a very different set of challenges to the links between lands, their material resources, and the communities of the living and the dead that were mustered to sustain subsistence, a point to which we will return later in the chapter.[3]

Burial sites and deserted villages were among many spaces that connected people to places because authority in early Botatwe communities mediated the relationships between the living and the dead. Deserted villages, *-tòngò [8], were prominent features of the landscape; they stood out as the theaters of older negotiations between communities and spirits. After the advent of cereal agriculture, *-tòngò marked locations of possible resettlement, for the debris of others' daily living eventually renewed the soil, creating fallow, farmable lands. Such associations between space, authority, and ancestors are remembered today: Chitonga speakers speak of *katongo*, "the relationship between a lineage and a defined area of land where it has rights of first settlement," and *sikatongo*, "earth priest; officiate for annual neighborhood rituals associated with the agricultural year."[4] As sites of earlier, deserted settlements, *-tòngò recalled the long-standing conceptualization of power that connected authority to the capacity to make lands and people fertile through the intersession of ancestor spirits, particularly those spirits connected to firstcomers.[5]

Ancestral spirits, *-zímó [9], literally glossing as "extinguished, lost ones," were among the most powerful figures in early Botatwe communities. Significantly, ancestors were not the inevitable outcome of kin's death. To effectively offer protection, ancestor spirits had to be remembered, and this required both the mobilization of relatives after a person's death as well as a person's best efforts to become memorable both during and after their lifetime. Anthropologists and historians of Africa have taught us a great deal about the practices, specialists, institutions, and interventions developed by communities to manage the attention of ancestral and other spirits. But we know decidedly less about the contingencies of efforts to *produce* spirits by families who counted among their numbers both the living and the extinguished. It is no surprise, then, that evidence from equatorial Africa inspired Jan Vansina to gloss the ancient Bantu root for ancestral spirits, *-dímó, as "hero."[6] The quest for ancestorhood likely inspired great creativity, generosity, and bravery in early Bantu communities. The material, social, and technological context of this creative accomplishment was a versatile, encompassing subsistence system.

An Inherited Tradition of Subsistence Eclecticism

Proto-Botatwe speakers' gardens and the grasslands, brush, and woodlands surrounding them constituted a robust larder. The earliest proto-Botatwe speakers, like their linguistic ancestors, were generalists who pursued a variety of strategies to feed their communities from nearby resources. Many of the subsistence strategies inherited by proto-Botatwe speakers were the products of their linguistic predecessors' experiences living in the northern, high-rainfall portion of the southern savanna belt. This point is easiest to discern by comparing the historical development of vocabulary for two forms of hunting: spearcraft and archery.

Proto-Botatwe speakers drew on two inherited pools of knowledge about hunting game, one ancient and the other a more recent elaboration on older technologies. From their earliest Bantu ancestors, proto-Botatwe speakers inherited and then passed on to their children a number of basic hunting strategies. Linguistic evidence suggests that proto-Botatwe speakers hunted with spears, *-gòngá [10] and *-sómò [11], a strategy that would become a focus of great creativity for speakers of Botatwe languages by the end of the first millennium. Likewise, proto-Botatwe speakers inherited the ancient Bantu term for "bow," *-tà [12].

Despite the antiquity of such hunting technologies, they were not unchanging. Most proto-Botatwe archery techniques and tools were developed by speakers of the Bantu protolanguages, such as proto-Savanna, that more immediately predated proto-Botatwe speech. Proto-Savanna hunters were inventive archers because they adapted an inherited form of forest hunting to the more open vegetation of the northern miombo.[7] Proto-Savanna marksmen innovated a new term for arrow, *-vóí [13], replacing an earlier Bantu term for arrow, *-bànjí. The new arrow point, *-vóí, may have been invented because it was constructed in a novel fashion; perhaps the point was joined to the arrow shaft in a new way or developed to travel farther distances in the open grasslands into which Bantu languages were being carried. The inherited proto-Savanna root *-vóí was used to invent a new word for "hunting by archery," *-vóím- [14], by either proto-Eastern Savanna speakers or, perhaps, as an areal between proto-Botatwe, proto-Mashariki, and proto-Sabi speakers. As the savanna environment came to be understood as the typical environment in which people settled, the word *-vóím- took on the generic definition "to hunt" in the languages that diverged from proto-Eastern Savanna, indicating the importance of archery in the hunting repertoire of the speakers of those languages. Proto-Botatwe archers inherited another kind of barbed arrow, *-gomba [15], and a new kind of hunting poison, *-lémbé [16], from their proto-Savanna or proto-Eastern Savanna linguistic ancestors. This new arrow point probably marks a shift in function from earlier dartlike missiles dependent on poison for killing the animal to a new potential for the missile itself to maim the animal when the barbs tore the animal's innards during its flight. Barbs also made poison all the more effective.

Hunting with spears or with bows and arrows was not the only way proto-Botatwe speakers brought meat to the cooking pot. Trapping, *-tég- [17], provided a predictable source of food and took far less effort than hunting. This more passive strategy was intimately connected to cultivation. Farmers planted traps in and near fields and stands of wild foods, exploiting the synergistic relationship between protecting crops from scavenging animals and birds and using the crops to attract game species preferred for their meat, skins, and horns.[8] As Jan Vansina observed of societies in the equatorial rainforest, farmers developed a complicated knowledge about which kinds of plants, and at what particular level of maturity, would attract which kinds of animals.[9] Farmers selected their traps to ensure that both gardens and larders remained full. Among the devices set to protect yam fields or stands of wild grains, *-pèto [18], a spring noose, was inherited by proto-Botatwe speakers, for its relict distribution within Botatwe languages and Savanna Bantu more generally attests to its age. The trap was easily built with simple materials (bent stick, rope) and little labor input. The simplicity of this device probably secured its place within the body of knowledge that enabled savanna Bantu farmers to practice shifting agriculture, frequently moving their fields and the technologies that protected them. Perhaps as early as the era of the proto-Bantu speech community, birds were trapped with the unctuous substance *-lìmbò [19], birdlime. Proto-Botatwe speakers also used a very old falling trap, *-líbá [20], in which a heavy stone or log was balanced to fall when an animal, attracted to the bait under the stone, shifted the sticks supporting the weight; the animal was crushed by the falling stone. Smaller versions of this trap were used to catch birds while larger ones were particularly effective traps for leopards and other cats. Spring noose, birdlime, and falling traps caught different kinds of animals attracted to the different plants within fields, gardens, and the lands between villages.

Knowledge and names of plant species were passed down from generation to generation, along with the seeds of preferred varieties and the location of particularly vigorous recurring growths of wild fruits and vegetables. The earliest Botatwe horticulturalists knew of edible gourds, probably eating the leaves as well as the fruit of the vines.[10] They likely grew cowpeas (*Vigna unguiculata*) and Bambara groundnut (*Vigna subterranean*) for protein and to revitalize fragile garden soils. Ancient Bantu terms for cowpeas and groundnuts, *-kóndè [21] and *-jògó [22], respectively, fell out of usage in Botatwe languages, though knowledge of them many not have been lost because the

Figure 2.1. Gathering wild grasses in the Gwembe Valley. Reprinted from Scudder, *Ecology of the Gwembe Tonga,* plate VI(a). Permission courtesy of the University of Zambia.

foods are known by different names today. Other foods were remembered and used across millennia. A common yam, *-pàmá [23], was named by proto-Bantu speakers while *lʊngʊ [24], another variety of yam, was a proto-Savanna innovation; both are still consumed in Zambia today.[11]

Many wild fruits, vegetables, fungi, greens, and medicines were available adjacent to houses, within gardens and fields, and along paths between settlements. Oleaginous trees like the baobab, *-bʊ̀jʊ́ [25] (*Adansonia digitata*), and castor bean tree, *-bónò [26] (*Ricinus communis*), supplied food and oil for cooking and smearing on the body. *Mobola* plum trees (*Parinari curatellifolia* and *Parinari capensis*) had long been exploited by eastern Bantu speakers and Botatwe communities spoke of these fruits in the earliest proto-Botatwe times as *-bʊda [27]. They ate the fruits and perhaps brewed them into beer, saving the nuts inside the endoscarp as another supply of food. Proto-Botatwe speakers certainly collected wild grains, as they continued to do in the twentieth century (fig. 2.1). Wild plants were also vital resources for making mats, bark-fiber rope, and storage containers. Some calabashes were also probably cultivated specifically for storage.[12]

In addition to wild game, legumes, and beans, proto-Botatwe householders inherited other strategies to add protein to their diets. Goats—

named by early Bantu speakers as *-bódì but called *-pòngó [28] in proto-
Botatwe—and guinea fowl, *-kángà [29], would have added to the cooking
pot. Dogs were likely kept for hunting.[13] Plentiful rivers and streams crossed
the savanna homeland of proto-Botatwe speakers, running with swift currents during the rainy season and forming well-stocked fishing pools as the
annual rains tapered off. Proto-Botatwe speakers angled with hook and line,
*-lób- [30], just as their linguistic ancestors had done for millennia.[14] They
also used baskets and traps. In the form of fishing proto-Botatwe speakers
called *-zòb- [31], or "dipping," fishers dipped round, shallow, plate-like baskets into the water to retrieve fish stunned by bludgeoning or by mixing
bottom sediments or poison into the water.

Proto-Botawe speakers inherited a robust, comprehensive approach to
subsistence. They integrated a diverse set of subsistence strategies together
in order to weather periodic and longer-term climate shifts, make productive
a range of environments, and easily incorporate novel technologies. Proto-
Botatwe farmers propagated edible tubers, planted legumes and gourds, secured their crops with traps, fished the swift waterways, and brought down
game in the open savannas. The longevity of the proto-Botatwe speech community, which spanned about fifteen centuries, attests to the success of this
versatile, encompassing subsistence system. But the success of this lifestyle
was also born of the unique climatological period in which the many generations of proto-Botatwe speakers lived.

The emergence of the proto-Botatwe speech community coincided
with the end of a long period of dry conditions as the climate underwent a
shift toward the warmer and wetter environment that would characterize the
next fifteen centuries.[15] The expansion of this warm, humid climate slowly
spread from north to south, from central Africa at the beginning of the first
millennium BCE to the northern Kalahari by the first centuries CE. As the
warm, wet climate regime of the proto-Botatwe era intensified over the first
five centuries of the first millennium, rainfall may have doubled over modern-
day averages.[16] Just as the new climate regime spread north to south so, too,
did the northern miombo environment it sustained. This meant that the
eclectic food system developed by proto-Botatwe speakers in the northern
miombo environment could be successfully carried southward, generation
after generation, across a millennium and a half, either opportunistically
or under pressure from the parallel southerly expansion of environments
with denser bands of vegetation to the immediate north of the miombo, an

environment for which proto-Botatwe subsistence was poorly suited. The opportunity to follow the shifting territories of broad ecological zones allowed proto-Botatwe speakers to move and interact with other speech communities who were also very slowly adapting the locations of their settlements and the strategies they employed to feed their families.

Innovations in Proto-Botatwe Subsistence Strategies

Continuity in language and subsistence strategies did not preclude inventiveness during the proto-Botatwe era. Indeed, the invention and adoption of new technologies had long been at the heart of the savanna subsistence system, as exemplified by the innovation of archery technology by the generations of Bantu speakers who lived before the proto-Botatwe era. During the very long span of proto-Botatwe speech, proto-Botatwe homesteaders, themselves, contributed their own innovations to savanna subsistence strategies. They borrowed new crops and adopted new by-products from bee's nests. These innovations demonstrate how proto-Botatwe speakers contributed to the long-standing inventiveness of savanna farmers' wide-ranging approach to subsistence.

Subsistence Innovations Dating from 1000 BCE to 500 CE

Sometimes, as in the case of honey hunting, proto-Botatwe speakers invented new words and products independently, elaborating on a form of work they already knew. Like fishing, trapping, hunting, and yam, gourd, and legume cultivation, honey collection was an ancient practice that proto-Botatwe speakers learned from their linguistic forebears and carried across a number of microenvironments over the course of three millennia. Much of the vocabulary describing honey collection was inherited, for few tools were needed to collect honey. Proto-Botatwe speakers conserved the very ancient Bantu word for honey, *-ócì [32]. Similarly, Botatwe people applied an old, inherited root for a tree hollow, *-pàkò [33], to refer to a natural hive, for these locations were frequently exploited by Botatwe speakers, who have no term for man-made hives. Proto-Botatwe speakers also innovated new words to talk about honey and its collection. Many of these were very basic terms. For example, proto-Botatwe speakers used *(ì)mpòká [34] for "honey bee," a word they shared with Bantu speakers living to the southwest. Proto-Botatwe speakers also renamed beeswax with the term *-ka(to) [35]. This innovation may have been related to innovations in archery, as beeswax is a common adherent in arrow making. Similarly, proto-Botatwe speakers used an older, inherited word for flower, *-lòbà [36], stretching the meaning of that word to talk about beebread, the pollen stored in a hive and fed to the bee larva as a protein to supplement the carbohydrates in their honey food.

The development of these new words for very basic honey vocabulary is surprising because we know that the ancestors of Botatwe peoples also collected honey. As proto-Botatwe speakers extended their settlements southward, they found the experience of hunting for and consuming honey to be novel enough to replace a number of the most basic terms their linguistic ancestors had used to talk about this work. Perhaps the locations of bees' nests and the kinds of products proto-Botatwe speakers found in those nests were significantly different in unfamiliar savanna ecologies because the pollens that bees used to make honey had changed. Perhaps knowledge of where one could collect these novel types of wax, beebread, and honey brought prestige. Or it may be that proto-Botatwe-speaking honey hunters who procured the honey, wax, and beebread of *impuka* bees played up the distinctive qualities of their products, encouraging their consumers to develop particularly discerning tastes and preferences for waxes used in crafting tools and the beebread and honey consumed as food. Interestingly, the term for calorie-rich honey— the main product that Botatwe people sought—did not change.

In other cases of innovation, particularly with domesticates like gourds, tubers, and cereals, proto-Botatwe speakers were learning of foods and products that were completely new to them. These technologies were borrowed alongside the words used to name them and the tools used to tend them. In particular, proto-Botatwe speakers shared cuttings, seeds, and roots with communities speaking eastern Bantu languages and living in an arc to the north, east, and south of proto-Botatwe communities. Through these exchanges, proto-Botatwe speakers came to eat a new kind of edible tuber, *-sɪabe [37], and gourd, *-óngò [38], and were introduced to the nutritious Livingstone potato, *-lʊmbʊ [39].

Subsistence Technologies Datable to the Early First Millennium
We know a great deal about the history of the spread of cereal cultivation and metallurgy compared to the histories of fishing, hunting, and plant collection. The detailed narrative offered here is not a result of proto-Botatwe speakers' emphasis on cereals or metals—the vocabularies we can reconstruct for these

technologies is no more robust than the vocabularies of trapping or honey hunting. Rather, scholars have sustained great interest in the histories of cereals and metals because of the transformative properties associated with the storable surplus supplied by cereals and the durability of metals combined with metals' great malleability, a feature that allows them to take an incredible range of shapes and, therefore, uses. Metals also have better survival rates in the archaeological record. Pithily, scholars have developed a detailed picture of the spread of cereals and metals because these technologies have long been thought to revolutionize how ancient peoples lived.[17] This book argues differently: societies develop their own categories of subsistence and elaborate on the social and material promise of such categories in unpredictable, contingent ways. However, the story of the diffusion of cereal agriculture remains significant to the history of proto-Botatwe speakers not because cereals and metals in and of themselves lead to economic or political complexity, but because many centuries later, Botatwe speakers harnessed the unique attributes of these technologies toward unexpected elaborations in other subsistence strategies, like spearcraft.

In the early centuries of first millennium, as proto-Botatwe speakers added cultivation and metallurgy to their subsistence repertoire, the economic, social, and political transformations so often associated with Neolithic lifeways in our civilizational narratives—increasing social stratification; the development of specialists like priests, artisans, and craftsmen; and the centralization of political authority—were not in evidence. Rather, cereals and metals remained a very minor part of the subsistence economy for centuries. To foreshadow the argument of later chapters, when farmers put cereals cultivated with metal tools at the center of their diet from at least the seventh or eighth century, the resulting economic, social, and political transformations unfolded in quite unexpected ways, around the activities of the spaces beyond fields and full granaries. In the early centuries of the first millennium, however, the adoption of cereals and metals were two options among many underpinning local combinations of food procurement strategies characteristic of the savanna subsistence economy.

Cereal cultivation spread from the eastern Bantu-speaking world along two major pathways of diffusion, probably as a result of both the extensive character of cereal cultivation in the miombo and through trade and contact. To the north, in the last centuries BCE and the earliest centuries of the Common Era, a set of loanwords describing a form of cereal cultivation that was initially developed in the Rift Valley of East Africa slowly diffused westward along the northern margins of the well-watered southern savanna. Farmers exchanged seeds, planting strategies, and vocabulary about sorghum (*Sorghum bicolor*), *-sàká, and finger millet (*Eleusine coracana*), *-lè, from the western shores of Lake Tanganyika as far as the upper reaches of the Lualaba River. A different pair of words for sorghum and finger millet—*-sángú and *-ku, respectively—connected farmers on the upper Lualaba to those cultivating in the Upemba Depression, along the upper Kasai, and even as far as the Atlantic coast into another zone of shared agricultural vocabulary and practice.[18] A second path of diffusion existed farther south, along the southern fringe of the savanna belt and the northern reaches of the Kalahari Sands system. This zone of contact and exchange probably developed slightly later, in the first centuries of the Common Era. Reflecting the drier environment of this path of diffusion, farmers in this zone exchanged sorghum, *-pú, and pearl millet, *-bèlé, from east to west.[19]

None of the of the word clusters that scholars have used to map cereal crop diffusion exactly match Botatwe cereal vocabulary, which includes roots for sorghum (*Sorghum bicolor*) and millet (probably pearl millet, *Pennisetum glaucum*): *-(y)ıla [40] and *-bèlé [41], respectively. This point carries three implications for early Botatwe history. First, Botatwe speaking communities were likely located somewhere between these two belts of diffusion, probably closer to the southern belt. This location fits well with the argument that the intensification of warmer, wetter climate conditions from the beginning of the Common Era opened opportunities for settlement to the south and facilitated the expansion of Botatwe languages in that direction. Second, borrowings from both the northern and southern zones demonstrate that proto-Botatwe speakers were in contact with communities to both the north and south. This is a simple point, but as we will see in chapter 5, proto-Botatwe speakers were among a number of communities living on a central frontier between these zones of diffusion, providing early and probably indirect links between them. Finally, the imperfect fit between Botatwe cereal vocabulary and the vocabularies marking the zones of diffusion reconstructed by other scholars serves as a reminder that the spread of cereals was a far more localized, contingent process than paths of diffusion would suggest. Cereals spread in the complicated ecological and social settings of existing communities. For speakers of proto-Botatwe, their location on a frontier at the center of these two paths of diffusion offered greater opportunities to diversify because they had access to the subsistence technologies of two agricultural traditions.

Although the distributions and phonologies of these terms within Botatwe languages attest to their status as very old borrowed terms, it is impossible to determine by phonology whether they were borrowed during the last centuries of the proto-Botatwe era or early in the history of the speech communities that developed as proto-Botatwe diverged: proto-Western Botatwe and proto-Greater Eastern Botatwe. Archaeological evidence, however, suggests that the introduction of cereals unfolded during the last centuries of proto-Botatwe speech and into the first centuries of proto-Western Botatwe and proto-Greater Eastern Botatwe speech. Archaeological remains of cereals are rare in south central and southern Africa, but sorghum seeds have been recovered from M'teteshi and dated to the first century CE, from Mondake dated to the early seventh century, from Isamu Pati dated to the seventh century (*Sorghum caffrorum Beauv.*), and from Nqoma dated to the late tenth century. Both sorghum and millet were found at Matlapaneng and dated between the ninth and eleventh centuries.[20] Grain storage bins recovered from lower levels of Isamu Pati suggest the cultivation of millet as sorghum does not store well.[21]

In contrast with areas farther north, the spread of ironworking technology across eastern and southern Africa diffused in tandem with cereal agriculture, or at least along commensurate paths in nearly overlapping periods. As David Killick has suggested, there may have been a delay in the southward spread of ironworking technology as farmers living on the northern fringe of the miombo belt that crosses southern Tanzania, Malawi, northern Mozambique, Zambia, and Angola experimented with growing cereals in the unfamiliar miombo environment. In the last centuries BCE, farmers in this zone conjoined the two technologies of metallurgy and cereal agriculture. They learned that the infertile soils of the miombo belt could be temporarily enriched by combining the cutting and burning of wood on future field sites, complex crop rotations, and long periods of fallowing. Iron axes were essential to this new miombo slash-and-burn agricultural system.[22]

South central Africans acquired their first iron and copper objects through trade.[23] The earliest iron items to circulate through the area were probably small items for personal decoration, but the importance of metal to the swidden style of cereal agriculture adopted in the miombo suggests that iron agricultural tools were especially significant trade items.[24] Iron hoes, an indirect indicator of cereal agriculture, were found at the Early Iron Age sites of Kumadzulo, Isamu Pati, and Fibobe and dated to between the sixth and seventh century, the seventh century, and the mid-eight to mid-tenth centuries, respectively. But iron did not displace stone tool technology. Farmers made use of weighted digging sticks well into the first millennium. Stone grinders, rubbers, pottery burnishers, stone hammers and even flaked stone blades, cleavers, scrapers, planes, abraders, and picks remained vital parts of the toolkit, including the toolkit developed for iron ore mining. Indeed, both stone and iron tools were linked to cereal agriculture.[25]

Linguistic evidence confirms the vital link between cereal farming and ironworking. The earliest set of loanwords borrowed into proto-Botatwe in the earliest centuries of the first millennium include *-gamba [42], "hoe," and *-jèmbè [43], "axe." These terms indicate why proto-Botatwe speakers traded for iron products and undertook laborious and rarely productive early attempts at smelting. The earliest adoption of ironworking by Botatwe speakers also included the technology of forging. Nearly all Botatwe languages attest a phonologically skewed form of the old verb *-tól- [44], "to forge," and *-(j)òndò [45], an ancient loanword for the smith's hammer or anvil. While scholars agree on the antiquity of these loans, a deep history supported by the Botatwe evidence, they offer widely divergent views on the direction of diffusion, even proposing contradictory histories of the same roots. For example, Jan Vansina argues for the diffusion of metallurgy and its vocabulary from the northwest across the Bantu zone toward the south and east. In contrast, Christopher Ehret posits diffusion from the western Rift Valley to the west and south. The Botatwe evidence contributes little to these debates, but we can be confident that proto-Botatwe speakers borrowed these technologies in the northern half of the southern savannas in the first centuries of the first millennium.[26]

Metallurgy was as slow a revolution as the adoption of cereal agriculture, for farmers in south central Africa acquired iron tools long before they mastered smelting locally. Slag is found in nearly all Early Iron Age sites, but usually in very small quantities, suggesting a persistent but not very productive interest in smithing and perhaps smelting in villages across the region during the first half of the first millennium.[27] Iron ores are common in lower grade forms, such as bog iron, throughout the region, and this abundance would have facilitated experimentation. The widespread regional pattern of persistent, local, small-scale smelting was eventually punctuated by centers of smelting expertise, such as the fifth-century smelting atelier at Kapwirimbwe, situated thirteen kilometers east of the modern day city of Lusaka and eight kilometers west of a particularly rich concentration of iron ore.[28] Kapwirimbwe was occupied only briefly, perhaps for a generation or two, and covered some one thousand to two thousand square meters, but its industry is evident from the abundant slag and unworked bloom recovered at the site compared to contemporary sites dating to the first half of the first millennium. Over eighty-one kilograms of slag and nearly eight kilograms of unworked bloom were recovered at a portion of the site thought to be the residential section. An even greater concentration of both products was discovered in a ploughed field within the site and adjacent to the excavations, the likely location of the majority of the smelting operations. Daga—burnt daga, daga fused with slag, and daga bearing wood impressions—was also abundant at the site, likely the remains of ancient furnaces.

It is important to point out at this juncture that smelting took place within the village until the end of the Early Iron Age. This is true of the Kapwirimbwe atelier and sites with abundant evidence of ironworking in the Zambezi Valley, including the late sixth- to early seventh-century site of Kumadzulo in the greater Victoria Falls region. These latter sites were adjacent to dambos rich in bog iron and close to two ancient ferricrete surface mines. Similarly, iron slag, ferricrete ore, tuyère, bellows nozzles, and other evidence of smelting were recovered from the settlement areas of two Kalomo culture mound sites on the Batoka Plateau, both near bog iron from local dambos and ferricrete deposits along the Kalomo River: Kalundu, which was occupied in the fourth century and reoccupied from the eighth to eleventh century, and Kabondo, which is undated. The same pattern obtained at the copper-smelting site of Kinsanshi until sometime between the eighth and tenth centuries, when metallurgists began to smelt iron beyond the limits of the excavated village. Beyond Zambia, the late eighth- or early ninth-century site D2–13, located in Dedza District of central Malawi, also exhibits evidence of smelting within the village limits.[29] This pattern stands in stark contrast with a pattern common to later Early Iron Age sites, most Late Iron Age sites, and the nineteenth- and twentieth-century ethnographic record in which smelting was undertaken outside the village, at a safe remove from the pollutants, fertile powers, jealousies, and interference of villagers, particularly women and sorcerers.[30] The shift in smelting from the village to spaces beyond its boundaries would be an essential part of the development of new ideas about the landscape at the end of the first millennium, after cereals became the center of the diet.

Despite evidence of some forging in most villages and a few ironworking ateliers, iron was rare in south central Africa up to at least the sixth century. Quantities of slag are low in most Early Iron Age sites and larger iron items, like hoes and axes, are rare compared to evidence for their use, such as abundant cutting marks on carcass bones. Such large tools are very worn when recovered, indicating the rarity of the metal itself and the likelihood that smiths reworked worn hoes and axes into smaller items.[31] The limited number but diffuse sources of borrowed terms suggest that early smelting was undertaken by itinerant specialists who traveled between villages, supplying local smiths who could afford to attract their services.

The Early Impact of Cereals and Metals

The story of the adoption of cereal agriculture and the ironworking technology that supported its practice is often told as a story in which hunting, fishing, and foraging "remained" an integral part of food production to supplement uncertain harvests and protect crops.[32] But for the earliest Botatwe speakers to sow seeds, this relationship was surely reversed: cereals were initially only a very minor part of the diet. Trapping, for example, was essential to farming, so we would expect evidence that farming and trapping technologies developed in parallel. If proto-Botatwe farmers adopted cereals as the center of their diet in the early centuries of the first millennium, they would have needed to adapt trapping tools and practices to the demands of new environments, cultivars, and the pests they attracted, adaptations that should be reflected in trapping vocabulary. Yet, innovation in trapping is more pronounced in later speech communities of the mid to late first millennium, when settlements became more sedentary and cereals provided the bulk of the diet.

Cereals opened new ecological zones to settlement and exploitation, to be sure, but they were taken up in the context of preexisting subsistence technologies. Like trapping, many of the activities supporting cereal agriculture were actually part of the subsistence repertoire of communities before the adoption of cereal because they were also important to other modes of procuring food. For example, shifting agriculture in the savannas has often been understood as a strategy to combat soil exhaustion, yet the movement of fields and villages to new areas may have also been a strategy to mitigate empty traps because animals living near human settlements quickly learned to stay away from field margins studded with snares. Jan Vansina estimates that south central African farmers probably moved every five years as soils depleted, game was scared away, and wild foods declined.[33] Early Botatwe farmers cultivated and harvested their garden crops but also the naturally occurring edible "weeds" and relishes that flourished in the ecotones produced for cereal crops and the care applied to garden plants. Early Iron Age farmers living between the upper Lualaba and middle Zambezi were familiar with sorghum and millet, but also harvested the seed heads of wild grasses.[34] Likewise, they burned the bush to drive quarry toward a pit or a line of hunters, to open pastures, to open and fertilize new fields, to control the habitat of disease vectors, to drive away pests like snakes, and to encourage the growth of fire retardant species and the tender shoots that attract low-grazing game nearer to homesteads, fields, and pastures.[35] For proto-Botatwe speakers employing these subsistence methods in the southern savannas in first five hundred years of the first millennium, the distinction between farming and using wild resources was not particularly clear.

Subsistence and Society in the Greater Eastern Botatwe Era, c. 500–750

Speakers spread the proto-Botatwe language about 350 to 400 kilometers south over the course of fifteen centuries. Sometimes, speakers of other languages adopted proto-Botatwe, but proto-Botatwe farmers also followed the slow expansion of the northern miombo environment southward during the long warm, moist climate regime that persisted through about the sixth century. Most of these moves were small-scale and averaged about six to eight kilometers per generation.[36] It was always possible to move back to familiar territories to the north. Undoubtedly some individuals, households, and even larger groups moved much longer distances from familiar lands, perhaps to pursue opportunities to establish new settlements or in response to the vicissitudes of climate, social relationships, and ancestors' demands. In spite of this mobility, the changing strategies of settlement adopted across south central Africa from the middle of the first millennium resulted in households extending their residence by a few years in a particular hamlet and investing in local ties, often to speakers of other languages. The frequency and intensity of proto-Botatwe speakers' contact with other members of their own broad speech community diminished in equal measure. Speech patterns diverged and dialects flourished as contact with non-Botatwe speakers increased, but this innovation unfolded across a time scale imperceptible to individual speakers. Localized pronunciations, word usages, and grammar distinguished regional speech patterns within what had once been a far more homogeneous speech community. If speakers from the eastern portion of the proto-Botatwe-speaking world could once understand speakers in the west, by the middle of the first millennium regionalized speech patterns rendered such communication impossible, marking the divergence of proto-Botatwe into proto-Western Botatwe, located west or southwest of the hook of the Kafue River, and proto-Greater Eastern Botatwe, spoken in the area between the Lukanga swamps, the hook of the Kafue, and the Kafue floodplain. The divergence of the long-lived proto-Botatwe language was the first in a rapid series of divergences that would occur every few hundred years into the first quarter of the second millennium as contacts with non-Botatwe communities intensified.

Seven changes mark the end of the long-standing proto Botatwe life-style in the sixth century: first, the divergence of proto-Botatwe into Greater Eastern and Western Botatwe described above; second, the abrupt shift to cooler, drier climate conditions; third, the development of more permanent house structures and increased sedentism; fourth, the commitment to cereals as the center of the diet; fifth, a limited adoption of cattle into a practice of animal husbandry that already included small livestock; sixth, an increase in the production of metal objects coinciding with new metallurgical technologies; and, finally, the adoption of new ideas about how to achieve and recognize successful living in the context of such changing material circumstances. The seven changes that constitute this major historical break are undoubtedly related. For example, cattle and some cereals, such as millet, thrived in the drier climate conditions of the third quarter of the first millennium, while the increasing availability of iron tools encouraged sedentism by facilitating swidden agriculture.

The widespread and near simultaneous development of these changes, even with localized differences, speak to the significance of contact and exchange in the transformations that mark the Greater Eastern Botatwe period. Linguistic evidence for borrowing substantiate this observation. Although there were many localized histories that would unfold in south central Africa after the sixth century—stories that are explored in the next two chapters—from the middle of the first millennium, south central Africa was increasingly characterized by contact across linguistic and material cultural boundaries. From the sixth through the thirteenth century, speakers of many different languages shared their ideas about proper social relationships, the most important attributes of those deemed worthy of respect, and the kinds of food technologies that could best sustain families. They opined on the latest fashions in bangles, exchanged techniques for decorating pots, cultivated common pools of stylistic conventions, and mimicked new ways to set up house in once ignored environments. This contact across linguistic and material cultural boundaries created a complex tapestry of diffused of words, technologies, and institutions and sustained the dispersal of homesteads across environmental zones and the rapid divergence of three successive speech communities. From a broad, regional perspective, the individual trajectories of loans crisscrossed and ran in parallel, preceded, followed, and moved together, sometimes overlapping and sometimes showing no similarities. But for the speakers who adopted novel techniques to unique, local problems, the jumbled character of loans on the regional level was anything but disorganized. The complex tracery of evidence for the diffusion of knowledge and practice across wide swaths of the central African savannas facilitated the development of a central frontier cultural zone enveloped by the two major pathways of technological and linguistic diffusion, a process revisited in chapter 5. The remainder of the story told in this chapter describes the beginnings of contact and exchange between those speech communities that would forge the famed savanna cultures of the late second millennium out of the technological and social innovations of the sixth to thirteenth centuries.

Rebalancing Old Subsistence Technologies:
Cereals, Metals, and Sedentism

If their ancestors' experiments with cereals were modest efforts contributing to a suite of food procurement strategies, between the sixth and mid-eighth centuries south central Africans put cereals at the center of their meals.[37] It was not inevitable that cereals would come to dominate the regional diet. The inhabitants of south central Africa might well have followed the slow, northward retreat of the northern miombo environment as the climate grew cooler and drier; indeed, some probably did, shifting their language as they joined Luban, Sabi, or other central Savanna speech communities. Although the mid-millennium climate shift was abrupt on the timescales of climate change, it would have been difficult for individuals to perceive the permanence of this shift until it was well under way—when grandchildren, who had known only the new conditions, heard from their grandparents stories of the way that gardens, fields, and the vegetation between villages used to look and the way seasons used to unfold.

Cereals were one of many foods to emphasize in the face of drier, cooler conditions. Farmers had long been making such adjustments to the relative proportion of foods they planted when pests, diseases, or the rains confounded families' best attempts to secure a predictable food supply. From the middle of the first millennium, however, cereals grew disproportionately significant to provisioning larders. Cereals provided a storable surplus and thrived in the climate conditions that threatened many of the older crops, particularly tuber crops. This new balance slowly became a permanent transition whereby cereals stood at the center of south central Africans' diet.

In committing to cereals, farmers slowly but quite profoundly reconfigured labor regimes, particularly around the clearing, planting, weeding, and harvesting seasons and around the daily processing and cooking of grain heads.[38] Dependence on cereal agriculture created an annual season of scarcity and the fearsome possibility of crop failure. Commitment to cereals also required some degree of seasonality in other subsistence activities in order to free up labor for work-intensive tasks during particular moments in the agricultural calendar. Farmers relegated iron smelting, large-scale hunting, potting, and other crafts to the dry season, but these activities were no less important to the social reproduction of the household for this new seasonality. Cutting out and burning fields and tending to planting, weeding, and harvesting was not only time-consuming, it required investment in soils, iron hoes and axes, heavy grinders and rubbers and winnowing baskets. And cereal agriculture required some degree of sedentism, even for farmers practicing swidden agriculture.

Before the sixth century, subsistence and settlement were organized around the prerogative—or perhaps even the imperative—of frequent mobility. Settlements dating to the first half of the first millennium contained very little daga and probably only housed three to ten families per village.[39] Between the sixth and mid-eighth centuries, communities farming the miombo wooded grasslands of south central Africa initiated an incremental but, cumulatively, quite radical transformation in their way of life. Over just a few generations, householders built more substantial houses. They completely enclosed their wattle-and-daub homes and plastered their floors, replacing the modest earthen floors and three-sided wattle-and-daub structures of previous generations. The overall population probably increased during this period, though cutting back woodlands for fields and villages surely changed the contours of disease distribution while increased sedentism may have also increased exposure to malaria vectors.[40] Potters produced finer wares, exercising their technological virtuosity with novel designs, tempers, and clay compositions. Indeed, early seventh-century ceramics from Mondake I represent the apogee of artisanship in the Mulungushi River Valley.[41]

The first occupation of the mound sites Basanga and Mwanamaimpa located on the Kafue flats dates from the sixth to the middle of the eighth centuries (uncal.) and provides a glimpse of what an mid-millennium farming village looked like.[42] While we will never know the language spoken by the inhabitants of Basanga and Mwanamaimpa, their economy bears striking resemblance to the kind of economy indicated by the subsistence vocabulary of proto-Greater Eastern Botatwe speakers. Small amounts of slag suggest a continued interest in smelting, although iron was still rather rare; archaeologists recovered no iron tools during excavations. These were cereal-farming communities, as indicated by fragments of domesticated sorghum as well as grindstones and rubbers. Yet domesticated foods were consumed alongside gathered vegetable foods, as indicated by the caches of *mobola* (*Parinari curatellifolia*) kernals and pits from *mushuku* fruit (*Uapaca cf. kirkiana*). The large faunal collections of these sites yielded evidence of cattle and goats at the lowest levels in addition to bones from fish, elephant, cane rat, buffalo, lechwe, impala, duiker, oribi, zebra and two species of wild pig. Some species, particularly wild pigs, are persistent garden pests; they were likely to be trapped by farmers using fields as bait.

Iron tools may have been rare in the middle Kafue at Basanga and Mwanamaimpa, but ironworking changed significantly from the sixth century.[43] By the third quarter of the first millennium, south central Africa was a meeting point of the pathways of diffusion of several new and distinct metal-working traditions. The outcome of this influx of technology was a slow increase in the volume and size of iron objects from the sixth century through the turn of the millennium.

Greater Eastern Botatwe communities learned technical knowledge developed by smelters and smiths from across central and eastern Africa. They borrowed words like *-kélwa* [46], meaning "tuyère" or "drain for slag," which was derived from an old Bantu verb, *-kéd-*, "to strain, to filter," probably referring to the overlapping roles of the furnace holes. Botatwe languages also attest more recent skews with focused distributions in the east in the form *-kélo and in the west as *-kéla. With such complicated, overlapping borrowings, scholars debate where this term was innovated: in the north between the Ubangi River and the bend of the Congo or in the eastern Bantu region?[44] Similarly, Greater Eastern Botatwe speakers learned of *-tále [47], a new term for "iron ore" or "iron bloom" developed from a proto-Bantu root for "stone."[45] The new meaning "iron ore" for this old root may have been invented in the southeastern rainforest region, and the term came to mean "bloom" among the skilled smelters of the corridor region between Lakes Tanganyika and Malawi. Botatwe languages use both meanings, "ore" and "bloom," indicating that the Botatwe zone was a meeting point for the different northern and eastern metallurgical traditions. Greater Eastern Botatwe speakers also borrowed the term *-gela [48], meaning "refined iron, iron ready for forging," that was invented by smelters in the corridor region. Smelters produced iron such as trade ingots, a semi-finished metal ready to be forged by village smiths. A final pair of borrowings may date as late as the last century of the first millennium, according to Botatwe attestations. It seems likely that *-vʊkʊt- [49], "to work bellows," and *-vʊba [50], "bellows," spread into the eastern Botatwe languages together as a pair from the corridor region, though this was not the case in other regions of eastern and southeastern Africa.[46] As we will see in the next chapter, metallurgy, particularly bellows work, would carry significant status by the end of the first millennium.

From the Greater Eastern Botatwe period, smelters in south central Africa honed their craft by adopting new technologies like tuyères and bellows to increase draught and, thereby, the quality and quantity of bloom they could supplying to local smiths. Smiths worked to meet the local demands for axes and hoes as farmers invested more time in cutting out new fields and cultivating miombo soils to nourish cereals. Metallurgists' efforts to improve their craft and satisfy famers' demands for iron left a record in the history of loanwords in ironworking vocabulary that spanned the mid to late first millennium. These efforts were part of savanna farming communities' broader strategy of rebalancing and refining familiar technologies and settlement patterns between the sixth and mid-eighth centuries. Another strategy of savanna farmers' encompassing subsistence practice was to learn technologies common among neighbors.

Cattle

As the climate shifted to cooler, drier conditions over the course of the third quarter of the first millennium, Greater Eastern Botatwe homesteaders also adopted a limited number of cattle into their subsistence repertoire.[47] This innovation was part of a broader regional trend. Very recent research has identified cattle in southern Africa in the early first millennium. It now seems that herders brought sheep and cattle to the Cape simultaneously as early as two millennia ago and that those herders were not Bantu speakers, who have long been attributed with introducing cattle to southern Africa.[48] The presence of cattle in eastern Africa and southern Africa in the early centuries of the Common Era does not, however, mean that cattle keeping spread uniformly across all the lands that lie between these two regions. The adoption of cattle was particularly uneven in the areas closer to the Botatwe region. By the middle of the first millennium, residents had already been keeping cattle for several generations at Lotshitshi in the south, east of the Okavango Delta. The inhabitants of M'teteshi, some twenty-five kilometers northeast of Kabwe in modern Zambia, adopted cattle around the same time. Over the course of the second half of the first millennium, farmers adopted cattle in small numbers at most sites between Lotshitshi and M'teteshi, including sites in the middle Kafue, on the Batoka Plateau, and in the Zambezi Valley. Residents at sites south of the Zambezi River, including Matlapaneng and Nqoma, began to keep very large herds. Christopher Ehret has argued that the spread of cattle keeping among Bantu speakers in the first millennium followed the paths of diffusion of cereals, which would once again place speakers of Botatwe languages between two technological traditions.[49]

The earliest words describing cattle appear in both western and eastern Botatwe languages today and were probably borrowed into proto-Botatwe in the first centuries of the first millennium from speakers of Bantu languages to the east: *-gombe [51], "head of cattle," *-kana [52], "calf" through a diminutive prefix added to the early Bantu term for "child," and *-lɪsa, "to pasture," a causative of the early Bantu verb *-dí-, "to eat."[50] These words are very general and signal limited acquaintance with the animals and their products. Some proto-Botatwe speakers may have kept a few head of cattle, but most traded with neighboring non-Botatwe speakers for meat, hides, and sour milk, *-bɪsɪ [53], which traveled better than fresh milk or cream, products for which words were invented later.[51]

Greater Eastern Botatwe farmers keep cattle in greater numbers than their proto-Botatwe-speaking linguistic ancestors; the earliest terms related to activities like breeding and housing herds can be reconstructed to this period. For example, the phonology and distribution of *-pʊızı [54], "heifer," indicate that the root was borrowed by proto-Greater Eastern Botatwe-speaking communities from speakers of an eastern Bantu protolanguage, Kaskazi, who themselves inherited it from their own eastern Bantu-speaking linguistic ancestors.[52] Proto-Greater Eastern Botatwe speakers adopted other words about keeping cattle and using their products: *-pʊmba [55], "dung," *-tàngá [56], "cattle pen, herd," and *-(y)aba [57], "cream."[53] Greater Eastern Botatwe farmers not only knew of cattle and some of their products, they were beginning to breed them, to consume fresh as well as soured milk, and perhaps to use manure as fertilizer, fuel, and house plaster.

Reconstructed cattle vocabulary indicates an initial investment in cattle keeping as one part of the subsistence economy of proto-Greater Eastern Botatwe communities at the beginning of the second half of the first millennium. This lexicon does not, however, represent the far more technical knowledge and naming vocabulary typical in vocabulary of specialist herders. Those terms would only develop in Botatwe languages after the divergence of proto-Kafue in the mid-thirteenth century.[54] Rather, for Greatern Eastern Botatwe communities feeding families in the middle of the first millennium, cattle were a novel component artfully blended into a much more diversified food system.

The archaeological evidence for cattle in sites with locations and dates overlapping the proposed homeland and chronology of Greater Eastern Botatwe speech is inconclusive. Brian Fagan observed that cattle bones were "surprisingly rare" in the first occupation levels of Basanga and Mwana-maimpa as compared to other mound sites of the Batoka to the south and compared to the numbers of goat bones recovered from the same levels. The modest Greater Eastern Botatwe breeding vocabulary suggests a minimum herd size not in evidence in the archaeology of such sites. Fagan posited that the absence of evidence for cattle could simply reflect a practice by which cattle were kept elsewhere, possibly on the Kafue flats.[55] Yet the pasturage of the flats was a particularly challenging disease environment for early cattle keepers in the Kafue region. Abundant grasses and their high buffalo and wildebeest populations would have created optimal conditions for the transmission of diseases like bovine malignant catarrhal fever, Rift Valley fever, East Coast fever, and foot-and-mouth disease to cattle and, in some cases, to humans.[56] Perhaps Greater Eastern Botatwe speakers kept their cattle with the neighbors from whom they were learning about cattle breeding. They may have used a system of cattle loaning similar to that of more recent centuries. If so, cattle, their offspring, and their products were for Greater Eastern Botatwe speakers a way to manage food security and to create ties to neighbors with knowledge of cattle keeping, rather than a part of the day-to-day labors of Greater Eastern Botatwe households. In south central Africa, the initial adoption of cattle and the subsequent shift to intensive exploitation of large herds unfolded in a staggered, uneven, very localized manner from the early first millennium to the seventeenth century.[57] Communities had distinct responses to cattle keeping. For Greater Eastern Botatwe farmers, a limited investment in herds managed elsewhere was a novel iteration of a very old strategy of subsistence diversification.

To sum, the material and social worlds of Greater Eastern Botatwe speakers were different than those of their proto-Botatwe-speaking linguistic forebears. Even if many of the strategies of subsistence were familiar, the climate had changed drastically by the middle of the first millennium. Farmers responded both by rebalancing the proportions of familiar crops, especially cereals, planted in gardens and fields and by trying out new subsistence strategies more familiar to neighbors, such as keeping small numbers of cattle. As a result of farmers' purposeful rebalancing and diversification of their eclectic food system, farmers resided for longer periods in more permanent homes. They were also in contact with speakers of many eastern Bantu languages.[58] After all, optimal farmlands were unevenly distributed across the landscape, and speakers of many different languages likely both competed for and shared such prized locations.

Greater Eastern Botatwe speakers lived between two important highways of technological diffusion, as their proto-Botatwe predecessors had earlier in the millennium. New knowledge about familiar technologies like cattle keeping and iron smelting were borrowed into Greater Easter Botatwe farmers' subsistence repertoires. Both of these technologies contributed to the cultivation of cereals. Metal tools facilitated cutting out new fields, preparing soils, and weeding. Manuring fields with cattle dung may have extended the fertility of fragile soils and delayed the laborious task of preparing new fields.

Farmers in south central Africa faced many novel challenges to making a living between the sixth and mid-eighth centuries: the threat of crop failure from lack of rains, insect and animal pests, and disease; the difficulty of mobilizing the quantities of labor demanded by cereal agriculture; and accessing both iron tools and the technicians who could repair and rework them, to name a few. In the face of these challenges, Greater Eastern Botatwe speakers thought anew about paths to prosperity and ancestorhood. What kind of person, Greater Eastern Botatwe speakers wondered, could secure rain for crops, placate ancestor spirits with new foods and drinks, and harness the forces of life to the productivity of fields and herds?

The Social Conditions of Success

The successful living required to secure ancestorhood—to continue living after one's death—shaded into related matters like elderhood and celebrity. And it is here, at the nexus of fame and reputation and the accumulation of the lifetime's worth of knowledge, material resources, and social ties required to achieve them that proto-Greater Eastern Botatwe speakers began to recognize some people with the name *-ámí [58]. Some scholars have argued that proto-Botatwe speakers inherited the root in the form *-àmí, "clan ritual leaders," from a far earlier ancestral speech community, but the Botatwe evidence supports neither such time depth nor this meaning for *-ámí within early Botatwe communities; moreover, there is no proto-Botatwe word for "clan."[59] The root *-ámí forms part of a large, polysemetic set of homophones and near homophones, all of which seem to derive from the same underlying root.[60] A full reconstruction of this underlying root across the entire Bantu domain lies beyond the scope of this study, but examining this polysemetic collection alongside the ethnographic and historical evidence from which previous reconstructions of the status of *-ámí have been formulated reveals the broad contours of the root's semantic history and the changing historical contexts in which Bantu speakers used the term. The history of *-ámí is important because it reveals the multiple historical strands of the core ideology of authority and achievement that would be inherited, reborrowed, mobilized, and revised by Botatwe-speaking communities as they invented new categories of subsistence underpinning novel paths to social influence between the mid-eighth and mid-thirteenth centuries.

Across the Bantu languages, nouns and verbs in the cluster of homophones and near homophones to which *-ámí belongs have related but different meanings, ranging from "chief" or "king" to "prostitute," "prophetess, spirit medium, rainmaker," "excellence," "independent, self-reliant person," "wealthy person," "to be fertile," "to protect," "to lean, to rely on" and "to shout, to cry," and "to suck (at the breast)."[61] The oldest and most widely distributed reflexes are associated with two likely related meanings: "to suck" and "to shout," "to cry," "kind of cry." These meanings have been reconstructed to the homophonous roots *-jámu "suck," with a variant in the form *-jám- "suck, suck at the breast" and *-jám- "shout," with a series of derivatives, including *-jámɪd- "shout to drive away (birds, animal)," *-jámò "cry," and *-jámʊdi "cry."[62] Extant Botatwe communities inherited the meaning "to suck" but have only indirect allusions to the significance of speech attached to this root cluster.

If the earliest meanings of words in the cluster associated with the root *-jám- connected shouting, crying, and speech to suckling, proto-Savanna speakers took that connection and created a new meaning, "to protect," for the verb *-jám- in the early second millennium BCE. Botatwe speakers inherited this meaning in the early first millennium BCE and conserved it across three millennia to the present day. We see this meaning in the modern-day Tonga verb *kuyaama*, "to lean, to rely on."[63] Proto-Savanna speakers determined that protection could best be provided by those with the capacity to initiate through their speech—perhaps, just as an infant does through shouts and cries—safe births, the careful husbandry of resources, and all manner of social and material acts that secured the abundance that protected people, an abundance that was represented metaphorically through the evocative image of an infant crying lustily and then sucking at the breast. The notion that speech and the prosperity represented by suckling constituted domains of effort, aspiration, and social judgment is best illustrated by the KiKongo attestation *nami*, "excellence."[64] This semantic innovation, which connected speech, human fertility, and the socially recognized capacity or even obligation to protect, is the first of many instances in which metaphors of human fertility shaped how central Africans thought about the related problems of authority, successful living and successful death, and creative acts worthy of the attention and admiration of others.

By the early first millennium BCE, proto-Mashariki speakers living west of the Great Lakes Region had developed the noun *-àmí to refer to the agent who could achieve excellence in the kinds of speech that brought many children to the breasts of mothers, that inspired infants to suckle lustily, and that extended a wider net of protection around those nearest him or her. This person, *-àmí, brought succor to her neighbors and, in turn, they gave her this name. But the verb form underlying this new title was now also used by proto-Mashariki speakers to refer more directly to sex and fecundity, broadening the actions and states that might lead to the forms of protective prosperity that developed out of such fertility. Great Lakes Bantu speakers, for example, later developed from the suite of ideas connected to *-jám- the verb *-yâm-: "to be fecund" or, literally, "to be clean or pure."[65] For proto-Mashariki speakers, the capacity to ensure fertility and fecundity required a body of knowledge and a pool of collaborators (and, perhaps, even competitors) rooted in the communities of living and dead and the natural resources of a particular place: from the proto-Mashariki period, *-àmí was tied to a territory or neighborhood. Therefore, in noun class 14, *-ámí—"chief's power or territory" in the Tonga gloss—was, as David Schoenbrun concludes for the related Great Lakes Bantu reconstruction, *-yàámí, "something ownable because it must be rooted in space, attached to a place at critical junctures in its life."[66] When the root was used to name a leader, *mwami*, his or her recognition stemmed from excellence in the capacity to mobilize those forces that ensured fertility and abundance within a particular territory, whether by knowledge of local spirits, nearby resources, or practical skills in planting, hunting, or medicine. The agent of protection and prosperity, *-àmí, may have been a word and concept invented early in the first millennium BCE by proto-Mashariki speakers, but the concept took on many lives as it was borrowed into neighboring societies. Proto-Greater Eastern Botatwe speakers were among those who borrowed *-ámí; the root was also eventually used to develop names for influential associations like the *bwámi* of the Lega and Bembe.[67]

The root *-ámí is only present in eastern Botatwe languages, so we can date it no earlier than the proto-Greater Eastern Botatwe speech community. Greater Eastern Botatwe communities lived in an uncertain world; rains did not always nourish crops to harvest, and as sources of water grew less certain, different kinds of people concentrated together around the predictable wetlands of south central Africa. The longevity of the proto-Botatwe speech community attests to its speakers' successful ways of living, but the flourishing culture developed by their linguistic ancestors offered little guidance to proto-Greater Eastern Botatwe speakers dealing with a rapidly changing climate. The imperative to rebalance and diversify the subsistence economy might have served as one kernel of advice that Greater Eastern Botatwe communities inherited from their linguistic forebears and put into use, as we have seen in this chapter. But as cooler and cooler winds chilled the months after meager, rain-starved harvests, Greater Eastern Botatwe speakers may well have wondered what kind of person could still manage to fill her *butaale* granary, hunt honey from the receding woodlands, and break up the hard soils of the southern miombo belt to nourish seeds to harvest in such a changing world. The answer, their neighboring Kaskazi or Kusi speakers taught them, was *-àmí. We can't know precisely what *-àmí meant to the donors who shared their ideas of success with struggling Greater Eastern Botatwe speakers on the wooded savannas between the sixth and mid-eighth centuries, but the range of words developed from *-ámí and used by eastern Botatwe speakers today reveal critical aspects of its meaning in the lives of their proto-Greater Eastern Botatwe speaking linguistic ancestors.

Modern Botatwe glosses insist that wealth and prosperity underpin the status of mwami. Mwami is often glossed today with the meaning "chief," a legacy of Indirect Rule. But mwami is more appropriately glossed as "wealthy person."[68] With the intensifying infix, Ila speakers use the agentive noun *mwaami* to talk of a "prophetess, spirit medium, rainmaker," figures whose speech directs efforts toward prosperous harvests and unties those whose potential prosperity is bound up by witchcraft and illness. Another form of the root, *mwaamu,* was a noun of quality with the intensive infix that was developed into a person with that quality: "an independent, self-reliant person." Without the intensive infix, *mwamu* is a "prostitute, precocious child" and a term of address for "my brother," perhaps an address that was used to lay claim to the fruits of *-ámí's labor or his ability and willingness to protect others. In noun class 14, *bwami* is "chiefship, authority" for Ila speakers and "chief's power or territory" for Tonga speakers. But as a noun of quality, *bwamu* is for Ila speakers "fornication, evil or precocious knowledge in children" and "lust" for Tonga speakers. These glosses teach us what missionaries penning dictionaries in the early twentieth century thought of local cultures of sexuality, but they also speak to Greater Eastern Botatwe speakers' understandings of the dual character of the power of fertility: dangerous to those who do not know how to control it but a source of protection and prosperity to those who do.[69]

Taken together, this evidence teaches us that for Greater Eastern Botatwe communities, *-ámí were accomplished in the arts of living; they were able to achieve excellence in the range of labors attempted by all but mastered by few. In a time of climate crisis, the fields of *-ámí were fertile, their stock fecund, and their wives brought pregnancies to term, infants into childhood, and children into adulthood and good marriage alliances. Their husbands brokered exchanges of labor and tools, identified and cleared the most fertile soils, crafted delicate but deadly arrows and smeared them with effective poisons. Their households had surplus to share and attracted dependents. Their sisters-in-law crafted pots with nary a crack that could hold for long hours the cool temperature of water collected in the early morning. Their siblings, cousins, or parents had knowledge of local medicines and the most powerful invocations, arresting the attention of lazy, indifferent, or offended mizimu, ancestral spirits. Their friends smelted iron and could target the shy duiker at great distances, sending the arrow home without damaging the hide. Their brothers surveyed and monitored the local area's resources: rock outcroppings and pools where spirits might reside, stands of fruit trees near to harvest, newly formed knotholes in once-solid tree trunks, likely to attract honey bees in a future season. Mwami had mastered the art of ensuring that the forces of life were brought to bear on their concerns and that they bore fruit, captivating neighbors with their own good luck and demonstrating a mature willingness to teach, learn, and provide for those around them.

The many changes to the subsistence strategies of the first two Botatwe speech communities, proto-Botatwe and Greater Eastern Botatwe, included those technologies usually associated with the transformative capacity of the Neolithic way of life: food production in the form of cereal agriculture and cattle keeping and the adoption of new technologies, like metallurgy, assumed to be the domain of specialists freed from toiling in fields by virtue of their talents and the storability of grains. But these changes were not experienced as revolutionary to the Botatwe communities who adopted them, often through contacts with neighboring communities. Not only had the linguistic forebears of proto-Botatwe speakers already been producing food, such as tubers and goats, the transition to cereal agriculture was a very slow process, as Jan Vansina observed nearly two decades ago.[70] Adopting new subsistence technologies was a long-standing facet of the early Bantu mixed farming system, a practical knowledge that proto-Botatwe speakers inherited. And, indeed, the distinction between food collection and food production was not entirely clear until well after the middle of the first millennium, when settlements grew more sedentary and later generations of Botatwe communities began to think in new ways about the differences between settlements and the lands beyond them.

If the earliest Botatwe communities sustained their experiments with cereals and cattle by relying on many familiar forms of food collection and horticulture, by the second half of the first millennium, their descendants established successful cereal fields and cared for small herds of cattle.[71] Between the eighth and thirteenth centuries, agricultural surplus underpinned innovation in the economic and social potential of particular forms of hunting, fishing, and metallurgy. The next two chapters explore how the stability of settlements inspired new ways of thinking about the spaces between villages and the labors that could be undertaken during the slow months of the agricultural calendar. Speakers of the next two generations of Botatwe speech— Central Eastern Botatwe and Kafue—drew on long-standing ideas about ancestorhood, fertility, and subsistence to invent an entirely new kind of space, the bush, and a new politics of fame and reputation developed from knowledge of the bush. The history of Botatwe bushcraft from the late first millennium reveals not only the affective dimensions of social influence and authority, but the ways in which ordinary people, or at least those who enjoyed a social status below or alternative to charismatic or ritual authorities, strived for recognition in an effort to be remembered.

3. Fame in the Kafue

*The Politics of Technology, Talent,
and Landscape, 750 to 1250*

From the middle of the eighth century through the middle of the thirteenth century, Central Eastern Botatwe communities and their linguistic descendants, speakers of proto-Kafue, participated in a regional revolution in the technologies of spear hunting, rapid-current fishing, and metallurgy. They invented a new category of landscape, the bush, which allowed them to cultivate a distinction between work undertaken in the fields and work undertaken in the bush. Celebrated spearmen, rapid-current fishers, and famous smelters sought to distinguish their activities from forms of related labor, such as trapping, smithing, and basket fishing, which were undertaken in or near the village and were more closely associated with agriculture. Counterintuitively, the commitment to a subsistence economy dominated by cereals sustained innovation in many of those domains of subsistence that agriculture is usually thought to replace. Bushcraft emerged out of and was not prior to the creation of a cereal-based savanna agricultural system. The invention of a distinction between the labors of agriculture and the work of the bush was transformative. With it, Central Eastern Botatwe speakers created a novel path to singularity, fame, friendship, and ancestorhood based on knowledge of the bush. This politics of talent and technology recast local understandings of the landscape and resisted the centralization of political and ritual authority around the agricultural economy.

Five related developments contributed to the invention of bushcraft as a unique subsistence category in the middle Kafue region between the mid-eighth and the mid-thirteenth centuries. First, Central Eastern Botatwe speakers settled the middle Kafue River region around the eighth century. The perennial waterways of this region mitigated threats to cereal agriculture posed by an increasingly dry and cool climate. But even in the better-watered environments of the middle Kafue, farming remained uncertain. Farmers tested out new ways of living near the lush grasslands of the middle Kafue by extending settlements into nearby woodlands. Here they learned about endemic species and local agricultural pests, and developed new strategies for fishing and hunting. Second, villagers' commitment to a cereal-based agricultural system demanded a degree of at least seasonal sedentism for those involved in different agricultural tasks, shaping access to different parts of the landscape by age, skill, and gender. Some Botatwe villagers created new ways to exploit the resources beyond village boundaries and field margins, but these opportunities were not open to everyone. As Central Eastern Botatwe speakers and, a few generations later, Kafue speakers developed new fishing technologies, their innovations were shaped by this novel distinction between food collection near fields and the village and food collection undertaken at greater distances from settled spaces. Third, as skilled practitioners developed new methods of food collection, they negotiated how their efforts were woven into the existing fabric of established subsistence activities and those ideals of dependency, obligation, and social association that sustained them. The histories embedded in hunting vocabulary illuminate the complicated process by which skilled spearmen and their celebrants argued that older, once-banal efforts at food collection practiced by a majority of households should become paths to distinction available to a minority who could claim intimate knowledge of the bush. Fourth, the association of certain subsistence activities with the potential for wealth and fame depended on both predictable sources of food, such as basket fishing and cereal agriculture, as well as regional developments in other technologies. By the end of the first millennium, Central Eastern Botatwe families understood the work of skilled huntsmen and smelters to be alike. Marksmen and metallurgists operated in similar spaces, shared kinesthetic experiences, and braved forces that others sought to avoid. All of these changes contributed to the last development: the invention of "the bush" as a category of landscape. The word speakers developed to name this space reveals how the coproduction of technological innovation in bushcraft and cultural ideas about gender, fame, and the politics of knowledge also depended on older ideas about landscapes, fertility, spirits, and the means by which individuals could safely combine and direct the powers of each to secure success in the bush and in the village, in life and in death.

Into the Woods: Middle Kafue Settlement from the Eighth Century

From the middle of the first millennium to about the tenth century, the climate shifted sharply to drier, cooler conditions. The southern miombo and mopane ecotones slowly extended northward, thriving in the more arid conditions that constricted the distribution of northern miombo vegetation. During these dry centuries, cereal famers in south central Africa faced a profound challenge to an agricultural system developed during the favorable climate conditions of the first half of the first millennium. Some farmers undoubtedly retreated north, toward regions with more predictable rainfall. Other farmers sought out landscapes with sufficient water to sustain their crops in the lands that now constitute central Zambia. Farmers' movements changed both population distributions and the linguistic landscape. Some speakers along the southern fringe of the Greater Eastern Botatwe speech community shifted their settlements into and beyond the middle Kafue River area, hampering intelligible speech between speakers at the extreme ends of the Greater Eastern Botatwe territory and facilitating its divergence around the middle of the eighth century into proto-Soli spoken to the southeast and proto-Central Eastern Botatwe spoken in the middle Kafue.

The material culture preserved from settlements in the middle Kafue River region records a parallel process of change around the mid-eighth century: a novel settlement pattern and the abrupt introduction of a new ceramic style unlike previous Early Iron Age styles. Archaeologist Robin Derricourt has interpreted these pronounced shifts as evidence that makers of a new ceramic tradition settled the middle Kafue region, displacing or absorbing preexisting Early Iron Age communities and establishing a new era in the middle Kafue culture sequence, the Middle Iron Age.[1] These new settlers— settlers we can confidently identify as proto-Central Eastern Botatwe speakers, according to direct associations between the linguistic and archaeological records—transformed the settlement pattern of the middle Kafue.[2] Although they continued long-established patterns of building homesteads in the grass-lands, Kafue Middle Iron Age people also opened new settlements in the miombo woodlands. As Derricourt notes, with access to a broader range of resources, villagers could better endure the cooling, drying trends characterizing weather patterns in the second half of the first millennium. The woodlands were punctuated by dambos, termite mounds, patches of mopane trees, and thicket and were probably infested with tsetse fly. But woodland sites offered better protection from floods, better access to game and fish, and plentiful vegetation to nourish poor soils when new fields were cut out and burned every few years. The settlement of a greater diversity of microenvironments around the middle Kafue resulted in a mutually dependent "dual-economy" between inhabitants of the grasslands and woodlands. Several centuries later, when climate conditions improved, this cooperative strategy would facilitate settlement across the Batoka Plateau and into the Zambezi Valley.[3]

In each microenvironment, Middle Iron Age Kafue people rejected the large, mounded grassland villages of the Early Iron Age in favor of smaller, more centralized villages. They clustered their round pole and daga huts together, sheltering a few families in each village. They lit their cooking fires in external hearth pits, perhaps shared by co-wives or across the generations of the household's women. These changes to the organization and construction of settlements mirrored similar changes in homesteads across the region: from the eighth century, hamlets and villages grew in size and duration. Groups of ten and even twenty families inhabited sites for longer periods of time than farmers of the first half of the first millennium, a degree of sedentism that shaped perceptions of and access to different parts of the landscape.[4]

A farmer who spoke Greater Eastern Botatwe and came of age near the end of the Greater Eastern Botatwe era, in the early eighth century, would have been quite familiar with some of the strategies employed at the home-steads of his Central Eastern Botatwe-speaking granddaughters in the early ninth century. As they had in generations past, fields and homesteads bustled with activities that bound cereal agriculture to other forms of food procurement. But learning to farm successfully in the woodlands was not without its challenges. The words innovated by Central Eastern Botatwe farmers for some animals attest to growing familiarity with the flora and fauna of the different environments into which farmers extended their fields and gardens.[5]

For example, Central Eastern Botatwe speakers innovated a new term for warthog, *nkólı [59], and retained the inherited term, *ngılı [60], applying it to the wild boar and river bush pig. Boars, bush pigs, river pigs, and warthogs have very specific habitats and are troublesome agricultural pests. Warthogs prefer drier areas with grasslands and open woodlands, which would have been increasingly common as Botatwe languages came to be spoken in the southern miombo woodlands. Warthog habitats were created each time homesteaders burned brush for hunting or field preparation, perhaps in just that integrated sequence.[6] Bush pigs inhabit the well-watered brush and dense woodland found in the river valleys draining into the Kafue and, farther south, into the Zambezi. Just as they are among the most determined field pests, wild pigs are also notoriously dangerous animals to hunt and kill; this threat to farming required action on the part of skilled hunters.

The modest flash of innovation around feral swine terminology continued during the proto-Kafue era, between the tenth and mid-thirteenth century, and attests to the durability of an encompassing, integrated approach to subsistence in efforts to protect fields and fully exploit the foods available in the middle Kafue. Hunting, fishing, and foraging had sustained proto-Botatwe speakers' earliest experiments in food production and, later, mitigated Greater Eastern Botatwe farmers' food shortages during the sixth-century transition to the cooler, drier climate conditions of the second half of the first millennium. Members of the short-lived Central Eastern Botatwe speech community, however, took a new approach, settling across environmental zones with such success that by the early second millennium, their linguistic descendants, speakers of proto-Kafue, established successful farms throughout the Kafue region.[7]

If our Greater Eastern Botatwe-speaking grandfather would have recognized his granddaughters' commitment to cereal agriculture and their more durable daga houses as innovations developed by his own grandparents, he would have wondered how his Central Eastern Botatwe grandchildren farmed the woodlands and worried over the possible dangers of his granddaughters remaining in their more centralized villages for longer periods of time. By the late eighth century, a young mother organized her day around different labors and movements than her grandmothers: she spent more time in her fields and at her homestead, growing and processing grains; her home was closer to neighbors and relatives; and she and her husband less frequently met the challenge of packing up, moving house, and starting their homestead afresh. Hers was a life more grounded in place. Central Eastern Botatwe and, later, Kafue farmers enjoyed a more sedentary lifestyle than their ancestors, organizing their lives around the two spatial poles of the village and the uninhabited bush beyond. They created new landscapes and generated through them original paths to successful living.

Farmers' Waterscapes: Skill, Visibility, and the Geographies of Fishing

Commitment to cereal agriculture changed how Botatwe communities worked in and on the landscape, but this change unfolded slowly, in stages. From the mid-eighth to the mid-thirteenth century, proto-Central Eastern Botatwe- and, later, proto-Kafue-speaking communities inhabiting the middle Kafue invented and learned new methods of fishing, often from neighboring Kaskazi and Kusi speakers. The different kinds of fishing tools invented by each speech community demonstrate that Central Eastern and Kafue people distinguished between fishing techniques on the basis of where in the landscape the fishing was undertaken. They separated fishing methods employed in the seasonal streams and small tributaries running near villages and fields from those employed in the swifter currents of the main channels of the Kafue River. Central Eastern fishermen and fisherwomen broadened their repertoire of fishing techniques to better exploit the swifter currents of the perennial waterways available to them in the middle Kafue region during the drier, cooler conditions of the second half of the first millennium. As the climate shifted to the warmer, wetter conditions of the early second millennium, proto-Kafue speakers' gardens thrived with a predictability their Central Eastern grandparents would have envied, but fish remained a vital source of protein in the local diet. Proto-Kafue-speaking fishers continued to develop new fishing techniques, though not of the same types as their Central Eastern linguistic forebears. Instead, Kafue fishers' innovations focused on slower, shallow, seasonal waterways nearer homesteads.

The distinction between fishing in low, slow waters and in swifter currents was captured in development of verbs available to talk about kinds of fishing. Between the mid-eighth and mid-thirteenth centuries, eastern Botatwe communities slowly elaborated the semantic domain of the inherited root *-zòb- [31], extending its meaning from "to fish with a basket" to "to fish with a basket, net, or trap." New techniques for fishing the seasonal

waterways came to be accepted as generic forms of slow, shallow-water fishing.[8] At the same time that Botatwe-speaking communities in the Kafue region were applying *-zòb- to a range of new fishing activities, they innovated
a new word, *-zèl- [61], to refer to this same cluster of fishing methods: fishing
with a trap or net.[9] While it may seem that Kafue speakers were inventing
a new word for the same kinds of fishing named by *-zòb-, the distinction
between the two lies in the different kinds of waterways in which fishers
deployed baskets, traps, and nets. Thus, by the close of the thirteenth century,
five hundred years of fishing innovation along the Kafue and its tributaries
yielded three significant forms of fishing: the old, inherited technique of angling, *kuloba;* the newer understanding of *kuʒuba,* or capturing fish in standing pools and along the banks with *-fombo, *masiko,* or communal fish drives
with *iʒubo* baskets; and the labor- and material-intensive techniques of
kuʒela, fishing with nets or weir and fish fence systems strung across major
tributaries, styles that relied on the current to push fish into traps and nets
accessed by dugout canoes. However, the technologies used in *-zèl- and
*-zòb- fishing were not invented simultaneously; the order of innovation
and relative contribution of each form of fishing to the cooking pot merits
closer scrutiny.

Fishermen who belonged to the short-lived Central Eastern Botatwe
speech community lived during a period of innovation that focused on swift-
current fishing methods. These techniques were necessary as Central Eastern Botatwe speakers settled along the middle Kafue River, a major tributary
of the Zambezi. During the drier conditions of the second half of the first millennium, slow moving seasonal waterways may not have been a predictable
source of fish, but innovations in swift-current fishing vocabulary suggest
that perennial waterways retained enough water for fishing. For example,
Central Eastern fishermen began to use *-sábwe [62], a smaller fishing net
that was likely thrown from a canoe in deep waters as opposed to the larger
trawling nets used in shallow waters along the riverbank and in seasonal
tributaries. Central Eastern Botatwe speakers learned about this kind of net
from a neighboring community of eastern Bantu speakers who used the
term *-(j)ábù for "hunting net," but adapted the technology to fishing. Indeed, overlaps between certain hunting and fishing technologies were quite
common at this time, as we will also see with the root *-wèz- [63], discussed
below. In addition to nets cast from *bwaato,* dugout canoes, two words, *buyeelo*
and *buyali,* have distributions that suggest that fishermen also developed weirs

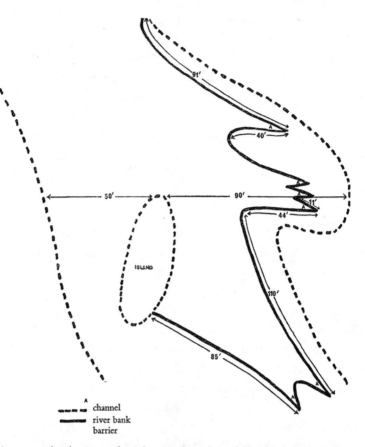

channel
river bank
barrier

Figure 3.1. The placement of weir barriers, buyeelo, in the Lusitu River near Sigongo in the Gwembe Valley, 1957. Note the narrow constriction points of the buyeelo (labeled A) into which traps, moono, were inserted. Reprinted from Reynolds, *Material Culture of the Gwembe Valley*, 44. Permission courtesy of the University of Zambia.

in the form of dams and fish fences between the mid-eighth and mid-thirteenth centuries.[10] Buyeelo, a dam, and buyali, a fish fence of reeds or sorghum stalks, were often quite long and tall; they represented significant investments of time and material and were built, maintained, and harvested by accomplished fisher-canoemen. Buyali were erected across flood lands and tributaries whereas buyeelo could be constructed across some of the small channels of the main river (fig. 3.1). Either could be fitted with valved and unvalved traps, *moono*, which depended on currents to trap the fish (fig. 3.2).[11]

As climate conditions improved with the turn of the millennium, Kafue speakers developed technologies for fishing the slow currents of returning

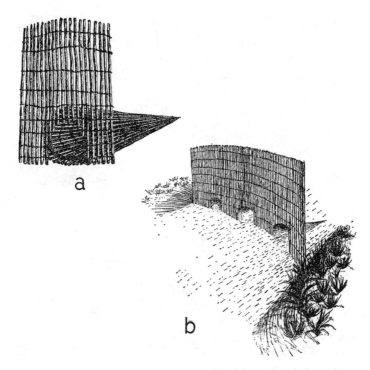

Figure 3.2. Constriction traps, moono (a), and reed fences, buyali (b), in the Gwembe Valley. Reprinted from Reynolds, *Material Culture of the Gwembe Valley*, 45. Permission courtesy of the University of Zambia.

seasonal streams and the still waters of pools left standing in depressions as minor tributaries dried up after the floods. Most of this innovation concerned basket fishing. For example, proto-Kafue speakers innovated a new kind of plunge basket, *-fʊmbo [64], probably as an areal form shared with their Sabi neighbors to the east. The *-fʊmbo plunge basket was a large reed cylinder with two open ends, tapering toward the top like an upside-down funnel. Fishers used this device in the shallow waters of flood lands or receding tributaries.[12] Proto-Kafue speakers also innovated a new kind of fish poison, *-bʊʊba [65].[13] The plant source for this poison seems to have varied from one community to another, but it may have included the *mundale* tree or a small, cultivated shrub, *Tephrosia vogelii*. Fish poison was used in the windy, hot season in the months before the rains to cull the last of the fish from standing pools left in dry riverbeds or those created by damming streams early in the hot, dry season. The poison, often taken from the roots of the plant, was pounded into mush and stirred into the water; it stunned the fish within thirty

Figure 3.3. Tonga women fishing with izubo baskets. Reprinted from Reynolds and Cousins, *Lwaano Lwanyika*, 106. Permission courtesy of the International African Institute, London.

minutes. Fish floated to the surface to be scooped up by a shallow, plate-like basket. This basket may have been named *-sɪko [66], a term proto-Kafue-speaking fishers inherited from proto-Central Eastern Botatwe speakers.[14] Proto-Kafue speakers invented a new term for trawling basket, *-zòbo [67], early in the second millennium by drawing on the ancient, inherited Bantu word for basket fishing, *-dùb- (*-zòb- in proto-Kafue; see fig. 3.3). Although any fisher could simply troll the *izubo* basket along the stream bottom, it was likely far more common to use the izubo when fishing as a group. Two lines of fishers arranged themselves bank to bank, perpendicular to its flow and facing each other. They held their baskets against the river bottom, forming a barrier from bank to bank. The trollers facing downstream swept toward the stationary line, herding fish into their own and the other fishers' baskets. Izubo and *masiko* baskets were used in minor tributaries, the slow seasonal streams feeding the floodplains and dambos, and the standing pools left as stretches of the streambeds dried up—the same types of environments settled during the Kafue Middle Iron Age. This method of fishing yields large catches and, importantly, predictable success. The innovation of a noun for the object of an inherited verb suggests that trolling for fish in shallow waters had become one of the most common forms of *-zòb-fishing. Innovations in trolling basket technology tell us that Botatwe fishers in the Kafue area in the early second millennium were concerned with developing modes of fishing that could be used in environments near their villages and cultivated fields to produce predictably large catches during the dry season, before the labor intensive work of the early agricultural season.

It is tempting to explain the innovations in kuzela fishing and, two centuries later, in kuzuba fishing as outcomes of climate dynamics. Central Eastern fishers perfected swift current fishing methods used in perennial waters that still flowed during the drier conditions of the late first millennium. While Kafue fishers could exploit such swift waters, they also had the luxury of fishing the smaller, seasonal streams and pools that returned to the area with better rains. Yet this environmental determinism does little to explain the relationship between different kinds of fishing and other forms of food procurement.

When eastern Botatwe speakers developed a verb for deep channel fishing, *-zèl-, they highlighted the different location in which it was undertaken and the more intensive investment in labor, materials, and skill, thereby distinguishing between ordinary fishing and more skilled forms. Of course, innovation was not only the domain of the skillful; Kafue speakers developed new techniques and tools for shallow-water fishing even after the development of the labor- and material-intensive swift-current fishing. This continued investment in the technology of lower-skill, less intensive techniques in the early second millennium suggests that the efforts of skilled fishers were valued, in part, because they were examples of great competence in domains of work undertaken to some degree by a majority of the population. After all, some fishers were surely identified as more skillful trollers or poison makers than others, and the parallel stories of technological dynamism in both forms of fishing demonstrate concern to improve the productivity of each form of fishing. But the distinction between the two also depended on new ideas about the landscape, ideas that developed out of the constraints of cereal agriculture.

When Botatwe-speaking men and women were broadening the semantic domain of words like *-zòb- and *-zèl-, they were thinking about how farmers might go about fishing. The orientation of the subsistence economy around fairly sedentary villages near agricultural fields created a dynamic in which some parts of the subsistence economy—notably planting, weeding, harvesting, trapping, and shallow-water fishing in the streams near settlements—were more visible than others; they were matters of common knowledge. This had a pronounced impact on the skills and knowledge developed by young children. The degree of sedentism associated with cereal agriculture transformed the extent to which different parts of the landscape were accessed, a tension captured in both local folklore and academic literature in the juxtaposition of the village and the bush, a cultural geography to which we will return. Some forms of food collection came to be practiced in landscapes that were no longer traversed in the daily or seasonal travels of the majority of community members. Knowledge about these activities of the bush came to be the purview of those who had not only the proclivity and skills but also the opportunities to learn it. Access to these opportunities was likely gendered.

It bears stating explicitly that we have no direct linguistic or archaeological evidence that men or women had exclusive control over different forms of fishing.[15] The ethnographic record teaches us that angling; fishing with some forms of nets, fences, weirs and traps; and *kuweʒa,* a verb for spearing game and fish discussed in greater detail below, were exclusively the domain of men in the eastern Botatwe region in the early twentieth century. They were undertaken in more swiftly running waters at the end of the dry season, when the shallow streams and pools had already dried up and women were busy preparing and planting fields in advance of the rains.[16] Both men and women used plunge baskets in the shallow waters of floodlands and receding tributaries, but only women used izubo and masiko in the twentieth century.[17] This evidence suggests that men and women developed *-zèl- and broadened the semantic domain of *-zòb- to better describe the different geographies of men's and women's fishing.

This argument seems to fit well with observations from comparative subsistence studies, in which the transition to agriculture allowed subsistence activities to be gendered and specialized in new ways according to the degree of danger, the predictable return on effort expended, and the range of mobility from the agricultural settlement necessary to carry out particular subsistence activities.[18] Cross-culturally, women's subsistence labors are usually more productive than men's. Similarly, specialists are usually thought to undertake dangerous activities that required greater labor and material inputs as well as longer travel from the home settlement, even though these efforts often contributed far fewer calories to the cooking pot than women's work in and around the fields.[19]

In spite of the seeming corroboration between Botatwe fishing history and observations from comparative subsistence studies, such universal explanations are decidedly unsatisfying to the historian. They assume that specialization is always the outcome of agriculture. They naturalize historically and culturally contingent ideas about danger. And they obscure women's investments in men's labors. These assumptions don't fit the evidence for the Botatwe case. In the middle Kafue region in the centuries around the turn of the first millennium, the distinction between fishing near the homestead and labor- and material-intensive fishing in the currents of major channels captures one iteration of a new geography associated with forms of food collection that predated agriculture. Although neither the linguistic nor archaeological records attest directly to the ways in which access to the landscape was gendered, swift-current fishing was inextricably tied to forms of hunting with spears. And it is here, in thinking though the kinesthetics of spearcraft, that Botatwe speakers created words that described the different opportunities available to those with the skills, knowledge, time, and desire to labor in the bush, opportunities that were tied up with ideas about masculinity and the different contributions of men's and women's bodies to the aspirations of technicians, lineages, and households.

Spearmen of the Kafue

Linguistic evidence that hunters were celebrated figures in central Africa in the late first millennium will not surprise those familiar with anthropological descriptions of central African hunters, with their potent metaphysical powers and distinctive autonomy.[20] Indeed, it is something of an axiom that hunters hold unique status in African farming societies. This is particularly true in the southern savannas, where foreign hunter-founders figure prominently in traditions of origin as bringers of civilization, generous givers, powerful magicians, alliance makers, and, of course, husbands and fathers of the heirs to newly established kingdoms.[21] With such charters, scholars have traced the spread of novel political ideologies, peoples, and titles to reconstruct regional political histories, in which hunter-founders symbolize both groups of actual political upstarts and hyperbolic "ideal men."[22]

Rather than assume that the symbolic significance of hunters in political charters stems from qualities inherent to their craft, we might ask how and when hunters and hunting developed such significance within the communities of the southern savannas. We know the end of this story well—the dramatic cults, powerful guilds, and mythical founders—but know considerably less about how hunters, as practitioners with a particular skill, came to be recognized as "ideal men" embodying the creativity and danger of autonomy and symbolizing the political capacity to found kingdoms. Decentralized Botatwe communities bound hunters' distinction to local politics in a manner that was different from the links developed between hunters and royal dynasties in familiar savanna traditions. If the political value of hunting varied across the southern savannas in the last centuries of the precolonial period, we might well ask *who* undertook the work of cultivating hunting reputations in early savanna societies and to what ends?

Good Shots and Generous Givers

From the mid-eighth to the mid-thirteenth century, Central Eastern and Kafue communities created an inventive tradition of spearcraft, a tradition that was both a product of and a catalyst in sweeping new ideas about the landscape, the social value of food collection within farming communities, and the relationship between talent and community well-being. As part of this innovation, proto-Central Eastern Botatwe speakers adopted the word *-pàdó [68], "celebrated, skilled hunter," in the late first millennium.[23] The fact that some hunters were more skilled than others was surely nothing new, yet the invention of a word to delineate this category of person was. The distribution and phonological form of this root in languages stretching across the savannas to the northwest, north, and east of the Kafue floodplain demonstrate that speakers of Botatwe, Luban, and Sabi languages innovated the term during a period of contact. In all but Luban attestations, the root is associated with skillful hunting. In Ruund, an inherited reflex, *cipar* (n. cl. 7/8), "ability, gift, or talent," suggests an association between talent and the root dating to the emergence of Ruund in the mid-first millennium, thereby supporting the antiquity of a semantic reconstruction emphasizing the talent of *-pàdó. Other attestations connect *-pàdó to the social process of recognizing hunters' aptitude. For example, Soli, Valley Tonga, and Chikunda speak of *cipalu* (n. cl. 7/8), the celebratory feasting, dancing, and reenactments performed after a successful hunt. The semantic domain of the root clearly indicates that their reputation for talent in their craft set *-pàdó apart from generic hunters, who were designated *muvwimi* in Botatwe languages, the agentive form of the verb "to hunt," *-vóím- [14].

Proto-Central Eastern Botatwe speakers derived *-pàdó from the ancient Bantu verb *-pá, "to give," with the extensive verbal affix. The extensive affix has been reconstructed on proto-Bantu verbs with the connotation "to be in a spread-out position."[24] Thus, the verb literally meant "to give or send across space" or "to give widely." In many southern Bantu languages, including Botatwe languages, the extensive affix connotes repetition of an action undertaken on a large scale.[25] In Ila, the affix invoking habitual, repetitive actions is created by simply inserting /-a/ before the final syllable to render *mwaalu* "he who repetitively, intensively gives."[26] The morphology Central Eastern communities mustered to invent the word also reflected the social, discursive nature of ascription: the /-ú/ suffix indicates that the root was used as a verb of quality able to function as an adjective of quality, glossing inelegantly as "hunt-ious."[27] Further derivation from the verb or adjective of quality produces both the noun of quality *bwaalu* ("huntsmanship," n cl. 14)[28] and the noun denoting a person who embodied huntsmanship, mwaalu (n. cl. 1/2). If the repetitive, intensive connotation of the extensive affix dates to proto-Central Eastern Botatwe, *-pàdó was the consummate huntsman, both a "good shot" and a "generous giver." The morphology of *-pàdó supported this polysemy because the verb's object—what the hunter "gives"—could be both his weapon and the game he distributed. Thus, *-pàdó poetically captured in one word fleeting scenes of the mwaalu's craft: his spear thrown across great distances, repeated stabbings of the close kill, and followers' expectation of his expansive and repeated munificence in sharing meat.

Mwaalu and his celebrants defined his status on the basis of his mastery of new technologies and techniques adopted at the same time as the invention of the appellation *-pàdó. Hunters speaking proto-Central Eastern Botatwe and their proto-Kafue-speaking descendants invented an elaborate lexicon to talk about spearcraft from the mid-eighth to the mid-thirteenth century, a lexicon that suggests these hunters radically transformed both their hunting technologies and the role of hunting in the local economy. The first example of this evidence is an innovation developed by proto-Central Eastern

Figure 3.4. Tonga spearmen, probably in the early twentieth century. Note that the men hold a variety of both fishing and hunting spears, demonstrating the relationship between spearcraft on water and on land, rather than the more familiar distinction between fishing and hunting. Reprinted from Reynolds and Cousins, *Lwaano Lwanyika*, 21. Permission courtesy of the International African Institute, London.

Botatwe speakers, *-wèz- [63], a mode of hunting or fishing with spears, possibly throwing spears (fig. 3.4).[29] This word was used alongside the inherited term *-vóím-, "to hunt with bows and arrows." By the turn of the first millennium, then, Botatwe communities living near the abundant game of the Kafue floodplains distinguished between at least two forms of hunting: archery and spearcraft, with the latter including fishing with spears. Like the establishment of the status of *-pàdó, *-wèz- was invented as part of a wider savanna project in the last quarter of the first millennium in which many societies shared across their linguistic boundaries innovations in hunting technology and ideas about the social implications of such creativity.[30]

The source of the verb *-wèz- is uncertain; its pronunciation in the Botatwe languages that inherited it supports its invention from two possible source roots. The most obvious derivation for kuweza in terms of meaning is also the least likely in terms of phonology. Kuweza could derive from the ancient Bantu verb *-bìng, meaning "to hunt or chase." The Central Eastern

Botatwe form does not follow the expected sound changes for inheritance, but it does match the sound changes undergone by some eastern Bantu languages.[31] If *-wèz- derives from *-bìng, it was borrowed by proto-Central Eastern Botatwe speakers from a now lost Kaskazi language spoken to the east. Yet the verb's phonology and its meaning in modern Botatwe languages supports another possible source, *-gèd-, a widespread Bantu root. As a verb, the root glosses across Bantu languages as "to try," "to think," or "to measure." In noun from, it means "wisdom" or even "guile" in central African Bantu languages. It is a root combined with suffixes to derive verbs with meanings such as "to liken" in some eastern Bantu languages and "to imitate" in some Bantu languages in central Africa. The phonology of the proto-Central Eastern Botatwe form indicates that it could have come from a widespread eastern Bantu form of the root *-gèdi, reconstructed with the meaning "to try."

Modern attestations of *-wèz- in Ila, the best documented language of the Central Eastern Botatwe branch, illustrate how hunting was first a path to and, later, a metaphor for social aspirations, the networks of assistance and dependency that supported social aspirations, and the forms of competition that laid bare the uncertainties of such strivings for recognition. In Ila, kuweza refers to the hunt for economic success and its use to launch and manage one's social position, precisely the process that could produce a status like *-pàdó. It is a term for wives' efforts to develop the kinds of intimate relationships that might attract gifts and wealth into their households. In the causative, kuweʒya not only means "to cause to hunt," it also means "to cause to help," calling to mind the social networks of dependency in which hunters both sought to be entangled and undoubtedly sometimes found themselves entrapped. Muweʒele, derived from the applicative of kuweza, "to hunt on behalf of," glosses elegantly as "a popular person." In a reduplicated form, Ila speakers use the verb kuweza-weʒa to talk about making light of difficulties, reminding us that hunting has a long history as a pathway out of difficulties, to more prosperous social ties and welcomed material wealth. To be sure, reduplication of the causative, kuweʒya-weʒya glosses with the expected "to hunt a little," but it also means "to deride" or "make light of," demonstrating the contingencies of hunters' aspirations.[32] Not all hunters' efforts were successful and even strenuous effort might not protect against ridicule in the face of failure. Nor did success ensure others' acceptance of the social status to which a hunter aspired. Ila speakers took an inherited word for a form of hunting with spears and developed out of that word a range of meanings conjuring up the lifelong pursuit of social status, the obligation of assistance, and the belittlement awaiting unsuccessful attempts at providing help and performing the status to which one aspired. Central Eastern Botatwe home-steaders developed the verb *-wèz- in the last quarter of the first millennium to talk about a new form of hunting with spears that was bound up with the social ambition of hunters, their kin, and their households.

Technological Innovations in Spearcraft

As *-wèz-, to hunt with spears, came to dominate innovation in hunting, proto-Central Eastern Botatwe speakers and their linguistic descendants, speakers of proto-Kafue, developed vocabulary for new types and parts of spears.[33] This efflorescence in spearcraft was supported by the development of an intensive smelting and smithing culture from the ninth through the eleventh centuries southeast of the Kafue floodplains, near modern-day Lusaka, and in the Zambezi Valley.[34] Indeed, archaeological evidence from woodlands sites in the Kafue region also show evidence of a local iron-smelting tradi-tion, with the greatest period of intensity beginning in the late ninth century and continuing at least through the tenth century, overlapping with the tran-sition between the Central Eastern Botatwe and Kafue periods.[35] For exam-ple, an ancient Bantu word for spear, *-túmò, was reborrowed at this time in the form *-súmò [11], probably because it now carried an iron point.

The savanna-wide world of technological innovation in which eastern Botatwe speakers participated was a world in which metallurgical, fishing, and hunting traditions spread and overlapped as technologies were exchanged. Central Eastern Botatwe villagers followed their neighbors in applying an ancient Bantu term for "stone," *-tádè, to "iron, iron ore, and iron bloom" but also converted the root into noun class 9/10 to produce *(ı)ntale [69], novel joints of iron taping or wire. Kafue marksmen a few centuries later adopted the *-sákò [70], a new spearshaft.[36] Hunters and smiths collaborated to de-velop at least two new spear points between the mid-eighth and mid-thirteenth centuries: *(ı)mpìla [71], "spear point," and *-bèjı [72], a "barbless point used on both spears and arrows" that was developed from the inherited verb, *-bàij-, "to carve" (fig. 3.5). The *(ı)mpòla spear was a throwing spear with a short, barbless point and perhaps an iron cone hafted onto the butt of the shaft. The cone facilitated digging and acted as a counterweight to improve balance and trajectory as the spearman lifted and steadied the spear, marked his target, and then hurled the spear. The large barbless *(ı)mpòla point was

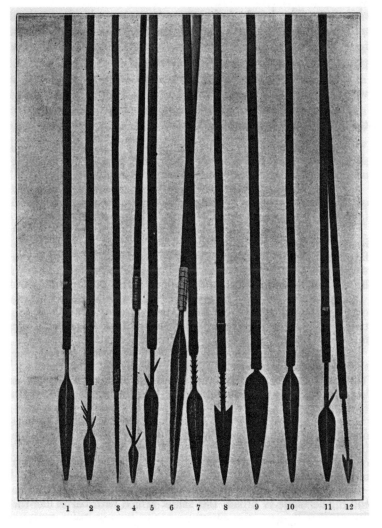

Figure 3.5. Some spears types used by Ila spearmen in the first decades of the twentieth century: 1. kapula (*(ı)mpòla), 2. lukona, 3. mumba, 4. chanza cha mpongo, 5. shichokochoko, 6. impengula, 7. chinkoshi, 8. shikamimbia, 9. chimpata, 10. kabezhi (*-bèjı), 11. inkombo, 12. shitwichinkoshi. Photograph by E. W. Smith. Reprinted from Smith and Dale, *Ila-Speaking Peoples of Northern Rhodesia*, vol. 1, 216.

well suited to hunting larger game without damaging the hide, as a barbed point is likely to do. A spearman who used these increasingly specialized points needed to know what animals he expected to hunt before he went into the bush, a decision that required detailed knowledge of environmental conditions and the seasonal and daily habits of game.

Elaborations in the technologies developed to ensure hunting success included new medicines, referred to by the common word *(mu)kana*. The modern-day distribution of this term in the nonadjacent languages of the Central Eastern Botatwe branch suggest that it dates to this period of innovation in spearcraft in the last quarter of the first millennium.[37] Though hunters had likely long been using charms and medicines to protect themselves and to ensure their success, probably speaking of them with the generic term for medicine, *musamu,* (mu)kana was different enough to merit a new name. The convergence of innovations around the technology of spearcraft strongly suggests that these innovations were related—that *-pàdó were hunters whose exceptional success in the activity named *-wèz- was secured by their ability to make or acquire technologies like (mu)kana or iron-tipped *-sómò.

The material cultural record of the Kafue and Batoka regions dating from the mid-eighth to mid-thirteenth centuries boasts similarly rich innovation in hunting technologies and new patterns of consuming meat.[38] As ironworking flourished between the ninth and eleventh centuries, smiths and spearmen collaborated to develop new forms of points, ferrules, and end spikes. The regional faunal record shifts toward higher mortality rates of gregarious antelope species, hippos, and elephants, all species hunted by groups armed with spears. Moreover, fully gown adults dominate mortality curves. Archaeologists interpret these faunal assemblages as indicative of the emergence of skillful communal hunting practices.[39] For example, though wild species outnumber domesticated species in the faunal assemblage throughout the occupation of the Middle Iron Age site of Kalala Island in the hook of the Kafue River, there is a spike in the ratio of wild to domesticates at stratigraphic levels dated from the last quarter of the first millennium into the mid-second millennium, levels that overlap with the proto-Central Eastern Botatwe and proto-Kafue periods, before the ratio returns in the fifteenth century to Early Iron Age levels. Finally, butchery patterns within late first millennium and early second millennium assemblages from the middle Kafue and Batoka Plateau regions exhibit a shift from an earlier pattern in which entire carcasses are represented in the assemblage to specific portions of the carcass being brought back to the village, skewing the portions represented in the faunal record.

Beginning in the Central Eastern Botatwe period and continuing through the Kafue period, hunters changed how they processed carcasses at the site of the kill. Three possible scenarios, or a combination thereof, can account for changes in the faunal record, but all three indicate that hunting and meat had taken on a new status. Hunters may have been hunting further from the homestead, eating some of the meat in hunting camps and drying other portions, returning with only preferred bones. This kind of long-distance hunting required great investment of hunters' time for very little return in calories. Moreover, all the species represented in the faunal record were likely abundant in the nearby Kafue flats, particularly in the dry season. Alternatively, hunters may have selectively, wastefully butchered game when it was bagged, particularly if innovations in hunting technologies increased the number and frequency of kills. Indeed, if animals were killed in ever-greater numbers but only selectively butchered, hunting was no longer merely a source of protein for ordinary people. It had a new value outside of nutrition. Or perhaps hunters butchered their kills in a way that followed local conventions of carcass division after communal hunts, though we have no indication of where other carcass portions went. In each scenario, the development of novel butchery and consumption practices demonstrate that hunting and meat had a value beyond nutrition for Central Eastern Botatwe and Kafue hunters and their households, kin, and neighbors. Likewise, the development of words that divided hunters into categories of talented and ordinary and linked spearcraft to social ambitions suggests that hunting was no longer a general pursuit strategically employed by farmers. Rather, some hunting and fishing, particularly with spears, was part of the work of distinguishing oneself and developing dependencies, of acting on the full suite of economic and social aspirations Ila speakers came to associate with the verb *-wèz-.

Hunting Reputations: The Social Contexts and Conceptual Contents of Fame

The unique status enjoyed by hunters across the southern savannas by the end of the second millennium would have confounded savanna farmers of the early first millennium, who labored to integrate the exploitation of game meats, skins, horns, and tusks into the work of protecting the ripening grain heads of the cereals with which they were experimenting.[40] Even after savanna farmers adopted sorghums and millets as the staples of their diet in the mid-first millennium, the distinct status of hunters was not a foregone conclusion to the admirers and dependents who first spoke of *-pàdó; to the inventive smiths who transformed the tools wielded in the pursuit of game; and to the gifted hunters who emphasized the sociality of the hunt, kindled the consumptive desire—even hunger—for meat, and built reputations as talented individuals within the community, living and dead. Charismatic leaders and lineage heads undoubtedly valued such talented individuals for their contributions to the circuits of redistribution, but the politics of knowledge and economies of subsistence looked different to those cultivating reputations for skill in hunting. Generations of speakers who inherited the word *-pàdó from their Central Eastern linguistic forebears layered new meanings onto it in their daily use of the term: "friend," "companion," "elder." These novel meanings reveal the discursive strategies deployed to bolster claims leveled at *-pàdó by members of the collectivities to which *-pàdó belonged or in which he claimed for himself a membership. As elders, friends, and companions, celebrated hunters developed personal associations that both bolstered and fell outside the control of those mwaami, lineage heads, and other notables who assured the well-being of hunters' neighborhoods and lineages. Hunters' strivings for recognition exemplify the affective dimensions of power, alternative loci of influence and dependency, and additional processes of network building that characterized authority in the southern savannas long before the development of its more familiar kingdoms.

Over the last two decades, studies of precolonial African societies have transformed our understanding of the relationship between knowledge, power, and community in the deep past. In an early, influential contribution to this scholarship, Jane Guyer and Samuel-Martin Eno Belinga argued that the familiar model of precolonial politics, "wealth in people," was best understood as the composition of "wealth in knowledge" by leaders building communities with good prospects for the future.[41] The shift beyond the accumulative nature of leadership bolstered research already underway on how Africans crafted dependencies through both the control of material resources and the manipulation of speech and knowledge, diffusing power across heterarchical networks with multiple nodes of authority and diversifying followers' opportunities for affiliation.[42] Historians have developed rich narratives about the paths by which leaders and followers invented clans, royalty, guilds, and healing cults around historically contingent ideas about what it meant to be a particular kind of person, such as a skilled drum maker, a descendant of a divine ancestor, an infertile woman, or a proven hunter. Underlying this scholarship is the cultivation, recognition, and transposition of individual distinction. The "wealth in people as wealth in knowledge" model explains how reputations for talent intersected with leaders' political aspirations; scholarship on heterarchical political traditions illuminates how adepts' investment in their own networks of obligation and dependency could undermine leaders' efforts to consolidate power. When initiated by figures like *-pàdó, such ambitious efforts may well have contributed to the persistently decentralized character of Botatwe societies.[43] Significantly, these approaches to precolonial political history do little to elucidate the experience of those cultivating reputations before or in the absence of a process whereby control of distinctive talents came to be a source of formal power. While we know a great deal about the politics of knowledge among leaders and groups of followers, we know decidedly less about the cultivation of individual distinction among peers.[44] This is particularly true of renown below the level of cultural heroes, founder figures, or charismatic and ritual leaders.

In the context of the small, decentralized Botatwe societies, struggles over paths to fame reveal a deep history of the informal power of local, even seasonal honorables, of primus inter pares.[45] Though Botatwe speakers celebrated some talented hunters as *-pàdó, we have no linguistic, comparative ethnographic, or archaeological evidence for the early use of such distinction as a basis for the development of guilds or cults of specialists or professionals, as was the case in neighboring societies. Peers' cultivation, contestation, and commemoration of hunting reputations foregrounds the affective dimensions of hunters' renown: the excitement of the chase; hunters' worry over success and their benevolent performances of distribution; dependents' anticipation, trust, or even ridicule; and remembrances of hunters past.[46] The invention of a concept like *-pàdó illuminates how communities and individuals struggled to redefine a once-banal form of labor as a path to distinction in the face of developments in the material, technological, and political context of hunting. The "wealth in people as wealth in knowledge" concept helps us imagine why local leaders and peers recognized and celebrated distinctive hunters for the meat, skins, security, excitement, and renown they brought to the community. Unfolding outside the familiar regional pattern of specialized professional and ritual institutions formalizing authority, the celebration of Botatwe hunters' reputations foregrounds the process of distinguishing peers, a process with strikingly affective power in small-scale communities. Later elaborations on the meaning of *-pàdó to include "elder," "friend," and "companion" after the divergence of proto-Kafue demonstrate the persistence of the affective, rather than the formally political, stakes for *-pàdó and the communities that esteemed them, even as the economic and political basis of hunting reputations drastically changed over the course of the second millennium.

The status of *-pàdó was an outcome of struggles to redefine the social and economic value of hunting. Rather than naturalize fame by assuming a universal ambition for its trappings, we might well ask what such celebrity was like in the closing centuries of the first millennium. How did celebrity articulate with preexisting ideas about fame and with established forms of authority? Who participated in building hunters' reputations, how, and why?

Lineages stand out in the ethnographic record among the many constituencies involved in matters of fame and commemoration because reputations are essential to the cult of ancestor spirits.[47] The social process of distinguishing peers and cultivating personal reputations lies at the heart of Botatwe speakers' ideas about the accumulation, storage, and transfer of remarkable capabilities from person to person through lineages. Hunting was among a number of other crafts, like canoe carving, ironworking, potting, and some forms of fishing, that were recorded in twentieth-century ethnography as being inheritable from ancestors known to have possessed particular knowledge and skill. [48] After decades studying Tonga communities, Elizabeth Colson notes: "If a person shows particular aptitudes, these may be attributed to the guardian *mizimu* [spirits], or other mizimu of the same lines may be thought to have given him the capacity to perform certain skills which they practiced during their lifetime. . . . As an extension of this belief, a man's successes and failures are not his alone, but belong to the groups which have supplied him with a guardian *muzimu* [spirit] and share with him a ritual attachment to it."[49]

Widespread ethnographic evidence for the practice of conducting talent in a particular skill through lineages suggests that the means by which certain individuals carved out paths to distinction had long been tied into the politics of kin groups.[50] The inheritance of skills from famous ancestors allowed lineages to make stronger claims to technicians' products in the face of competing claims from their households, friends, and dependents. By binding skill to the politics of inheritance, both lineage leaders and practitioners masked the very real, very difficult labor that hunters, fishers, smelters, and others invested in developing their skill through practice. Lineages' active participation in making, curating, and celebrating the fame of ancestors and linking that fame to living aspirants alerts us to the importance of talent and fame in the quest for ancestorhood, both for the individuals seeking remembrance after their death and for the lineages to which they belonged. Indeed, the imperative to strive for ancestorhood on the part of talented individuals and the need to produce ancestors on the part of lineages was undoubtedly complicated by the changing standards, meanings, and material underpinnings of talent and fame.

How, then, did fame work in the closing centuries of the first millennium, as the first *-pàdó were named? How was fame recognized and what did it feel like to both the celebrated and their celebrants? Central Eastern Botatwe speakers inherited a very old metaphor for speaking about fame: the wind. They spoke of fame, *mpʊwo [73], with an inherited word that ultimately derived from an older Bantu word, *-pòʊp-, meaning "blow, wind, breath from lungs." Significantly, this single root for fame encapsulates a nested set of ideas that shaped how Central Eastern communities thought fame worked. From the broadest, oldest meaning of "wind, breath and lung," many central Bantu languages, including some eastern Botatwe languages, developed meanings like "spirit," "news," "opinion," "talk," or a "thing well-known." These meanings connected the discursive mechanisms by which fame was literally called into being with the social circuits of living and dead through which it was conducted.

If proto-Central Eastern Botatwe speakers reconfigured the relationship between fame and the politics of knowledge in the last centuries of the first millennium, as subsistence technology changed and the cultural value of metals grew, we would expect Central Eastern Botatwe speakers to have invented new ways to speak about fame.[51] Moreover, we might expect such a new vocabulary to mirror the ties between technology and fame exhibited in the innovation *-pàdó. Following these expectations, the innovation *-vʊbɪ [74], "famous, rich person," demonstrates that new conceptualizations of fame depended on developments in technological knowledge. Similar to and contemporaneous with the invention of the status of *-pàdó, Central Eastern Botatwe speakers invented the status of *-vʊbɪ from knowledge about metallurgy. This new word for famous, rich person derived from an object used in metallurgy: either an older eastern Bantu root, *-gùbà, "smithy, bellows," or an ancient eastern Bantu areal form,

°-vuba, "bellows."[52] The development of new forms of fame from the tool used to blast air through a smithy or smelting furnace clearly built on older ideas about the blustery, aerial character of fame encapsulated in the term *mpʊwo, even as the knowledge and materials through which one could build up great fame and wealth shifted at the end of the first millennium. Like the status of *-pàdó and other crafts whose expertise was inheritable, the fame of *muvubi* was tied to the politics and ritual responsibilities of lineages through aspirations for acestorhood. As Toka speakers explained in the late 1960s and early 1970s, *bavubi* seek wealth as a way to become widely known in order to be remembered by posterity, a goal achieved, in part, through kin groups. Indeed, *-vʊbɪ proved to be a particularly flexible term. It took on new meanings as the material basis of fame shifted over the course of the second half of the second millennium, as cattle keeping and slavery became more important to the regional political economy.[53]

The links between *mpʊwo and *-vʊbɪ seem rather clear, then, but *-pàdó's relationship to them deserves closer scrutiny. While it shares the semantic field of fame and celebrity based on knowledge of bushcraft, *-pàdó may not conjure up a sense of breathiness or windiness as easily as the blustery bellows work of *-vʊbɪ. Yet the windiness of hunting with spears becomes clear by thinking about the qualities of the moving body and tools of the celebrated hunter, *-pàdó.

The hunter, who is also a farmer most of the year, works in the dry season, part of which constitutes the windy season in south central Africa. He and his wife or lover initiate his task by abstaining from sex the night before hunting. But he might empower his hunt through incest with his mother or sister.[54] In the morning, he makes an offering at a shrine dedicated to the ancestor spirit from whom he inherited his craft (fig. 3.6). The shrine, a forked branch near his homestead or in the bush, also functions as his spear rest and trophy rack. He asks his ancestor, whom he cannot see but whose affects are as visible as the wind for which spirits and fame are also named, to be the source of what Clapperton Mavhunga calls "guided mobility" in the "transient workspace" of the bush.[55] The hunter runs with his dogs, heaving air to chase down quarry, stilling himself perhaps by controlling his breath as he stalks the animal. His knowledge of the wind's changing direction is of upmost importance, for just as the vibrating air of the speech of his admirers carries the hunter's reputation like the wind, so the wind might carry his scent

Figure 3.6. An Ila hunter's spear rest, *lwangu*, in front of an ancestor shrine in a homestead in the early twentieth century. Photograph by E. W. Smith. Reprinted from Smith and Dale, *Ila-Speaking Peoples of Northern Rhodesia*, vol. 2, 171.

to his quarry in warning, undermining the hunter's efforts and threatening his reputation for skill and success.[56] His spear moves through the air, shaped by the wind and directing new air currents, eventually wounding the animal. When the wounded animal is found, cutting its throat redirects the felled animal's breath and changes its sonorous quality to the heaving tones and vibrations of wet membranes, muscle, and skin in the long minutes it takes for the animal's breath to cease, ensuring that the hunter will be greeted with the singing and breathless excitement of the village when he returns. The hunter's return includes laying his spear to rest in the forked branch of his ancestor shrine, accompanied by a gesture or word of thanks directed at the protective spirit whose influence mitigated the possible dangers of those precarious forces stirred to action in the bush during the chase and in the animal's death. The hunter's success circulates on the lips of those living in the homestead and those residing beyond its fence, simultaneously creating and sustaining his reputation, just as his hunts will be commemorated by future generations' talk in the stories and petitions that will secure the hunter's place in his family's community of efficacious ancestral spirits. Like metallurgy, there is, then, some breathiness to the experiences of the celebrated hunter, to the creation of his fame, and to the objects he works in and on in life and in death. Botatwe speakers emphasized such similarities when they invented words to distinguish categories of subsistence labor in the centuries around the turn of the first millennium.

Why did some talents and not others come to be paths to status, the focus of celebration and the kinds of social talk—the exchange of news, stories, and nicknames—that engendered fame, in the closing centuries of the first millennium? While it would be simple to assume that some activities were more significant to the subsistence economy, this crude instrumentalism belies the complicated ways Central Eastern Botatwe speakers and their linguistic descendants thought about the similarities between hunting, canoe carving, smelting, or other labors. Spearcraft and metallurgy seemed particularly alike. Indeed, for Central Eastern Botatwe speakers in the late first millennium, the work of hunters, metallurgists, fame, spirits, and wind resembled one another. The sensuous qualities of wind and breath materialized in an airborne spear, a working bellows, an animal's last gasp, or a furnace's blustery blue flame were captured in the etymologies and meanings of *-pàdó, *mpʊwo, and *-vʊbɩ, however distinct their technological or material basis. But when marksmen and smelters wielded bellows and spears—both new material objects and new iterations of older ones—in crafting fame in the last centuries of the first millennium in south central Africa, they also opened up new ways of categorizing, acting, and being in the world. Technicians created these opportunities by observing that the kinesthetic experience and tools of spearcraft and metallurgy had more in common than their windy, aerial qualities. Each tool, each body's action when performing these technologies was necessarily, by virtue of their materiality, bundled together with additional qualities.[57] Hunters and smelters seized on such further overlaps to identify what, exactly, was unique about their labors compared to work in the fields, fishing in shallow waters, house repair, and the many other activities that contributed to the subsistence economy and the well-being of families. Celebrated practitioners and those connected to them used these overlaps to craft another link between the technologies of *-pàdó and *-vʊbɩ in the closing centuries of the first millennium, a link that neither directly included nor excluded *mpʊwo. This link was both spatial and conceptual. It lay at the man-made intersection between the geographies of spearcraft, smelting, and spirits' influence: the bush.

Inventing the Bush: New Landscapes of Fame

Spearcraft and metallurgy shared a particular geography by the close of the first millennium. Although metallurgy was an ancient technology dating to at least the first centuries of the first millennium, by the last centuries of the millennium, smelting underwent a dramatic change: the location of smelting shifted from the village to sites beyond the village margin, sites that were probably in the bush, according to the ethnographic record.[58] While it is difficult to distinguish whether the root from which *-vʊbɪ was derived indicated an association with smithing or smelting because bellows are used in both, it is significant that the innovation occurred at the same time that the geography of smelting changed. None of the excavations at Middle Iron Age Kafue village sites recovered evidence of smelting activity, indicating that smelting was undertaken outside the village in the Kafue region centuries before that same shift in location took hold in Zambian sites farther south. Indeed, the shift to smelting outside village boundaries in southern Zambia actually corresponds to the period when an intrusive material cultural tradition with roots in the middle Kafue region arrives on the Batoka and in the Zambezi Valley. This evidence strongly suggests that inhabitants with historical ties to the middle Kafue region were responsible for the diffusion of this transformation in the geography of smelting practices. Middle Iron Age Kafue people did not develop this innovation alone; they were participating in a wider, regional shift in the geography of metallurgical practice that unfolded across south central Africa between the seventh and eleventh centuries.[59] Central Eastern Botatwe *-vʊbɪ and *-pàdó invented new paths to renown and influence on the basis of their connections to wider networks of technological innovators, a point to which we will return in chapter 5, as well as their ability to travel through and make productive landscapes that lay beyond the day-to-day bustle of the village. The reputations of *-vʊbɪ and *-pàdó depended on the same contrast between the village and the bush captured in the distinction between kuzuba and kuzela fishing. That contrast was established late in the first millennium, when the bush was first described with a new name: *-sókwe [75].

In the last quarter of the first millennium, Central Eastern Botatwe speakers who undertook forms of hunting and metallurgy associated with fame and wealth did so under the cover of the bush. To better understand the interlocking politics of talent and fame and the interlocking technologies of spearcraft and smelting, we need to understand the historical development of the idea of the bush. For those Botatwe communities about which we have a rich ethnographic literature, the bush is a key concept for understanding the social, economic, and ritual dimensions of the landscape because it is associated with metaphysical forces implicated in acts of transformation, such as hunting, initiation, smelting, and, in other central African societies, chiefs' investiture. Entry into and activities undertaken within this space require careful planning and ritual management to be successful. The landscape itself contributes to that success because it contains such potent, potentially generative powers.

Elizabeth Colson's description of Tonga ideas about the bush has much in common with ideas shared by most Botatwe societies, so it is worth quoting her at length. For Tonga speakers living on the Batoka Plateau in the twentieth century, the bush was "a metaphor for the great nonhuman sources of power pervasive of the wild," a space that "carried connotations of wilderness and of absence of human control," and "the embodiment of power antithetical to human power."[60] The bush was the "habitat of *basangu* [spirits] and ghosts (*ʒelo*)"; though "people seek out basangu at *malende* [shrines] and through their mediums, in other contexts they fear contact with them." Colson explains: "[The] bush is still an ambivalent metaphor, for while it harbours much good, it also stands for matters out of human control, danger, and evil. It also stands for illicit activities. Children born of an affair are called 'children of the bush.' And . . . the bodies of children born with certain physical anomalies and adults who were rejected by society [lepers, suicides, strangers] were once disposed of by throwing them away in the bush." Thus, "ghosts and the spirits of the unmourned adult dead who died away from home are associated with the bush." While the bush is "unpredictable and contains malevolent forces," it is also a place "to which [Tonga] turned for extra empowerment" through medicine. Colson teaches us: "medicines and charms, whether for protection or witchcraft, are primarily associated with the bush," and "the use of such charms opens [users] to accusations of witchcraft, for they mobilize power stemming from outside the village." Botatwe speakers today understand the bush as a place imbued with, in the words of Eugenia Herbert, "unrestricted power," a power of great social potential and possible danger.[61]

Across Bantu-speaking Africa and even beyond, scholars have observed the link between ambivalent power and the bush, especially in rituals associated with technologies like hunting and smelting that are undertaken in the bush.[62] They have reconstructed histories in which the bush is tamed, traversed, or transformed. For example, both Emmanuel Kreike and Clapperton Mavhunga demonstrate in studies of regions near Botatwe lands how environments and social lives were coproduced when men and women practiced particular subsistence technologies in particular kinds of places.[63] As Susan Kent notes, the bush, as a particular kind of space, is often considered to be a place within which to build a social career.[64] This career—as a hunter, a smelter, a medium, a political innovator—depends equally on ideas about the power and productivity of the bush and one's ability to harness and manage them. Scholars tend to focus on the latter. For example, in a cross-cultural study of "transformative" activities like smelting, hunting, and potting, Eugenia Herbert argues that these activities are conceptualized as analogous to the "drama of human fertility" and governed by a common cosmology. They are made successful through the technician's careful management of homologous activities, like sex and menstruation, and those forces related to or involved in matters of human fertility, such as ancestor spirits and life forces like *nyama, koyo,* or *asa.*[65] Herbert's "transformative model" is useful, but, as she admits, it takes for granted the dangerous and powerful qualities of the bush as somehow universal, natural, symbolic, or simply beyond our ability to historicize. To be sure, scholars often read the danger and unrestricted power of the bush and particular activities like hunting and smelting into the deep past on the basis of their "inherent" risks. But this approach naturalizes cultural ideas about fear, risk, and danger. Rather than being merely the setting for potent, even dangerous, activities, the bush is a particular cultural space with qualities unique unto itself, a spatial concept whose development can be historicized. The words Botatwe speakers used to describe their environment allow us to discern what homesteaders living in the middle Kafue between the mid-eighth and mid-thirteenth centuries thought about the bush, the village, and the spaces in between.

When Central Eastern Botatwe families moved into the unfamiliar ecologies of the middle Kafue region, they began to think about the landscape in new terms. The Kafue floodplain dominated the area and as Central Eastern Botatwe speakers established homesteads within its lush margins, they named it with an older, inherited word, *-nyíka [76], that had long been used by Bantu speakers for just this kind of landscape, a floodplain or grassland. Although some Bantu speakers eventually applied this root to the concept of the bush, Central Eastern Botatwe homesteaders changed its meaning to "country," a far more generic gloss in environmental terms but one which carried a sense of political or cultural territory. With this semantic innovation Central East-ern Botatwe farmers announced their ideal homeland and, perhaps, their claim to the well-watered territories of the middle Kafue at a time when the climate posed a challenge to cereal agriculture. Significantly, Central Eastern Botatwe homesteaders developed this new understanding of the significance of grass-land environments at the same time that they extended their villages into the woodlands adjacent to the Kafue and its tributaries, cutting and burning the trees and brush to carve out new fields in areas hospitable to their style of agriculture. Central Eastern Botatwe families conceptualized these hospi-table woodlands and the nearby grasslands—these *-nyíka lands—in con-tradistinction to another new category of environment, *-sókwe.[66]

In modern Botatwe languages, *isokwe* is the quintessential "bush"; it is an open space with the scrub vegetation that indicates that it is neither set-tled nor cultivated. In the closing centuries of first millennium, Botatwe villa-gers derived *-sókwe from an older, more widespread verb, *-còk-, "to incite," which, itself, derived from an ancient Bantu term that glosses as "to poke in, put in, prick with a point, hide, ram in." Contemporary attestations in the best documented Botatwe languages reveal a complicated network of meanings tying together ideas about "provoking," "inciting," and "stabbing" with "being first," "establishing," or "originating." In the late first millennium, Botatwe men and women imagined acts of creation within the landscape they named "isokwe" to require provocation by poking or spearing. Modern attestations make explicit the link to hunting. As a transitive verb, *kusoka* means "to examine trap(s)" and "to start a quarrel," and *kusokoma* means "to poke, as with a spear in a burrow, or in an animal's chest to kill it."[67]

When Central Eastern Botatwe and Kafue communities named the open bush around them with the passive tense of the verb, *-còk-, they imagined this landscape to be a place of potential creation, a place that was literally "the poked, the prodded, the hidden, the entered" place. It was a setting for and ingredient in acts of origination incited by the plunging action of spears thrust into quarry stalked, netted, or trapped in the bush, the pricking of furnaces with bellows' (tuyères') nozzles or the rhythmic push of air goading the flames of the smelt. The old aerial qualities of spearcraft and metallurgy were still present, but they were bundled with the pricking, piercing, poking, and in-citing qualities of the actions of marksmen and bellows workers. It was this latter cluster of kinesthetic and material qualities experienced through and by the bodies and the objects of bushcraft that speakers drew upon to describe the quintessential encounter with the bush. *-Sókwe was a place of great potential power that could be incited and activated by those spearmen and smelters capable of prodding such generative forces toward acts of creation and social significance. *-Sókwe was the space where the geographies of the spirit world and excitable life forces met and overlapped in a way that could support the unique status sought by skilled hunters and smelters, thrusters of spears and blustery inciters of flames.

Farming communities' invention of *-sókwe at the close of the millennium drew on older associations between landscapes, activities, practitioners, and the ways that the forces of the world worked. The widespread distribution of ideas connecting the bush to ambivalent, unrestricted power might, itself, be an historical outcome of a very old conceptualization of the landscape among Bantu-speaking farmers. Kairn Klieman's history of early interactions between Bantu-speaking farmers and autochthonous hunter-gatherers suggests that the ability to control spirits living beyond the social and spatial boundaries of the village was a very ancient source of authority mustered to ensure the success of humans' efforts. This was an authority associated with first-comers. It depended on an understanding of the landscape that distinguished between those lands, practitioners, and spiritual forces affiliated with immigrant Bantu-speaking farmers' villages and those that were not.[68] Likewise, Eugenia Herbert's model of transformative power depends on mediating restricted human fertility and other kinds of unrestricted life forces, often associated with the forest or the bush in a widespread distribution that may indicate great antiquity.[69] But ancient associations between particular landscapes, activities, and understandings of how different powers were activated or mitigated were neither unchanging nor reconfigured in the same way across the Bantu world, however similar they appear.

The widespread distribution of the village/bush dichotomy across Bantu-speaking regions of Africa (and beyond) speaks to its antiquity, yet the words used to name the bush changed over time, demonstrating the ways in which the space was refashioned by its users. Botatwe speakers probably already had a concept we might gloss as "the bush" when they invented a new name for it in the centuries around the turn of the first millennium, during a time when novel meanings and tools were grafted onto far older technologies. Even in the face of a broad, long-standing consensus about the utility of the idea of "the bush," it worked as a boundary object, with slightly different meanings for different members of the speech community describing it with the same name.[70] Although many villagers traveled through the bush, harvested its wild fruits, and sought out ingredients for relishes and medical treatments, speakers also recognized what was novel about some people's experiences of and in the bush—novelties that were dependent on changing technologies. In response to a shared agreement that the experience of the bush was different for a particular subset of the village population, spearmen, metallurgists and their kin, neighbors, and households marked the bush with a new name, *-sókwe, that could describe the social significance of the new experiences of the space enjoyed by a few.

Technicians helped to establish the atmosphere of the uncertain and potentially dangerous power of the bush even as they drew upon it to protect and ensure the success of their labors. The invention of isokwe was partly a mechanism of control. This idea fits well with evidence that different Bantu communities associate hunters' success with antisocial behaviors like witchcraft and their lack of success with the antisocial behaviors of others, such as the infidelity of wives and the jealousy of witches.[71] Perhaps ambitious spearmen and metallurgists carefully describing the dangers of the transformative power saturating *-sókwe sought to guard access to the wealth and social influence available to those who could render productive their efforts in the bush. Yet we could equally imagine the concerns of villagers who sought to limit the wealth and social influence of ambitious, skilled spearmen and smelters through talk about the dangers and antisocial powers of the bush and those who hide their wealth-generating labors in its shadows. Both of these explanations hold merit because they conform to our assumed contest for control over paths to social mobility, power, and influence. But such contests— as likely as they were—do little to address the extreme uncertainty, fear, triumph, and celebrations that were shared across the community upon the completion of a successful smelt or hunt and in anticipation of sharing in the fruits of such labors. That is to say, an instrumental reading ignores the community's desire for hunters' fame and wealth in favor of hunters' personal ambitions and the affective outcomes of bushcraft in favor of the material outcomes, though all such distinctions were likely far more blurred.[72]

Fame was as significant a product of bushcraft as skins, meat, and bloom. Among eastern Botatwe communities in the centuries around the turn of the first millennium, access to the economic and social value of technological innovation was not mediated through professional groups or exclusive guilds, as they were in other parts of the savanna in the second half of the second millennium. Rather, access to reputations for skill in bushcraft was mediated through local ideas about talent and fame that were intimately bound up in lineage politics and preexisting ideas about the relationship between kin, subsistence, and social reproduction. As the scale and success of hunting and ironworking increased, these technologies offered new ways to build up a following and to cultivate a reputation, both of which secured one's future position as a remembered, commemorated ancestor. Hunters and smelters contributed to their lineage's patrimony knowledge and reputations that could prod older spirits to action and be inherited by future generations. Renowned individuals had the potential to become remembered and, therefore, efficacious spirits, but achieving renown, the hunt for reputations, took great effort on the part of the technician and their communities of admirers. Ideas about the potency and potential dangers of the bush actually buttressed the politics of reputation building that served to populate the spirit world, which loomed so powerfully in local understandings of the bush and ensured the success of efforts undertaken within it. Just as some women were able to secure their own and their lineage's social place by giving birth to children and even pots, some men "birthed" not only meat, skins, and ivory but also ancestors.[73]

Hunters, smelters, wives, spirits, kin, and neighbors shared existential concerns about the significance of individual achievement in the bush. These concerns were captured in the very morphology used to invent the name *-sókwe for the landscape of the bush. Here, comparison with another attestation of the old Bantu root *-còk- sharpens the point. Bashu communities in eastern DRC also use this old Bantu root *-còk- to talk about "the bush," but they developed the noun from the verb as isoki, the agentive noun. For Bashu, the bush itself is the inciter, the piercer, the provoker in acts of creation.[74] For Central Eastern Botatwe speakers in south central Africa in the last centuries of the first millennium, isokwe was the object acted upon by the piercer, the inciter, the provoker: the hunter or the smelter capable of entering the bush. It is difficult to assess whether the Bashu attestation suggests that isoki is a far more ancient form transformed by marksmen in south central Africa at the close of the millennium or whether it was an independent, convergent innovation. Regardless, the comparison demonstrates that what was unique to south central Africans was a different set of ideas about what entities were subjects and what entities were objects. South central Africans insisted that the bush was an *object* of human's actions, a place marked by a firm boundary laid out between the bush and the village, a boundary that needed to be pierced but was pierce-able only by certain kinds of subjects. The sensuous, affective qualities of technology mattered because the kinesthetic resemblances between being the agent of poking and prodding as an act of origination in the use of new iron-tipped spears and bellows and in sex were experiences available to men, a point elaborated more fully elsewhere.[75] The morphology mustered to name the bush "isokwe" supported a kind of authority and agency rooted in novel performances of skill, a celebrity available to a new kind of man.

What was new about the bush in the late first millennium—what inspired Botatwe speakers to name it *-sókwe—was its gendering as a masculine space, a place where men drew on older ideas about the creative powers associated with fertility to contribute in new ways to social reproduction. In many central African societies, hunting is associated with childbirth. Likewise, Ila speakers' application of *-wèz-, spear hunting, to sexual relationships initiated to augment wealth and social status explicitly connect hunter's productivity with the power of fertility to achieve social ambitions. Ila speakers use the root *-sókwe in noun class 3/4, *cisokwe,* to refer to men's pubic hair, a source of virility requiring protection.[76] The landscape named with the novel word *-sókwe simultaneously conjured up the thrusting action of spears and bellows and the virility associated with those who could provoke its generative powers to bear fruit in activities, such as hunting, that were understood through the lens of human reproduction, as Eugenia Herbert so eloquently describes.[77] The invention of bushcraft, then, was both an assertion of a technological feat and a social achievement by marksmen who claimed a potent virility. But the opportunity to be the kind of man who could provoke the bush depended on intimate negotiations within and between households because it may have demanded particular forms of sexual comportment from marksmen and the women closest to them.[78] Community investment in the safe and productive exploitation of the bush became all the more pronounced in the early centuries of the second millennium as proto-Kafue speakers extended their settlements beyond the middle Kafue. They elaborated on their Central Eastern Botatwe-speaking ancestors' innovation in spearcraft and their inventive mobilization of the landscapes of fame and geographies of power to establish communal hunts as a mechanism of social integration, a story told in the next chapter. The bush, *-sókwe, and efforts undertaken within it may well have been the domain of men, but its activities were of great interest to men's households, lineages, social betters, peers, and neighbors.

Central Eastern Botatwe agriculturalists were inventive hunters, fishers, and smelters, for the shift to food production undertaken in the first half of the first millennium both required efforts in food collection during food shortages and sustained experimentation in the technologies of food collection during times of plenty. In the last quarter of the first millennium, Central Eastern Botatwe farmers, some of whom were also skilled fishers and hunters, began to describe their landscape in novel terms as they constructed settlements in new environments and committed to more sedentary styles of living. Indeed, the landscape of the middle Kafue region looked very different to Central Eastern Botatwe homesteaders who saw local environments in terms of the kinds of soils and amount of water necessary to sustain their cereal crops and their more stable villages. Some methods of food collection took practitioners out of the visual range of their fellow farmers and inspired a reconceptualization of food procurement that distinguished work undertaken in the fields from labors in the bush. This novel reconfiguration of the landscape of subsistence relied on an elaborate series of innovations around spear hunting and rapid-current fishing. Those who proved talented in spearcraft, metallurgy, and other crafts undertaken away from the village opened paths to wealth and fame in activities that had once been the purview of the majority, or at least part of village life. Indeed, in the early eighth century, a young boy living in a village blessed with a metallurgist who had a knack for smelting would have heard the heaving, rhythmic whoosh of air forced through the bellows and into the furnace and perhaps even caught a glimpse of the smelter draining the bloom. But such memories would have seemed incredible to his disbelieving adult granddaughters in the early ninth century, for they could expect to see no such sight. They lived in a world in which the success and scales of hunting and smelting had increased, a world in which such activities' geographies and socialities had changed. By the late first millennium, inhabitants of the middle Kafue had used skill in spearcraft and smelting in the bush to develop new categories of local notables, *-pàdó and *-vʊbi, who were famed for their wealth in knowledge and, certainly, material. Yet the new forms of status and fame developed by creative technicians also mobilized older ideas about gender, fame, and the social institutions and geographies of power, a process that coalesced around the invention of the landscape category *-sókwe.

Skilled and celebrated hunters, smelters, canoe carvers, and other craftsmen were not the only people invested in their endeavors; friends, dependents, and kin were also involved in the affective, social dimensions of the subsistence economy. Indeed, reputations, as matters of fame connected to the mechanisms that guided the transmission of knowledge across generations, bound the politics of kin groups to wider audiences of friends, neighbors, and in-laws, as we will see in the coming chapters. As celebrated technicians and their constituencies, peers, and leaders all understood, fame was transitory because it relied on wealth, knowledge, and audiences whose sources, valuation, and organization changed as historical circumstances changed. This chapter has described the social, sensuous, and affective dynamics of technological changes in the subsistence history of eastern Botatwe communities from the mid-eighth to the mid-thirteenth centuries. The next chapter narrows our focus to explore how men and women reconfigured the social and political implications of skill in bushcraft in the particular historical circumstances of the early second millennium, as proto-Kafue speakers settled areas beyond the middle Kafue, using marriages, friendships, new ideas about kinship, and communal hunts to facilitate social integration across linguistic and material cultural boundaries, especially on the Batoka Plateau.

4. Of Kith and Kin

Bushcraft and Social Incorporation, 950–1250

The aspirations of *-pàdó and *-vʊbı were tied to the interests of their kin, friends, betters, and admirers. How did technicians' labors in the bush articulate with those relationships, like kinship and friendship, that bound technicians to other people through affection, obligation, and dependency? And how did changes to social relationships shape the practices and status of those skilled in bushcraft? This chapter explores the social context of bushcraft for Kafue speakers between the mid-tenth and mid-thirteenth centuries. This was a particularly dynamic period when the language of social ties expanded to capture new social practices as middle Kafue lifeways were adopted across the region and preexisting populations were displaced or absorbed into Kafue-speaking communities, permanently transforming the human and linguistic geographies of a large portion of south central Africa.

The history of south central Africa during the proto-Kafue period, then, is a story about the consolidation and scaling up of social and economic ties and the loss of other societies' languages and well-established material cultural traditions. The first people to change the language spoken in their homestead and the forms of their pottery could not have anticipated that three hundred years later the ways of speaking and crafting familiar from their own childhood would be completely lost. Even if the cumulative outcomes were unintentional, we need not assume that the many individual choices about language, house building, and pottery style that aggregated into major demographic and cultural changes were entirely peaceful or always went unchallenged. Unfortunately, linguistic evidence for the process by which families of the middle Kafue extended the influence of their language and life-style into neighboring communities is available only from the language of those whose culture gained hegemony from the middle Kafue, to the Victoria Falls, and beyond. In other words, we must study this process through the language of the dominant group.

Three social innovations—the adoption of new institutions of kinship, the development of networks of bond friendship, and changes to the scale and sociality of hunting—helped both Kafue speakers and their non-Botatwe neighbors integrate their communities. By the end of the thirteenth century, the inhabitants of the region shared a single pool of linguistic and material cultural conventions, masking the earlier, far more diverse histories of individual lineages, neighborhoods, and populations. Even as they sought to consolidate local ties, Kafue families and their non-Botatwe neighbors simultaneously worked to broaden regional social networks. New forms of the long familiar local bonds of kith and kin were scaled up as families began to recognize members of the same *mukowa*, or matriclan, and as individuals established *mulongo*, a form of bond friendship. For Kafue speakers, these ties formally extended the social and economic horizons that had governed the trade, travel, and social obligations undertaken by their Central Eastern Botatwe linguistic forebears. In the dramatically changing social world of Kafue speakers, opportunities for mobility, for learning, inheriting, practicing, and demonstrating skills, for ancestorhood and marriage—all the social acts and understandings underpinning the status of *-pàdó and *-vʊbɪ—also changed. Bushcraft persisted as a category of subsistence practice and aspirational effort, but access to it was opened up to new participants. Kafue speakers reconfigured the scales of community by transforming everyday practices, from the reckoning of kinship and the crafting of friendship, to the best method to butcher a carcass or clothe a loved one. Bushcraft both contributed to and was refashioned by these changes.

Living on the Margins

The history of proto-Kafue speakers begins at the very end of the first millennium. As warmer, moister climate conditions returned to the wooded grasslands of south central Africa, proto-Central Eastern Botatwe diverged into three new speech communities. Proto-Kafue speakers continued the long settlement of lands adjacent to the middle Kafue River—both grasslands and woodlands—but also began to expand their speech communities to the northeast, toward the Lukanga swamps north of modern-day Lusaka, and to the south and southeast of that homeland, onto the Batoka Plateau and along the lower Kafue. Proto-Lundwe-speaking communities expanded into lands south and east of the Kafue floodplain on the northeastern edge of the Batoka Plateau. Proto-Falls speakers extended their communities southwest, along the western edge of the Batoka Plateau, eventually reaching the Victoria Falls area. In each case, speakers of Botatwe protolanguages extended their ways of living and speaking into areas inhabited by other linguistic groups. At this time, speakers of a distantly related eastern Bantu language of the southern, or "Kusi", cluster inhabited the Batoka Plateau. Similarly, speakers of other eastern Bantu languages inhabited lands to the north and east of the middle Kafue, lands into which some proto-Kafue speakers were extending settlement.[1] We know less about contact to the west as the phonologically conservative western Botatwe languages formed a buffer between Kafue and speech communities of the upper Zambezi and beyond. Contact and exchange between Kafue speakers and speakers of Bantu languages far to the north remained common, but interactions with speakers of Bantu languages nearer to the middle Kafue eventually led to the complete replacement of non-Botatwe languages with Kafue languages, from the Lukanga swamps in the north to the Zambezi Valley in the south.

The process by which non-Botatwe languages were lost or replaced and by which their speakers were either absorbed into Botatwe communities or pushed out of the region unfolded over a substantial area. Yet the nature of the evidence does not allow us to reconstruct this history evenly across space. Although similar stories undoubtedly occurred in new settlements to the northeast, the archaeological evidence is richest for contact between makers of different material cultures and the eventual replacement of preexisting material cultural traditions in the Batoka Plateau and Zambezi Valley regions. Similarly, the extension of Botatwe speech onto the Batoka and the eventual absorption of its inhabitants into their communities was an important achievement of the speakers (and linguistic descendants) of all three of the daughter languages that diverged from Central Eastern Botatwe because each of them extended settlement onto the plateau. But the small size and limited phonological innovations by speakers of the Lundwe and Falls branches mean that we can know very little of their participation in this demographic process.

The richest, most compelling evidence for the human actions that underpinned changes in language and lifestyle is the linguistic archive of proto-Kafue speakers and the material cultural archives of the Batoka Plateau and the Zambezi Valley dating from the middle of the tenth to the middle of the thirteenth centuries. This chapter mines that rich vein of evidence to elucidate the changing history of bushcraft during a dramatic, though perhaps quite common, demographic process in the history of central Africa's southern savannas.

Two late first millennium village sites, Basanga and Mwanamaimpa, have the earliest evidence of the kinds of human actions that undergirded the broader demographic and cultural shifts that unfolded across lands radiating out from middle Kafue in the early centuries of the second millennium. It is worth a slow walk through these village sites, just as the many residents of the middle Kafue had reason to do in the early second millennium, when they traveled to the nearby saltpans. In the mid-eleventh century, an older Kafue-speaking man might have risen in the dark of night to begin his journey from his rather unassuming, traditionally styled middle Kafue village to the saltpans near Basanga. If he timed the journey right, arriving early in the season, he could simply scrape up the white crust of salt that rose to coat the black earth of the lands north and west of the mounded village of Basanga. Too early a trip might result in undifferentiated black soils, for the rains had not yet drawn the salt up to the surface. A journey too late into the dry season risked losing the easiest deposits to others, for all that would remain were salty soils that needed to be refined through a labor-intensive process of mixing, boiling, and evaporation. As he neared the pans, our salt seeker would have observed a cluster of at least ten mounded villages that had been built up along the slope that marked the transition between the elevated woodlands and the lower-lying grasslands adjacent to the river's floodplain.[2] These villages were in a different style from his village; indeed, they looked much more like those mounded villages located farther south, on the Batoka Plateau. Most of the salt seeker's Kafue-speaking neighbors would have followed the Middle Iron Age settlement pattern established by their Central Eastern Botatwe linguistic ancestors, establishing small, centralized villages in diverse ecological zones. But from the middle of the tenth century, at the beginning of the era of the proto-Kafue speech community and in the later phase of the Kafue Middle Iron Age archaeological sequence, some villagers lived in a cluster of mounded sites south of the Kafue hook, along the margins dividing woodlands and grasslands.

Even if it was rare in the middle Kafue region to pass through the shadow cast by a mounded village in the early morning sun or to raise one's eyes upward from a village edge in order to identify the source of a shouted greeting, the glimpses of village life our traveler would have caught as he walked past were recognizable enough. Basanga and Mwanamaimpa residents of the early second millennium practiced mixed farming. They kept a few dogs, chickens, and goats near the mud and clay huts of their compounds, though never in great numbers. Mound dwellers probably kept or had access to small herds of cattle tended beyond the village.[3] As in other villages, early morning conversations within homesteads and across fences were punctuated by the dull, rhythmic thuds and scraping sounds of women processing sorghum, grinding their flour with base stones and rubbers that would eventually be left behind by their descendants when the sites were abandoned in the thirteenth and fourteenth centuries.[4] Traveling since the early hours, the salt seeker might have pondered the likely relishes to sauce the morning porridge. Like everyone else in the area, the villagers of Basanga and Mwanamaimpa collected a wide range of wild fruits and vegetables, though archaeologists a millennium later would recover only fruits of the *mobula* (*Parinari curatellifolia*) and *mushuku* (*Uapaca kirkiana*) trees. Of course, it was also well known that Mwanamaimpa villagers were especially fond of catfish and ate it in great quantities as a relish; their women had only to walk a short quarter mile to an oxbow of the Nanzhila River to catch it.

Now walking past the fields beyond the village, our traveler would have trod more carefully, for the field margins were dotted with traps that the unsuspecting person might spring.[5] Perhaps he recognized some of the newer snares that trappers set around the game runs near grain fields and gardens: *-kole [77], a spring noose snare named from the verb *-kód-, "to take, to touch," and *-kooze [78], which applied an inherited root for bark string, *-ooye from *-gòdí, to the noose trap made with that material (fig. 4.1).[6] The phonology of modern attestations date the innovations to the proto-Kafue speech community, but residents of the middle Kafue region in the early second millennium might have better known them as innovations trappers had developed to work in tandem. The latter protected ripening crops from larger antelope and other game while the former were set—perhaps by enterprising children—to snare birds and cane rats (attested in the archaeological record at Mwanamaimpa) and small animals like duiker. To the eye of any pedestrian passing through the neighborhood of Basanga, located near the

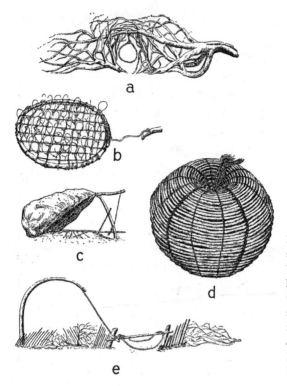

Figure 4.1. Hunting traps and snares used in the Gwembe Valley: a. kakoka noose snare, b. citendele noose snare, c. fall trap, d. valved citendele trap, e. spring trap (*-kole). Reprinted from Reynolds, *Material Culture of the Gwembe Valley*, 61. Permission courtesy of the University of Zambia.

Kafue flats, and Mwanamaimpa, nearly adjacent to the smaller Nanzhila River, local farmers' fields looked like particularly appealing habitat for wild boar, perhaps already called by the common term *munyemba,* and riverine bush pigs, *-ngılı [61], common to the well-watered bush and dense woodlands of river valleys draining into the Kafue.[7] Everyone in the middle Kafue region, it seemed, struggled with these tenacious pests. Archaeologists teach us that residents of Basanga and Mwanamaimpa caught at least two species of wild pig. In fact, the faunal record is dominated by wild game species: elephant, buffalo, impala, lechwe, duiker, oribi, and zebra were also identified. But this reliance on hunted game was common across the region. The faunal records of contemporary sites in the Kafue and on the Batoka follow this trend.[8] Of course, any resident of the middle Kafue region between the mid-eighth and mid-thirteenth centuries would have already understood the important contributions that hunters had long made to the larder, feeding grumbling bellies as well as shaking up the mundane rhythms of daily life with adventures to captivate audiences, inspire youngsters, woo belles, and give reason to pause and recall ancestors and hunts past.

Our wayfarer might have known that some of the mounded villages he passed were built on very old *-tòngò [8], abandoned village sites. The settlement history of the mounds corresponds with astonishing accuracy to the pulse of Botatwe language change, suggesting a regional history punctuated by common periods of change in human geography. Archaeologists teach us that the earliest inhabitants of the mound sites crafted objects with close affinities to contemporary Early Iron Age materials on the Batoka Plateau. These first residents established the mound sites around the sixth century as the northernmost frontier of the Batoka Early Iron Age culture but abandoned them by the middle of the eighth century, corresponding with the era of Greater Eastern Botatwe speech. The mounds remained deserted between the mid-eighth and mid-tenth centuries, when Central Eastern Botatwe speakers moved into the middle Kafue region. The mounds were resettled at the beginning of the proto-Kafue era and abandoned soon after its close. A Kafue speaker of the mid-eleventh century, like our salt seeker, might have heard stories of the resettlement of the first mound from grandparents who watched industrious homesteaders renovate the ancient *-tòngò for occupation in the mid-tenth century. It would have been quite a sight as archaeologists suggest that the sandy, sterile deposits between the first and second occupations—nearly a meter and a half of material at Mwanamaimpa!—may have been purposefully deposited by tenth-century settlers, perhaps to improve drainage during the onset of the moister climate of the Medieval Warm Epoch.

Even as they mimicked a mounded settlement form that had long been in practice on the Batoka Plateau, settlers of the mounded sites from the mid-tenth century to the mid-fourteenth century also used the material cultural traditions of the middle Kafue. They used the same range of vessel forms as their proto-Kafue-speaking neighbors, including necked pots, small bowls, and even a few carinated, or amphora-shaped, vessels. A traveler passing by Basanga or Mwanamaimpa in the eleventh century would have recognized the delicate comb-stamped and incised designs on pots carried to collect water as typical of the pots used by everyone else in middle Kafue area. Archaeologists tell us these designs are reminiscent of pottery produced in earlier periods far to the north at Naviundu, near Lubumbashi in southern Democratic Republic of the Congo, and Kangila ware produced in later periods across the Batoka Plateau.[9] Sherds of this delicately decorated pottery were recovered across three meters of the reoccupation deposits at both sites, demonstrating cultural continuity across the Middle Iron Age.

What was novel about the settlers reoccupying the abandoned mound sites near the Kafue hook was the way that they blended the material cultural traditions of the Kafue Middle Iron Age with the mounded style of the villages of the Early Iron Age (Kalundu) and early Late Iron Age (Kalomo) traditions practiced farther south, on the Batoka Plateau. The origins of the settlers who reoccupied mounds like Basanga and Mwanamaimpa at the turn of the millennium are unknown. Perhaps families from the Batoka Plateau, where mound settlements had been common for centuries, moved into the middle Kafue area and adopted some aspects of their lifestyle from proto-Kafue-speaking neighbors. In this case, such families were vanguards of a wider demographic shift, for makers of Kalomo pottery extended their settlements northward, toward the Kafue pastures of the middle Kafue in the early centuries of the second millennium at just the time that middle Kafue residents extended their settlements southward.[10] Perhaps the mounds were reoccupied by proto-Kafue speakers with a long family history of occupation in the middle Kafue region but also with an eye toward mimicking parts of the lifestyle of Kalomo makers living to the south, with their mounded villages and growing cattle herds. Such Kafue families may have had relatives, friends, or even a few of their own head of cattle living within Kalomo villages on the Batoka Plateau. Of course, categories like "Kafue speakers" and "Kalomo makers" hold more meaning for modern researchers than for the populations whose histories we seek through such heuristics. These creative homesteaders may have been among the earliest families to negotiate marriages across cultural and linguistic frontiers, reminding us that ways of speaking and making are learned and forgotten in the actual goings-on of life. The homesteaders who resettled mounds near the Kafue hook may have had a different linguistic or material cultural heritage than either their middle Kafue neighbors or the Batoka villagers whose settlements they mimicked, but they could and did speak with communities in both the middle Kafue and Batoka regions. They made the most of living on the margins, both the sloping transition zone between the low-lying grasslands and elevated woodlands where they built their homes and the linguistic and cultural frontier they crossed to learn, borrow, and blend two lifestyles, crafting something of a borderlands in the process.

The blended settlements crafted by those living on the margins at the mound sites south of the Kafue hook was one iteration of a processes that unfolded in different ways across the Batoka Plateau, reaching the settlements of the Zambezi Valley by the close of the era of the Kafue speech community. On the Batoka Plateau, makers of Kalomo and middle Kafue wares lived in distinct but neighboring villages in the eleventh and twelfth centuries before settlements with ties to the middle Kafue became dominant. In the Zambezi Valley, settlement styles and pottery with origins in the middle Kafue ("Early Tonga" ware) simply replaced preexisting material culture from about the thirteenth century. Despite the varied iterations of this process of contact and mixing, its culmination speaks to the linguistic and cultural hegemony of populations from the middle Kafue; their material culture replaced those of both the Batoka and Zambezi Valley, just as Botatwe languages were adopted by all speakers in the area.[11] How did Kafue speakers convince others to adopt the middle Kafue way of life? Although some people may well have been pushed out of the area, those who remained were convinced or made to learn how Kafue speakers lived. What social institutions created and the kinds of sustained intimate contact in which such inspired or coerced learning could take place?

The Terms of Social Integration

As they extended their settlements southward, into lands occupied by speakers of a language belonging to the Kusi branch of the eastern Bantu languages, the first generations of frontier families speaking proto-Kafue contributed to the linguistic and cultural diversity of life on the Batoka Plateau, just as mound dwellers at sites like Basanga and Mwanamaimpa contributed to the diversity of the middle Kafue region. The social ties that made such movements possible allowed the descendants of the pioneers who crafted blended settlements to create a more homogeneous cultural and linguistic landscape. This demographic and cultural process was a slow and likely incremental one, unfolding over about three hundred years. But it was also a process that could be recalled across a period of four or five lifespans. At the very end of this period, a grandfather could recall for his grandchildren the stories that his own grandparents had told him about the first uncertain steps their own Kafue- and Kusi-speaking parents and grandparents took to blend their ways of living in order to mitigate the challenges to belonging precipitated by population movement, language shift, and the myriad other choices that contributed to the changing human geography of the lands between the middle Kafue and middle Zambezi.

Forgetting languages and ceramic motifs or building a foreign style of house or a village in an unconventional location were outcomes of far more complicated and subjective negotiations around the concepts that governed identity and belonging. These negotiations accumulated into changes in the way families claimed children, communities fed themselves, neighborhoods commemorated heroes, and friends valued the unique qualities of their association in order to allay the critical social condition of alienation—linguistic, cultural, geographical—as the frontier of social integration moved beyond the middle Kafue into areas like the Batoka Plateau in the early centuries of the second millennium. All such changes were captured in the novel terms of social integration invented by proto-Kafue speakers.

Mukowa and Inventions of Matrilinearity

Societies whose members speak extant Botatwe languages live in an area of central Africa where it is common to reckon family ties through one's mother. Like other communities living in the "matrilineal belt," an area that stretches from Angola in the west, through southern Democratic Republic of the Congo, parts of Zambia and Malawi, and east to the coast of Mozambique, speakers of modern Botatwe languages have particular terms for talking about the kin of their mothers. Of course, this does not mean they ignored members of their father's family. In fact, anthropologists have documented a slow adoption of patrilineal practices among some Botatwe-speaking societies during the twentieth century, such that many Botatwe speakers today emphasize relationships reckoned through their fathers in matters of inheritance and succession. This is nothing new: Tonga, Ila, and other Botatwe speakers had long recognized ties to fathers and fathers' kin as important to an individual's social network of rights and obligations.[12] To be sure, the labels "matrilineal" and "patrilineal" and the systems they describe have been roundly critiqued for obscuring the situational nature of claims to belonging and assistance through the idiom of kinship. Kinship is more a negotiated practice than an idealized system.

Sensitivity to the contingent nature of kinship has inspired great debate about two topics of significance for this story: the antiquity of matrilineality in Bantu-speaking Africa and the meanings and uses communities attach to familiar units from the anthropology of kinship, such as clans, lineages, and even mothers.[13] In each case, scholars emphasize the ways in which ideals of kinship were used to both include and exclude those who could potentially count as family members in particular social contexts.

Scholars have come to different conclusions about the antiquity of both matrilineality and clanship in central Africa. As described in chapter 2, some historians suggest that political life in the earliest Botatwe era, the era of proto-Botatwe speakers, was organized around ritual clan leaders, *-àmí [58], and that the institution of matriclans governed by ritual specialists was inherited by subsequent generations of Botatwe speech communities down to late pre-colonial times. Indeed, they see the linked institutions of matriclans and *-àmí as far more ancient than proto-Botatwe speech communities, dating them to the proto-Eastern Savanna speech community of the early first millennium BCE.[14] As we have seen, the evidence for matriclans in the earliest Botatwe communities is inconclusive at best because there is no certain proto-Botatwe term for the institution, though influential men and women, *-ámí, were a part of Botatwe communities from the Greater Eastern Botatwe period. In west central Africa, Jan Vansina and Wyatt MacGaffey insist that matrilineality and, in the case of Vansina, matriclans are far more recent social innovations.[15]

These different perspectives on the antiquity of matrilineality are, in part, a matter of terminology and methodology. Scholars using the comparative historical linguistic method reconstruct different terms for clanship as well as different time depths for the same term and even disagree on the features of the institution such terms reference.[16] Debates about the antiquity of matrilineality are also matters of definition, for, as MacGaffey, Vansina, and others have pointed out, reconstructions of terms for matrilineages or matriclans mean very little if we cannot know what it was that people living long ago did with such institutions. There were likely as many "versions" of matrilineality in the past as there are today. Therefore, the historical question should not be about the antiquity or origins of matrilineality but, rather, about the antiquity of the many institutions and practices that people invented, combined, reconfigured, and forgot in order to make or deny claims on other people who were viable candidates for the status of mother's kin in specific historical contexts.[17] One such institution for communities speaking eastern Botatwe languages was the *mukowa*, matriclan.

Mukowa is an attestation of *-kóba [79], a root that can be found widely across the western half of the matrilineal belt, usually glossing as "(matri-)

lineage" or "matriclan," though in its earliest form, *-kóba was the proto-Bantu root for "skin." Vansina has reconstructed the history of this root among speakers of the Njila languages of west central Africa, to the west of, though not adjacent to, the Botatwe languages. Shortly before the eighth century, speakers of an ancestral Njila language in the region of modern-day southern Angola used the inherited root *-kóba, "skin," in a new way, to describe the umbilical cord connecting mothers to their newly born infants, a connection between the child and mother with a permanent and visible reminder at the navel.[18] Out of the semantic shift from skin to umbilical cord, Njila communities invented a new meaning for *-kóba: "group of matrilineal descent," either a corporate matrilineage or a dispersed matriclan, depending on the area of west central Africa. Vansina argues that this institution must have been invented in response to the problem posed by new forms of inheritable wealth. Ethnographic descriptions of the inheritance of cattle through the mother's line in the southern parts of west central Africa supply Vansina with an explanation for this innovation in social organization: speakers of ancestral Njila languages invented *-kóba matrigroups in concert with the adoption of pastoralism. Early Njila speakers could better manage risks to herds, such as localized disease outbreaks and water shortages, by loaning them within the wider matriclan and better protect the herd from dissolution by limiting claimants during inheritance to members of the matrilineage.

The semantic innovation developed by Njila speakers in west central Africa was one chapter of a wider regional history that included speakers of eastern Botatwe languages. That *-kóba demonstrates the phonology, distribution, and semantic outcomes of a word that has undergone wide diffusion and borrowings in multiple directions is documented in languages across the region.[19] Among Botatwe languages, attestations of the root with the meaning "matriclan" or a more general reference to "mother's kin," show skewed phonology, which indicates borrowing. But these phonological skews are slight and occur in a sound contrast that is often not even recorded in dictionaries.[20] The phonological evidence and typical loan patterns between Lenje and Soli suggest that Botatwe communities living in the greater Kafue area borrowed both the word and the idea of distinguishing maternal kin as a particular kind of family relationship sometime between the middle of the eighth and the middle of the thirteenth century, the period corresponding to the settlement shift of the Kafue Middle Iron Age and the periods of proto-Central Eastern Botatwe and proto-Kafue speech. Another term, *-tʃɪСɪa [80], does, however, show phonological and semantic consistency to at least proto-Kafue, indicating that Kafue speakers distinguished their "maternal uncle" as a relative distinct from their mothers' and fathers' other siblings, a characteristic considered typical in matrilineal systems.[21] Regardless of whether some preexisting practices we might label as "matrilineal" predate these innovations, Kafue families of the early second millennium were developing new ways to distinguish and put into use categories of relationships within the wider grouping of maternal kin. Unlike the complex morphology sustaining the development of *-pàdó or the telling semantic shift applied to *-vʊbɪ, there is little evidence embedded in the term mukowa itself to explain why proto-Kafue speakers adopted mukowa as the root spread from the Njila-speaking communities of west central Africa into south central Africa.

Different terms, institutions, and practices of matrilineality likely originated in several distinct centers at different times but were adopted by communities across the southern savannas for unique, local purposes. Perhaps the logic of Njila speakers' invention of *-kóba around the eighth century to manage the labor and social demands of the new pastoralist economy applied to communities along the Zambezi River and on the southern Batoka Plateau. The Kusi languages spoken by communities on the Batoka Plateau constituted evidence of Batoka communities' historical ties to the cultural world south and east of the middle Zambezi, a zone of contact along which cattle keeping spread into Angola in the late first millennium. Yet the spread of cattle keeping within south central Africa was quite uneven across time and space. Some of the most famous herders in the Botatwe-speaking group— the Ila—were quite late adapters.[22] Intensive pastoralism spread in this smaller region from south to north, from the hook of the Zambezi and Machili River system, to the Batoka, reaching the Kafue area only in the second half of the second millennium, after the divergence of proto-Kafue. Perhaps some Kusi-speaking cattlemen of the Batoka looked north to the dependable grasses of the Kafue floodplain during the unpredictable rains of the eighth to the tenth centuries, extending their *-kóba networks to include some Central Eastern Botatwe farmers. It may be more likely that middle Kafue men and women used ties of mukowa to keep a few head of cattle with herds on the Batoka, for archaeological evidence for cattle remains sparse in the middle Kafue for centuries longer and the Kafue floodplain harbored many disease vectors. Vansina argues that *-kóba spread through the region to manage cattle loans and to limit inheritance, but there is little linguistic or archaeological evidence that Kafue speakers were intensifying their modest investment in herds.[23] While an explanation linking the adoption of *-kóba to pastoralism makes sense for the Kusi cattle keepers of the Batoka and the southern Njila context about which Vansina writes, something different was brewing in the middle Kafue region at the close of the first millennium. It bears considering, as Vansina does, how Botatwe speakers have used mukowa in the recent past to imagine how Kafue speakers in the early second millennium mobilized mukowa.

The ways in which speakers of extant Botatwe languages talk about and use mukowa today signals a very flexible institution for reckoning relatedness to mother's kin. Lest we reconstruct to the early second millennium an anthropological ideal of matrilinearity or matriclanship, we would do well to consider the range of relationships invoked when speakers talked about mukowa in recent times. Lenje speakers in the early twentieth century understood mukowa to refer to a "fetish, clan, family."[24] Ila attestations of mukowa gloss as "clan" but also mean "family, generation," suggesting that the distinctions between family, generation, and clan on the mother's side were not organized into tidy hierarchical units of increasing scale, units in which lineages nested neatly into a container-like clan. Rather, these multiple glosses hint that "clan" was more a flexible ascriptive affiliation for Ila speakers, invoking Ego's lateral links to a network of kin in which references to shared ancestors created cohorts of relatives, perhaps especially those in the same generation. Ila mukowa were widely dispersed across villages and did not assemble for ritual or other purposes, though they claimed some "vague attachment to a specific locality," usually a burial site of an important clan founder or eminent clan member. The clan played no role in inheritance or succession; it was significant for the reciprocal responsibilities accepted by clan members. As Jaspan summarized, "The functions of the matrilineal clan as organizing principle are limited."[25]

Similarly, Elizabeth Colson explains that for the Tonga, clans "are not corporate bodies. They own no property, have no ritual centers or leaders, and never on any occasion assemble as a group." A mukowa, Colson clarifies, is a dispersed, unnamed matrilineal group, a much smaller kinship group "guiding inheritance, succession, provision and sharing of bridewealth, vengeance and common ritual responsibility," though ritual events are not communal enterprises. This definition relates well to the ephemeral sense of "clan as family as generation" in the Ila use of mukowa. Indeed, Colson notes "matrilineal groups [mukowa] are bound together, however, by ties which are purely temporal and tied to the life-span of particular individuals."[26] Other Botatwe speakers in the early twenty-first century also deployed mukowa to delineate lineage, clan, and extended family on the mother's and, sometimes, father's side.[27]

The multiple English meanings that have been attached to *-kóba capture the wide range of family relations belonging to mukowa in the recent past. Ethnographic descriptions teach us about the value of mukowa in mobilizing help and connecting relatives whose exact relationship is often uncertain or even unimportant. Mukowa are not defined, organized, or called into being by carefully remembered recitations of historical genealogies as is common in societies where there is a link between descent and formal political power. Rather, mukowa incorporate into one social group a wide range of living kin and ancestors available to a particular individual, with an emphasis on those relatives and spirits who are regularly accessible and, therefore, "effective."[28] A person's mukowa has the potential to include whatever kin can be traced as being related to one's mother. In practice, the clan is a network of lateral links between Ego and several matrilines of only a few generations each. Non-kin can be accommodated as easily as kin can be forgotten or ignored on the basis of personal differences because mukowa relationships are created through participation in the affairs of one another's marriages and disputes. Members share an ancestor at enough of a historical remove from the present that those without the right biology but with the correct social knowledge to stake a claim of belonging can be easily incorporated. In recent times, mukowa were communities of protection created and maintained by travel and the commitment to inquire about and support the lives and needs of other members. The ethnographic and linguistic records teach us that speakers who inherited the institution of mukowa from their linguistic ancestors valued its flexibility.

Homesteaders in the early second millennium likely saw in this foreign concept of reckoning relatedness through one parent a new mechanism to organize cooperation and assistance. Mukowa were mobilized by proto-Kafue speakers in two contexts: the familiar middle Kafue homeland and the expanding cultural and linguistic frontiers. For residents of the middle Kafue, matriclans scaled up social ties to match the geographic scales of settlement pioneered by Central Eastern Botatwe speakers. Matriclans linked the residents of villages dispersed across the grasslands, islands, and woodlands adjacent to the Kafue River, facilitating trade in the unique resources of each environment and the seasonal travel of clan members seeking salt, medicines, fish, or game in the areas inhabited by relatives. Indeed, clans helped farmers cope with the risks of committing to a more sedentary way of life.

Although Kafue speakers enjoyed the better climate of the Medieval Warm Epoch, they still endured disasters. Rain shortages, flooding, locust and other pest infestations, disease and illness—even the vagaries of the movements of elephant herds—created localized shortages of food, seed, and even water. Clan members could be called upon to rebuild houses, to supply food and water, and to provide hospitality to those in desperate need. Clans may have been mustered to claim indemnities for injustices to other members or to make such payments on behalf of their own. Mukowa also formally opened up a wider network of people on whom members could lay claim to nonmaterial resources. Neil Kodesh's work on Ganda clans as "networks of knowledge" ensuring members' and communities' well-being helps us to imagine why Africans living long ago valued ties we gloss as "clanship" without reverting to the older anthropological paradigm of clans as scaled-up lineages.[29] It may well be that clans expanded the pools of potential ancestors from whom living aspirants could inherit knowledge and reputations in crafts like hunting, smelting, potting, healing, divining, or canoe making and on whom such talented individuals could call to ensure the success of their dangerous, transformative pursuits. The uncertainties of living—whether the result of human behavior or the capricious wills of the spirits—were best borne by large, dispersed groups and best managed when the ideals of reciprocity were formalized through clan ties.

For those Kafue homesteaders pushing out the frontier of the familiar middle Kafue way of life, belonging was a more precarious condition to secure. The flexibility of mukowa ties would have proved to be a particularly important mechanism of social integration for Kafue speakers seeking to settle on the Batoka Plateau or those Kusi speakers extending Batoka ways of life northward. Indeed, the fact that *-kóba was borrowed supplies the evidence that matriclans became a valuable way of connecting people of different linguistic and cultural backgrounds. It may be that the multiple meanings attached to *mukowa* today among acephalous Botatwe societies reflect the adoption of *-kóba in a similarly fluid social context in the deeper past. By adopting matriclans organized around the principle—if not the actuality—of shared descent, Kafue speakers and their Kusi neighbors could make claims on each other's help, expertise, land, hospitality and, significantly, could pool the metaphysical powers and special skills of their now common ancestors without disrupting the territorial claims of firstcomers and their ancestors.

In sum, by reckoning relatedness through one parent, Kafue speakers and their non-Botatwe neighbors created social relationships across broad geographic and vague, uncertain, or nonexistent genealogical distances. Homesteaders in the late first and early second millennium adopted mukowa to support new patterns of mobility and sedentism. While ties to neighbors and preceding and succeeding generations were built over time, a Kafue-speaking pioneer on the Batoka Plateau who invoked membership to a known mukowa could immediately access help and protection in communities where he was otherwise a stranger. Individuals and families also initiated ties of clanship with neighbors who seemed as closely integrated into their families as blood kin but without relying on detailed genealogies to explain exactly how the status of "family" applied. Mukowa ties were not instantiated through formal clan rituals or embodied in clan leaders. Rather, clanship was created and sustained by members' commitment to knowing about and visiting each other to offer support and exchange news. Ties of clanship extended quickly, tracing out networks across landscapes, following the footsteps of young brides carrying a cooking pot to their husbands' homesteads and retracing their journey back home as new mothers, presenting their babies to their own mother's family as the youngest members of the clan. But just as mukowa scaled up the networks of assistance, they also excluded non-members from the benefits of belonging, restricted the children one could claim as family, and even reduced those who might inherit the wealth built up by the preceding generation. As exogamous institutions, they also constricted the field of potential spouses. Therefore, Kafue speakers could not adopt *-kóba without other innovations in the practice of crafting social ties.

Kin and Cohort

Kafue speakers preserved many ways of speaking about kin: terms for mothers and fathers, siblings, and lineages were all inherited from their linguistic ancestors. What would have struck those ancestors as new in the way Kafue families thought about relatedness at the turn of the millennium, however, was both mukowa, which supported flexible claims to relatedness through maternal kin, and a pair of words used to talk about the lateral ties of generation and cohort embodied in cousins: *-kwésʊ [81] and *-kwàshɪ [82]. These terms can be glossed with reference to well-known anthropological systems of kinship, specifically Iroquois: they named parallel cousins (the children of mother's sisters and father's brothers) and cross-cousins (the children of mother's brothers and father's sisters), respectively. But such one-to-one matches between reconstructed terms and the precise relative(s) they label on a classic kinship diagram foreground relationships between individuals within a family group at the expense of mid-level cadres of kin within larger, multigenerational units like clans or lineages. They obscure the underlying ideas that Kafue speakers used to invent such categories of kin, which often invoked such cadres.[30]

The older, inherited words Kafue speakers combined to invent new names for categories of parallel and cross-cousins reveal the concerns that worried families in the early centuries of the second millennium. As families traced out kin across wider geographical and social distances through mu-kowa, as they pioneered settlement in unfamiliar regions inhabited by people who spoke and ate and lived in foreign ways, and as they accepted into their communities new households that blended regional lifestyles, Kafue speak-ers invented categories of kinship that located classificatory brothers and sisters in space, as well-known and accessible relatives responsible for generating and managing the flow of bridewealth from and for new marriages. They also in-sisted that cross-cousins understood their responsibilities as helpmeets and as ideal marriage partners. The contemporaneous use of *-kwésʊ and *-kwàshɪ indicate that Kafue speakers and the families who learned Kafue languages used a new ideal of marriage between cohorts of cross-cousins as a mecha-nism to bridge in a mere three centuries the linguistic, geographical, and genealogical distances that had separated communities of the middle Kafue, Batoka Plateau, and middle Zambezi Valley in the early tenth century.

A young man in the early eleventh century who sought a bride and was anxious to make his way into adulthood would have known all too well how changing practices of marriage complicated matters like bridewealth nego-tiations and residency, matters that governed opportunities to amass wealth, access land, and secure the support of the spirits who meddled in the lives of the living. We can imagine a family history for our bridegroom: a member of the first generation of children born at the southern frontier of Kafue speech; the child of one of a group of sisters who braved a life far away from familiar faces, landscapes, and speech in order to one day be remembered as a founding ancestress of a new branch of the mukowa; a child of a Batoka villager whose family agreed to relinquish claims to any children of the marriage in return for wives who brought substantial bridewealth in skins, meat, beer, and iron and who, it was said, knew how to reap harvests in almost any landscape. Perhaps the young bridegroom's *-tʃɪCɪa, his mother's brother, had already arranged for him to marry one of the *-tʃɪCɪa's own daughters, a female *-kwàshɪ, or cross-cousin, of the bridegroom. Such a marriage would strengthen the ties between the two families across the long distance between the middle Kafue, where his *-tʃɪCɪa lived, and the Batoka Plateau, where the bridegroom would remain. But the bridegroom's marriage also depended on what bridewealth, *-kó [83], could be mustered among the family, both through the good marriages of his own female *-kwésʊ, the parallel cousins he grew up with, and the *-kwésʊ of the generation of his mother and *-tʃɪCɪa.

In the early eleventh century, some elders may well have wondered how marriage had gotten so complex and whether the ancestor spirits blessed marriages between so-called *-kwàshɪ, cross-cousins. After all, didn't the meaning of this name—"the seizers"—say enough about what these dangerous new marriages entailed, as women were carried away to live with the families of their new husbands? Such skeptical older neighbors and family members had married at a time when Kafue-speaking elders were first debating the merits of mukowa, *-kwésʊ, and *-kwàshɪ and may not have observed the rules of exogamy governing mukowa or followed the new practice of marrying into the same cohort of cross-cousins as their parallel cousins. Kafue speakers promoting the idea of distinguishing *-kwésʊ and *-kwàshɪ crafted the names of these kinship categories by describing the attributes which, promoters argued, made them advantageous.

When speakers of extant Kafue languages use the term *bakwesu,* they refer to a category of matrikin that belongs to one's (classificatory) generation.[31] However, when proto-Kafue speakers first invented the term, they compounded the locative *-ku with the possessive *-esu and applied the noun class pair for people (n. cl. 1/2); the novel term glossed roughly as "those from our place." This innovation suggests that the practice whereby a cohort of male relatives (classificatory "brothers") married a cohort of female relatives (classificatory "sisters") recorded in the twentieth century probably dates to the early second millennium. In the context of virilocality, a bride lived with her husband's family. Thus, the children of marriages in which a cohort of parallel cousins all married into the same cohort of cross-cousins created a new cohort of parallel cousins who grew up in the same village.[32] They were, quite literally, "the same generation of family from our place" as reckoned matrilineally with virilocal residence. When proto-Kafue speakers spoke of *-kwésʊ, they were naming family members of their own generation who were located nearby and could easily be called upon to strategize about the challenges of shared life stages and the pressing concerns of living in a particular place. For a cohort of female kin who extended their family's marriage ties to new lands, *-kwésʊ might be the only matrikin living in a village that may have felt to a young bride to be overpopulated by the prying eyes of in-laws.

The accessibility of *-kwésʊ mattered because they were important allies as one moved through the stages of life and set one's children up to do the same. Indeed, other words in the proto-Kafue vocabulary allowed speakers to parse *-kwésʊ a bit differently. To give bridewealth, *-kwa [84], was already a well-established institution, ensuring the intentions and supporting the claims of the large family groups involved in the marriage.[33] The family giving their daughter and receiving bridewealth, *-kó, could expect to distribute those gifts widely: to *-tʃɪCɪa (mother's brother), to those in the generations above the parents of the bride, even to the mother's bakwesu, women who shared the classificatory status of "mothers" to the bride and other maternal uncles. Though the syntax was not exact, the term contained elements that could gloss as "those given our bridewealth," a pun likely not lost on matrikin with outstretched hands. But bakwesu who received the wealth circulating when the lineage's daughters married would also be ready to contribute *-kó, bridewealth, mustered to secure a good marriage with esteemed in-laws, *-kwe [85], for their own classificatory sons. The polysemy emphasizes once again the significance of accessing one's kin cohort or generation of relatives. Bakwesu could refer to the circuit of relatives participating in the giving and receiving of *ciko*, bridewealth, that is, all the classificatory parents of the generation marrying. It could also refer to the parallel cousins of either gender of marriageable age, cousins whose own good marriages and social standing depended on the ciko attracted by their classificatory sisters and the social connections fostered by marriages of both male and female bakwesu. As one aged, the material and social obligations of bakwesu might change, but the cohort of lateral kin supporting each other's social aspirations persisted.[34]

When speakers of modern-day eastern Botatwe languages use the term *mukwashi,* an attestation of the proto-Kafue innovation *-kwàshɪ, they refer to in-laws of one's own generation (brothers- and sisters-in-law) and to cross-cousins, suggesting a preference for cross-cousin marriages.[35] Muk-washi derives from an older Bantu root, *-kóat-, "to seize, grasp," with the agentive suffix yielding a rough gloss as "the seizer" or "the holder." Cross-cousins, proto-Kafue speakers insisted, seized and held something that did not belong to them, namely, a spouse who was not of their family. But attestations of *-kóat- in the best-documented Kafue languages also carry a particular connotation of assistance. In Tonga, the root with a causative suffix glosses as "to help" while in Ila, the root carries the additional meanings of "to have, hold; to seize, grasp; to arrest; to keep, preserve; to possess, as a spirit" and is a verb that can be used to talk about looking after another person.[36] In modern Botatwe communities, when the ideals of matrilineality and virilocal residence are followed, children grow up as outsiders in the village of their father's lineage but remain preferred marriage partners to the daughters of their father's sisters. Thus, a child's father's lineage had a stake in the child's well-being, even if the child was not a member of that family. When proto-Kafue husbands, wives, parents, and siblings drew on the obligation of assistance embedded in the verb *-kóat- to name the group of relatives designated by *-kwàshɪ, they assigned to them the role of a "caretaker" or "guardian" group, a role still observed by ethnographers in the early twentieth century.[37] If proto-Kafue speakers who borrowed the institution of matriclans were also adopting unilateral descent for the first time, the name for cross-cousins was all the more poignant. For the first to adopt these new ways of reckoning kin, the name *-kwàshɪ reminded preferred marriage partners that even if they were no longer considered blood kin, they were privileged as the ideal "bride seizers." They could not and should not forget their obligations those who had until recently been counted amongst their kin. For those who became *-kwàshɪ, in-laws, through marriage and were not already cross-cousins, the expectation of assistance embedded in the word's meaning was a forceful reminder about the obligations of the families connected through marriage, even if they were strangers and the marriages were the outcome of the violent seizure of women from a distant village.

The invention of *-kwàshɪ created a group of in-laws that contrasted with the class of in-laws named with the inherited term *-kwe. Together, *-kwàshɪ and *-kwe demarcated alternating generations with different stakes in (and potential for conflict over) the marriage that created the in-law relationship.[38] Among eastern Botatwe communities today, *bakwe* negotiate, sanction, and assess the success of marriages and are avoided until the birth of a child, at which point the relationship is respectful, if reserved. In contrast to bakwe, mukwashi are affines (brothers- and sisters-in-law) without a conflicting interest in the children of the marriages that created their relationship.

For Kafue men and women living in the early second millennium in villages dispersed widely across the many environmental zones of the middle Kafue, mukowa, bakwesu, mukwashi, and virilocal residence successfully spanned the wider geographical distances between villages and the wider genealogical distances between neighbors of different linguistic and cultural backgrounds. Elders of a Kafue-speaking lineage settling onto the Batoka Plateau in the early second millennium could marry their children, a cohort of its lineage's classificatory brothers and sisters, to a set of siblings or cousins from a nearby village of Kusi-speaking firstcomers. Such elders used the principles of matrilinearity and the practice of virilocality to secure the protection of firstomers' ancestors for members of their own immigrant lineages. The mukwashi of an immigrant, Kafue lineage—the children of its sons—became the newest generation of an established firstcomer lineage as well as the spouses and affine cohort of the immigrant lineage's own children. The immigrant lineage's children—the offspring of its daughters—were raised in the villages of their fathers, cared for by the firstcomer lineages of their fathers, and recognized as the preferred spouses of the children that firstcomer lineage.

Matrilinearity has long been considered an integrative kinship system; foreign men, the thinking goes, can easily be absorbed by local lineages. The kinship terms that survive from the process of social integration initiated by proto-Kafue speakers and their neighbors on the Batoka a millennium ago teach us that attempts to harness the integrative potential of matrilinearity relied on the efforts and support of cohorts of male and female cousins, who stood as classificatory brothers and sisters within their cohort and as cross-cousins to the other cohort. Of course, there were many generations, alive and dead, invested in marriages and the children such marriages produced. But the virilocal residence suggested by the ethnographic record and the spatial distances captured in the etymologies of *-kwésʊ and *-kwàshɪ meant that the form of matrilineality practiced by Kafue speakers in the early second millennium was most useful to families who aspired to extend the influence of their lineage across environmental and cultural boundaries, perhaps sometimes when cohorts of male *-kwésʊ made themselves into *-kwàshɪ by seizing the women of distant villages as brides. If they were women, these cohorts of *-kwésʊ left their natal villages for alien ones. The lilt of speech, the marks decorating pots, the more frequent lowing of cattle, even the elevation of villages and the distances from major rivers would have all felt unfamiliar to young Kafue brides coming to settle among their husband's families on the mounded Iron Age villages of the Batoka. The linguistic and cultural homogeneity that characterizes the lands from the Kafue across the Batoka Plateau and into the Zambezi Valley today was the outcome of the efforts of small groups of female cousins leaving behind the villages of their fathers, supporting each other's marriages, and caring for each other's children—their own mukowa's youngest generation—under the watchful eye of their husbands' families.[39]

Mulongo: Individuals and Their Networks

Kafue speakers extended the frontiers of their speech and the lands throughout which their families could travel and settle through large-scale aggregates like mukowa, through the marriages of smaller cohorts of cousins, and at the individual level through a new form of friendship: *-lòngó [86].[40] In contrast to *-kóba, *-lòngó, or bond friendships, were a local innovation limited to Kafue speakers and those speakers of Kusi Bantu languages living on the Batoka Plateau and eventually incorporated into Kafue communities. A *mulòngó was a particular kind of formalized friendship that could even be inherited among Tonga and Ila speakers of the early twentieth century. Edwin Smith and Andrew Dale defined the word in the early decades of the twentieth century as a "covenant of friendship" and noted that such friendships among Ila people temporarily facilitated the exchange of wives, medicines, and food, but that they were far more formalized and enduring than the materials and assistance exchanged, particularly if they were *mulongo we maninga*, sealed by blood.[41] Elizabeth Colson glossed *mulongo* as "bond friendships" initiated by Tonga men and women to meet a number of needs, all related to "mutual assistance and sharing the good things which either one possesses." They ensured life and property on travels far from the pressures that *-kóba, *-kwésʊ, and even *-kwàshɪ relations might bring to bear on threats to the traveler's safety. Mulongo provided newcomers with a mechanism to access assistance in resettlement, linked residents of distant neighborhoods who were not kin, and established a deep and lasting claim on local neighbors who were not obligated through clanship or some other tie to assist with work parties, funerals, and other activities requiring substantial cooperation.[42]

Significantly, this root carries additional meanings in other noun classes and as a verb. The range of Ila meanings are typical of Kafue languages. In Ila, the word mulongo is also used to talk about "a queue, line, row." In another noun class, the root becomes *kalongo*, "a queue of people." *Cilonga-longa* (n. cl. 7) is the "wattle around the top of the wall of a house, to which the roof-poles are attached" with the secondary meaning "friendliness." In verb form, to *kulonga* is "to abandon a village and settle elsewhere." With a suffix locating the action in relative space, the verb *kulongela* means "to emigrate; to transfer things into a box or bag." When a passive suffix is combined with the relative, the verb kulongela becomes *kulongelwa:* "to be happy; to be made happy, be blessed." The root can also carry a causative suffix; thus, the verb *kulongezya* translates as "to make happy, to bless," with the connotation that one causes happiness in process of emigration.[43] Together this range of synchronic meanings encapsulates a more recent trajectory of the longer history of this ancient Bantu root, from its earliest meanings associated with packing, heaping, and arranging to glosses related to movement through space and emigration to more recent ideas about the social ties, affections, assistance, and gifts facilitating mobility.

As Kafue peoples settled among communities of Kusi speakers living in lands south of the middle Kafue at the turn of the first millennium, they learned the Kusi word *-lòngó (n. cl. 1/2), which has been reconstructed with the meaning "brother" or "sibling." For Kafue newcomers, kinship—both fictive and real—was not the only path of successful social integration with established Batoka communities. Proto-Kafue speakers would have recognized that they could not pursue ties through marriage to all the many neighbors, notables, itinerant specialists, and peers with whom relationships of dependency and assistance were valuable. Kafue speakers who had no hope to assert claims as close kinsmen took this word into their languages but changed the meaning in the first noun class from "brother," a formalized kin relationship already described by *-kwésʋ, to a formalized friendship based on affect, exchange, and assistance.[44] For proto-Kafue communities, *-lòngó—be it the physical framework of wattle for roof poles or the friendliness that supported building new settlements—was the *matériel* from which communities were successfully formed, perhaps even the social and physical context in which one could expect to feel, or was expected to feel, happiness.

But let us move backward in time and consider the meanings tied to this root before Kafue communities of the early second millennium used it to describe a new, formal bond of friendship. In other Bantu languages, the root from which *-lòngó derives, *-dòngò, carries some of the same meanings it has in Botatwe languages, especially those tied to packing, moving through space, and identifying lines of objects. But the social relationships talked about with this root are startlingly different outside the Botatwe languages because they describe a range of ascriptive relationships, including family, lineage, clan, and tribe. Historian Christopher Ehret argues that "lineage" is the underlying meaning of *-lòngò in proto-Savanna, a linguistic ancestor to both proto-Kusi and proto-Kafue. Ehret rejects the more general meaning of "kinship" for *-lòngò because a more widely distributed and, therefore, an even older meaning of this root refers to objects in a line, a meaning still conserved in Botatwe languages, including the Ila glosses discussed above. When proto-Savanna speakers in the second millennium BCE started applying this known word for "objects in a line" to groups of kin, they were applying the notion of "a sequentially ordered set" to groups of kin and, Ehret argues, the "only logical analogue in kin relations is the line of forebears that leads back to the a founding ancestor, in other words, a lineage."[45]

In surveying all the meanings of the root and its derived forms across the entire Bantu domain, other linguists identify the oldest, most general meaning of the root as "heap up, arrange, pack up," a meaning that predates Ehret's proto-Savanna gloss as "lineage."[46] Indeed, this ancient Bantu root carries a large number of meanings tied to the movement and arrangement of people in physical space: it is the root word for settling new villages; for packing up, moving, and unpacking; for leading, guiding, and preceding others (through space); for teaching others and speaking to them. Even the references to lines and queues are imbued with motion.[47] When people were busy *longa*-ing, they were moving through space, working to organize and arrange the settlement of new areas by determining who could or should follow whom and on what basis they could expect support in their endeavors. It was *moving* that produced the context in which new meanings were layered upon this ancient root as novel dependencies and opportunities for social ties emerged in the context of shifting settlements.

Throughout most of Bantu history, kinship and friendship were both ways to make sense of who could settle where and from whom settlers could expect support. After all, the gloss "line, queue, row" can just as easily depict houses along a village avenue, riverbank, or ridge top or the movement of people on footpaths as they visit between hamlets as it can depict the "line of forebears" to which Ehret alludes. What was "lineal" about "lineages" emerged from the context of moving peoples' bodies, social networks, and effects. The proto-Kafue understanding of *-lòngó connects lineality to friendship and ascriptive ties to crafted affective ties. To be sure, the distinction between "friends" and "lineages" may be more important to anthropologists than it was to the first Kusi and Kafue speakers experimenting with strategies to make claims in negotiating land access, exchanging knowledge and tools, teaching new skills, honoring ancestors and local spirits, and reconfiguring what and whom they valued in the process of building new settlements on the Batoka Plateau in the first centuries of the second millennium.[48] This root has also been applied to male friendships that include sharing sexual access to wives, the payment for such access, and the names given by the sexual partners involved, further blurring the boundary between the social relationships and physical experiences that governed concepts that we gloss in English as friendship and kinship.

Of course, relationships like bond friendships may be more ascriptive than the English gloss "friend" can connote. The corporeality of ascriptive status is as evident in Smith's and Dale's description of the cutting, sucking, and ingestion of blood between committed Ila mulongo as it is in the birthing of children. Like the navels that had served as marks of a new form of matrilineal kinship, *-kóba, among Njila speakers in the eighth century in west central Africa, scars inscribed during the initiation of mulongo were visible years after the establishment of the social relationship they marked. As physical mnemonics announcing particular forms of association and likely triggering heightened moments of emotional subjectivity, such bodily markers might have been as central to the success of Ila mulongo as the exchange of material gifts and assistance. It may be that the affective basis of both kinship and friendship, a basis that supported expectations of exchange and assistance, helped speakers craft the changing meaning of *-lòngó from a brother, sibling, or lineage to a covenant of friendship. What was affective about *-lòngó proved more resilient than meanings tied only to the idiom of corporeal relationship. The history of *-lòngó illuminates how the expansive character of associations like mulongo or mukowa have often been disguised or reduced by the idiom of kinship.[49]

In many ways, *-lòngó functioned much like *-kóba clan ties, cementing relationships of obligation and assistance across broad geographical and uncertain genealogical distances—even the lack of genealogical connections. Yet with *-lòngó, proto-Kafue speakers established significant networks beyond those forms of kinship called mukowa, mukwashi, and bakwesu. These were lateral links par excellence that could, when inherited across generations, create a shared history of association between the original friends and the generations of successors inheriting their storied friendship, thereby joining unrelated families beyond the lifetime of individuals and outside the commonly recognized principles of kinship. Such mulongo ties also strengthened intrafamily links between living and recently deceased kinsmen through the mechanism of inheritance. Perhaps these enduring ties inspired Tonga speakers to use the *-lòngó root to speak of the "eternal" in noun form.[50] If mukwashi and bakwesu described cohorts of relatives supporting a person's path through the recognized stages of the life cycle, ensuring well-being and spiritual support, mulongo offered the opportunities and support necessary to orient that path toward particular personal aspirations, pleasures, and gratifications not easily met through ties of kinship. Mulongo friendships bring to our attention the emotional stakes of the many individuals, households, friends, lineages, and clans whose actions ensured that communities speaking different languages and making distinct forms of material cultural objects nevertheless became speakers and makers of the same cultural traditions by the middle of the second millennium.

Summing Up the Terms of Social Integration

In innovating *-lòngó, *-kóba, *-kwésʋ, and *-kwàshɪ, proto-Kafue speakers transformed the scales of geographical, genealogical, and cultural distance that they could span through ties of obligation and dependency. If the borrowing of *-kóba marks the initial shift to unilateral descent, the first few families in an area to adopt the practice of reckoning family through only the mother's line may well have angered the father's kin, who lost rights to the children of the marriage. Perhaps the ideal of virilocal cross-cousin marriage was developed to mollify the disgruntled kin of young fathers, who were cut off from their sons' children.[51] Children that had also once belonged to fathers' families would still grow under their care and, within a generation or two of the *-kwésʋ of each lineage marrying their cross-cousins, the families' wealth and children would be tightly bound to one another.[52] The ideal marriage between the *-kwésʊ cohort of one lineage and their common cohort of *-kwàshı was not easy to achieve among individual foreigners, the kinless, or lineages with few children, for such people had few ties to offer. Women who married into a family alone because no other classificatory sister married into the same family faced the challenge of reaping large harvests and bringing difficult pregnancies to term quite far from the help of female kin. Infertility or accusations of witchcraft would have been social stigmas they faced in isolation from a network of support. Indeed, the ideal marriage in the Kafue era benefited the largest, most influential families, whose many children probably seemed both a product of and a justification for their social clout.

The fact that the middle Kafue way of life came to predominate in the area supplies evidence that the ideal of cross-cousin marriage was not always followed in the early second millennium. Some Kafue-speaking *-tʃıCıa undoubtedly had other ambitions for the alliances that might be made through the marriages they could negotiate for the daughters of the lineage. Some cohorts of female *-kwésʊ traveled to the distant villages of complete strangers. Women whose marriages brought them to distant villages had good reason to travel back to the villages of their mothers and those of their maternal uncles: they needed to advocate for their children. Plying the footpaths in the dry season, such women perhaps had more need of the ties of mukowa and mulongo for hospitality in their travels than their male relatives. Women whose marriages carried them to foreign lands may not have received a warm welcome in their new villages. Locals may well have been wary of the strangers brought to the village by new marriage practices, for such foreign women taught their children a different language, crafted pots in unconventional styles, and might even draw the attention of malevolent spirits. What did anyone in the village know of the kin who pledged for the comportment of these strange women? Those Kusi speakers who did not embrace the social innovations of Kafue speakers might have been outraged to be told that the ties of brotherhood they valued as *-lòngó could not do the same socially meaningful work within families as *-kwésʊ. Rather, non-Kafue speakers may have been told that *-lòngó were the ties that bound individuals together, not cohorts within larger family networks. Perhaps marking mulongo as inheritable was a compromise between the positions.

As fraught as the adoption of these new social ties may have been, Kafue speakers' vision of what a family looked like and how its members should

behave came to dominate the collective imagination of all residents of the region in the early second millennium. These broad social ties dispersed risks
across the landscape, combating localized threats to subsistence as they simultaneously reshaped and were shaped by new kinds of settlement, marriage,
and patterns of long-distance travel. But Kafue speakers' social innovations
also changed quotidian practices. Groups of *-kwésʊ lived near each other and
could depend on each other's assistance to mitigate the seasonal labor bottlenecks of the agricultural calendar. Male parallel cousins probably helped each
other cut fields and repair houses; female parallel cousins may have prepared,
planted, weeded, and harvested each other's gardens and perhaps collaborated in the kinds of communal fishing developed in the early second millennium and described in chapter 3. These are some of the instrumental benefits
to subsistence that Kafue speakers might have realized in the social ties they
innovated. But how did the increasing scales of Kafue speakers' social institutions impact the older politics of fame and social status built around knowledge of the bush and embodied in figures like *-pàdó and *-vʊbɩ? Could such
individuals work in foreign isokwe? If family members most invested in the
celebrity and products cultivated by *-pàdó and *-vʊbɩ now lived in distant
lands, particularly the children of the family's daughters, could ancestors
still be made? Kafue speakers met these challenges with innovations in two
aspects of bushcraft. A new emphasis on communal hunting grew the scale
of bushcraft and created opportunities for broad participation and learning
even as they expanded the audiences witnessing, recalling, and retelling
*-pàdó's feats. Simultaneously, Kafue speakers used a new lingo that gendered
antelopes to reassert the cosmological valence of bushcraft.

Hunting Communities

From the middle of the tenth through the middle of the thirteenth century,
speakers of proto-Kafue used their Central Eastern linguistic ancestors'
innovations in spearcraft to profoundly recast the social stakes of spear
hunting, adding to the familiar status of *-pàdó a new emphasis on the social outcomes of communal hunts.[53] In the process, proto-Kafue speakers
innovated words for their preferred quarry and for the tools and organization of group hunting, which intensively exploited several species of antelope, a point to which we'll return. This vocabulary is rich, like the cluster
of Central Eastern Botatwe innovations relating to spearcraft; the two

vocabularies are undoubtedly connected. As we learned in the previous chapter, the archaeological record of the Middle Iron Age in the Kafue region independently attests to the significance of communal hunting in the high mortality rates of gregarious species like antelope as compared to other species. The predominance of full-grown adults in the faunal record suggests skillful communal hunting methods.[54]

Chila

Kafue-speaking hunters in the early second millennium conserved a culture of bushcraft that depended on and celebrated technology, fame, and skill. But the practice of bushcraft was developed in dialogue with the cultural world of the central African savannas to the north and west—the cultural world that would eventually give rise to the familiar hunter-founder figures and important metallurgists populating the origin traditions of the well-known savanna kingdoms. From this world, Kafue speakers borrowed a term for a very large hunting net, *-kìdà, just as their Central Eastern Botatwe-speaking linguistic forebears had collaborated with hunters of the north to name celebrated hunters *-pàdó several centuries earlier. When proto-Kafue speakers borrowed *-kìdà, they pronounced it in the form *cìlà [87], adopting it into noun class 7 without adding a noun class prefix. Kafue speakers used *cìlà to talk about a communal hunt, rather than the hunting net more commonly used in the denser wooded savannas to the north.

These communal hunts were probably large, seasonal enterprises. In the early twentieth century, chila dry season hunts drew scores and even hundreds of participants, attracting enough attention from conservation officers to be banned by the colonial government.[55] While beaters chased animals toward an entrapment—a bog, a long net or pitfall, a river, a fire—other hunters waited there, prepared to spear the animals, a classic formation in *battue* hunting, or hunting with beaters. Proto-Kafue speakers invented a new generic word for hunting entrapments, *-pàndo [88], by combining an older Bantu transitive verb root *-pànd-, "to split," with the deverbative suffix denoting the action, result, or instrument of the verb. Indeed, Tonga and Lenje speakers now use the word in the form *lwaando* to refer to the dry season communal hunt itself. In addition to using *-pàndo, proto-Kafue battue hunting parties also encircled game. The bodies of the hunters themselves served as the entrapment, though this method of hunting was distinct enough from using *-pàndo to merit unique vocabulary. Commencing in two facing lines

Figure 4.2. Ila spearmen honing their skills in a formation like chila during a throwing competition in the early twentieth century. Photograph by E. W. Smith. Reprinted from Smith and Dale, *Ila-Speaking Peoples of Northern Rhodesia*, vol. 2, 242.

at some distance apart, one line of hunters advanced, beating the animals forward as both lines curved tighter, encircling the animals (fig. 4.2). As the hunters closed in, they stabbed their prey. While all modern-day Kafue languages refer to this form of hunting as *kuoba banyama*, it is impossible to reconstruct the entire phrase through the comparative historical linguistic method. It is only with the common Kafue noun *ibalo* [89], "circle of hunters in a battue hunt," which derived from *-bada, "ring," and with an areal form developed in the western Batoka after the thirteenth century, *-yala [90], "to hunt by surrounding," that we have evidence that explicitly refers to battue hunting by encirclement, typical of precolonial elephant hunting.[56]

This evidence of innovation around the technologies and techniques of communal hunting with spears is surprising. Why did proto-Kafue speakers invent new vocabulary to talk about communal hunting, when archaeological evidence suggests that it was probably already a strategy in local hunting repertoires?

Chila belonged to the skill set of both great spearmen and local participants and is best understood as the social context in which celebrated hunters' actions were carefully followed by relatives, neighbors, wives, lovers, and even competitors. These observers consumed meat, skins, and stories of the hunt, celebrating the hunter and buoying his fame through their own actions. But with chila, observers, consumers, and celebrants could become participants. Large-scale communal hunting provided one context for social cooperation among proto-Kafue speakers whose small, centralized villages were dispersed across large neighborhoods encompassing different microenvironments. Large-scale seasonal neighborhood hunts afforded participants the opportunity to trade local resources; visit with relatives, dependents, and friends; arrange future marriages; and exchange gifts between mulongo. As Kafue speakers extended settlements across the environmental zones of the middle Kafue and into lands inhabited by speakers of other languages, their relatives now lived some distance away. Lineages' daughters moved to the homesteads of in-laws and lineages' sons may have ventured out to found villages elsewhere. Young mothers may have returned to their natal homes for the neighborhood chila, taking advantage of their proximity to male kin to demand a share of the hunt's bounty and to introduce to kin the children for whom they would negotiate marriages, amassing and distributing bridewealth through bakwesu networks. Mothers may have wanted their children to see, hear, and learn the heroic feats of their family's men and to meet the relatives who would one day become ancestors shaping the world of the children's own offspring. Indeed, these events were probably as significant a seasonal festivity in the past as they were in recent decades.

Chila also offered opportunities to engage with communities speaking other Bantu languages, as the very borrowing of the term indicates. Kafue speakers might well have sought to include villages in which some Kafue families had begun to build homes and marry. Indeed, the timing of this new emphasis on communal hunting in the context of establishing new settlements across linguistic and material cultural boundaries suggests that one of the ways immigrant Kafue speakers met the social and ritual imperatives of settling in the occupied lands of the Batoka Plateau was through massive communal hunts. Chila offered opportunities to cooperate and generated in vast quantities prized resources that could be shared. Proto-Kafue speakers began to emphasize communal hunting in the context of continued innovation in the technologies and techniques of spearcraft described in the previous chapter. For example, Kafue speakers invented the *-bèjɪ [72] carving spear point, which suggests that butchery and meat distribution may have become a more formal and perhaps more ritualized process. Faunal remains from the Kafue and Batoka region in the late first and early second millennium demonstrate clear preferences for particular carcass parts.[57] The traditions of butchery accompanying these hunts may have followed particular alliances forged across communities, such that participants from one region, clan, or speech community traditionally took the foreleg, while those from another group took the cranium, and so forth. The carving and sharing of the carcass, sinew, and skin would have been a way to recognize the new boundaries of family and the ties crafted between bakwesu and bakwashi, allowing those in command of carving to publically and materially meet the obligations such ties demanded.

Chila participants harnessed the creative, transformative powers of the bush and the skill of individual hunters to productive, social ends, affirming bonds of reciprocity and dependency. Colson observed that among Tonga in the twentieth century, a communal game drive might occur after the building of a ritual fence against the bush in *kusinka,* a ceremony used by the Tonga in times of stress to defeat witchcraft or call for rain. This communal hunt was "a statement of community solidarity and strength in the face of the forces of the bush, just as the fence built during *kusinka* separates the human space of the *cisi* from the wild."[58] We can imagine that by sharing the dangers of the hunt as manifest in stampeding herds and the unpredictable interventions of ancestors, the wealth of meat, skins, and horns such hunts could produce, and the celebrations of hunters flushed with success and communities hungry for meat, established firstcomers and Kafue-speaking newcomers enacted a similar community solidarity in the uninhabited lands of the Batoka in the early second millennium. The heightened affective state of these moments of community building could be renewed in future hunts and even actualized when recalled through stories told around the evening fire, when skin aprons and ivory bangles adorned the bodies of favored wives and lovers, and when foreign beads and copper were exchanged for horns and tusks traded into the regional economy. By traversing the bush together, large hunting groups asserted solidarity and shared claims to the spirits protecting their endeavors in the bush.

The democratizing effect of chila provoked, quite literally, an existential crisis, for the quest for ancestorhood looked very different for hunters vying for recognition in the wider pool of celebrated heroes and ancestors called into being by the larger audiences of chila. The audiences were not only larger, they were more culturally and linguistically diverse on the Batoka in the early second millennium. The move to the Batoka posed a challenge to the politics of reputations tied to knowledge about the bush that were first developed by Central Eastern Botatwe speakers and subsequently conserved by Kafue speakers. Reputations could always travel, but they now traveled through landscapes populated by other local notables, infamous hunters, and wealthy smelters. Those who drew on the knowledge and power of their own ancestors to ensure the success of their activities in the bush began to work in landscapes studded by the graves of others' ancestors and controlled by their willful spirits.[59] For the earliest Kafue families to live among strangers, it was not at all certain how ancestors and heroes engaged with non-kin and newcomers. How could one be remembered in lands traversed by unknown muzimu and their living descendants? Communities used chila to establish in a very public setting those hunting heroes who would become the ancestor spirits protecting future generations and bestowing great skills in return for the commemoration of their own talents, feats, and fame. Shared heroes may well have smoothed over the inconvenient problem of lack of access to firstcomers' ancestral spirits for the earliest Kafue settlers participating in chila, but the inheritance of their skill may well have been limited to kin at a time when the categories of kin were in flux.

Chila allowed a wider public to see and participate in the violent and competitive aspects of bushcraft. Certainly the larger body of participants could regal audiences of those who didn't particpate—those who supported the event or were too old or young to serve as beaters and carriers—with stories of the masterful feats of established and aspiring *-pàdó. No doubt the vast audience of the day's events also circulated less savory stories of poor huntsmanship. For some, chila opened a social space for collaboration across social and linguistic boundaries. Yet others who attended a middle Kafue chila or observed recently settled neighbors mounting a chila hunt near their villages might well have watched with some trepidation as large groups of spearmen, beaters, carriers, and children put on a show that, in essence, exhibited masterful coordination in the corralling and killing of swiftly fleeing animals. These were technical skills transferrable to warfare, a message that may have been particularly clear to non-Kafue communities who felt that middle Kafue ways of life were being forced upon them by those collaborating with Kafue speakers, whether ambitious juniors or large, influential lineages already well tied to Kafue families. And for some non-Kafue-speaking families, chila may have been deeply emotional reenactments of the same coordination and skills that groups of young Kafue-speaking men had exploited when they seized their daughters as brides, returning to claim the status of in-laws, the *-kwàshı and *-kwe of the victims' families.

Chila opened the path to the status of *-pàdó to more young men, including those in lineages lacking tales of accomplished hunters and ancestors whose talents might be inherited. As a venue of participatory learning, chila taught skills and shared talented folk across the linguistic and cultural boundaries that Batoka and Kafue communities were slowly dissolving. But young men who observed and practiced the maneuvers of older *-pàdó might also show them up. Established *-pàdó practiced their best strategies in the public venue of chila or kept them secret at the risk of offering a sub-par performance. Among young men, huntsmanship was something to strive for because it was tied up with other ideas about what kind of man one might prove oneself to be. Through a strong performance in chila, a young man exhibited a particular kind of virile maturity for the benefit of lineage elders busy initiating marriage negotiations for the lineage's most promising children. Young men performed under the appraising gaze of young women, whether married or still several years from such demanding ties. Chila changed the scale of the politics governing the tangible and intangible products of hunters' pursuits; it also shaped understandings of the meaning of the products sought by hunters.

Hunters' Pursuits

A young, unmarried hunter living in the middle Kafue at the dawn of the second millennium might have practiced his craft as often as he could if he aspired to one day be recognized as a *-pàdó. He might have set out early in the morning in the dry, windy season to bag a lechwe in the boggy dambos and muddy floodplains the animal prefers. The young hunter would have carried his spears and brought his dogs, already fortified with their own medicines. Not only would the shy antelope supply ample relish for the many dependents of his mother's and aunts' cooking pots, but a buck might provide a shapely set of horns to ornament the hunter's spear rest before the next visit of his *-tʃıCıa. The skin of the lechwe's elongated torso could be worked into a particularly supple apron for the hunter's preferred bride, but his *-tʃıCıa's perceptive eye would be assessing the hunter's accomplishments carefully before committing a daughter in marriage to a young nephew.

Our young hunter's quarry was typical of the period. Kafue hunters in the early second millennium—whether low-skill beaters joining the festivities of a neighborhood chila or *-pàdó expertly weighing the merits of particular spear points, hunting grounds, and medicines to ensure their success—increasingly used their knowledge of spearcraft, archery, and poisons to target species of antelope with strict preferences for wetland margins. For these quarry, Kafue speakers innovated new names. They integrated into their vocabulary and environmental knowledge a name for sitatunga, *-jóbé, reconstructed to proto-Kafue as *-zóbé [2].[60] They adopted a regional term for *Kobus lechwe*, *n(y)anjá [91], that was circulating across the wooded savannas from the Okavango River through the Zambezi hook and into the Sabi-speaking areas east of Botatwe communities. Similarly, the broad savanna form *mbàbàlá [92] was likely borrowed by Kafue communities from Kusi speakers and used to talk about bushbuck, which inhabited areas of well-watered thick brush and forest near permanent water, like the Kafue River and its tributaries. *Mbololo*, a common Kafue word for the numerous kudu that graze the woodland and thickets along the edges of the floodplain grasses, may well date to the proto-Kafue period.[61] The phonology of *n(y)aluvwɪ [93], a new term for reedbuck, secures its status as a Kafue innovation. This term is a compound word combining an old feminine pre-prefix for "mother of" or "female" with the noun class 10 prefix and an old, inherited proto-Savanna term for arrow, known as *-vóí [13] to proto-Kafue speakers. The proto-Kafue name for the reedbuck may allude to what it was that hunters sought when they decided to hunt in the style of *-vóím- [14]. Named from the same Savanna root for arrow, *-gúí, the verb *-vóím- probably originally referred to archery. After the breakup of the proto-Kafue speech community, it slowly transformed into a term for communal hunts and fire drives (a specific form of communal hunt). Antelope like those Kafue speakers named in the early second millennium were the quarry of trappers, independent spearmen, and chila.

The addition of a feminine pre-prefix to antelope names seems to have been something of a linguistic fashion in Kafue speech about certain kinds of antelope. In addition to *n(y)aluvwɪ, proto-Kafue speakers added the feminine prefix to the borrowed term for kobus lechwe, *n(y)anjá, and an old inherited word for duiker, *-síá [94]. Though many neighboring communities also used these latter two roots, Kafue people were the only speakers to add gender prefixes to them. Although it may have originated as part of an argot defining *-pàdó who were in the know, this lingo was certainly common parlance only a generation or two later. We might imagine Kafue hunters adding this linguistic flourish to the names of antelope species they hunted with decoy whistles. Indeed, Kafue speakers living near the large herds of antelope found in the Kafue grasslands used a decoy whistle to hunt duiker in the twentieth century, speaking about it with the common root -*Nyele*.[62] The common root -Nyele is difficult to date because it is onomatopoeia; it might have been independently invented numerous times in the recent past as speakers produced seeming cognates by approximating the sound of the whistle. However, we know onomatopoeia to be a result of culturally influenced perceptions of sound. When we consider the relict distribution of this root, we might hypothesize that the root developed as onomatopoeia in the proto-Kafue period, undergoing common changes like reduplication in more recent centuries, though this dating remains very uncertain. A Kafue hunter crouched in the bush, would have used a carved, clay, or rolled-leaf whistle to mimic the duiker calf's cry in order to lure a mother duiker toward him, adding to the name of the species he lured the sex of the animal the hunter bagged when hunting with decoy whistles. However, the luring of mother duikers is a less convincing explanation for the application of the feminine prefix to other antelope species because the decoy whistle was most commonly used in hunting duiker.

In traveling from his village to the receding floodplain pastures where his quarry would be passing an active morning grazing, our ambitious young hunter might have reflected upon what it would mean for him to bag the lechwe buck he sought outside the context of chila, where even those with little skill had the chance to land the first hit on an antelope. Where the ethnographic record is richest, we learn of the practice of hunters giving wives and lovers the skins of lechwe and reedbuck to fulfill the obligation of men to provide clothing, especially skins for aprons, for women and young girls to whom they were betrothed (fig. 4.3).[63] The feminine prefixes attached to particular species might indicate both the preferred species for making women's aprons and the antiquity of this gendered form of gift giving. It may well be that the produce of hunters' efforts afforded them a way to meet the mundane material needs of their female dependents and affirm social ties of responsibility and obligation with an exemplary and perhaps even coveted kind of apron leather.

Figure 4.3. Tonga woman "sewing beads on a skin skirt" in 1950. The material is probably a cow hide. Photograph by Nigel Watt. Reprinted from Reynolds, *Material Culture of the Gwembe Valley*, plate IX. Permission courtesy of Zambia News and Information Services.

The gifting of women's aprons to wives, would-be wives, and lovers specified an existing or future sexual relationship, which adds another layer of meaning to such gifted skins. When stalked and hunted, rather than snared along field margins or game paths, these species were bagged in the uninhabited bush, *-sókwe [74].[64] When Kafue hunters began to mark with feminine gender the names of antelopes whose hides could be worked into supple leather and cut into aprons donned by favored wives and skirting the hips of desired lovers, they may have summoned up in the minds of their listeners ideas about the virility and productivity associated with the bush and with its technicians. Coveted hides may have been as precious for their material attributes as for their production by a successful hunter and their provenance in the bush, a place of uncertain but potentially transformative power. Within burials from this region dating from the late first through the second millennium, products of the bush, such as ivory bangles, most often adorned the bodies of girls and young women approaching or at the height of their fertile years.[65] It may have been at women's behest that antelope skins became requested gifts and meaningful markers of sexual relationships.

Attuned to the meaning of the bush for Kafue communities, we catch a glimpse—albeit through the haze of inadequate sources and long spans of time—of the convergence of ideas connecting the transformative powers associated with the bush with new patterns of human mobility, kinship, and sexuality and with long-established cosmologies valuing powerful but unreliable human fertility.[66] The convergence of the kinds of ideas associated with the bush made gifted skins circling and masking the bodies of sexual partners quite potent, even aspirational, social statements. Perhaps Kafue hunters and their wives, lovers, and betrothed understood markers of their relationship expressed in products of the bush to be claims to a potent sexuality associated with the bush, connecting material wealth, sensuous affect, and social status. Chila communal hunts may have been a way to more intensively exploit and also open up access to the kinds of virility and fertility associated with the bush and evoked by its products.

The early centuries of the second millennium in south central Africa were a period of profound demographic change. Residents of the middle Kafue slowly extended the influence of their lifestyle beyond the old heartland of Central Eastern Botatwe speech through migration, intermarriage, and the adoption of Kafue speech by non-Kafue speakers. These actions carried the potential to be violent and may have included the seizure of land and people. Successful social integration was not a foregone conclusion to the men and women balancing the possibilities of migration and marriage and enduring the trauma of lost lands and daughters wrought by aggressive expansionists. Kafue speakers developed three innovations that nurtured enduring social integration: changes in the scale and sociality of hunting, the development of networks of bond friendship cultivated by individuals and rooted in the uneven distribution of talent and expertise, and the creation of ties of kinship that could sustain claims on the material wealth and social influence of others.

The new opportunities and threats to the quest for communal belonging and remembrance by future generations must have been profound for these men and women. The geographic proximity and cultural homogeneity of their predecessors' homesteads in the middle Kafue allowed their Central Eastern Botatwe ancestors to meet challenges to the fertility and fecundity of the people and the land posed by periodic drought, witchcraft, and other threats through immediate access to lineage elders and other intercessors to the ancestors. The settlement of Kafue peoples among established communities with

foreign languages and different material cultures posed a distinct social challenge to accessing strategic resources, including the protection of firstcomers'
ancestral spirits. The different social and geographic ties bound through
mulongo, chila, mukowa, bakwesu, and mukwashi constituted a flexible range
of strategies to protect social and physical mobility and open multiple access
points to farmlands, hunting grounds, medicines, shared heroes, beads and
bangles, spirits, and audiences for the stories of one's own and others' achievements.[67] These innovations proved to be so successful that speakers expanded
Kafue languages as far as the Lukanga swamps in the northeast and the
Zambezi Valley to the south before proto-Kafue dissolved into extant Zambian languages after the thirteenth century.

Bushcraft was changed by and for the men and women who reconfigured the social world of south central Africa. This is a testament to the social
influence of practitioners of bushcraft and the status of bushcraft itself as both
a symbol of productive powers that sustained communities and a tactic for
harnessing that power to actualize the well-being of communities. Chila was
potentially an integrative institution, but it also endangered the status of established *-pàdó. Achievements mattered at chila because the size of the audience made for higher stakes; reputations were on the line but so, too, were
all the tangible and intangible outcomes of noteworthy feats. Chila hunts may
have been a way to scale up production in and democratize access to the
products—skins, meat, tusks, and horns—of favored species. In a demographic context in which marriage was expected to create social stability,
efforts to intensify the production of antelope skins through chila may have
inspired large-scale public acts of magnificent, sexually potent gifting to fertile women. Bond friendships may have served to reconcile an older politics
of fame and social status with the wider communities created through mukowa. Perhaps *-pàdó initiated *-lòngó ties, trading on one another's notoriety to extend their own fame or improve the caliber of a chila hunt by building
up participation or swapping new tools and methods.

Kafue speakers borrowed many of the words discussed in this chapter.
Some of them, such as terms for antelope species, describe the kind of environmental knowledge Kafue speakers learned from speakers of other, nearby
Bantu languages. Others loans locate Botatwe lands in a central frontier between the cultural worlds of central and southern Africa. Kafue speakers, like
their linguistic forebears, looked to these two worlds for different kinds of
learning. Residents of the middle Kafue looked to the north to learn about

and collaborate on the prestige, techniques, and tools of hunting, such as the *-kìdà hunting net, but they adapted them to local contexts. From the cultures of pastoralism located south of the Zambezi, Kafue speakers adopted new names for kith and kin, but they manipulated for their own purposes the fuzzy, affective boundary between the ties of friendship and brotherhood that connected men.

Significantly, the same institutions that facilitated relationships within the Kafue-speaking world could be used to tie regular visitors to members of the communities they frequently passed through. If bakwesu and mukwashi facilitated access to spirits and ensured that familiar faces were nearby in unfamiliar social territory, mulongo and mukowa had the potential to work across far greater linguistic, cultural, and territorial distances. We can imagine that mulongo and mukowa relationships were used to draw in from central and southern Africa the many itinerant workers, frequent visitors, and others regularly passing through the region: hunters, healers, smelters, salt seekers, the kinsmen of neighbors spending the dry season on a tour of relatives, ambitious would-be Big Men, and vulnerable but potentially loyal outcasts. Our models of precolonial social organization do not account well for such passers-through; we tend to assume newcomers sought to stay, attracted by leaders, or to leave, registering dissatisfaction through their departure.[68] These ties equally allowed Kafue speakers to travel with protection and hospitality across long distances in central and southern Africa during the dry season. The broader archaeological and historical contexts of the southern and central African worlds bridged by the inhabitants of the middle Kafue, Batoka, and middle Zambezi offer many tantalizing hints of just this sort of regional mobility, association, and exchange.

5. Life on the Central Frontier

*The Geographies of Technology, Trade,
and Prestige, 750 to 1700*

From the early first millennium, Botatwe speakers lived in a territory that constituted a frontier encircled by multiple and changing heartlands of political and technological innovation. Archaeological and linguistic evidence demonstrate that residents of this central frontier, including Botatwe speakers, contributed to the development and reconfiguration of the trade, politics, and technologies of both central and southern Africa between the middle of the first and the middle of the second millennium. But the story of the central frontier has been obscured because, with few exceptions, the interior regions of central and southern Africa before the sixteenth century are studied in isolation from one another, with the northern escarpment of the Zambezi often serving as a boundary between the two regions. Moreover, the character of the central frontier is impossible to discern when frontier communities are studied as the hinterlands or even the backlands of only a single polity or industrial center. Although the early histories of central and southern Africa have never been told from the perspective of the residents of the lands that bridged them, the history of the central frontier changes how we understand familiar political and economic processes in both regions, from the emergence of early long-distance trade networks linking the Indian Ocean to the western Kalahari, to the founding of the famous savanna kingdoms of central Africa.

The material cultural record suggests that the central frontier was something of a backwater, for its communities developed nothing like the sumptuous caches of ceramics, jewelry, ceremonial objects, and, later, currencies discovered at sites in the Upemba Depression, the Limpopo Valley, and the Zimbabwe Plateau (fig. 5.1). The central frontier did not boast the multitier settlement patterns or the great cattle herds known from Toutswe Iron Age sites in eastern Botswana. It did not contain sites with the degree of industry found at Tsodilo Hills around the turn of the first millennium, where miners carved out specularite to dust skin and hair, smiths beat out beautiful metal jewelry in industrial quantities, and nearby craftsman rubbed strings of chipped ostrich eggshell within troughs worn into rocks to smooth the chips into round disc beads. And the communities of the central frontier did not invent the kinds of elaborately titled societies, principalities, and ranked sodalities of initiates governing members' movement through life's cycle of statuses developed by men and women in west central Africa. Inhabitants of the central frontier did, however, contribute in key ways to the many political, economic, and technological innovations that characterized central and southern Africa in the first and second millennia. Furthermore, by selectively participating in and borrowing from the changes wrought by inventive technicians and leaders living well beyond the central frontier, Botatwe speakers crafted a durable, but ever-changing political culture valuing worldliness, fame, wealth, and skill as the foundation for efficacious claims to status, however ephemeral.

To appreciate this history, we need to understand the nature of the central frontier as a geographical, cultural, and political phenomenon. We also need to understand the relationship between trade and subsistence on the central frontier before the eighteenth century. Pithily, the central frontier was a "backlands with options." Unlike a hinterland, it was not defined in relation only to the center from which it was hinter. The central frontier was not the internal frontier described by Igor Kopytoff, a land beyond the hinterland of a single metropole, inviting would-be leaders to reproduce the culture of the center from which they migrated. It was not like the "oasis" refuge described by Jan Vansina in the lands upstream of the confluence of the Okavango and Cuito Rivers, where continual influxes of people bringing "impoverished reminiscences" of the social and political features of the their homelands ensured that residents developed "nothing original to the region itself." The central frontier was rich with the work of invention, cultural bricolage, and active participation in the affairs of the communities beyond its boundary.[1]

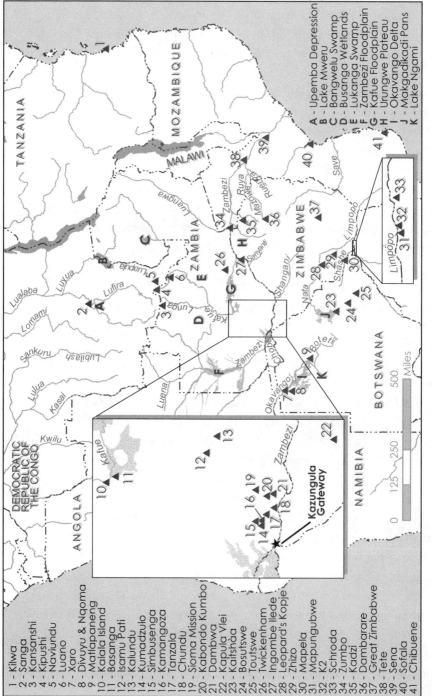

Figure 5.1. Natural features and major centers of settlement, trade, industry, and politics in central and southern Africa, c. 500 to 1700.

1 - Kilwa
2 - Sanga
3 - Kansanshi
4 - Kipushi
5 - Naviundu
6 - Luano
7 - Xaro
8 - Divuyu & Nqoma
9 - Matlapaneng
10 - Kalala Island
11 - Basanga
12 - Isamu Pati
13 - Kalundu
14 - Kumadzulo
15 - Simbusenga
16 - Kamangoza
17 - Tanzala
18 - Chundu
19 - Sioma Mission
20 - Kabondo Kumbo
21 - Dambwa
22 - Kapula Vlei
23 - Kaitshàa
24 - Bosutswe
25 - Toutswe
26 - Twickenham
27 - Ingombe Ilede
28 - Leopard's Kopje
29 - Zhizo
30 - Mapela
31 - Mapungubwe
32 - K2
33 - Schroda
34 - Zumbo
35 - Kadzi
36 - Dambarare
37 - Great Zimbabwe
38 - Tete
39 - Sena
40 - Sofala
41 - Chibuene

A - Upemba Depression
B - Lake Mweru
C - Bangwelu Swamp
D - Busanga Wetlands
E - Lukanga Swamp
F - Zambezi Floodplain
G - Kafue Floodplain
H - Urungwe Plateau
I - Okavango Delta
J - Makgadikadi Pans
K - Lake Ngami

The central frontier was close enough to political and technological centers to attract in or thrust out ideas, objects, and people across its boundary, but it lay at a distance beyond the hinterland of any one center. It was out of reach of the efficacious force of important metropoles, whether the coercive enforcement of tribute or the ridicule that might censure local attempts to master the rituals and styles of the metropole. The distance to and numbers of political, industrial, and trade centers beyond the central frontier shaped life in this unique place. Sometimes the central frontier had the feel of a borderland between many competing—and, therefore, waxing and waning—centers. At other times, its residents acted as a bridge between major cultural and economic zones to their north and south. Residents could not always maintain the boundaries of the central frontier: sometimes the central frontier simply dissolved into a hinterland under the sway of a single center. This dissolution occurred when the trade emporium of Ingombe Ilede was reoccupied in the fourteenth and fifteenth centuries, dominating the flow of ideas and materials and relegating the lands of Botatwe speakers to the periphery of its own networks. Botatwe speakers lived in a backlands, to be sure. But because those backlands constituted a central frontier, residents could be more cosmopolitan, flexible, and creative in their lifestyles and politics than residents living in the surrounding metropoles. For nearly a millennium, Botatwe speakers on the central frontier sustained a decentralized political culture that depended on manipulating the unique geography they enjoyed.

The residents of the backlands continually reconstituted the central frontier through the movement of people, ideas, and things. Sometimes ideas and objects moved slowly, from village to village. At other times, they moved with the seasonal travels of residents of the central frontier, especially the travels of skilled technicians who journeyed to acquire new tools, learn new techniques, rekindle ties of affection or the fires of competition, and honor those who were masters of their craft. As Clapperton Mavhunga has observed, such technicians often labored in transient workspaces; mobility was central to the practice of their craft.[2] Movement also required the kinds of exchanges that honored hospitality, recognized spiritual and political authorities, and cemented ties of kith and kin through gift exchanges. In other words, many of the skilled practitioners, from hunters to bone setters, who journeyed to undertake or improve the practice of their craft in the dry season, had to "trade" along the way. Farmers and those who took time to collect salt, honey, fruits, and medicines might bring some of their produce with them in the hopes that they could exchange such surplus during annual dry season visits to relatives and friends. They, too, were bound by the demands of hospitality and expectations of gifting. The economic changes often invoked to define the "revolutionary" character of Neolithic transitions to cereal agriculture, such as "craft specialization" and "trade in surplus," fail to capture the complicated social context in which people exchanged products that were cultivated and collected as matters of everyday subsistence. People "traded" knowledge and acquaintances alongside material goods and, for some, such nonmaterial exchanges were far more integral to the journey. The activities hunters undertook during their travels exemplify the blurry boundaries between subsisting, trading, learning, and the social performances of associating that, together, sustained such journeymen's movements through space and gained them recognition upon their return home.

This chapter offers four stories that place the history of the middle Kafue in the context of better-known narratives about the precolonial past of central and southern Africa. The first two trace out evidence for connections between the central frontier and the communities of southern and central Africa between the seventh and thirteenth centuries. One story connects the middle Kafue to emerging evidence for a first millennium long-distance trade network that linked the Kalahari to the Indian Ocean along a route oriented through lands well north of the expected Shashe-Limpopo region. The second story explores the fate of intermediate statuses and figures in the political culture of the communities residing in the northern miombo savannas that lie to the north and northwest of the middle Kafue. The third story explores the impact of the best-known trading entrepôt to develop near Botatwe lands, Ingombe Ilede, on central frontier communities during the fourteenth and fifteenth centuries. The final story of the chapter considers how Botatwe communities engaged with the political ideas and objects available from emerging polities and trade centers on the ever-constricting periphery of the central frontier during the sixteenth and seventeenth centuries. In each of these four stories, the location of Botatwe communities on the central frontier shaped their involvement with and contribution to the watershed events of central and southern African history before the eighteenth century, from the emergence of the northern and southern regional economies and their integration to the rise of the famed savanna kingdoms and the emergence of the states of the Zimbabwe Plateau.

Looking South

By the end of the first millennium, the lands inhabited by Botatwe speakers and others on the central frontier formed a transitional zone between the northern miombo-wooded savannas common to the north and the mopane and scrub grasslands of the southern velds. Linguistic evidence for complicated histories of contact, language shift, and word borrowing together with the diversity of pottery styles characteristic of the region have led many archaeologists, historians, and linguists to conclude that the central frontier was a meeting point for the two broad eastern and western "branches" or "streams" into which the diverse regional forms of speech and pottery can be classified. We might debate the details, but these scholars insist on the importance of the central frontier as a place of contact and borrowing. In its earliest iteration, the central frontier was created by communities living between and borrowing from the two major (and much debated) north-to-south eastern and western streams of linguistic and material cultural diffusion and the two major east-to-west paths along which technologies like metallurgy and farming diffused. As discussed in chapter 2, one of these east-to-west paths crossed the central African savannas south of the equatorial forests and the other crossed the lands south of the Zambezi River.[3] The most recent archaeological research now shows that from the middle of the first millennium, communities south of the Zambezi crafted a surprisingly early trade network that connected the western Kalahari to the Indian Ocean. The story told here traces the creation of that network and presents evidence that residents of the central frontier, far to the north, participated in its establishment and its growth. Indeed, residents of the central frontier served as a bridge between the vast trade routes south of the Zambezi and the inventive copper industries emerging in central Africa.

Although it did not boast the industrial centers of contemporary regions in the western Kalahari or the Copperbelt, the central frontier was not an undifferentiated space during the second half of the first millennium. The distribution of evidence for the production and consumption of ivory and copper bangles, two ornaments crafted from products of the bush, reveal networks of trade and communication that crossed linguistic and material cultural boundaries both within and beyond the central frontier. These networks belie the uneven degrees of connectivity and participation sought by inhabitants of different regions within the central frontier. The level of detail we can muster to identify centers of production and trade on the central frontier

matters to specialists. For the general reader, two important points emerge
from the details of the archaeological record. First, the evidence for the production and consumption of common artifacts like ivory and copper bangles
do not overlap. Second, the evidence for working ivory, copper, and smelting iron generally do overlap. In the last centuries of the first millennium,
some sites in the middle Kafue and in the middle Zambezi northwest of the
Victoria Falls shared a common status as centers of manufacture and regional
and long-distance trade while neighboring sites tended to be consumers of the
finished objects, especially bangles, crafted—but generally not consumed—
in regional centers.

Networks within the Central Frontier

Copper and ivory are among the oldest decorative materials that have
survived in the archaeological record of the continent's interior.[4] The relative
rarity of copper is clear from the decorative forms into which it was usually
worked. In some large, wealthy villages, opulent copper necklaces, bangles,
pectorals, beads, chains, and rings adorned the necks and waists and encircled the fingers, arms, and ankles of residents. Such objects were recovered
from the lavish graves and households excavated at Sanga, Mapungubwe, and,
later, at Great Zimbabwe and Ingombe Ilede, dating from the late first millennium and into the middle of the second millennium. The most widely
distributed form of copper adornment on the central frontier in the Early
Iron Age, however, was the wound copper bangle.

In the fourth century, coppersmiths in Naviundu, the earliest known
site of copper smelting in central Africa, crafted the earliest known examples
of wound copper bangles. A few centuries later, smiths fashioned copper bangles at Chondwe in the Copperbelt and Kumadzulo in the Zambezi Valley
upstream of Victoria Falls. This fashion of ornamentation spread fairly rapidly to sites located between these two regional copper-smelting centers. By
the centuries around the turn of the millennium, wound copper bangles were
worn at Twickenham Road near Lusaka; at the mound sites of Kalundu and
perhaps also Isamu Pati on the Batoka Plateau; and at Chundu, Dambwa,
Kamangoza, Tanzala, Simbusenga, and Kabondo Kumbo in the Zambezi
Valley, upstream of Victoria Falls. At Kabondo Kumbo, fragments from at
least twenty wound copper bangles were recovered from trenches spanning the ninth and tenth centuries. This is a surprisingly high number for
the region and may represent a cache for trading rather than the typical con-

sumption habits of the valley's inhabitants. Unfortunately, only the tally and not the context of fragments' recovery was reported.[5] Beyond the central frontier, copper strip bangles were recovered at the turn of the first millennium at Mapungubwe Hill in the Limpopo Valley, at the early Tsodilo Hills site of Divuyu and its successor, Nqoma, and even as far as the Shire Valley in Malawi and the highveld of South Africa, albeit in lower numbers.[6]

Perhaps unsurprisingly, some of the best evidence for copper smithing on the central frontier comes from regions that were also known for smelting, such as the Zambezi Valley and, to a lesser degree, the middle Kafue. Copper probably circulated in a trade form, mostly likely a bar ingot, but these ingots have been recovered from very few sites: a solid copper bar from Naviundu, a fourth-century copper-smelting center, and two additional bars from Kumadzulo, known as a sixth- to seventh-century iron-smelting and smithing center.[7] All three of these bars were partial and showed signs that they were in the process of being reworked into the copper artifacts recovered from the sites. In the Zambezi Valley, the generations of smiths inhabiting a series of successive metalworking sites dating from the late sixth through the twelfth century left behind the best evidence of the production of wound copper bangles. This evidence teaches us that smiths worked portions of trade bars into flat hammered copper ribbons and sheets of hammered foil, portions of which were recovered from Kamangoza and Simbusenga. In the next step in the production process, hammered sheets of copper foil were cut into stocks of thin strips, a few of which were discovered at Kumadzulo, before being wound around fiber cores of palm to create the popular bangles.[8]

Kalala Island and Itezhitezhi in the middle Kafue region were among the only other regional sites to contain worked copper in forms reflecting stages of the wound copper bangle production process, besides, perhaps, Twickenham in the Lusaka area. Here, archaeologists found copper slag, a roll of wound copper wires, and copper in semi-processed wire and strip states. From the late eighth through the ninth century and perhaps into the tenth century, craftsmen in the middle Kafue may have produced wound copper bangles, but local villagers didn't wear them. Only one bangle was recovered from the Middle Iron Age trenches of Kafue sites and neither it nor any other copper objects in the copper collection were made of copper strip. Producers were rarely the consumers of wound copper bangles in the middle Kafue.

Ivory bangles served as a form of personal adornment in the central frontier from as early as the middle of the sixth century and are a fairly common find during excavations. Although the technology used to produce them did not require such consistency, where cross sections are recorded by archaeologists, ivory bangles recovered from the middle of the first millennium through the middle of the second millennium from the Copperbelt to the Zambezi Valley, at sites as dispersed in time and space as Chondwe, Twickenham, Chundu, and Simbusenga, share a common form: a rectangular cross section with a slightly convex exterior surface and slightly rounded edges.[9] This regularity suggests a widespread stylistic convention that crossed the boundaries of material cultural traditions. The only possible exception to this pattern before the mid-second millennium is the slightly more oval cross section of bangles recovered from the Batoka Plateau mound site of Isamu Pati and dated between the eighth and fourteenth centuries, perhaps indicating a localized style and production process or links to a different exchange network than the one that linked the inhabitants of the middle Kafue and middle Zambezi. In the few instances where archaeologists recorded measurements, bangle diameters from the Copperbelt to sites just south of the Zambezi River cluster at intervals with surprising regularity across time and space: 80–85mm, 60–65 mm, and 40–45 mm. Perhaps future research will reveal that, for nearly a millennium, ivory turners crafted bangles not only in a common style, but in a standardized set of sizes across the central frontier. The exception occurs, once again, on the Batoka at the mound site of Isamu Pati. Here, the eight recovered bangles from burial and trenches dating from the eighth to the fourteenth centuries have a much larger diameter of about 114 mm.[10] Although this larger size suggests that the bangles may have been worn as arm bands or anklets, six were recovered from the left forearm of a burial dated to the thirteenth or fourteenth century. This large bangle style would have fit loosely on the wrist, sliding much farther up the arm and falling with a loud clacking sound upon gesticulation or during daily activities like pounding grain.

As was the case with copper bangle manufacturing, sites with evidence of ivory bangle production yield fewer or no finished products of those labors. For example, there were no ivory bangles recovered from the Kafue Middle Iron Age sites of Basanga, Mwanamaipma, Kalala Island, or Itezhitezhi. This is surprising because it corresponds with the era of the Central Botatwe and Kafue speech communities, a period of great innovation in hunting technology. It is the period when mwaalu and isokwe were invented to sustain the argument that hunting, as a form of bushcraft, was a socially valuable enter-

Figure 5.2. Ila ivory turner and lathe in the early twentieth century. Photograph by E. W. Smith. Reprinted from Smith and Dale, *Ila-Speaking Peoples of Northern Rhodesia*, vol. 1, 181.

prise. Yet ivory was worked: ivory fragments were recovered from middle Kafue sites at levels dating from the late eighth through the tenth century.

The fragments from the middle Kafue are meager evidence of ivory working compared to the two large ivory blocks recovered from sites in the Zambezi Valley. The block recovered from the late sixth- to mid-seventh-century site of Kumadzulo had been carved into a rectangle but was not (yet?) worked. Tool marks on the sides of the block speak to its purposeful creation and other ivory fragments evince ivory working. The ivory block recovered from the ninth- and tenth-century site of Kabondo Kumbo was partially worked and its corners had been smoothed. These blocks match those inserted into lathes by Ila ivory turners in the early twentieth century (fig. 5.2).[11] The blocks are rare finds and may have been a trade form of the sort used to craft the elaborately carved pendants and cylinders found in the Upemba Depression.[12] Although ivory bangles were recovered from other sites in the Zambezi Valley, including the late first-millennium site of Chundu and the early second-millennium site of Simbusenga, these sites contained no evidence for ivory working. Rather, the two large blocks were recovered from important sites of iron smelting and iron and copper smithing. Downriver, inhabitants of Ingombe Ilede were keen elephant hunters, for both elephant bones and ivory fragments are abundant in deposits dated from the eighth to the eleventh centuries, periods contemporary with the evidence for ivory working from the middle Kafue and from Kabondo Kumbo in the Zambezi Valley. With pottery sherds that resemble wares produced in the middle Kafue in later centuries, it may be that some communities with ties to the middle Kafue used Ingombe Ilede as a seasonal hunting camp. Indeed, the excavators posit that the village "came into being as a base for elephant hunting."[13] Elephants may have been more abundant in the Zambezi Valley downstream of the falls than upstream of the falls or in the middle Kafue, as early European travelers reported and as the patterns of loaning among mid to late second-millennium terms for professional ivory hunter suggest.[14]

To sum up, copper smithing and ivory turning were not technologies practiced uniformly across the central frontier. The evidence for ivory procurement and ivory working largely overlap with the geography of wound copper bangle manufacture and iron smelting in the middle Kafue and middle Zambezi regions. Kumadzulo was the first regional center for iron smelting and forging, copper smithing, and ivory working, perhaps including the rough, initial processing of tusks into trade blocks. The eighth century marked a transition. Kumadzulo was abandoned, surpassed in the late eighth or early ninth century by the smelters, smiths, and hunters of Kabondo Kumbo, who intensified the processing of ivory and iron ore and the manufacture of copper and ivory bangles. Residents of the middle Kafue also took up iron smelting, copper smithing, and ivory processing from the early eighth century. At this time Ingombe Ilede was first used as an elephant-hunting camp.

Blooms and tusks, semi-processed trade ingots and blocks, and finished copper and ivory bangles were certainly not produced at major industrial centers on the central frontier—the sites show nothing like the quantities of tools, semi-processed materials, or finished artifacts found at contemporaneous larger copper and specularite mining and processing centers like Nqoma or Kansanshi. After all, iron ores and elephant herds were much more widely distributed than copper ores and specularite. Rather, middle Kafue and middle

Zambezi sites were minor, regional centers of production for objects manu-
factured from the products of bushcraft. As they did in the middle Kafue,
smelters, hunters, miners, and perhaps ivory turners and smiths of the middle
Zambezi sites might have understood their labors to be related to each other
and to the bush, although smelting near the Zambezi continued to be undertaken near or in the village. At the very least, the networks circulating copper ingots, ivory blocks, and iron bloom overlapped and intensified on the
central frontier from the eighth century, revealing links between residents of
the middle Kafue and the Zambezi Valley upstream of the falls and a surprising disconnect from sites on the Batoka Plateau. In comparison to the mound
sites of the Batoka Plateau, the patterns of consumption and production shared
by sites in the middle Kafue, the Lusaka and Ingombe Ilede areas, and the
middle Zambezi Valley suggest that between the eighth and the tenth or eleventh centuries, trade and communication were conducted along a route to
the east of the plateau and another route on its western fringe, exactly the pathways of diffusion for the early Soli- and proto-Falls-speaking communities
in the late first millennium. The uneven geographies of ivory and wound copper bangle production and consumption within the central frontier reveal
the different networks to which technicians belonged, both within the central frontier and, as we'll see, well beyond it.

South of the Zambezi

A series of archaeological studies over the last five to ten years have traced
the chemical, mineral, and biological composition of glass beads and pots recovered from sites across southern Africa.[15] These technical studies have
changed how we understand the history of the lands between the Zambezi
and Limpopo Valleys during the first millennium by demonstrating that a surprisingly early and unexpectedly northern trade route linked northwestern
Botswana to the Chobe-Zambezi confluence, Okavango Delta, Makgadikgadi
Pans, and the Indian Ocean coast from as early as the seventh century. This
extensive trade network operated several hundred years before the large,
cattle-rich sites of the eastern Botswana hardveld and influential communities
of the Shashe-Limpopo region dominated the flow of wealth to and from the
Indian Ocean. This new evidence has not yet been incorporated into syntheses of southern African prehistory so it is worth examining it in some detail.
For the purposes of Botatwe history, however, the most significant finding is
the unexpected role within this trade network of communities living in the

lands immediately south of the middle Zambezi River, for societies of the central frontier had historical ties to these communities during the first millennium.

The chronology and geography of the raw materials of bushcraft on the central frontier suggest that residents of the middle Kafue and middle Zambezi traded some of the iron and ivory they produced and some of the copper they secured from the north into this late first-millennium Kalahari-to-coast network. This vast web of exchange may have influenced the timing of innovations in bushcraft in the middle Kafue and the character of the prestige associated with its practitioners, who were best positioned to participate in such trade. Indeed, the collapse of the northern portion of the trade network coincided with the demographic changes undertaken by middle Kafue peoples in the early second millennium, as they expanded their settlements onto the Batoka Plateau. Following the richest vein of evidence for late first millennium trade south of the Zambezi, this story is best begun at a solitary cluster of hills rising out of the Kalahari Sands upstream of the Okavango Delta's fan, about twenty-five miles west of the river's main channel.

In the seventh century, a small community, perhaps with cultural roots in central Angola, founded an entirely new kind of settlement on the cluster of rocky hills, caves, and shelters that constitute the Tsodilo Hills.[16] The inhabitants of the first village, Divuyu, may have been attracted to settle the rather sparse Tsodilo landscape to mine the deposits of specularite found in the rocky hills and long exploited by local stone-tool-using communities. The site also offered a strategic defensive position. Divuyu peoples introduced or perhaps intensified metalworking and brought a new form of pottery. The newcomers attracted a degree of wealth to the Tsodilo region that took the form of iron and copper jewelry. Some Tsodilo residents settled lower down the hill, on the plateau, founding the village Nqoma.

Up to about the tenth century, the Tsodilo villages were diverse places, attracting settlers who crafted pottery from several different traditions, all of which originated to the north or east. An eight-century resident of Nqoma, for example, would have seen her neighbors using one of four different styles of pottery. Divuyu wares were related to the pottery recovered from sites in coastal Angola and Democratic Republic of the Congo. Xaro pottery shared affinities with the complex tradition of Bambata wares common to the Botswana-Zimbabwe border region as early as the last centuries BCE. Matlapaneng ceramics were also used by sorghum farmers living south of the

Okavango Delta between the seventh and ninth centuries and were related to Dambwa-style pottery used in the Victoria Falls region and Northern Zimbabwe sites like Kadzi. A final style of pottery visible to our eighth-century Nqoma denizen was similar to ceramics used at the Chobe-Zambezi confluence between the seventh and eleventh century, ceramics that are related to the pottery crafted by residents of the metalworking atelier of Kumadzulo on the central frontier between the late sixth and mid-seventh centuries. Makers of these discrete pottery styles shared connections to the cultural traditions of the Chobe-Zambezi confluence, central Angola, and the widespread Gokomere tradition of the middle Zambezi south of the river. They were contemporaries at Nqoma for about two hundred years, from the eighth through the ninth centuries. Yet they lived in discreet precincts of the Nqoma Plateau. Their distinct cultural heritages may have been easier to assert, honor, or police because Nqoma residents remained well connected to most of the lands from which their pottery styles originated.

For all the diversity carefully maintained within the ceramic assemblages of Divuyu and Nqoma from the seventh through the ninth centuries, there was no source of clay near the Tsodilo Hills from which to craft these vessels. Residents either imported their pots or imported their clay and fashioned their own pots. Using a method called optical petrography to examine the mineral and biological inclusions in pots' materials, archaeologists can develop signatures of the various fabrics (clay pastes, tempers, slips, and surface finishes) from which excavated pottery sherds were crafted in order to determine the sources of the materials from which a pot was made. From this information, archaeologists can determine whether a pot was crafted on site or made elsewhere and imported. The results of optical petrography map out sections of the transregional networks connecting communities that exchanged raw materials and products fashioned in the interior of the continent. For example, the earliest users of pottery in the Tsodilo Hills crafted their early thin-walled vessels between the third and seventh centuries from clays sourced in the middle Zambezi near the confluence with the Chobe River, about 250 miles to the northeast. In contrast, makers of Xaro wares crafted their pots from clays sourced in the panhandle of the delta, near the site of Xaro. By the eighth century, finished Xaro pots were imported to Nqoma and Divuyu. The thick-walled Divuyu pottery was often crafted of clays sourced from vlei deposits in the sandveld to the west of Tsodilo, perhaps from the Kaudum fossil river valley some sixty miles away. Sherds recovered from Kasane, near the Chobe-Zambezi confluence, and the Nqoma and White Animal Shelter sites at Tsodilo Hills were crafted of a fabric found in similar Gokomere-styled pottery common at Kapula Vlei, about 100 miles southeast of Kasane in northern Zimbabwe. Similarly, on stylistic grounds, archaeologists suggest that from the seventh through the tenth centuries, the inhabitants of Kaitshàa in the Makgadikgadi Pans produced a style of pottery that reflected their cultural affiliations with communities to the northeast that produced a ceramic style called Zhizo. However, early Kaitshàa residents also used ceramics with stylistic features common on the pottery used by residents of Nqoma in the Tsodilo Hills, Matlapaneng on the southern fringe of the Okavango Delta, and Nyungwe on the Chobe River near its confluence with the Zambezi.[17] The multidirectional exchange of raw and finished materials and stylistic elements belie the complexity of first millennium trade networks. These networks expand dramatically when we track objects foreign to the continent.

Imports from the Indian Ocean, including cowrie shells and glass beads were durable stores of value in precolonial Africa. Demand for these ornaments facilitated the exchange of local products across hundreds of miles. Traders living in the port town of Chibuene, located on the Mozambique littoral, dominated early trade between Indian Ocean merchants and southern Africa. Between the seventh and mid-ninth century, Chibuene traders tapped into the trade network that linked Tsodilo, the middle Zambezi, and the Makgadikgadi Pans. They traded a kind of glass bead archaeologists have dubbed "Chibuene" into the interior in exchange for raw materials like skins, horns, metals, perhaps slaves, and especially ivory. Crafted from a sub-type (v-Na 3) of low-alumina plant-ash soda glass with less magnesia and more potash than other plant-ash soda glass, these beads came from the Persian Gulf and may have been exported from a succession of ports that dominated Persian Gulf trade in the late first millennium: Ubulla, Sohar, and Siraf. Chibuene beads were traded into the interior in small numbers and have been recovered from the Makgadikgadi site of Kaitshàa at levels dating to the seventh and eighth centuries and from Nqoma at levels dating to the mid-seventh or eighth centuries. Imported Zhizo series beads replaced Chibuene beads in the early eight century and are found in even higher numbers at Nqoma, Kaitshàa, and many other sites of the interior.[18]

Together, the distribution of glass beads and the clays, tempers, and stylistic features of pottery indicate that by the seventh or eighth century an extensive network of trade spanned over half the continent, connecting the Indian Ocean port of Chibuene to the Tsodilo Hills more than a thousand miles away. The sources of clay used in Divuyu pottery extended the network even farther west. Archaeologists posit that the route ran from Chibuene inland, across the Zimbabwe Plateau toward the Makgadikgadi Pans.[19] From here, most traffic probably followed the Boteti River toward Lake Ngami, the Okavango Delta, and the Tsodilo Hills beyond.

Sources of clays and the stylistic features of pottery remind us that some trade also connected to the middle Zambezi, perhaps moving north from the Zimbabwe Plateau toward Kapula Vlei but certainly connecting sites on the Makgadikgadi Pans, the southern Delta, and in the Tsodilo Hills to lands between the Chobe-Zambezi confluence and Victoria Falls. The trade route connected several distinct environmental zones: the dry sandveld sites of the Tsodilo Hills, the saltpans of the Makgadikgadi region, the eastern Zimbabwe highveld, and the waterveld communities of the Okavango Delta, its panhandle, and middle Zambezi communities stretching from the Chobe confluence to Victoria Falls and northern Zimbabwe.[20] Men and women who traveled segments of this vast network traded for the clay, pottery, and animal skins, horns, and meat of the waterveld. Villagers in the Makgadikgadi region exported ostrich eggshell beads and salt. And from the Tsodilo Hills, men and women demanded ground specularite—a shimmering, glittery cosmetic powder mixed into oil or fat and applied to the body and hair. The Indian Ocean system was but one node in this network; Chibuene and Zhizo glass beads smoothed the unpredictable bottlenecks of excess and scarcity that could hold up the flow of trade. The early dates, the sheer size, and the geography of this first millennium trade route are significant to the early history of southern Africa. This route both predated and bypassed the Shashe-Limpopo region and the hardveld of eastern Botswana, areas that have long been accepted as the incubators of the kinds of long-distance trade that undergirded the wealth and statecraft of southern Africa in the early second millennium.[21]

The first millennium Kalahari-to-coast route was not unchanging. Its reconfiguration at the turn of the millennium is best understood by studying the zenith and collapse of Nqoma. Trade brought unprecedented wealth to residents of Nqoma in the centuries spanning the turn of the millennium. In the early tenth century, the material cultural diversity that had once characterized life on the Tsodilo Hills abruptly vanished. The only pottery crafted at Nqoma and at Matlapaneng in the delta during the peak of Nqoma's wealth and influence in the tenth and eleventh centuries was made from panhandle clays and styled in a fashion similar to pottery from Sioma Mission, a village on the Zambezi River in western Zambia, nearly two hundred miles from Victoria Falls. It is difficult to determine whether the change in pottery at Nqoma and Matlapaneng was a result of one faction of the Nqoma population taking control of the village and emphasizing ties to communities of the middle Zambezi or an influx of people from the central frontier, north of the Zambezi River.

Regardless of their origins, the residents of Nqoma at its zenith during the tenth and eleventh centuries intensified specularite mining. Between the eighth and twelfth centuries, nearly one thousand tons of granite rock were removed from the mines and crushed to extract specularite, which was then pulverized into a usable, tradable powdered form. Nqoma commanded great wealth in cattle and continued to attract Zhizo beads, marine shells, ostrich eggshell beads, and more than twenty-seven hundred copper and iron artifacts, mostly jewelry. Resident smiths probably made at least some of these ornaments by reworking imported iron and copper. Indeed, through the end of the tenth century, residents at Nqoma were the richest in iron and copper jewelry of all the sites in southern Africa.[22] They imported copper from the Kwebe Hills of Namibia and probably more distant mines in eastern Botswana. At least one ornament in the Nqoma collection demonstrates that Nqoma residents were wealthy enough to attract objects from even greater distances: this ornament was fashioned of a high-phosphorous ore such as those found in both the Transvaal lowveld of the South Africa and the ores used to make Early Iron Age artifacts in the Upemba Depression in southern Democratic Republic of the Congo.[23] Visitors would have been dazzled by the ornaments and cosmetics worn by Nqoma residents at the turn of the first millennium, even if some of these objects, such as Zhizo beads and specularite, were also available to the inhabitants of less wealthy villages.

During the tenth and eleventh centuries, at the same time that Nqoma rose to prominence on the trade in specularite, enterprising cattlemen in eastern Botswana, skilled ivory hunters in the Shashe-Limpopo region and beyond, and merchants in the Persian Gulf reconfigured the geography, objects, and volume of trade in southern Africa. These changes had a profound effect on the communities of the interior. In the tenth century, communities living on the hardveld of eastern Botswana at sites like Bosutswe joined the vast trade network to the north of their cattle-rich country. At the same time, they formed regular trade connections with settlements like Schroda to their east, in the Shashe-Limpopo area.[24] From the tenth century, the pottery of residents at Bosutswe on the eastern Botswana hardveld included both specimens with Nqoma styling crafted from middle Zambezi clays and Eiland style pottery from the Limpopo Valley. In fact, the Nqoma-style ceramics were recovered from just one part of the site during a period that was also characterized by the import of water antelope, despite nearby herds of game (Tsodilo residents at Divuyu had also had a taste for water antelope). It seems that traders from Nqoma and the delta lived in their own precinct within the Bosutswe settlement during the tenth and eleventh centuries, and they may have imported their preferred meats during their residence at Bosutswe.

When residents of the Shashe-Limpopo joined the old first millennium trade network in the tenth century, they changed the character of trade with the coast by focusing production on materials—first ivory, and later gold—specifically for export into Indian Ocean networks. By the early second millennium, residents at sites like Mapela, K2, and Mapungubwe dominated trade with Chibuene, cutting off the older northern route. As the geography of trade shifted southward, the terms of trade no longer favored those communities that had built the late first-millennium networks on the exchange of regional products like pots, clay, and specularite, whose circulation was facilitated by Indian Ocean imports, like glass beads.

Changing patterns of trade at the Makgadikgadi site of Kaitshàa exemplify the shifting character and geography of trade in southern Africa in the early second millennium. By the tenth century, Kaitshàa salt had so declined in value relative to the goods in demand among communities in the eastern Botswana hardveld and the Limpopo Valley that Kaitshàa villagers began to export more ivory than salt in order to attract glass beads. In the tenth century, however, Kaitshàa residents were far less successful in their efforts to access glass beads than in the centuries before hardveld and Limpopo communities entered the southern African trade network. Kaitshàa was increasingly cut off from the circuits of wealth as trade began to flow through the Limpopo Valley.

The changing geography of trade reverberated across the Kalahari. By the eleventh century, Toutswe sites on the hardveld sourced specularite from local mines in eastern Botswana, rendering Nqoma redundant. Nqoma went into decline at the beginning of the second millennium, just as communities in eastern Botswana and Zimbabwe, such as Toutswe, Malumba, Mapela,

Mapungubwe, and Zimbwbe Hill began to amass wealth. In the first millennium, the inhabitants of even small commoners' sites in the Makgadikgadi, on the hardveld, and in the Limpopo Valley could amass caches of glass and eggshell beads and ivory bangles; wealth generated by trade in the first millennium was fairly widely distributed. In contrast, the early second millennium trade benefited those who claimed the authority to direct trade, the power to command labor, and the right to keep ornaments of great value; it sustained elites.[25]

Bridging Two Worlds: The Middle Kafue
in Southern African History

The northernmost reach of this first millennium trade network is unknown because mineral, biological, and chemical analysis have not been undertaken on artifacts from sites north of the Zambezi River. We await the kinds of analyses that might trace the origins and movement of clays, glass, ostrich eggshell beads, and ores within and beyond the central frontier. Yet patterns in the geography, chronology, and materials produced north of the Zambezi suggest that from the sixth or seventh century through the tenth century, sites in the middle Zambezi and middle Kafue participated in the trade networks linking the Indian Ocean coastal site of Chibuene, the Tsodilo Hills, the Makgadikgadi Pans, and the Chobe-Zambezi confluence.

The Chobe-Zambezi confluence was one of the most important sources of clays for sites in the Tsodilo and delta regions up to the tenth century, and pots with Chobe-Zambezi clays reached as far as Bosutswe after the tenth century. The Zambian iron-smelting centers of the middle Zambezi—sites whose pottery styles were carried to the Okavango and Tsodilo areas throughout the mid-first millennium—were located about thirty miles from the Chobe-Zambezi confluence. This was the journey of a day or two and included a crossing at Kazungula, one of the few places upstream of the falls where the Zambezi River constricts down to a narrow, easily navigable channel. Sites like Kumadzulo also show surprisingly early evidence of Indian Ocean trade, including perhaps the only known first-millennium glass shard of the interior dating between the mid-fifth and late eight century. Significantly, the inhabitants of Chibuene on the Indian Ocean coast left behind glass shards in high numbers beginning in the late sixth or early seventh century.[26] From the mid-fifth through the late tenth centuries, a succession of sites shifted across the iron-rich dambo margins and river valleys of the middle Zambezi, just northwest of Victoria Falls, as smelters followed the most accessible veins of ore. They smelted quantities of iron but did not have a similarly active forging industry. As discussed above, those sites with active smelters also contained ivory blocks and evidence of copper bangle manufacture. The Zambian middle Zambezi sites likely exported iron bloom, ivory, and perhaps copper bangles and salt to lands south of the river, but they sourced some of those goods from communities to their north.

Residents of the middle Kafue, some 100 to 120 miles directly north of middle Zambezi sites also smelted iron throughout the Middle Iron Age, though in smaller quantities. Middle Kafue sites share the ivory and copper production patterns of the most active middle Zambezi sites: Kumadzulo from the mid-fifth through the late eighth centuries and Kabondo Kumbo from the late eight to the late tenth centuries. Middle Kafue residents exported high-quality Basanga salt, ivory, and perhaps hides, bushmeat, and copper. The residents of the middle Kafue were in communication with sites to the north; copper bars and ornaments crafted in the Copperbelt may have passed through middle Kafue communities on their way into the Zambezi Valley and sometimes even farther south, to Nqoma.

Middle Kafue hunters may also have produced dried or smoked water antelope segments that were in high demand at Divuyu from the mid-seventh through the eight century and at Bosutswe between the eleventh and mid-twelfth centuries. Although residents of those locations could have sourced water antelope closer to their homes, the demand from Bosutswe, for example, overlaps with the dates during which Kafue hunters innovated new names for water antelope like lechwe and sitatunga, many of which were borrowed from speakers of Kusi languages to the south of the middle Kafue. If middle Kafue hunters were not provisioning sites so far to the south, the scattered evidence for interest in these species among inhabitants of the sandveld, hardveld, and middle Kafue may attest to a common culinary culture. This is also the period when Kafue speakers, uniquely among their neighbors, applied feminine prefixes to preferred antelope species, reminding us that even if water antelope was valued more broadly by communities linked through trade, any such high-status items were also reinterpreted in local contexts.

Middle Kafue products may not always have reached trade networks south of the Zambezi. When they did, they likely passed through sites in the middle Zambezi region and on to the Kazungula gateway, from which point they could continue south to the Makgadikgadi or west to the

Chobe-Zimbabwe confluence. In return for their exports, middle Kafue men and women were able to secure ostrich eggshell and glass beads and perhaps specularite.[27]

The timing of changing patterns of trade among villages north of the Zambezi further supports their connection to trade networks south of the river. When communities in the Shashe-Limpopo and eastern Botswana hardveld took control of trade to the coast in the early second millennium, the reverberations were felt as far north as the middle Kafue. For example, men and women living north of the Zambezi River were no longer able to access ostrich eggshell beads from about the twelfth century. Around the same time, ostrich eggshell beads were no longer imported by residents of Eastern Botswana and the village of Nqoma rapidly declined in status from a center to a backwater, marking the collapse of the northern and western portions of the old first-millennium trade network.[28] Although elephants had long been hunted in the region, in the eighth century, around the time that Central Eastern Botatwe speakers developed words to talk about the prestige and value of hunting and bushcraft, hunters began to processing tusks in the middle Kafue, at Ingombe Ilede, and in the middle Zambezi ivory in greater quantities and in forms that may have been for trade. But evidence for ivory hunting and processing ends abruptly in the tenth century in all three regions north of the Zambezi, corresponding to the time when Kaitshàa began to produce ivory to supplement or replace its salt trade and the period when hunters at Schroda developed an ivory industry that served as a closer source of ivory to merchants at Chibuene and offered a volume of production aimed specifically at coastal trade.

Practitioners of bushcraft in the middle Kafue undoubtedly produced materials with local meanings to meet local demands. Yet Central Eastern Botatwe speakers developed new ideas about the power of the bush and celebrated the achievements of those who practiced their technologies in its embrace within a wider regional context. Between the eighth and tenth centuries, products of the bush—ivory, skins, meat, bloom, perhaps honey and dried fish—could be converted into glass and eggshell beads and perhaps specularite when middle Kafue hunters and smelters exchanged them into southern trade networks. A few centuries later, in the early second millennium, Kafue speakers expanded their settlements beyond the middle Kafue at a time when lands to the south of the Zambezi Valley were losing easy ac-

cess to Indian Ocean trade. As they sought their fortunes beyond the middle
Kafue, families may have looked for new trade networks. Or perhaps they
saw in the growing cattle herds of the Batoka a new opportunity to amass
wealth and sustain social ties, for herds grew rapidly after the first few centuries of the second millennium, when Botatwe languages had come to dominate the plateau. There were undoubtedly many reasons for the expansion
of Kafue speech beyond the middle Kafue. As they shifted settlements and
incorporated non-Kafue speakers into their villages, Kafue speakers democ-
ratized hunting through chila communal hunts, applying skills once mustered
to build individual reputations and access novel imports to the local problems
of social integration and, perhaps, demonstrations of military power. The late
first millennium was not the last time Botatwe speakers participated in long-
distance trade. Nor did the celebrity of technicians of the bush disappear. To
understand the persistence of this celebrity, we turn to stories of the status of
copper smelters and hunters in central Africa, to the north of Botatwe lands.

Looking North

The extensive trade network linking the middle Kafue to the middle Zambezi, Tsodilo Hills, Okavango Delta and panhandle, Makgadikgadi Pans and
the Indian Ocean during the last few centuries of the first millennium offered
a measure of material wealth to skilled hunters and metallurgists trying to
convince neighbors that the work they did was unique in the subsistence landscape of the middle Kafue. But hunters and even metallurgists relied on partners in the far northwest, north, and northeast—inhabitants of the northern
miombo savannas—for the copper bloom, tools, technical know-how, and
even the language they used to lay claim to the status of masterful huntsmen
and metalworkers. The evidence for connections between the central frontier and the northern miombo is different from evidence for links to southern
trade routes. Although we await the level of detail that archaeologists have
reconstructed for the movement of clays, stylistic motifs, pottery, and glass,
shell, and metal ornaments available in southern Africa, shared vocabulary
and enigmatic patterns in the material cultural record of central Africa reveal a regional culture that valued achieved status, exchanges among networks
of friends and technicians, and knowledge of the bush as a measure of men's
maturity. Aspects of this culture were shared widely across central Africa in

the centuries around the turn of the millennium. Centuries later these cultural ideals shaped the practice of power in the polities crafted by Luba, Lunda, and related savanna societies in the mid to late second millennium.

Glimmers of Contact and Prestige across the Land of Copper

Just as communities living south of the Zambezi slowly extended the geographic range of networks of trade and aesthetics during the last half of the first millennium, so, too, did the inhabitants of the central African savannas. Networks of communication and shared aesthetics can be traced, for example, in the adoption of the intricate guilloche designs that decorated first millennium pottery recovered from the early copper-smelting center of Kansanshi in Northwestern Province, Zambia. The story of the rise and fall of guilloche wares encapsulates an important trend in central African history in the centuries spanning the late first and early second millennium. The history of this stunning pottery illuminates a brief moment in the late first millennium when technicians of the bush—in this case, copper smelters—enjoyed both widespread prestige and great autonomy. Significantly, this period overlaps with the prestige and fame of metallurgists among Central Eastern Botatwe speakers living almost three hundred miles to the south, who adopted at this time the status named *-vʊbɪ [74]. The prestige of copper smelters using guilloche pottery was part of a wider social experiment in central African history in which intermediate statuses associated with the prestige of bushcraft existed independent from other, more formalized institutions of authority. But this was a brief moment, as the elimination of guilloche pottery from copper-smelting sites demonstrates. From the early second millennium, the prestige of bushcraft was incorporated into the political aspirations of elites across much of central Africa. Botatwe communities stand out as an exception.

Guilloche is a difficult style to produce, involving a complex pattern of carefully interlaced lines. The design was first used by potters in Kansanshi in the early seventh century as one among many decorative motifs applied to pottery. Some hundred miles to the east, villagers living in the Luano area near Chingola in Copperbelt Province, Zambia, also kept pottery decorated with guilloche designs among their many Early Iron Age pottery styles. Luano dates between the fourth and eighth centuries, but pots decorated with guilloche designs were not evenly distributed across the site and probably date to the seventh or eighth centuries. Guilloche pottery was kept in a "spatially limited" cluster and at least one of these guilloche pots was created from clays sourced back in the Kansanshi area, about one hundred miles to the west. As archaeologist Michael Bisson suggests, this cache of guilloche ware "may have been produced by an immigrant potter."[29] The contexts in which Kansanshi residents used guilloche wares teach us much more about the possible significance of the cache of guilloche wares recovered at Luano.

By the ninth century, the guilloche design dominated the Kansanshi ceramic collection, "a degree of specialization in design that is very unusual in the Zambian EIA."[30] The potters who crafted these ninth-century pots drew up thinner walls with the guilloche wares than they or their predecessors had done in sculpting the sides of the other Early Iron Age ceramics used by Kansanshi residents. They tempered the clay with a large amount of mica so that the dark pots would sparkle and shine in the sunlight. The complex guilloche design on recovered sherds exhibited surprising uniformity: potters impressed the guilloche design with bangles—perhaps of brilliant copper?— as well as other tools, and they did so with great and very deliberate care. Significantly, the ninth-century guilloche pottery was not recovered from village sites. Rather, it was found in association with copper-smelting furnaces, suggesting that it might have served as a specialized ware for copper workers.[31] This singular pottery began to dominate the ceramic assemblage of the Kansanshi area, marking the prestige of metallurgists at the same time that smelts in the Kansanshi area were moved beyond village confines, into the bush. As copper smelters began to build their furnaces in the bush, they carried with them to the sites of their smelts the graceful, sparkling guilloche wares in preparation, perhaps, to feed the hungry work of goading the furnace flames or to celebrate the conclusion of a successful smelt.

The prestige of this design traveled quickly, far to the west of Kansanshi in the same century. Inhabitants of the upper Zambezi, nearly three hundred miles west, attempted to render in rock engravings in the ninth century the prestigious guilloche pattern that had become the signature design of Kansanshi copper smelters. Trade in copper objects was already well established between the wealthy Upemba communities to the north and copper regions like Kansanshi in the ninth century. A western branch of this trade grew, following the trail of guilloche designs westward, reaching the communities of the upper Zambezi, Lwena, Kasai, and Kwilu Rivers after the turn of the millennium.[32] But by this time the glittery guilloche wares had been eclipsed by Late Iron Age (LIA) Luano pottery back in the Copperbelt.

The cache of ceramics at Luano predates the emergence of guilloche as a symbol of Kansanshi smelters in the ninth century. After the eighth century, the guilloche design was eliminated from the repertoire of potters and consumers of Luano ceramics. Perhaps this elimination at Luano was a rejection of the symbols of competing smelters at Kansanshi. By the early second millennium, demand for copper increased significantly, as elites in the Upemba Depression amassed caches of copper ornaments and emblems of great prestige and power. In the early second millennium, Luano, Kansanshi, and Kipushi, at the headwaters of the Kafue River, formed a triangle of important copper-working centers, with Kipushi at the northern tip. From the twelfth century, the pottery at Kansanshi, over one hundred miles west of Luano, and at Kipushi, about seventy miles northwest of Luano, was replaced by a contemporary pottery originating at Luano; this was "a full-scale expansion of Copperbelt potting practices into part of Northwestern Province, replacing the indigenous tradition." Although a very few sherds with guilloche decoration (less than 1 percent) were recovered from Kansanshi and Kipushi in levels dating from the twelfth century, the hegemonic status of Luano style ceramics was firmly in place, perhaps representing the control of Kansanshi and Kipushi mines and smelts by the leaders of Luano communities.

The brief glimmer of prestige materialized in guilloche wares had intrigued earlier generations of Luano residents and, once associated with copper smelts undertaken in the bush, had caught the eye residents as far away as the upper Zambezi in the ninth century. By the turn of the millennium, however, this glimmer was extinguished by the shadow of the expanding LIA Luano tradition, which belonged to a community that probably grew powerful by meeting a demand for copper ornaments emanating from the Upemba region, a demand that only increased between the eleventh and eighteenth centuries. The role of this brief story in illuminating the culture of prestige developed around copper smelters working in the bush in the last few centuries of the first millennium becomes clearer when set alongside the history of hunting and of the associations, guilds, and statuses developed by west central Africans in the same period.

Iterations of Huntsmanship and Leadership in Central Africa

Communities speaking languages of the Eastern and Kwilu blocks of the Njila branch of Bantu languages lived in those lands where the upper Kwilu, Kasai, and Lulua Rivers met the upper reaches of the Zambezi watershed.

The history of these communities has already been told in breathtaking detail by Jan Vansina, but the story of Botatwe bushcraft foregrounds a different narrative strand in the development of the collective governance so carefully chronicled by Vansina.[33] In the mid to late first millennium, Vansina teaches us, communities in this region organized themselves into vicinages that developed from the way family-based villages aggregated on the better agricultural soils along rivers, creating neighborhoods in the valleys that cut through the landscape. If the demands of cereal agriculture concentrated settlement into river valleys, swidden agriculture on the poor Kalahari Sands soils of this region also required great mobility. Families had to relocate every few years as soils were depleted. Although all forms of food collection were important to local subsistence, hunting was particularly prized: "All the men would have been expected to be thoroughly familiar with what the bush had to offer and they were all hunters to some degree. But only some became professional hunters." Such professionals were named by two roots, *-yanga and *-binda, whose phonology and distribution betray great antiquity. On the basis of comparative ethnography and the observations of early travelers, Vansina suggests that professional hunters enjoyed high status and practiced their craft year-round, forming associations to initiate apprentices who had mastered the supernatural forces that could affect the hunt. Professional hunters were considered by their communities to be "creatures of legendary skill and the most illustrious of men."[34]

In the late first millennium, perhaps in the eighth or ninth century, Eastern Njila and Kwilu communities built upon the local social institutions of family-based villages aggregated into riverside vicinages and professional hunters' associations. They developed matrilineages and established the lineage's men and their households as the ideal residential group. Such residential clusters of male matrikin were crosscut by vicinage-wide sodalities organized by age and gender. These sodalities administered rites of passage, such as funerals and initiations into new age and gender based statuses. Their elaborate training regimens, masked dances, and public displays fostered a sense of cohort, particularly among men who were members of different residential areas and matrilineages. Sodalities' impact on the social mechanisms of belonging eventually resulted in a system of age sets and vicinage representatives, *mwene*, that further fostered the sense of cohesiveness within the neighborhood. Matriclans connected members across vicinages, ensuring their safety and support beyond the vicinage.

Vansina argues that the risks of cereal agriculture inspired sodalities to put bushcraft at the center of the education of young girls and boys. Perhaps earlier associations of professional hunters served as a model for the age and gender-based sodalities developed in the eighth or ninth century. Be that as it may, bushcraft remained central to men's performances of successful adulthood, performances that included hunting and, especially, initiation into professional hunters' associations. Bushcraft was an enduring path to status for men in west central Africa from before the eighth century, just as it was for their Botatwe-speaking contemporaries living in the middle Kafue region and aspiring to the status of *-pàdó [68] by adopting new tools and improving their hunting practice, *-wèz- [63].

Between the end of the first millennium and the middle of the second, Njila speakers living near the confluence of the Kasai and Lweta Rivers—the linguistic forebears of Lweta and Ruund speakers—dramatically changed the inherited system of governance organized into matrilineages, vicinages, and sodalities. They reconfigured the relationship among residential matrilineages to form House-like villages led by *kalamba*, Big Men, and they bundled villages into named and sloganed vicinages ruled collectively by members of the premier rank of the male sodality, *ngongo munene*. While any man could join the lowest ranks of ngongo munene, initiation into higher ranks required membership in one of the founding matrilineages of the vicinage, approval of other members of the rank, and the wealth to pay exorbitant initiation fees. As they, themselves, must have argued, the highest-ranking members of ngongo munene, *mutúmbú*, were in the best position to assure the well-being of the community because they claimed ties to the ancestral and territorial spirits governing fertility and had the wealth and means to protect dependents. Mutúmbú collected fees and fines assessed by the association and leveraged such wealth to pay for the care of neighbors and followers. They also mustered young men of the lowest ranks, who served as warriors. This oligarchy may have controlled local decision making and undoubtedly conferred great status on its members, but its authority and prestige was highly localized. As contemporaneous Botatwe politics suggests, other identities offered decidedly wider influence.

The hunters' association in the Kasai-Lweta area was known by the old name *-yanga. *Buyanga* connected hunters on the basis of their talent, creating networks that extended far beyond the authority of the ruling ranks of a particular vicinage's ngongo munene. Viewed through the lens of what we know of Botatwe bushcraft, the aspirational, knowledge-based component of buyanga comes into full relief. In the twentieth century, the root -yanga carried many additional meanings in northeastern Njila languages: "to chase, to pursue," "specialized hunter with a charm," and, significantly, "to be expert." Although the terms are different, the knowledge, skill, and training associated with -yanga mirrors the meanings of *-pàdó and *-wèz-. In fact, an attestation of *-pàdó from Ruund, a language belonging to the family of languages whose story we are considering, was glossed as "ability, gift, talent" and bears witness to the participation of communities of the Kasai-Lweta area in the exchange of ideas that gave rise to the adoption of *-pàdó by Central Eastern Botatwe speakers in the eighth century.[35] Villagers in this area may well have shared the older ideas about power, virility, and productivity that undergirded Central Eastern Botatwe and Kafue communities' understanding of bushcraft. Just as villagers in the middle Kafue debated the meaning of hunters' status and the significance of what they did in the bush, families of the Kasai-Lweta region also hoped that their sons would become great hunters, even if they were cut off from the highest ranks of ngongo munene.

Buyanga was an older source of status that stood outside of but could compete with or compliment the prestige and perhaps even the authority of ngongo munene. Vansina glosses the sodality's name, ngongo munene, as "great territory," but a footnote elaborates on the range of meanings that the noun ngongo carried in Eastern Njila languages and Kimbundu: "suffering, danger, world," "woods," "rough bush shelter," "initiation," "large deserted stretch of land," "place of terror or fear," "wild beast," and "land without chiefs." As Vansina concludes, "the whole title means either 'wilderness' or . . . 'land without chiefs.'" In other words, "ngongo" was to these communities of eastern Njila speakers similar to the concepts invoked in Central Eastern Botatwe and Kafue speakers' use of the term *-sókwe [75]. When Eastern Njila men invented a sodality with lower ranks open to all men but higher ranks accessible only to wealthy men of established lineages and then named that sodality "ngongo munene," they were claiming that their members had mastered the "great wilderness." Ngongo places were the kinds of uninhabited lands devoid of chiefs and, a mutúmbú might have wryly observed, overrun with members of buyanga. The highest-ranking members of ngongo munene asserted their status as the best representatives of the vicinage and most qualified guarantors of the fertility of the people and of the land using a very old measure of standing: their claims rested on being the best of those who could successfully control the bush. They claimed the virility and status such accomplishment had conferred to men in central Africa since the last centuries of the first millennium. To the ears of professional hunters, this claim may well have sounded like an assertion of control over those who worked within ngongo lands. The role of mutúmbú in organizing collective hunts would suggest just such an appropriation of bushcraft, although some mutúmbú may have also been members of buyanga.

Mixing claims to authority on the basis of mastery of the bush with claims tied to wealth and lineage produced an uncomfortable tension. Just as speakers of Botatwe languages layered meanings onto the words they used to talk about skilled technicians of the bush, savanna leaders would again and again confront the challenge of incorporating the practitioners of bushcraft—hunters, smelters and sometimes smiths—into the coalitions and governments they sought to build. In some cases, leaders attempted to lay claim to the status such figures enjoyed. Leaders managed this tension differently across the northern miombo savannas, sometimes using the same vocabulary and often using shared metaphors.[36] They learned from each other's successes, leaving behind a meshwork of borrowed stories of foreign hunters founding kingdoms, shared titles for metallurgist-councilors, and emblems and rites of royal investiture that have captivated generations of observers who recorded this rich tapestry in the patterns studding *lusaka* memory boards and the words filling academic books. The precolonial savanna stories we know best developed from a common culture that stretched from the upper Kwilu to the Upemba Depression and as far south as the middle Kafue as early as the eighth century.

Middling Figures: The Middle Kafue in Central African History

Central Eastern Botatwe and Kafue speakers borrowed some of the most transformative words in the lexicon of bushcraft through conversations they had with speakers of Bantu languages living in the northern miombo savannas. In the last centuries of the first millennium and partly on the basis of the way communities of the north used the same words, Central Eastern Botatwe speakers developed their own understanding that the skills of *-pàdó and *-vʊbɪ were worthy of fame and celebration and that efforts known as *-wèz- required deep knowledge, even cunning, and were saturated with social potential. Later, Kafue hunters learned the technology of *-kìdà from speakers of Bantu languages of central Africa, but Kafue hunters adapted the technology and the word to incorporate neighbors and newcomers into their communal hunts, *cìlà [87], as they created new kinds of blended communities beyond the middle Kafue. The distribution and meanings of such words teach us that Central Eastern Botatwe, Luban, Eastern Njila, Sabi, and other communities of the south central African savannas crafted the culture of bushcraft in conversations across networks of great huntsmen.[37]

Hunters brought home to their own villages foreign ideas and technologies that were integrated into the local practice of bushcraft and local structures of authority, creating a tapestry of variations on common cultural themes. In the earliest period, from the seventh or eighth century through the tenth or eleventh century, the men who cultivated the knowledge and wealth that underpinned the culture of bushcraft and the wives, parents, dependents, and peers who celebrated their achievements created a viable pathway to wealth and status that seems to have stood out as an alternative to forms of social influence vested in the authority of family leaders, elders, and ritual specialists. In other words, they created a social middle, a middle that likely included many other sorts of persons who did not work in the bush but were, nevertheless, welcomed and celebrated for a skill or perhaps for a singular achievement.

This moment of an emerging social middle is exemplified in the burials of intermediate wealth uncovered in the Classic Kisalian necropolis at Sanga and dated to the tenth, eleventh, and twelfth centuries. Taken together, the efflorescence of sodalities among eastern Njila communities in the eighth and ninth centuries, the middling status of many of the Classical Kisalian burials between the tenth and twelfth centuries, the welcoming of potters who had mastered the guilloche style associated with smelters working in the bush, the careful attempts to mimic that prestigious guilloche design by distant communities in the eighth and ninth centuries, and, finally, the celebrity but lack of formal authority granted practitioners of bushcraft among middle Kafue communities from the eighth century all suggest that in its earliest form, practitioners of bushcraft enjoyed an intermediate status. The status crafted by technicians of the bush in the south central African savannas rarely persisted into the early second millennium independent of the aspirations of other kinds of leaders; the social middle was an unstable innovation. The glimmering guilloche vessels of Kansanshi were extinguished in the twelfth century by the dull wares of Luano potters extending the reach of their smelting culture across the copperlands. Burials of intermediate wealth disappear from Sanga by the thirteenth century. In the early centuries of the second millennium, members of buyanga suffered outrageous claims of mastery over the bush from men in the highest ranks of ngongo munene. In the Kafue, however, *-pàdó and *-vʊbi continued to exist alongside older statuses like *-ámí [58], even as new statuses were adopted in the late second millennium and the meanings of *-pàdó and *-vʊbi were broadened to accommodate developments in the subsistence economy.

Interlude: Networks and Aspirational Technologies of the Savanna

How did the inhabitants of the central frontier and beyond move objects and ideas between such far-flung places as they crafted a unique status built on their distant connections? As early as the middle of the first millennium, but certainly by the eighth century, south central Africans reconfigured relationships of space and cultures of mobility in the context of increasing sedentism. Counterintuitively, increasingly sedentary people and more permanent villages inspired rather than diminished modes of connectivity. The degree of human mobility is particularly clear in the rate of language change. Rather than languages growing more static and conservative, this period was the most dynamic in Botatwe language history: a series of three protolanguages emerged and diverged over the course of seven or eight centuries, about every two hundred years, or every six to seven generations. This astounding level of linguistic innovation speaks to the numbers of Botatwe speakers in contact and on the move within the central frontier as well as the degree to which knowing about and being able to speak in the terms of worlds beyond one's settlement was valued from the sixth to the mid-thirteenth century. Importantly, this linguistic dynamism stands in stark contrast to the significant linguistic stability that characterized Botatwe speech communities after the mid-thirteenth century, when increasing numbers of foreign objects and copper currencies partly replaced the social relationships like mukowa and mulongo that had once sustained contact and exchange.

Just as increasing sendentism supported cereal agriculture and created the conditions for new conceptualizations of the landscape, including isokwe, it also created the conditions for new forms of seasonal mobility. Seasonal travel linked the products and producers laboring in more permanent villages, industrial centers, and the spaces in between. Kafue speakers invented new kinds of relationships like mulongo and mukowa to expand the social networks undergirding mobility, learning, and exchange. As cereals came to supply the bulk of the diet in the second half of the first millennium, farmers enjoyed a season dedicated to travel and the pursuits that might sustain seasonal journeys. Perhaps it is no surprise that modern Botatwe languages apply the old verb for walking, *kuenda*, to the economic and social activities obscured by the English gloss "to trade." In the last centuries of the precolonial period, Tonga-speaking men and women would travel and visit, journeying up to three hundred miles in the dry season, seeking out products that were rare in their home settlements or that catered to the sensibilities of consumers, particularly with respect to the different tastes of products like salt.[38] Seasonal production, journeying, exchanging, and socializing had long sustained one another.

The social networks undergirding mobility, learning, and exchange between the mid-eighth and mid-thirteenth centuries took two forms. Products moved slowly and indirectly from village to village through relay, exchanged from one person to the next along networks connecting neighbors, extended family, and friends.[39] This kind of indirect trade balanced the uneven distribution of natural resources and skill, but it probably differed in volume and frequency according to the products exchanged, particularly when the products traded were produced seasonally. The graduated distribution of some objects, such as the decreasing frequency of ostrich eggshells on the central frontier beyond sites in the middle Kafue and Zambezi Valley, illustrate the village-to-village character of most trade beyond such better-connected places. In addition to the indirect relay networks that connected villages, more exclusive networks of technicians linked sites across greater distances. Technicians of the bush serve as an example of this kind of network and reveal the local and transregional stakes of belonging to them.

In general, labors in the bush in the Botatwe-speaking areas were likely seasonal and fairly local affairs because these technicians were also farmers. But *-pàdó and *-vʊbi may have traveled during the dry season to visit or apprentice for a span of weeks or months with fellow technicians who lived hundreds of miles away.[40] What can we know of the character of connections between such technicians? It is unlikely that individual hunters or smelters traveled the entirety of the great distances that were linked by common words, tools, and techniques in the centuries surrounding the turn of the millennium. Guilds and professional associations, which developed in many parts of the savanna, did not exist in Botatwe-speaking areas until the eighteenth or nineteenth century. Rather, technicians were connected to one another by disjointed and uneven circuits of objects and knowledge that were linked in patchwork fashion across a vast region by the seasonal travel of hunters and metalworkers along small portions of the larger network. This form of association and belonging was as much born of mutual knowledge of others as it was of direct acquaintance, whether those others were known by reputation or formed part of an undifferentiated group of members understood to share certain talents and sensibilities.[41]

The various communities to which celebrated technicians belonged existed simultaneously on two different but interrelated geographic scales: the local and the more remote but terribly significant wider savanna world. We learned in the last two chapters how and why Botatwe hunters and metallurgists were honored as *-pàdó and *-vʊbi when they brought home the products of their labors in the bush. Yet these skilled technicians became teachers, peers, and learners in relation to other members of the regional networks of technicians that connected people with shared interests and skills. Colleen Kriger has traced out the material and intellectual underpinnings of the relationships binding distant west central African smiths to each other through common cultures of technology and technique, form and fashion in the nineteenth century.[42] As a rejoinder to symbolic scholarly approaches to central African metallurgists that remove them from history, Kriger's study insists that smiths were first and foremost involved in a historically contingent form of *work* and that the many ritual aspects of metallurgists' labors were among the kinds of practical knowledge developed and exchanged along the circuits connecting technicians. This is undoubtedly true, but shared ideas about parallel domains of work, such as hunting and smelting in the bush, also drew on common ideas about how the world worked and could be worked upon. This shared cosmology has drawn the attention of scholars interested in the contribution of symbols to our understanding of the dynamics of power in central Africa.[43] Uniting anthropologists' interests in how symbols and metaphors of violence, uncertainty, and antisocial activities shaped the character and balance of power with the social historian's interest in the material conditions and labor relations connecting people to one another in specific historical contexts is the equally contingent affective domain, from which Kriger titled her book, *Pride of Men*.

Skilled practitioners of bushcraft living on the central frontier and their counterparts living beyond its boundaries shared a transregional affective culture connecting technological innovation to social striving, with both local and transregional consequences. Word histories from the Botatwe languages teach us that technicians practicing bushcraft across the southern savannas shared a common interest in and knack for directing the powers associated with the bush and fickle spirits in order to transform the fearsome violence of the hunter's craft and the uncertainties of the smelter's actions into creative, socially productive acts. Hunters, smelters, honey hunters, and fishers sharing the affective vocabulary of bushcraft understood their efforts in the bush to be a difficult, uncertain, but possible pathway to the kind of wealth and status that could attract dependents, storytellers, lovers, and ancestors' support, a mutually reinforcing cycle of obligation and admiration that might secure one's future as an ancestor spirit. These technicians were bound together as much by a cultivated worldliness and the common sensibility of trying to do something extraordinary, something worthy of fame, as they were by the raw materials, finished products, and the novel tools, rituals, and social technologies that passed between them. The aspirational nature of technologists' networks was captured when Central Eastern Botatwe speakers developed a new word, *-wèz-, for hunting, honey collection, and fishing that derived from an old root for trying to do something. The affective dimensions of bushcraft were asserted in the invention of words like *-pàdó and *-vʊbi that honored celebrated technicians on the basis of their unique skill and knowledge. Similarly, speakers of Luban languages used an ancient word for fishhook—the tool of the solitary angler—to craft a new way to name a "hero."[44] Perhaps the best evidence for the aspirational, celebratory character of bushcraft was its appropriation into the practice of power when ambitious central African leaders crafted new forms of governance, from mutúmbú oligarchs to kings whose veins contained precious *bulopwe*, Luba royal blood.

Foreign ideas and objects were given meaning in local contexts, but those who could perform the kinds of work that linked them to distant people and places also "lived" on those transregional geographic scales. To be a practitioner of bushcraft was to belong to an infamous network that called into being prestige and fame with important local repercussions. But belonging to this dispersed transregional community of skilled, celebrated technicians and innovative strivers did not ensure equal kinds of participation. The fact that many of the central words in the Botatwe lexicon of bushcraft were borrowed suggests that Botatwe speakers did not invent such technologies as often as they extended the geographic reach of new tools, techniques, and statuses. Yet all members benefited when technical achievement and virtuosity increased as the size of the network itself grew. Belonging conferred social status in part through the sheer scale of the network and its reach into places beyond the ken of kinsmen and neighbors. Objects, technologies, and relationships rooted in knowledge about the bush were one pool from which to access the linguistic, material, and intellectual proof of one's belonging to worlds greater than the central frontier. They were means to call forth the collective experience of aspiration that constituted belonging to worlds beyond as much as symbols and objects for local performances consumed by others in the here and now.

Hinterlands and Borderlands: The Changing Periphery of the Central Frontier

The integration of the northern and southern cultural and economic zones around the fourteenth century is usually told as a story of the expansion of trade between major political and industrial centers like Sanga and Great Zimbabwe that were linked by entrepôts like the fourteenth- and fifteenth-century reoccupation of Ingombe Ilede. Yet the evidence described in the first half of this chapter demonstrates that the central frontier had served as a bridge indirectly linking communities like Sanga and Nqoma centuries earlier. Enigmatic objects like the Nqoma copper object with a chemical signature indicating origins in the Katanga region of the Democratic Republic of the Congo and the ostrich eggshell beads at Sanga passed through the central frontier.[45] Thus, what was new from the fourteenth century was not the distance covered by the trade networks but, rather, the increasing frequency and volume of long-distance trade within the interior and between the interior and the coast.

The growth of trade was fueled by demand for ivory, slaves, and metals like gold and copper in the Indian Ocean—demand that gave rise to new coastal trading towns like Kilwa—and by the invention of copper currencies used in the interior of the continent (fig. 5.3). If social ties like mulongo and mukowa had smoothed settlement and trade within and beyond the central frontier before the fourteenth century, the invention and standardized of copper currencies in the early fourteenth century facilitated a rapid expansion of trade that tied the economies of central and southern Africa together. Currencies could flow between people without the social ties that supported delayed gifting between mulongo and within mukowa. Currencies kept products

Figure 5.3. Copper currency from Katanga. Photograph by and
courtesy of Sean de Luna. Permission to photograph the objects
courtesy of the National Numismatic Collection, National Museum
of American History, Smithsonian Institution.

and, to a lesser degree, people on the move, increasing the frequency of exchanges, the kinds and quantities of products circulated, and the distances
those products might travel. There is good reason, then, that scholars have
pointed to the development of copper currencies linking the distant centers of
the Upemba with those of the Zimbabwe Plateau as among the most important evidence of the integration of the once far more discrete zones of the
central African savannas and the southern African velds.[46]

Smiths, political elites, and traders used currencies to facilitate the movement of other kinds of objects. Archaeologists and historians have traced the
distribution of emblems of political power, like ceremonial axes and clapper-
less gongs, and objects of personal adornment, like gold beads, *impande* shells,
and drawn wire copper bangles, to argue for the significance of trade to the
creation of social stratification and political ideologies supporting the ideal
of centralized power.[47] Of course, the practice of power did not always con-
centrate instrumental control over trade, production, or even matters of great
ritual and jural consequence into the hands of an individual or a small group
of people. Nevertheless, the lands stretching between the Inner Congo basin
and the Limpopo River valley are known for the diverse outcomes of experimentation in political scale, particularly since the fourteenth century. The
most famous results of these experiments include the hierarchies of stone

enclosures dotting the gold-rich farming and cattle lands of the Shashe-Limpopo and the central Zimbabwean plateau. Their many successor states, such as the Mutapa, Torwa, and Rozvi-Changamire states, further elaborated on the centralization of power first attempted on the stone-walled and terraced hilltops to the south. We know well traditions celebrating the oft-ephemeral ties linking outposts of the Luba-Lunda world to the "divine" king at their centers and chronicling the sometimes uncomfortable relations between the chieftaincies and cults of east central Africa. Leaders concentrated power on the Zambezi floodplain both before and after the arrival of military upstarts fleeing the collapse of pastoralism on the southern African highveld. Likewise nineteenth-century traders and warlords provisioning ivory and slave caravans established small predatory states across central and southern Africa.

The story of the central frontier complicates the familiar narrative of increasing scales of trade and political complexity from the fourteenth century. We have come a long way from the idea that states and trade developed in lockstep. Yet even as we draw on new models like heterarchy to explain the development of political complexity, the early histories of central and southern Africa are disproportionately tied to the story of statecraft at centers like Great Zimbabwe, Dhlodhlo, and Upemba Depression, to name a few. The increasing volume and frequency of long-distance trade after the fourteenth century brought political opportunities, to be sure, but it did so in uneven ways. Residents of the central frontier who participated in long-distance trade, provisioning raw materials like gold, ivory, and copper and consuming both local ornaments and foreign imports lived in a world shaped by the bridge-like character of the central frontier crafted by their ancestors. As they had in centuries past, the inhabitants of the central frontier found that, in most periods, forging ties beyond the central frontier brought great opportunity for wealth and prestige.

But the boundary of the central frontier was, itself, a mercurial beast from the fourteenth through the nineteenth centuries. It shifted location over time as new trade and political centers developed and collapsed, jockeying for position between the central frontier and the networks of the Indian Ocean and, later, the Atlantic Ocean. Such centers consumed great wealth, but, as we will see, their successes were often short-lived and fraught with the uncertainties of competition. Indeed, after the fifteenth century, it was often the inhabitants of the central frontier, who were poorer in relative terms than the residents of great trading centers like Ingombe Ilede or important political centers like the Luba court, who could pass on to their children some measure of political and economic stability and gradually rising wealth.

In the Shadow of Ingombe Ilede

The fourteenth and fifteenth centuries were a very precarious time for the inhabitants of the central frontier because a local iteration of the global Little Ice Age brought very cool and dry conditions to the region. Much like the northward spread of cattle keeping associated with the fifteenth century in the northern Batoka and middle Kafue regions, the trade emporium built up by a new community that reoccupied Ingombe Ilede in the fourteenth and fifteenth centuries may, in part, have been an alternative strategy to withstand the difficulties of cereal agriculture in this climate regime.[48] Ingombe Ilede in the fourteenth and fifteenth centuries was a settlement unlike any that had previously existed in the region: it was an important, if short-lived, trade emporium.[49] Its inhabitants were among the first in the region to exploit the Zambezi River trade route to the Indian Ocean coast, rather than the Save and Limpopo River routes that had connected Great Zimbabwe and the older settlements like Schroda, K2, and Mapungubwe to coastal trade networks. Among Ingombe Ilede's inhabitants were successful exporters who conducted trade in copper, ivory, and probably gold and slaves with buyers based at Kilwa on the Swahili coast. In return, Ingombe Ilede merchants accepted glass beads, beautiful cloth, conus and cowrie shells, and rare items like amulets. Adept smiths either belonged to or worked alongside Ingombe Ilede's community of traders, transforming flanged copper ingots and perhaps gold into a variety of ornaments.

The coppersmiths of Ingombe Ilede developed an entirely new form of copper bangle crafted of very fine-gauge wire created through a process of wire drawing and wrapped around a palm fiber core. This form was a different style from older hammered ribbon and foil strip copper bangles. Based on their regular and more durable form as compared to older wound copper bangles, their collection in vast quantities, and their distribution on the copper-rich Urungwe Plateau south of the Zambezi River, archaeologists agree that these new drawn wire copper bangles were used as a form of currency by people who traded with Ingombe Ilede.[50]

Evidence from burials upholds the unique currency status of drawn wire copper bangles, for they adorned the bodies of the dead in great numbers.

Moreover, no ivory bangles were recovered from the Ingombe Ilede burials, further distinguishing consumption patterns among the site's inhabitants from those of other central frontier communities. Like the extravagant burials of the Upemba Depression, the rich graves of Ingombe Ilede inhabitants include copper objects in the burials of men, women, and children.[51] The wealthiest residents of Ingombe Ilede wore their bangles in a new fashion as well, with hundreds of bangles creating a cuff of three, thirteen, and even fifteen inches on bearers' forearms and ankles, recalling the cuffs of iron bangles worn by wealthy Sanga denizens. Although residents of more modest villages of the central frontier wore multiple bangles and circlets, the objects did not create the uniform cuffs gracing the bodies of Ingombe Ilede men and women.

Ingombe Ilede residents amassed great wealth on the central frontier through the profitable ivory, copper, and gold trade they conducted with communities of the Copperbelt far to the north, the Zimbabwean mines to the south, and the Indian Ocean networks to the east. Counterintuitively, the material cultural record of much of the central frontier grows uncannily quiet during this reoccupation of Ingombe Ilede. Bangles and copper crosses are frequent at archaeological sites in the southeastern hinterland of Ingombe Ilede, on the Urungwe Plateau south of the Zambezi River. Ingombe Ilede residents used copper bangles to purchase ivory, smelted copper, and smelted gold from their neighbors to the south.[52] In sharp contrast, in the lands that constituted the western hinterland of Ingombe Ilede, including the Batoka Plateau, the middle Kafue, and the neighborhood of the middle Zambezi upstream of the falls, archaeologists have recovered only one specimen of copper currency: a lone drawn wire bangle.[53] Trade between Ingombe Ilede merchants and communities of the middle Kafue, Batoka, and the northern bank of the Zambezi, upstream of the falls was so limited that it did not warrant the use of copper currencies.

Although most residents of modest villages on the central frontier appear not to have shared in the great wealth of Ingombe Ilede, there was likely some interaction. For example, more ivory fragments were recovered from the few trenches associated with the fifteenth century at Kalala Island in the middle Kafue region than the many trenches associated with the longer, more intensive use of the site during the Middle Iron Age.[54] Hunters of the middle Kafue may have been trying to trade ivory with Ingombe Ilede merchants, but Ingombe Ilede agents could acquire ivory from any number of hunters living in and around the central frontier. And, of course, they resided in one of the richest elephant-hunting grounds on the central frontier. Their material culture demonstrates that when they were conducting trade or seeking emblems of power and ornaments marking status, Ingombe Ilede residents faced north toward the Copperbelt, Katanga, and the Upemba Depression, east toward Indian Ocean entrepôts like Kilwa, and south, toward the copper mines of the Urungwe Plateau and the goldfields beyond. Ingombe Ilede was near enough to have tied communities of the middle Kafue and Batoka more closely into Indian Ocean networks. But Ingombe Ilede had its back to the west. As residents of the hinterland of a single trade center that dominated the flow of raw materials and rare imports, speakers of Botatwe languages were marginalized from the kinds of trade networks their linguistic forebears had once crafted between communities of the far north and far south. That marginalization ended as the numbers of trade and political centers on the edges of Botatwe lands increased from the fifteenth century, allowing residents of the central frontier to once again enjoy the benefits of creating multiple networks of exchange and communication beyond the central frontier.

Borrowing on the Borderlands: The Central Frontier through the Seventeenth Century

Ingombe Ilede collapsed by the end of the fifteenth century, probably as towns on the Swahili coast, particularly the coastal town of Kilwa, endured a period of poor trade. Even as demand from the coast floundered in the fifteenth and sixteenth centuries and Ingombe Ilede was deserted, smelting production remained at high levels at Copperbelt sites like Kansanshi up to the seventeenth century, when surface malachite deposits were finally depleted.[55] Enterprising residents of the Upemba Depression and the villages beyond reconfigured their croisette currencies into lighter forms circulated in ever-greater quantities, pulling north the copper that might have once been sent south to Ingombe Ilede.[56] To the south of the Zambezi, the confederacy of Mwene Mutapa emerged in the mid-fifteenth century on the northern edge of the Zimbabwe Plateau, east of the Urungwe settlements that had been so closely tied to Ingombe Ilede. The Mutapa confederacy may have had roots in the Great Zimbabwe culture to the south, but the character of trade relations on the northern plateau changed in the face of civil wars and political interference by the Portuguese. Portuguese merchants eager to cut off Swahili middlemen established trading posts along the Zambezi River; the closest to

Botatwe-speaking lands was Zumbo, founded in the seventeenth century. Copper from Katanga, Urungwe, and perhaps the Kafue hook was exported to the coast through Zumbo, comprising the bulk of the two or three tons of copper exported from the Zambezi area.[57] Entrepreneurs of Portuguese, African, and mixed descent established market towns scattered across the territories of the Mwene Mutapa confederacy at sites like Dambarare, Luanze, and Baranda during the sixteenth and seventeenth centuries.[58] Autonomous "back country traders" may have provided further options for trade outside the control of the Mutapa confederacy. Indeed, communities on the central frontier north of the Zambezi River remained autonomous from tributary demands even after Changamira pushed the Portuguese off the Zimbabwe Plateau and took over control of trade at Zumbo in the late seventeenth and early eighteenth century.[59]

In this sweeping summary of very complicated and well-documented historical changes two points stand out as trends that would characterize life on the central frontier in the sixteenth and seventeenth centuries. First, although some trade still crossed the central frontier, linking central and southern Africa, most long-distance trade was oriented to the coasts, both the Indian Ocean and the Atlantic. The geography of trade dramatically recast opportunities for inland communities because the central frontier lay at the furthest remove from growing coastal trade. In other words, the central frontier was surrounded by many different political and industrial centers oriented toward either coast (or both). Second, the size of the central frontier constricted as novel centers jockeyed for a place on its periphery. The central frontier became a borderlands par excellence: it was close enough to forge ties to different political and economic centers, but distant enough to remain beyond the coercive reach of states demanding tribute or the meddling of specialists who might critique the way Botatwe speakers put into practice the words, rituals, and objects they borrowed from afar.

With the abandonment of Ingombe Ilede in the late fifteenth century, residents of the central frontier were no longer living in the hinterland of a single center monopolizing Indian Ocean trade but were once again living in central lands surrounded by many other places. This commercial and political geography meant that inhabitants of the central frontier were well positioned to trade with and borrow simultaneously from established and emerging centers for their own enrichment, edification, or pleasure and to pass objects, foods, emblems, even lingo between these different cultural and political worlds. The inhabitants of the central frontier never came to control inter-regional trade, but efforts to extend one's social, economic, and technological networks were bolstered by ever more numerous opportunities to use objects and knowledge that signaled connections to other, distant cultures. Foreign words, objects, and styles could be used to assert, display, and aspire to another social status in this life or in the future elsewhere of the spirit realm.[60] The waxing and waning of these multiple and ever-closer centers on the edge of the central frontier offered Botatwe speakers novel concepts, practices, and when they could afford them, objects to adopt for local purposes. The archaeological, ethnographic, and linguistic records each attest to this period as one of opportunity and creativity. Material cultural objects recovered by archaeologists bring great precision to localized and fleeting consumer trends. For methodological reasons, ethnographic and linguistic data cannot easily be dated to the period between the sixteenth and eighteenth centuries. Yet these forms of evidence also evince robust contact and the borrowing of ideas and practices in nonmaterial domains of life. Even without the wealth to attract or direct great volumes of trade, communities on the central frontier participated in the cultures and histories of societies outside the central frontier.

As the scale of Indian Ocean trade increased from the late sixteenth and into the seventeenth century, the consumption of foreign objects and practices also increased on the central frontier. The changing centers of trade beyond Botatwe lands created unstable geographies of exchange in long-distance commodities like ivory, copper, gold, cowries, conus shells, glass beads, and cloth and ample opportunities to engage in trade on terms more favorable to the householders of small villages. The central frontier grave goods and village artifacts that postdate the collapse of Ingombe Ilede's trade monopoly in the late fifteenth century are far richer than those of the Ingombe Ilede era. For example, glass beads and conus shell discs, impande, are most abundant in graves dating from the seventeenth century onwards. The richest sixteenth- to nineteenth-century burials of Zambezi Valley sites included solid copper rings and bangles of thick curved wire—some even four times thicker than solid wire bangles of previous centuries.[61] Residents of these villages probably traded ivory across the Zambezi River in exchange for copper. Indeed, late seventeenth-century documents suggest that African chiefdoms with trading centers between the confluences of the Zambezi with the Kafue and Luangwa Kafue Rivers produced nearly two hundred bars of ivory a year, competing with the exports of fairs under Portuguese influence on the Zimbabwean plateau.[62]

The shifting fortunes of traders and leaders south of the Zambezi opened opportunities for inhabitants on the central frontier to selectively participate in the long-distance trade and regional exchanges that made copper, ivory, and other commodities signals of wealth and extensive social relationships. The unequal distribution of wealth in the few burials that postdate the Ingombe Ilede cemetery remind us that this was not an even process. However, women and children were among those who could command objects of value. One woman who died in her twenties was buried in the middle Kafue in the mid-seventeenth century with eleven of a new style of ivory bangle decorating her right arm and multiple strands of glass beads around her neck.[63] If such objects as copper and ivory bangles circulated only as gifts in marriage negotiations, the wealth embellishing the bodies of women and children may have said as much about the status of their male kin as the women and children themselves. Yet the exchange of lechwe skins between lovers and Ila speakers' use of the inherited hunting verb *-wèz- sometime after the mid-thirteenth century to talk about creating sexual ties outside marriage to bolster wealth and social status suggest that some kinds of objects circulated in an economy of wealth, status, fertility, and virility that was not always transacted within the institution of marriage. Women and young girls in the middle Kafue and on the Batoka Plateau may well have adorned themselves to communicate social networks and circuits of wealth of their own cultivation.[64]

Not all inhabitants of the central frontier could afford the degree of material consumption undertaken by its wealthiest inhabitants, much less that of elites in economic and political centers beyond the central frontier. By the sixteenth or seventeenth century, many other quite powerful states and entrepôts stood between Botatwe speakers and the sources of the rarest objects and the most prestigious emblems. Words and practices were far cheaper imports and the distances spanned by such loanwords ensured that no one could police the accuracy or purity of their use as central frontiersmen and women adapted such borrowings into local practice. Borrowing in the non-material domain often involved ideas and practices that underpinned the centralization of authority in other societies. We might imagine that Botatwe societies borrowed such ideas and practices as Lunda positional succession or emblems of authority like Luban ceremonial axes to claim membership to prestigious centers. But Botatwe societies rarely accepted wholesale the ideologies and values associated with foreign words and practices in the places where they originated. The fact that Botatwe speakers borrowed simultaneously from different centers suggests that such decisions were less about claiming to belong to a specific polity than fitting objects and ideas from afar into a local politics that valued connectivity and a worldliness demonstrated through unique skills, broad networks, and foreign and esoteric knowledge.

Botatwe societies and other savanna communities elaborated on the political and social consequences of the ideologies and status associated with bushcraft, even borrowing them back and forth, but with very different outcomes. Botatwe speakers did not follow northerners' lead in using the older forms of distinction and social influence tied to bushcraft to legitimize subsequent ideologies of royalty embodied in the hunter-founder figures of charter myths. However, some Botatwe societies shared the strategy to make more explicit the links between institutionalized authority and the social prestige of practitioners of bushcraft sometime after the divergence of proto-Kafue in the thirteenth century. For example, Tonga speakers invented the status of *ulanyika*, "eater of the bush," a ritual leader who could claim the fruits of the bush and the right to initiate certain seasonal forms of hunting and fishing.[65] Central African ideologies of royalty and sacral kingship were inherently exclusive, constricting and concentrating political power, at least in theory. In contrast, Botatwe speakers continued to politicize and control knowledge by debating claims to talent, wealth, and fame. Although the Tonga office of ulyanika, like those of other central African societies, tied a form of ritual authority to control of the bush, the Tonga ulanyika jockeyed for position on a political stage crowded by mwaalu, muvubi, mwami, healers, and diviners. And this cast grew over the centuries. In Tonga communities, mediums of new basangu spirits joined the many leaders seeking to cultivate followings on the central frontier. Famed basangu mediums entered into Tonga communities from the Zimbabwe hills perhaps in the late seventeenth century, as communities speaking languages related to Shona established a strong trade presence near the abandoned site of Ingombe Ilede at settlements like Angoa, Mudzimu, and Mburuma.[66] In Botatwe societies, fame and its socialities remained a viable form of inter-peer influence into the present day, for statuses like muvubi, mwami, and mwaalu persisted even as the economic and material context of their celebrity changed and new statues were adopted into local social and political repertoires.

As new symbols and practices of status were invented and borrowed by Botatwe societies, older routes to distinction changed. This is particularly clear in the vocabulary for high status practitioners of bushcraft, *-pàdó and *-vʊbi. The intensification of long-distance trade in products of the bush supported new means to acquire reputations in bushcraft, transforming earlier paths to renown in the Botatwe-speaking area. Older kinds of celebrated hunters, *-pàdó, were redefined as "friends" and "elders" as new entrepreneurial elephant hunters like *nkombalume* and *sinyanga* came to be celebrated hunters, building up great wealth and repute, often through professional organizations and guilds. Similarly, the various meanings of *-vʊbi changed over time. In Plateau Tonga, the term eventually came to mean domestic animal in noun class 3/4, probably after the fifteenth or sixteenth century, indicating the role of large cattle herds in acquiring wealth, status, and fame.[67] Tonga speakers also used a verb form of the root to talk about owning slaves, an innovation indicating another shift in the sources of wealth sustaining fame. This change may date to the second half of the nineteenth century.[68] Significantly, the affective, social character of repute persisted throughout the second millennium. When Botatwe speakers associated words like *-pàdó and *-vʊbi with concepts like "famous one" and "friend," they joined the value of material wealth, knowledge, and affect to the many, sometimes contesting collectivities to which skilled practitioners belonged.

In summary, the story of Botatwe speakers in the sixteenth and seventeenth century is a story of the inventiveness of borrowing. Even as societies in central and southern Africa experimented with social exclusion, social inclusion and association remained an important strategy for Botatwe communities of the central frontier. The unique geography of the central frontier ensured a constant flow of objects, practices, and technologies that residents used to craft new forms of local and long-distance affiliation and to claim new statuses. Indeed, forms of inherited, centralized power would have been quite difficult to sustain on the central frontier because there were opportunities to forge a link or to borrow a new political emblem, high-status ornament, or social institution from distant centers of political and economic innovation every few generations. The patterns of borrowing from different sources, often simultaneously, suggests that participation in the networks of trade and political prestige developed by communities well beyond the central frontier— from the Luba-Lunda world in the north to the healing cults to the south and east and the shifting capitals of southern Zambezia—was a matter of choice and opportunity for inhabitants of the central frontier between the sixteenth and the late seventeenth or early eighteenth century.

In the late eighteenth and nineteenth centuries, the central frontier was shattered. Ivory and slave caravans provisioning coastal markets pushed farther inland, devastating interior communities as they chased the receding frontier of elephant herds and raided for slaves to feed markets abroad or to labor at the port docks and fields at the coasts. Under the protection of powerful warlords, guilds of professional ivory hunters monopolized local ivory procurement. Political upstarts from the south African highveld toppled local leaders across the region. Some Botatwe speakers participated in these transformations, but the vast majority merely endured them as objects of ridicule, cattle raiding, and enslavement. These are the best-known histories of Botatwe communities in the precolonial period, and they are important chapters in the Botatwe story. But they mask the long legacy of a politics of skill, celebrity, and worldliness that had organized Botatwe communities since at least the eighth century and that shaped the fortunes of Botatwe communities as they endured and sometimes participated in the rapidly changing world of the eighteenth and nineteenth centuries.

The communities of the central frontier never boasted the concentrations of wealth or the evidence of social stratification so common on its periphery. The central frontier was, in part, a creation of those, like technicians of bushcraft, who built networks outward from its center. This process helps to explain why political life at the heart of the central frontier, in the Botatwe-speaking areas, did not follow the many centralized practices of power that were initiated in central and southern Africa in the early second millennium and elaborated over the following centuries. Throughout the second millennium, the unique position of the central frontier as a place surrounded by many inventive economic and political centers ensured that an older politics of celebrity and fame remained the foundation of ephemeral claims to authority and social influence among Botatwe-speaking societies. This politics was predicated on a culture valuing the capacity to secure ties beyond local communities and competition for celebrity. Hunters, smelters, and ordinary homesteaders used social ties like mukowa and mulongo to travel and to share technologies, stylistic conventions, and a sensibility of striving and worldliness. Claims to success were expressed through learning, practicing, and demonstrating unique skills and acquiring and displaying novel objects. Networks and singular individuals added to the complexity of local relationships governing affiliation, dependency, social influence, and reciprocity. And they did so in ways that highlight the seasonally contingent, highly mobile, even transient forms of status and association crafted by skilled practitioners of bushcraft, bone setters, green thumbs, and others who were merely neighbors most of the year, at least in Botatwe lands.

The position of the central frontier offered Botatwe speakers a steady supply of political and social resources, for there were many options available for men and women to connect to and borrow from networks spreading out in multiple directions. Often, Botatwe speakers invented their own versions of common statuses, landscapes, and technologies, developing new words or changing foreign words' meanings. By facilitating borrowing and bricolage, the political culture and geography of the central frontier ensured that power remained highly localized, decentralized, often ephemeral, and even seasonal. But it was a political culture that was crafted from a widespread tradition of the late first millennium celebrating the prestige of technicians of the bush.

The history of Botatwe bushcraft illuminates new aspects of central and southern African history. The story of Tsodilo communities and of residents in the Makgadikgadi Pans and even as far as Chibuene looks different in light of their connections north of the Zambezi. The participation of residents of villages in the middle Kafue and in the hinterland of the falls in the first-millennium trade network south of the Zambezi dramatically extends the northern limits of that trade. Moreover, residents of the central frontier served as a bridge between central and southern Africa, moving objects between centers as distant as the Upemba and Tsodilo. The argument that the economies of central and southern Africa were connected only after the fourteenth century through the efforts of members of large-scale states is untenable in light of the history of first millennium connections between the central frontier and communities to their north and south. The history of Botatwe bushcraft transforms how we understand those cosmologies and materials that savanna communities living to the north of the central frontier drew upon as they invented new ideologies of power out of older ideas about the status of hunters and metallurgists. Central Africans reconfigured long-standing ideas about the power of the bush and the inheritance of skills that made some people suited to protect others and able to harness dangerous, fickle forces toward socially productive ends. Luba *bulopwe*, "sacred blood," constricted authority to the few, but it did so by reconfiguring an older, more open path to celebrity and its social and political responsibilities.

The political culture of the central frontier was viable as long as the central frontier remained at a distance from sites of political and economic innovation. But perhaps as early as the mid-eighteenth century and with increasing frequency through the nineteenth century, its own frontier had been breached. By the early twentieth century, the latest political innovators to reach the central frontier were simply blind to the forms of decentralized, ephemeral politics and affiliation that had flourished within the unique geography of the central frontier. For British South Africa Company officials and, later, district commissioners and missionaries, provincial Botatwe societies lacked government and, therefore, they lacked history.

Epilogue

In 1977, Chief Chona of Nampeyo, a neighborhood in BuTonga about ten miles east of Monze in Southern Province and abutting the Gwembe Valley escarpment, asked the eminent anthropologist Elizabeth Colson to write a history of his area.[1] Nampeyo was the location of several local shrines and, after 1937, the seat of a Tonga chieftaincy recognized by the British Colonial Office. It was also the site of Colson's fieldwork for portions of 1946–47 and 1948–50. The historical information Colson collected in the 1940s described the previous hundred and fifty years and was supplemented by narratives collected in later years by her longtime collaborator, Benjamin Shipopa. Colson's 1977 history of Nampeyo was organized around the lives of the "big" people of the neighborhood. Stories of the twentieth century focused on the deeds of chiefs. Stories from the late eighteenth and nineteenth centuries also described the exploits of leaders, but they were men and women who rose to local prominence for their ability to provide for others, especially, but not only, as skilled rainmakers and diviners.

In one such story, Colson reconstructed the life history of Chona Mupati, the earliest historical figure the people of Nampeyo could recall in the 1940s. Colson estimates that Chona Mupati was born around 1810 and died between the two major Ndebele raids of 1888 and 1891. Chona Mupati came to power as a skilled diviner whose dreams revealed efficacious strategies to protect people in a time of terrible raiding, slaving, and violence. Although it was agreed that Chona Mupati was not entered by *basangu* spirits, the guidance he received from his dreams seemed similar to the guidance of possessed mediums. Therefore, when Chona Mupati died, his followers decided he must be treated like a basangu medium. So they built a shrine to ensure that he could continue to provide for the living.[2]

The succession of Chona Mupati was something of a difficult affair because no one wanted to inherit his name and position. Chona Mupati's family came for the funeral and accused the inhabitants of his neighborhood of killing him through witchcraft. After three people were executed for Chona Mupati's murder, his family began to debate who would inherit his position. In the late nineteenth century, people in Nampeyo, like many other BaTonga and, indeed, many other central Africans, practiced positional succession, an institution in which a family member inherited the name, social position, relationships, and obligations of the deceased. Three likely candidates were debated by Chona Mupati's kin, but the one who was eventually selected, Nankambula, died before he could move to Chona Mupati's village and take up his new responsibilities. Again, the family met to select a successor, but some family members now feared that the death of the second Chona Mupati, Nankambula, had also been caused by witchcraft. So a slave of Chona Mupati, Hamatu, was chosen. Hamatu moved into Chona Mupati's homestead and married all of his widows, except the senior wife, the *namalelo*. The namalelo was married by another relative and her death later in the story creates an important twist in the plot. Hamatu suffered from homesickness, however, and soon left Chona Mupati's area to return to his natal country with Chona Mupati's widows. There, Hamatu founded his own village, perhaps in no small part because he now, with the four widows, had the human resources and status to do so. For some time after Hamatu's departure, no one held the place of Chona Mupati. The village had begun to disperse: "there were only young men and children left." Around this time, a few years after the death of Chona Mupati, his namalelo, his senior wife, also died.[3] Here, we take up the story in Colson's words to explore an intriguing subplot in the story of Chona Mupati's succession and the death of his namalelo:

> Before she [the namalelo] died, there had already been trouble among some of the men living at Makwembo village [in Nampeyo]. Chileka, Hankombo, and Nacibote were brothers. They were rivals for the girls who lived in the village of Chona Mupati and were jealous of each other. Hankombo killed a buffalo and Nacibote, his rival, said, "All the girls will prefer him because he killed a buffalo." He [Nacibote] began to hate his brother and was said to have killed him with sorcery. Hankombo's younger brother, by a different

mother, began to proclaim that Nacibote had killed his brother with sorcery. He came to report the matter to Moonga Bbuleke, the oldest son of Nangoma. Moonga Bbuleke lived in Chona Mupati's village as a boy, but he was already a married man at the time of Chona Mupati's death.

Then the *Namalelo* wife of Chona Mupati died. The people said, "It is this man (Nacibote) who is using sorcery here because he wants the place of Chona Mupati." They went to call the Bwengwa Bukonka who were of the lineage of Chona Mupati. They held a divination and found that it was Nacibote who had killed her. They returned and said, "Why are you still talking about this matter? We will take this man for another divination." They took him towards Chiyobola and speared him on the path. He did not die immediately. The son-in-law of Nangoma, Magabba who was a Mudenda and the father of Paul Chisuwo, speared him again and he died. As the men returned to Nampeyo they sang, "*Twapwaya, Twapwaya.*" This was to show they had killed the witch.[4]

After this, the people of Nampeyo dispersed and no longer claimed to be Bakonka but, rather, "began to take back their own clans and deny that they were Bakonkas." Moonga Bbuleke was asked to take Chona Mupati's place, but he refused and nominated his younger brother, Mahachi Namukamba, who became the accepted successor of Chona Mupati: "He therefore was the leader of Nampeyo for over thirty years, but he never acquired the power or ritual authority of Chona Mupati." In fact, Namukamba's mother, Nangoma, was more influential. She had her own village and regulated the ritual life of all of Nampeyo because she had been possessed by a basangu and offered sound counsel to local residents.[5]

In 1948, in one of her first publications on the Tonga and drawing on the same field notes from which she would write the 1977 history of Nampeyo quoted above, Colson famously claimed that the Tonga of Northern Rhodesia were a "non-historical people." "On the whole, the Tonga might be defined as culturally a have-not group," Colson quipped.

> They have never had an organized state. They were unwarlike and had neither regimental organizations nor armies. They were and are equally lacking in an age-grade set-up, secret societies, and social stratification of all kinds. The Tonga would not even attract those

fascinated by the intricate rules of lineage organization, for while they have clans and smaller matrilineal kin-groups, they have them in a characteristically unorganized fashion which leaves the investigator with a baffled, frustrated desire to rearrange their social structure into some more ordered system. It is only in the rain-rituals and their associated shrine that the Tonga show a half-hearted groping towards the establishment of a larger community than that which existed in the village or in the ties of kinship.[6]

Of course, the acephalous nature of Tonga social and political organization would, in time, bring both the Tonga and their foremost student fame in the discipline of anthropology.

As Colson's career unfolded, she carefully examined and documented the political and social organization of Tonga communities residing on the Batoka Plateau and in the Gwembe Valley, arguing that their form of amorphous acephalous society should be added to the known typology of African political systems.[7] As Colson observed, leaders who were identified as "chiefs" in twentieth-century BuTonga were merely inventions of the colonial government, sometimes bolstering other claims to authority embedded in rain shrines or local influence.[8] According to Colson, there were no formal precolonial institutions, offices, or bureaucracies that could maintain legitimacy in the eyes of subjects beyond the lifespan of the incumbent, even with the practice of positional succession. Freedom to move and shift associations and alliances was at the heart of Tonga social, political, and religious life. This pragmatic approach to making a living, rather than preserving current conditions, characterized the flexible, casual use of institutions like neighborhood and kinship, which provided the idioms of association and authority that made good living possible.[9]

Colson also identified a causal relationship between decentralized political organization and a lack of a deep historical consciousness among Tonga communities.[10] History for the Tonga, Colson claimed, was a local affair of relatively recent time depth. There were no "origins" myths or stories of settling a Tonga homeland to connect Tonga-speaking communities as a "People." Oral narratives were both "short" and "particularistic," referring to local neighborhoods and restricted kin groups, narratives of exactly the sort from which she wrote the history of Nampeyo.[11] As Colson explained in the 1980s, it was probably difficult for a community to be historically conscious "in the absence of a centralized state or some other device that provides a time scale for ordering individual and local experience."[12] Woe betide the would-be historian of the Tonga!

Subsequent students of the Tonga and "related peoples" took issue with Colson's claims that the Tonga lacked both historical consciousness and hierarchical political organization.[13] The second generation of Tonga specialists, many trained under the careful tutelage of Colson and Thayer Scudder, used local narratives associated with shrines and "chiefly" families to write centripetal forces back into the precolonial political history of Tonga speakers and their neighbors, including Toka, Nkoya, and Goba communities. In almost all such revisionist work, the authors argued that religious institutions were part of the political domain and that earlier evidence of more centralized leadership, particularly oral historical evidence, must have once existed but was likely forgotten during the extreme disruptions of the nineteenth century.[14] As a result of this historical research, few today would question the political dimensions of ritual life, its institutions, and forms of authority and leadership in the precolonial past of Tonga communities. Similarly, the impact of colonial warrant chiefs on local practices of power now seems self-evident. Such revisionist work on acephalous societies also opened the intellectual space to explore the centripetal forces at work in centralized states and the great organizing capacities of heterarchical societies, important research trajectories in other parts of the continent.[15]

The debate about Tonga history was something of a red herring, of course, for it turned on a discrepancy of scale. Colson wrote of the Tonga as a unit but was well aware of the complications of doing so.[16] Colson's characterizations of the early history and political organization of the unit were critiqued with particularistic examples confined in time and space: the Monze cult, the BanaMainga kinglets, and the slave-raiding chieftaincies of the Gwembe. Like parts of BuTonga, many other Botatwe societies have chiefly institutions, sometimes with very elaborate rituals, courts, and regalia, but the words for such offices, objects, and practices tend to postdate the reach of the comparative historical linguistic method, which is around the mid-thirteenth century in the Botatwe language family. As in many other parts of Africa, a large number of these now "traditional" institutions are of very recent origin, indeed. By adding another scale to our interpretation of the past—that of a deep history in which Tonga speakers may claim a place, but which also extends well beyond them—the local, particularistic histories of places like Nampeyo offer up for our consideration the contingencies of de-

centralized politics, the often ambivalent ambitions for power, and the durability of ancient idioms for success and influence.

In the subplot of Chona Mupati's succession, quoted at length above,
the rivalry between Hankombo and Nacibote over women in Chona Mupati's
village comes to be tied up with accusations of sorcery, debates about the
death of Chona Mupati's namalelo, and the identification of an appropriate
successor to his place. Underlying this story is an older history of the politics
of fame and talent associated with bushcraft and those ends toward which such
fame and talent are mobilized by the different constituencies who recognize
them. This was a politics that stood both within and outside the institutions
Tonga communities either lacked or had developed in localized forms in recent centuries. It was a politics tied to the cultivation of distinction and the
affective character of social influence and, ultimately, power. It was a politics
archived not in traditions of figures founding or populating offices but in those
stories that became folktales and local legends about individuals' exploits and
their masterful episodes of good living. The notoriety captured in such
stories was especially, but not only, associated with those who had mastered
bushcraft.

Hankombo's demonstration of talent in bushcraft transformed the rivalry between Hankombo and Nacibote over the young women in Chona
Mupati's village. The story of Hankombo's feat recalls other widespread
regional folktales about hunters' success: the story of Monga who was hunted
down by his friends because "all is meat"; the cautionary tale of the boastful,
unskilled old man, who insisted on celebrating his meager kill to the amuse-
ment of his neighbors; the fable of the hunter who sought to be gazed at every
day until his life's desire so infuriated the mythical "chief of the fishes" that
he was eaten by the angered beast.[17] When Hankombo killed the dangerous
buffalo, he opened for himself social opportunities not available to his brother
because he secured for himself a reputation as a successful hunter. Hankombo,
Nacibote assumed, would be admired for his success in an endeavor that had
long been a pathway to social standing. More specifically, Hankombo would
be able to acquire the marks of maturity: the admiration of his peers and a
wife or, perhaps, a lover (we are never told the nature of the relationships
sought with the young women). Given that Nacibote was accused of such
jealousy that he was suspected of witchcraft against his brother, it seems
likely that the social opportunities opened by Hankombo's success threatened Nacibote's ability to access any of the women in the village. Perhaps

Hankombo, now an admired hunter, would be able to seduce or even marry them all! We also don't know whether Nacibote was accused of killing Chona Mupati's namalelo and attempting to succeed to Chona Mupati's position because he was already accused of witchcraft against his brother and made an easy scapegoat or whether Nacibote actually tried to inherit Chona Mupati's place in an effort to become "preferred" by the village women. We do know, however, that for either Nacibote or the kin of Chona Mupati who leveled the accusation of murder against him, and certainly for the people of Nampeyo who recalled the story in the 1940s, that an attempt by Nacibote to succeed Chona Mupati was understood to carry a status equivalent to Hankombo's magnificent kill. Inheriting the relationships and responsibilities—the legacy of such a person as Chona Mupati—was a parallel means to attract the attention of the desired young women of the village.

We have little indication that Nacibote and Hankombo sought out status because they were ambitious, would-be Big Men. Perhaps being preferred by a woman was a step along that path. But the casting of this subplot as a story about rivalry among young men over women suggests instead that Nacibote and Hankombo were concerned with undertaking the necessary work to begin their paths into adulthood. By trodding a well-worn path to fame that cut through the bush, Hankombo was able to do so first and with a measure of artfulness and consequence unavailable to Nacibote. Personal careers were acts of social and political creativity, to be sure, but they were tied to individuals' bodies, desires, and vulnerabilities in social and political contexts that shifted abruptly, day to day, in the brief moment it took to cast a spear straight and true, to exhale a last breath, or to make public a suspicion of witchcraft.

Skill was embodied, but bodies were not equally skilled, for skill exhibited an uneven geography. Moreover, skill was a product of great effort; it took learning and practice to create bodily habits to transition between a hunter's absolute stillness and the movement of rapid fire. In contrast, the fame that was born of skill was a matter of social recognition, not the automatic outcome of personal effort and physiology. This tension between the embodied dimension of skill and the social quality of fame is mirrored in the story of Chona Mupati's succession, into which the Nacibote and Hankombo subplot is embedded. The very difficult business of securing a successor to Chona Mupati's intimidating legacy betrays an ambivalent attitude among his relatives toward an institution, positional succession, which supported the creation of a stable political center among other societies, particularly the nuclear

Lunda some centuries earlier. The problem may have turned on the fact that succession to the place of the deceased did not include those skills the deceased had cultivated and brought to bear in the creation of the social relationships and responsibilities the successor would inherit. The inheritance of skill was an entirely different social institution. And not all skills were inheritable. Mahachi Namukamba, Chona Mupati's eventual successor, knew this all too well, for he was recognized as the "leader" of Nampeyo even as he lived in the shadow of his mother's innate "good sense" and ritual authority, both of which earned her great respect, influence, and affection.[18]

The story of Chona Mupati's succession is the opposite of the succession struggles known from the dynastic traditions of more centralized polities. There seemed to be little ambition among the men and women of Nampeyo to build on the publics created by others in order to secure power for power's sake. The story of Chona Mupati's many burdened inheritors raises a number of questions: why would anyone would want to take on the obligations of a Big Man without the talents he used to amass his influence or without a specific ambition toward which such precarious prestige might be directed? To what degree did so-called Big Men influence matters of day-to-day living like subsistence? What ideas, materials, and feelings held together other kinds of relationships besides those governing leaders and followers, elders and juniors, men and women? Can they teach us anything new about life in the deep past of acephelous societies?

Like the many twists and turns in the story of Chona Mupati's succession, the history of Botatwe speakers teaches us that ephemeral, decentralized social and political organization was as much a domain of effort and creativity as the invention of royalty, the founding of kingdoms, or the tidy scaling up into empires and nation-states that had served as the destinations in social evolutionary models. Acephelous politics in precolonial Botatwe-speaking communities was the product of great innovation around the mechanisms and practices of association over the course of three millennia. This innovation depended on contact with and learning from other communities, a degree of engagement and creativity that is reflected in records of language, material cultural, and technological change. Botatwe societies did not "conserve" decentralized politics in the face of neighboring societies' experiments with concentrating authority as a way to keep in check some disembodied force toward centralizing power or some naturalized ambition for it. Rather,

Botatwe speakers added into their repertoire new activities, objects, names, and feelings about status and novel ways of imagining what good living looked like. Perhaps these efforts constitute a political tradition that idealized ephemeral forms of authority, but, as the history of Botatwe bushcraft demonstrates, the idea of preservation and conservation masks the inventiveness and contingencies of acephelous politics.

Precisely because subsistence is a domain of life where social, political, and material concerns shade into one another, subsistence was fertile ground for developing potent identity categories in both Botatwe-speaking and European communities over the past several millennia. Like their contemporaries in Europe, men and women in precolonial central Africa invented novel categories of subsistence to meet in new ways the personal and collective challenges of much older concerns. For central Africans, these concerns were about feeding families as technologies changed, harnessing life forces and rejuvenating populations of fickle spirits, and mitigating the uneven distribution of the talent necessary to accomplish such work. The way that speakers of Botatwe languages used certain kinds of food collection techniques to develop novel forms of association and social influence complicates the narratives we might expect from a deep history of decentralized societies and a deep history of food collection in farming communities. For example, not all aspects of political and social life unfolded at the local level in decentralized societies. Mwaalu and muvubi lived in highly localized communities, but they also belonged to large networks of practitioners that tied together peers across very long distances through shared technologies, skills, and vocabularies and that connected the living with the chance to be counted among the efficacious, consequential dead. Although the status of belonging to such networks undoubtedly carried important and changing local meanings, they also reveal the quite vast geographic scales of affiliation available to some members of societies we usually describe as small scale.

It would be easy to describe technicians of the bush as alternative kinds of Big Men. Yet the seasonality of their labors, the ambition to find agency in death as much as fame in life, and the dependence of their influence on the recognition of others—the many contingencies of their labors, particularly in communities without professional guilds, cults, or other groups—may better reveal the forms of authority and mobilizing clout that hover betwixt and between leaders and their followers. Alternative paths to distinction and social influence shaped the lives of villagers alongside, beyond, or in tandem with the authority of charismatic ritual leaders, lineage heads, or local Big Men. The political geographies of millennia past were likely as complicated and frequently changing as those described by historians of more recent periods. Just as historians have discovered with respect to the "nation," precolonial political institutions, such as kingdoms and clans, that we assume to have drawn people together, may well elide alternative and coexisting configurations of association, such as mulongo or being counted among those called mwaalu. These forms of status and association were just as important in the day-to-day business of living meaningfully.[19] The pluralistic politics of precolonial south central Africa can be traced through the coercive demands of ambitious Big Men for tribute and their competitors' exchange of protection for loyalty—and also in the celebration of a successful hunter, the hunger for meat, the formalization of dependencies among friends, and a shared fear of the forces of the bush. We see the significance of these latter social practices and statuses in the contests surrounding them, from the ways that technicians' skills were tied to lineage politics through the mechanism of inheritance to the expansion of the meaning of words like mulongo and muvubi. The social and political dimensions of talent, of task-based mobility, of friendship, of descendant's strivings for ancestorhood and ancestor's efforts to shape the world of the living, even of supple skins wrapped around a most-desired lover's hips together reveal the social networks that existed outside and alongside forms of authority grafted onto local settlements, households, spirits, formal clan ties, and marriage alliances.

The history of Botatwe bushcraft suggests that in ancient south central Africa, corporate action depended on celebrating and even inventing new forms of individual distinction just as the honors and responsibilities of leadership flowed beyond individual politicians to his or her communities of supporters, living and dead. If ambition for power obtained in the early communities of south central Africa, it was a social and not only an individual phenomenon. If competition for power obtained, power was a created and nurtured resource, sometimes, but not always, limited by instrumental and coercive authority. With these insights in mind, we can begin to incorporate into our precolonial histories the experiences of "small" men and women, of seasonal notables, of primus inter pares, of the diversity of statuses, dignities, and capacities valued by our historical subjects, a "popular politics" of very distant pasts.[20] We may well find, as generations of Botatwe speakers did, that these are affecting histories to curate.

Appendix

The following list of reconstructed words functions as a glossary. It is intended to help the reader recall key features of particular reconstructions, such as their derivations or distributions, when those reconstructions are encountered again in later chapters. A root's appendix number is provided in brackets the first time the root is discussed in each chapter. Entries include basic details about the reconstruction, including its form in the earliest Botatwe protolanguage to which it can be reconstructed, its noun class, and notes on derivation and distribution. Reference numbers for the two largest compendia of Bantu reconstructions—the Bantu Lexical Reconstructions database (abbreviated here as BLR-3), created by the team of linguists at Tervuren, and Guthrie's Comparative Bantu—direct the reader to attestations and related or alternative reconstructions.[1] Following conventions in the field, reference to Guthrie's forms are listed by his Comparative Series (C.S.) and partial series (p.s.) numbers. Letters refer to the revision of Guthrie's Bantu zones as listed in Bastin and Schadeberg, "Bantu Lexical Reconstructions." A more detailed bibliography of Botatwe-language dictionaries, grammars, and word lists is available elsewhere.[2] Citations in this appendix direct the reader to some sources for Botatwe attestations, further historical analysis of reconstructions, and debates about specific reconstructions. An etymological dictionary is in preparation to supplement this book and will include the published and unpublished attestations underlying the word reconstructions based on revisions to the Botatwe-language family classification and its diachronic phonology.

1. *-kúmú (1/2)[3]

   Botatwe Protolanguage: predates proto-Bantu; was not inherited by proto-Botatwe speakers

Gloss: simultaneously "bringer of honor" and "honored one," an ancient name for a kind of leader, variously achieved or ascribed, secular or ritual

Etymology: from *-kúm- "to be honored, to be rich"

Distribution: widespread across Bantu with attestations in wider Niger Congo (notably Akan)

BLR-3: 2118, see also 2113–17

C.S.: 1265, see also 1263, 1263a, 1264, p.s. 336

2. *-zóbé (7/8)[4]

Botatwe Protolanguage: Kafue, borrowed

Gloss: "sitatunga"

Etymology: as *-jóbé in northern cluster of eastern Bantu languages; unidentified antelope species in A; replaces earlier Bantu *-búdí?

Distribution: A, D, F, G, J, M

BLR-3: 1601

C.S.: 947

3. *-pogʊ(e/a) (9/10)[5]

Botatwe Protolanguage: Kafue and perhaps Western Botatwe or Machili, borrowed

Gloss: ostrich

Etymology: multiple borrowing episodes from different eastern Bantu languages, including the Shona cluster and southeastern Bantu

Distribution: depends on the form of the root, but innovation focused on Shona and southeast Bantu clusters

BLR-3: 7163, 7781, 8933

4. *-mpe (9/6)[6]

Botatwe Protolanguage: Kafue, borrowed

Gloss: wild dog

Etymology: from *-pumpɪ, "wild dog"

Distribution: southeastern cluster of Bantu and L M. Although attestations take the form *-pumpɪ in extant Kusi languages, the word appears as *-mpe in Kafue languages, losing the first syllable and exhibiting the characteristic weakening of the final vowel, which is common in borrowings from Kusi languages. Soli speakers later borrowed this term, surely from neighboring Lenje speakers on the eastern edge of the Batoka Plateau.

BLR-3: 5001

5. *siʊmbwa (5/6)[7]

Botatwe Protolanguage: Kafue, borrowed

Gloss: lion

Etymology: from narrow eastern Bantu *-siumba, perhaps a skew of the old Bantu root *-címbá?

Distribution: widespread in narrow eastern Bantu. Attestations of the term in Lundwe have a phonological form that suggests later borrowing from Tonga speakers. Similarly, Soli speakers borrowed the root from Lenje speakers. The form *ihumbwa* in Totela and Subiya might result from independent proto-Machili borrowing but are more likely recent borrowings from Lozi or Thimbukushu because they gloss, like the Lozi attestation, as leopard or cheetah and have the wrong phonological form for an inherited root.

BLR-3: *-címbá: 613

C.S.: *-címbá: 355

6. *-sí (7/8)[8]

Botatwe Protolanguage: proto-Botatwe, inherited

Gloss: "country, territory"; also "ground"

Etymology: early Bantu, probably proto-Bantu

Distribution: widespread in Bantu

BLR-3: 562–64, see also *-cí, 584

C.S.: 330, see also 343

7. *-éné (1/2)[9]

Botatwe Protolanguage: proto-Botatwe, inherited

Gloss: "owner of," a kind of leader, generally drops out of eastern Botatwe

Etymology: from older Bantu *-jéné, "self, same"

Distribution: widespread as a term for leader in narrow eastern Bantu and southwestern Bantu: E F G H J K L M N P R

BLR-3: 3298, see also 3296–97, 3299

C.S.: 1971, see also 1970

8. *-tòngò (5/6)[10]

Botatwe Protolanguage: proto-Botatwe, inherited

Gloss: deserted homestead or village site

Etymology: probably from an older term for "sleep": *-tòngò

Distribution: widespread in eastern Bantu and across the southern savannas; proto-Eastern Savanna?

BLR-3: 6820, see also 3001
C.S.: see also 1796

9. *-zímú (3/4)[11]
Botatwe Protolanguage: proto-Botatwe, inherited
Gloss: ancestor spirit
Etymology: from the older Bantu verb *-dím-, "to be extinguished, to get lost"
Distribution: widespread in Bantu, probably proto-Bantu
BLR-3: 1050 see also 1046
C.S.: 619, see also 617–18

10. *-gòngá (5/6)[12]
Botatwe Protolanguage: proto-Botatwe, inherited
Gloss: spear
Etymology: proto-Bantu; originally a stabbing spear?
Distribution: widespread and relict, including A B C H K L M R. The root *-gòngá later took on a specialized meaning in Tonga and Ila to refer specifically to elephant spears. As with many ancient inherited roots, the limitation of Botatwe attestations to the Tonga and Ila languages is likely a result of the better documentation of these two languages, rather than any conservative character of two.
BLR-3: 1448
C.S.: 857

11. *-súmò (5/6)[13]
Botatwe Protolanguage: proto-Botatwe, inherited but also reborrowed into Central Eastern Botatwe, probably to designate a new iron point
Gloss: spear
Etymology: from proto-Bantu *-túm- "to stab"
Distribution: widespread in eastern Bantu, including D E G J L M N S
BLR-3: 3109, see also 3108
C.S.: 1867, see also 1866

12. *-tà (14/6)[14]
Botatwe Protolanguage: proto-Botatwe, inherited
Gloss: bow
Etymology: from *-tá "to throw," proto-Bantu

Distribution: widespread in Bantu

BLR-3: 9207 as *-táà, see also 2708

C.S.: see also 1633

13. *-vóí (3/4)[15]

Botatwe Protolanguage: proto-Botatwe, inherited

Gloss: arrow

Etymology: unknown; Savanna Bantu innovation as *-gúí or very ancient areal form, replaces earlier Bantu *-bànjí

Distribution: D E G J K M N R S

BLR-3: 1523

C.S.: 903y

14. *-vóím-[16]

Botatwe Protolanguage: proto-Botatwe, inherited

Gloss: to hunt, probably originally referred to archery

Etymology: narrow eastern Bantu innovation as *-gúím- from *-gúí with the addition of -ma to fix the transitive effect of the arrow's capacity to kill onto its target.

Distribution: eastern Bantu, including E R G M S. The Nkoya attestation is a borrowing from Ila, based on both its phonological form and its narrow semantic meaning.

BLR-3: 1525; see also 4028

C.S.: 904

15. *-gomba (9/10)[17]

Botatwe Protolanguage: proto-Botatwe, inherited

Gloss: barbed arrow

Etymology: unknown

Distribution: narrow eastern Bantu with some attestations in other Savanna Bantu languages; with attestations in Botatwe languages following appropriate sound shifts, this root may now be tentatively reconstructed as a proto-Eastern Savanna Bantu innovation.

16. *-lémbé (14/6)[18]

Botatwe Protolanguage: proto-Botatwe, inherited

Gloss: poison, probably *Apocynaceae strophanthus* (sp. *nicholsonii?*)

Etymology: from an ancient Bantu root *-démà, "invalid, physical disabil-ity," which also produced verbs like *-démad-, "to be lame, to be injured," with a wide distribution, including A B C D E F G J K L M N R S
Distribution: C F J S
BLR-3: 922 as "birdlime," see also 914–15, 917–18.
C.S.: p.s. 161, see also 531–34

17. *-tég-[19]
    Botatwe Protolanguage: proto-Botatwe, inherited
    Gloss: to trap, to set a trap
    Etymology: unknown; early Bantu
    Distribution: B D E F G H J L M P S
    BLR-3: 2825
    C.S.: 1698

18. *-pèto (3/4)[20]
    Botatwe Protolanguage: proto-Botatwe, inherited
    Gloss: spring noose trap
    Etymology: from an older Bantu root *-pèt-, "to bend tr., to fold"
    Distribution: relict across narrow eastern Bantu and southwestern Bantu
    BLR-3: *-pèt-: 2482
    C.S.: *-pèt-: 1495

19. *-lìmbò (14/6)[21]
    Botatwe Protolanguage: proto-Botatwe, inherited
    Gloss: birdlime
    Etymology: proto-Bantu?, from an older verb *-dɪmb-, "to trap with bird lime, to stick to something," with a distribution including B C F G H J K L M N P S
    Distribution: B C G H J L M N P S
    BLR-3: 985; see also 976–78
    C.S.: 575, 578

20. *-líbá (5/6)[22]
    Botatwe Protolanguage: proto-Botatwe, inherited
    Gloss: falling trap
    Etymology: unknown
    Distribution: widespread in Savanna Bantu and beyond; C E G J K M N P R S

BLR-3: 955
C.S.: 558

21. *-kúndè (5/6, 9/10, 11/10)[23]
Botatwe Protolanguage: fell out of use in Botatwe languages
Gloss: cowpeas
Etymology: unknown
Distribution: A C D E G K L M N P R
BLR-3: 2048
C.S.: 1222

22. *-jʊ̀gʊ́ (9/10, 11/10)[24]
Botatwe Protolanguage: fell out of use in Botatwe languages
Gloss: groundnuts
Etymology: unknown
Distribution: widespread but relict distribution across Bantu, including
B C E G S
BLR-3: 1621
C.S.: 961

23. *-pàmá (5/6)[25]
Botatwe Protolanguage: proto-Botatwe, inherited
Gloss: yam sp.
Etymology: uncertain; proto-Bantu?
Distribution: A C M and widespread in narrow eastern Bantu

24. *lʊngʊ (7/8)
Botatwe Protolanguage: proto-Botatwe, inherited
Gloss: yam
Etymology: uncertain; early Savanna?
Distribution: relict in northeastern languages of narrow eastern Bantu; com-
mon in K L M R
BLR-3: 3872

25. *-bʊ̀jʊ́ (3/4)
Botatwe Protolanguage: proto-Botatwe, inherited
Gloss: baobab
Etymology: unknown

Distribution: more common in eastern Bantu languages; C G M N S

BLR-3: 354

C.S.: 214

26. *-bónò (3/4)[26]

Botatwe Protolanguage: proto-Botatwe, inherited

Gloss: castor oil plant and/or castor oil bean

Etymology: proto-Bantu but better conserved in eastern Bantu.

Distribution: more common in eastern Bantu; B E F G J H M

BLR-3: 268–70

C.S.: 166

27. *-bʊda (3/4)[27]

Botatwe Protolanguage: proto-Botatwe, borrowed or inherited (unresolved by phonology)

Gloss: mobula tree and/or fruit (*Parinari curatellifolia*)

Etymology: Savanna or early narrow eastern Bantu with borrowing into Botatwe

Distribution: F G K N M P S

BLR-3: 4562

28. *-pòngó (5/6)[28]

Botatwe Protolanguage: proto-Botatwe, borrowed

Gloss: goat (he-goat?)

Etymology: replaces earlier Bantu *-bʊ́dì in early narrow eastern Bantu

Distribution: G K L M N S

BLR-3: 2609

C.S.: 1581

29. *-kángà (9/10)[29]

Botatwe Protolanguage: proto-Botatwe, inherited

Gloss: guinea fowl

Etymology: onomatopoeia?; proto-Bantu

Distribution: A B C D E F G H J K L M N P

BLR-3: 1720

C.S.: 1010

30. *-lób-[30]

Botatwe Protolanguage: proto-Botatwe, inherited

Gloss: to fish with a hook and line, angle

Etymology: proto-Bantu

Distribution: widespread, including A B C F G H J K L M R S. The Fwe attestation, *kulaba,* exhibits retrogressive assimilation, a process that is common to this language (but most frequent in the stabilizer vowels of absolute pronouns)

BLR-3: 1088

C.S.: 638

31. *-zə̀b-[31]

Botatwe Protolanguage: proto-Botatwe, inherited, but with semantic shift in Central Eastern and Kafue periods to broaden the forms of fishing to which the root referred

Gloss: to fish with a basket

Etymology: proto-Bantu or early Bantu

Distribution: B C D E F G J L M S

BLR-3: 1244

C.S.: 731

32. *-ócì (14/6)[32]

Botatwe Protolanguage: proto-Botatwe, inherited

Gloss: honey

Etymology: proto-Bantu

Distribution: widespread

BLR-3: 6225

C.S.: 962

33. *-pàkò (5/6)[33]

Botatwe Protolanguage: proto-Botatwe, inherited

Gloss: natural beehive, a hallow in a tree

Etymology: from *-pàkò "tree hallow"

Distribution: D E H J K L M N P S. It is difficult to determine when speakers began to use this root as the generic term for a natural beehive. The distribution stretches to Mashariki languages that are not adjacent so the innovation could be proto-Eastern Savanna or an areal between proto-Botatwe and proto-Mashariki. With an attestation in Thimbukushu, it is even possible that the semantic innovation is proto-Savanna. However, Thimbukushu frequently follows western Botatwe languages. Of course, the semantic extension from "hole in tree" to "natural beehive" is not surprising. Therefore, the distribution could be a result of convergence.

BLR-3: 2374

C.S.: 1425

34. *(1)mpòká (5/6, 11/10)[34]

Botatwe Protolanguage: proto-Botatwe, semantic shift to focus only on honeybee

Gloss: honeybee

Etymology: Bantu applied to various insects; replaced *-jíkì

Distribution: widespread distribution referring to different insects, including D H J K L. This root could have been borrowed later, into languages bordering the Botatwe to the northwest, west, and southwest, including Nkoya, Mwenyi, Lozi, and Thimbukushu. Yet an attestation in Rumanyo suggests that the word could have been an ancient areal between proto-Botatwe or proto-Western Botatwe speakers and speakers of proto-Luyana/Southwest Bantu. Despite its replacement in proto-Eastern Botatwe by a transformation of the old root *-júkì, the retention of *(1)mpòká in Soli (subsequently borrowed into Lenje) further supports the place of *(1)mpòká as a proto-Botatwe form. Furthermore, just to the east of the Botatwe domain Sabi speakers use a completely different term. M N R S.

BLR-3: 2638, 2638–41

C.S.: 1596

35. *-ka(to) (14)[35]

Botatwe Protolanguage: proto-Botatwe

Gloss: beeswax

Etymology: replaced older Savanna term *-púdá

Distribution: Botatwe and Lamba

36. *-lòbà (14/6, 11/6)[36]

Botatwe Protolanguage: proto-Botatwe semantic innovation

Gloss: beebread

Etymology: from older Bantu term *-dòbà "flower, pollen" with a wide distribution in Savanna, including D E G J K L M N P S

Distribution: semantic innovation seems restricted to Botatwe

BLR-3: 1158

C.S.: 681

37. *-sɪabe (3/4)[37]

    Botatwe Protolanguage: proto-Botatwe, borrowed
    Gloss: edible tuber
    Etymology: narrow eastern Bantu
    Distribution: relict in narrow eastern Bantu

38. *-óngò (7/8)[38]

    Botatwe Protolanguage: proto-Botatwe, borrowed
    Gloss: gourd
    Etymology: early narrow eastern Bantu
    Distribution: relict in narrow eastern Bantu

39. *-lʊmbʊ (7/8) [39]

    Botatwe Protolanguage: proto-Botatwe, borrowed
    Gloss: Livingstone potato
    Etymology: unknown.
    Distribution: relict in northern narrow eastern Bantu
    BLR-3: 4249

40. *-(y)ɪla (5/6)[40]

    Botatwe Protolanguage: proto-Botatwe, borrowed
    Gloss: sorghum (*bicolor*)
    Etymology: narrow eastern Bantu or Kusi
    Distribution: F M N S
    BLR-3: 5778 var. of *-bɪda, 5736

41. *-bèlé (5/6)[41]

    Botatwe Protolanguage: proto-Botatwe, borrowed
    Gloss: pearl millet
    Etymology: narrow eastern Bantu
    Distribution: E F G J L M N R S
    BLR-3: 122–23
    C.S.: 70

42. *-gamba (5/6)[42]

    Botatwe Protolanguage: proto-Botatwe, borrowed
    Gloss: hoe
    Etymology: variant of widespread *-gèmbè

Distribution: see discussion in citations in n. 42
BLR-3: var. of 1356
C.S.: var. of 803

43. *-jèmbè (5/6)

Botatwe Protolanguage: proto-Botatwe, borrowed
Gloss: axe
Etymology: borrowed from narrow eastern Bantu
Distribution: G E L M N S
BLR-3: 1581 var. of 1356
C.S.: 933, var. of 803

44. *-tǔl-

Botatwe Protolanguage: proto-Botatwe, borrowed
Gloss: to forge
Etymology: semantic innovation from the early Bantu meaning "hammer"
Distribution: very widespread across the Bantu domain
BLR-3: 3101
C.S.: 1861

45. *-(j)ǒndò (9/10)

Botatwe Protolanguage: proto-Botatwe, borrowed
Gloss: smith's hammer or anvil
Etymology: probably carried the original meaning "hammer"
Distribution: very widespread across the Bantu domain
BLR-3: 1628
C.S.: 965

46. *-kélwa (9/10)

Botatwe Protolanguage: Greater Eastern Botatwe, borrowed
Gloss: "tuyère" or "drain for slag"
Etymology: from an old Bantu verb, *-kéd-, "to strain, to filter"
Distribution: see discussion in citations in n. 42
BLR-3: *-kéd-: 1756
C.S.: *-kéd-: 1030

47. *-tále (14/6)

Botatwe Protolanguage: Greater Eastern Botatwe, borrowed

Gloss: "iron ore" or "iron bloom"

Etymology: semantic innovation from an older root for stone

Distribution: widespread convergence across the Bantu domain

BLR-3: 2727–30; see also 2726

C.S.: 1643–44; see also 1642

48. *-gela (7/8)

Botatwe Protolanguage: Greater Eastern Botatwe, borrowed

Gloss: refined iron, iron ready for forging

Etymology: from an older verb, *-gèd-, "to flow"

Distribution: A C D E F G J L M N P

BLR-3: 1349–50

C.S.: 800

49. *-vʊkʊt-

Botatwe Protolanguage: Greater Eastern Botatwe, borrowed

Gloss: to work the bellows

Etymology: areal eastern Bantu, centered on the corridor region?

Distribution: F G J S

BLR-3: 373, var. of 1253

C.S.: p.s. 54, var. of 738

50. *-vʊba (3/4)

Botatwe Protolanguage: Greater Eastern Botatwe, borrowed

Gloss: bellows

Etymology: narrow eastern Bantu

Distribution: E F G J M P S

BLR-3: 1526

C.S.: 905

51. *-gombe (9/10)[43]

Botatwe Protolanguage: proto-Botatwe

Gloss: head of cattle

Etymology: much borrowing; onomatopoeia?

Distribution: C D E F G H J K L M N P R S

BLR-3: 1434

C.S.: 849

52. *-kana (9/10)

Botatwe Protolanguage: proto-Botatwe
Gloss: calf
Etymology: semantic extension from the early Bantu root *-jánà, "child"
Distribution: narrow eastern Bantu
BLR-3: 8251, der. of 3203

53. *-bɪsɪ (3/4)

Botatwe Protolanguage: proto-Botatwe
Gloss: sour milk
Etymology: unknown
Distribution: Botatwe

54. *-pʊɪzɪ (5/6)

Botatwe Protolanguage: Greater Eastern Botatwe, borrowed
Gloss: heifer
Etymology: narrow eastern Bantu; perhaps innovated among northern language cluster?
Distribution: narrow eastern Bantu, Sabi, Botatwe
BLR-3: 4803 as "sheep" for S zone attestation

55. *-pʊmba (5/6)

Botatwe Protolanguage: Greater Eastern Botatwe, borrowed
Gloss: dung
Etymology: unknown
Distribution: middle Zambezi, Njila, eastern Botatwe
BLR-3: related to 3810 "burning material"?

56. *-tàngá (5/6)

Botatwe Protolanguage: Greater Eastern Botatwe, borrowed
Gloss: cattle pen, herd
Etymology: southern cluster of narrow east Bantu (Ehret's "Kusi")
Distribution: diffused east to west from southern cluster of narrow east Bantu to include Botatwe, and Njila languages, including G K L M N S
BLR-3: 2795–96
C.S.: 1678

57. *-(y)aba (11/6)

Botatwe Protolanguage: Greater Eastern Botatwe, borrowed

Gloss: cream

Etymology: uncertain; Ehret posits that the root is a late Kaskazi (northern narrow east Bantu) innovation

Distribution: Takama and Botatwe

58. *-ámí (1/2)

Botatwe Protolanguage: Greater Eastern Botatwe, borrowed

Gloss: leader, a bringer and achiever of prosperity and fertility

Etymology: part of a wider polysemetic cluster of roots that elaborate on *-jám-, "to shout, to suck(le)"; connection to leadership developed in narrow eastern Bantu

Distribution: D F H J K M

BLR-3: 3183

C.S.: 1911

59. *nkólɪ (9/10)[44]

Botatwe Protolanguage: Central Eastern Botatwe

Gloss: warthog

Etymology: from an older Bantu root, *-kód-, "to be strong, to be hard, to be difficult" (undoubtedly describing the temperament of this agricultural pest), often combined with the masculine pre-stem element reminiscent of the feminine pre-stem element added to many antelope species around this time, as the bush, its inhabitants, and labors undertaken within it are gendered in new ways.

Distribution: Central Eastern Botatwe only

BLR-3: *-kód-: 1874

C.S.: *-kód-: 1104

60. *ngɪlɪ (9/10)[45]

Botatwe Protolanguage: Central Eastern Botatwe

Gloss: feral swine (wild boar, river bush pig)

Etymology: semantic innovation from inherited meaning "warthog"; root of Savanna Bantu origin?

Distribution: as "feral swine": Central Eastern Botatwe only; as "warthog": E F G J K M N S

BLR-3: 1377

C.S.: 814

61. *-zèl-[46]

Botatwe Protolanguage: Kafue

Gloss: to fish with nets, traps, and baskets in swift-running waterways

Etymology: perhaps derived in a similar manner *-jéd-, "to float," which was derived in the P zone from an older root, *-jédɪd-, "to float." The floating describes both the traps set in swift waters and the fishers casting nets and hauling baskets from canoes.

Distribution: Kafue; Bemba, Lungu

BLR-3: consider 3274–75

C.S.: consider 1960–60a

62. *-sábwe (11/6)[47]

Botatwe Protolanguage: Central Eastern Botatwe

Gloss: small fishing net, probably tossed from a canoe

Etymology: Botatwe attestations of this word indicate that it was a loan because *j does not shift to /s/ and the /u/ had already shifted to /ʊ/. Two possible (related?) sources include a common term for "hunting net" in eastern Bantu, *-(j)ábù, or a cluster of related roots common across the Savanna Bantu languages for river crossing: *-jàbʊk- "to cross a river" and *-jàbʊ́ (7/8) "crossing place."

Distribution: Central Eastern Botatwe

BLR-3: 3142 or 1553, 3140–41.

C.S.: 1887 or 916, 1885–86.

63. *-wèz-[48]

Botatwe Protolanguage: Central Eastern Bantu

Gloss: to hunt or fish, probably with a spear (throwing spears?)

Etymology: perhaps from the ancient Bantu verb *-bìng, meaning "to hunt or chase." More likely from a widespread eastern Bantu root, *-gèdi, "to try."

Distribution: eastern and western Botatwe with slightly different semantic fields: "to hunt or fish" and "to spear," respectively; distinct borrowings, given the pattern of lenition of /g/ in western Botatwe languages

BLR-3: 213–14 or 1346, but see also 1345.

C.S.: 129 or 797 and 797a

64. *-fʊmbo (5/6)[49]

Botatwe Protolanguage: Kafue

Gloss: plunge basket

Etymology: from an old Bantu verb, *-kúmba, with the meaning "to bend," which is also the source for old, widespread derivatives like *-kúmba, "to enclose or embrace," and *-kúmbat, "to hold in arm, hold in hand"
Distribution: Kafue and some adjacent Sabi languages
BLR-3: consider: 2120, 2122, 3825
C.S.: consider: 1266

65. *-bʊʊba (14/6)[50]
Botatwe Protolanguage: Kafue or, perhaps, Central Eastern Botatwe
Gloss: fish poison (mundale tree or *Tephrosia vogelii*)
Etymology: unknown.
Distribution: Kafue and adjacent Falls, Soli, and Sabi languages

66. *-sɪko (5/6 or 11/6)[51]
Botatwe Protolanguage: Central Eastern Botatwe
Gloss: shallow, plate-like fishing basket
Etymology: perhaps derives from a common verb in Luban languages: *-tɪkʊd-, "to pull off, to take," whereby the basket, with the -o suffix, becomes the object or tool for enacting the verb
Distribution: Central Eastern Botatwe
BLR-3: consider 6251

67. *-zòbo (3/4)
Botatwe Protolanguage: Kafue
Gloss: trawling basket
Etymology: from the inherited verb *-zòb- with a suffix indicating the instrument of the action
Distribution: Kafue

68. *-pàdó (1/2) "celebrated, talented hunter"[52]
Botatwe Protolanguage: Central Eastern Botatwe
Gloss: skilled, celebrated spearman
Etymology: from the ancient Bantu root *-pá, "to give," with an extensive affix indicating spread or distance from the source of the giving developed into an adjective to describe the instrument (also *-pàdó) and person who wielded it. Sometimes, an intensifying infix is added to describe the spearman in class 1/2. The use of the root to talk about the instrument has a far

more widespread distribution beyond the nexus of contact that supported the innovation of the person who wielded it to acquire fame.

Distribution: Central Eastern Botatwe, Ruund, Luban, Sabi, Chikunda, Lozi (the instrument extends to narrow eastern Bantu and Bobangi)

BLR-3: 8982, 8909; for *-pá, see 2344

C.S.: for *-pá, see 1404

69. *(ı)ntale (9/10)[53]

Botatwe Protolanguage: Central Eastern Botatwe

Gloss: ferrule or joints of iron taping or wire connecting the spear point to its shaft

Etymology: from an older Bantu root, *-tádè, for "iron, iron ore, iron bloom," with an earlier meaning "stone"

Distribution: relict Central Eastern Botatwe

BLR-3: for *-tádè, see 2726–30

C.S.: for *-tádè, see 1642–44

70. *lusákò (11/6)[54]

Botatwe Protolanguage: Kafue

Gloss: spearshaft

Etymology: derived from an older root for thicket, dense woodlands, forest, or "wild area," *-càká, itself a derivative of the older Bantu root *-sàk-, "to hunt by chasing or driving animals"

Distribution: parallel derivations using the same root in different noun classes abound in Sabi and southwest Bantu

BLR-3: *-càká: 423; see also 420, 424.

C.S.: *-càká: 260

71. *(ı)mpòla (9/10)[55]

Botatwe Protolanguage: Kafue

Gloss: spear point (barbless?)

Etymology: from *-pùd-, "to dig," with nasal prefix stabilizing /p/? An alternative may be *-pódɪk-, a verb meaning "to hear, to listen in silence" with a narrow east Bantu distribution, including F G J H N. The second possibility follows the Ila nickname for this spear: "the silencer," for this spear is used to finish the wounded animal.

Distribution: Kafue

BLR-3: *-pùd-: 3961, 4621; *-pʊ́dɪk-: 2626–27.

C.S.: *-pʊ́dɪk-: 1589a

72. *-bèjɪ (5/6 or 11/6)[56]

Botatwe Protolanguage: Kafue

Gloss: barbless point used on both spears and arrows

Etymology: from an older Bantu root, *-bàij-, "to carve" with the agentive affix to form "the carver"

Distribution: Lenje, Ila, Lamba

BLR-3: consider 8930

73. *mpʊwo (9/Ø)[57]

Botatwe Protolanguage: Central Eastern Botatwe

Gloss: fame

Etymology: derived from an older Bantu word, *-pòʊp-, meaning "blow, wind, breath from lungs"

Distribution. with the meaning fame, Central Eastern Botatwe

BLR-3: *-pòʊp-: 2660–62, 4823, 2690, 2691, 2693, 4797, 4381, 2469

C.S.: *-pòʊp-: 1605.

74. *-vʊbɪ (1/2)[58]

Botatwe Protolanguage: Central Eastern Botatwe

Gloss: famous, rich person

Etymology: from an older eastern Bantu root, *-gùbà, "smithy, bellows," or an ancient eastern Bantu areal form, °-vuba, "bellows"

Distribution: Central Eastern Botatwe

BLR-3: 1526

C.S.: 905

75. *-sókwe (5/6)[59]

Botatwe Protolanguage: Central Eastern Botatwe or, perhaps, Kafue with loaning in Lundwe

Gloss: the bush

Etymology: from a narrow eastern Bantu verb, *-còk-, "to incite," distributed across E J R S, which, itself, derives from an ancient Bantu term, *-còk-, reconstructed with a range of meanings, including, "to poke in, put in, prick with a point, hide, ram in," and a distribution that includes A F H J K L M N

R S. The verb was put into the passive form to create "the landscape that is prodded or incited." Another related root derives from this stem: *-còkó (n. cl. 1/2, 9/10), "monkey," with distribution restricted to south central Africa and the Shona-Venda cluster. This distribution mirrors that of later trade goods, including currencies, and indicates an ancient contact zone bridged by Botatwe speakers and discussed in chapter 5.

Distribution: Lundwe, Lenje, Tonga, Ila
BLR-3: *-còk-: 644–45; see also 648
C.S.: *-còk-: 370–71; see also 373

76. *-nyíka (9/10)[60]

Botatwe Protolanguage: Central Eastern Botatwe semantic innovation
Gloss: country, suggesting that savanna environments were understood to be generic lands for settlement
Etymology: semantic shift of an earlier root, *-jìkà, meaning "grassland, desert"
Distribution: Central Eastern Botatwe and some Sabi with this meaning
BLR-3: 3347
C.S.: 2002

77. *-kole (5/6 or 7/8)[61]

Botatwe Protolanguage: Kafue
Gloss: noose snare
Etymology: from the verb *-kód-, "to take, to touch," with a distribution including attestations in zones C G J M N
Distribution: Lenje, Tonga, Ila, adjacent Sabi and Bemba
BLR-3: *-kód-: 6999

78. *-kooze (12/13)[62]

Botatwe Protolanguage: Kafue
Gloss: noose trap
Etymology: from an inherited root for bark string, *-ooye, itself a form of the ancient Bantu root *-gòdí
Distribution: Kafue
BLR-3: *-gòdí: 1417
C.S.: *-gòdí: 839

79. *-kóba (3/4)[63]

Botatwe Protolanguage: Central Eastern Botatwe or Kafue

Gloss: matriclan or kin grouping reckoned through the mother's line
Etymology: developed by Njila speakers to the west of Botatwe communities; derives from an older Bantu term for skin, *-kóba "skin"
Distribution: block distribution from west central to east central Africa
BLR-3: 1861
C.S.: 1095

80. *-tʃıCıa (1/2)

Botatwe Protolanguage: Kafue (possibly Greater Eastern Botatwe)
Gloss: maternal uncle
Etymology: difficult to determine due to the outcome of spirantization in eastern Botatwe languages; the consonant in the C3 position remains uncertain. Replaces or instead of an older term for maternal uncle in Bantu languages, *-dómè, which has a distribution in A B J M N S.
Distribution: Kafue, Soli, Lundwe, Toka
BLR-3: *-dómè: 1184
C.S.: *-dómè: 698

81. *-kwésʊ (1/2)

Botatwe Protolanguage: proto-Botatwe, inherited
Gloss: a category of family that belongs to one's (classificatory) generation; narrowed to parallel cousin in Kafue era
Etymology: compound of the locative *-ku combined with the possessive *-esu
Distribution: Botatwe, Sabi, eastern Bantu

82. *-kwàshı (n. cl. 3/4)

Botatwe Protolanguage: Kafue
Gloss: in-laws of one's own generation (brothers- and sisters-in-law) and cross-cousins, suggesting a preference for cross-cousin marriages
Etymology: from an older Bantu verb *-kóat-, "to seize, grasp," with a very wide distribution across Bantu
Distribution: Kafue and some eastern Bantu languages to the southeast of Kafue languages
BLR-3: *-kóat-: 1974
C.S.: *-kóat-: 1172

83. *-kó (7/8)[64]

Botatwe Protolanguage: proto-Botatwe, inherited

Gloss: bridewealth

Etymology: proto-Bantu

Distribution: widespread; see citations in n. 64 for different distributions of *-kwé and *-kó in both noun and verb forms

BLR-3: 7240

84. *-kwa[65]

Botatwe Protolanguage: proto-Botatwe, inherited

Gloss: to give bridewealth

Etymology: from early Bantu *-kó, "to give bridewealth"

Distribution: see citations in n. 65 for different distributions of *-kwé and *-kó in both noun and verb forms

BLR-3: 7240

85. *-kwe (1/2)[66]

Botatwe Protolanguage: proto-Botatwe, inherited

Gloss: in-law; those affines of an adjacent generation who hold a stake in the marriage that created the relationship

Etymology: from proto-Bantu *-kó, "to give bridewealth"

Distribution: widespread derivation, but likely skewed by some convergence given the variety of forms

C.S.: 1174

86. *-lòngó (1/2 and 14)[67]

Botatwe Protolanguage: Kafue

Gloss: bond friend, bond friendship

Etymology: from a very old Bantu root, *-dòng-, "heap up, arrange; pack up" related to moving house. The widespread eastern Bantu root for lineage, kinship, or clan, *-dòngò, also derives from this root. Borrowed from eastern Bantu languages into Kafue, probably languages using the derivative *-dòngó, "brother," distributed in L N P S.

Distribution: Kafue only with the meaning "bond friendship"

BLR-3: *-dòng-: 1120; see also 1135, 1137, and many other related roots

C.S.: *-dòng-: 658; see also 665, 666, and related roots

87. *cìlà (7/8)[68]

Botatwe Protolanguage: Kafue

Gloss: communal hunt, game drive

Etymology: from *-kìdà (14/6), an older term in equatorial Bantu languages for "hunting net"

Distribution: Kafue with this meaning; as "net" or "hammock" in B C D J L M (but with different VI)

BLR-3: 5807, 6130 (different VI)

88. *-pàndo (11/10)[69]

Botatwe Protolanguage: Kafue

Gloss: hunting entrapments

Etymology: derives from older Bantu transitive verb root *-pànd-, "to split," with the deverbative suffix denoting the action, result, or instrument of the verb

Distribution: Kafue

BLR-3: *-pànd-: 2387–89

C.S.: *-pànd-: 1433

89. ıbalo (5/6)[70]

Botatwe Protolanguage: common Kafue form

Gloss: circle of hunters in a battue hunt

Etymology: related to *-bada, "ring"

Distribution: Lenje, Tonga, Ila

BLR-3: *-bada: 9139

90. *-yal-[71]

Botatwe Protolanguage: eastern Batoka areal form developed after the thirteenth century

Gloss: to hunt by surrounding

Etymology: from *-jàd-, "to spread"

Distribution: Soli, Lenje, Tonga

BLR-3: *-jàd-: 3147

C.S.: *-jàd-: 1890

91. *n(y)anjá (9/10)[72]

Botatwe Protolanguage: Kafue; the addition of a feminine pre-stem element was a Kafue innovation

Gloss: kobus lechwe

Etymology: skewed phonology in Kafue indicates borrowing. Possibly related to *-jànjá, "lake," with attestations in D F G J M N P S, indicating the preferred wetland habitat of the kobus lechwe.

Distribution: Kafue with the feminine pre-stem element; also Bemba, Lamba, Yeyi. It may well have been borrowed by a now lost eastern Bantu language, for the root would have produced *-nza if inherited by proto-Kafue speakers and is likewise skewed in Lundwe.

BLR-3: *-jànjá: 3221–24

C.S.: *-jànjá: 1934 and p.s. 490–91

92. *mbàbàlá (7/8)[73]

Botatwe Protolanguage: Kafue; possible Savanna inheritance (phonology does not resolve)

Gloss: bushbuck

Etymology: borrowed from southern narrow east Bantu languages?

Distribution: Kafue, narrow east Bantu; Lunda, Lozi. Although phonologically the root could be proto-Savanna or proto-Eastern Savanna, the block distribution in languages spoken along major swamps and rivers in south central Africa (Kafue, Zambezi, and Luangwa) suggests two borrowings into Botatwe languages in the early to mid-second millennium CE: one in the east among proto-Kafue and proto-Soli speakers and one in the west.

BLR-3: 13

C.S.: 8

93. *n(y)alʊvwɪ (11/6)[74]

Botatwe Protolanguage: Kafue

Gloss: reedbuck

Etymology: combines old feminine pre-stem element with inherited proto-Savanna term for arrow, *-gúí (see above)

Distribution: Kafue, Sabi, Thimbukushu (?). This root spread to two Sabi languages, Lamba and Bemba, via Lenje. A possible Thimbukushu attestation of this root, *-ruvi, may suggest an older origin or be an outcome of independent innovation. Regardless, the root with the feminine pre-prefix was certainly a Proto-Kafue innovation.

94. *-síá (12/13)[75]

Botatwe Protolanguage: Kafue innovates feminine pre-stem element

Gloss: duiker

Etymology: Early Bantu or Proto-Bantu

Distribution: without the pre-stem element, widespread: B E F G H J L M
N P S

BLR-3: 1823

C.S.: 1075

Notes

Introduction

1. Term from Homewood, *Ecology of African Pastoralist*, 49.
2. But consider the approach of Finlayson and Warren in *Changing Natures*.
3. Though not framed in this way, Kairn Klieman's study of the complicated, intertwined history of "autochthones," "hunter-gatherers," and "Batwa" in *"The Pygmies Were Our Compass"* stands out as an exception.
4. Baloglou, "Tradition of Economic Thought."
5. Rudebeck, *Tilling Nature*.
6. Such schemes occur in the writings of Diodorus Siculus, Lucretius, Hesiod, and Virgil, among others, sometimes as a narrative of decline and in other cases with an underlying progressivism. See discussions of these texts in Pluciennik, "Invention"; Rudebeck, *Tilling*, 37–46; Vencl, "Problem."
7. Cited in Zvelebil, "Invention of Hunter-Gatherers," 129, n. 1. Ideas about the value of hunting offer another example of differing classical views on subsistence. Compare Greek and Roman attitudes toward hunting in Cartmill, *View*, 30, 42–45.
8. Ferguson, *Utter Antiquity;* Janko, "Two Concepts of the World"; Kuper, *Invention of Primitive Society;* Pluciennik, "Invention"; Rudebeck, *Tilling;* Vencl, "Problem."
9. This and the next two paragraphs draw on Barnard, "Images of Hunter-Gatherers"; Barnard, "Hunting-and-Gathering Society," 36, 40; Meek, *Social Science;* Kuper, *Invention;* Pluciennik, "Archeology, Anthropology and Subsistence"; Pluciennik, "Invention"; Pluciennik, "Meaning of 'Hunter-Gatherers'"; Rudebeck, *Tilling*.
10. Monboddo, *Of the Origin,* cited in Cartmill, *View*, 25–26; 76–91. Hobbes and Locke articulated similar views in the previous century. See also Klieman, *"Pygmies,"* 11–12.

11. Jean-Jacques Rousseau, "Essay on the Origin of Languages in Which Melody and Musical Imitation Are Treated," cited in Pluciennik, "Invention," 109.

12. Pluciennik, "Meaning of 'Hunter-Gatherers,'" 27.

13. Ferguson, *History of Civil Society;* Millar, *Origin of the Distinction of Ranks;* Monboddo, *Of the Origin;* Robertson, *History of America.* There were many antecedents to these thinkers. All cited in Barnard, "Hunting-and-Gathering."

14. Adam Smith, *An Inquiry into the Nature and Causes of the Wealth of Nations,* 2 vols. (London: W. Strahan and T. Cadell, 1776), cited in Barnard, "Hunting-and-Gathering." Of course, the idea that a fundamental purpose of government derives from its role in guaranteeing private property rights undergirds many economic policies aimed at developing contemporary African economies.

15. Consider, for example, Barnard, "Through Radcliffe-Brown's Spectacles"; Trigger, *History of Archaeological Thought.*

16. Klieman offers a history of hunter-gatherer studies in *"Pygmies,"* ch. 1.

17. The idea was popularized with the 1911 publication of Sollas's *Ancient Hunters and their Modern Representatives.*

18. Kuper, *Invention.* In *Myth of the Noble Savage,* Ellingson, argues that the noble savage was developed by proponents of social Darwinism rather than by its critics.

19. For a classic treatment, consider Stocking, *Race, Culture, and Evolution.*

20. Childe, *Man Makes Himself.* See also Rudebeck, *Tilling,* 154–60.

21. Though the Killer Ape theory is most frequently associated with Raymond Dart, the earliest iteration can be traced to Lord Monboddo (see above). Dart, "Australopithecus Africanus." A number of other scientists, notably Charles Morris, Harry Campbell, and Carveth Read, made similar suggestions between the world wars. The thesis was overturned by the Man the Hunter thesis: Washburn and Lancaster, "Evolution of Hunting." For a summary, see Cartmill, *View,* chs. 1 and 10. The Man the Hunter conference in 1966 reinvigorated the field of hunter-gatherer studies; published proceedings demonstrate the variety of hunter-gatherer research at mid-century: Lee and DeVore, eds., *Man the Hunter.* On the Original Affluent Society thesis, see Sahlins, "Original Affluent Society," 85–89; Sahlins, *Stone Age Economics.* On the Woman the Gatherer thesis, see Dahlberg, "Introduction." The conflation of gender and subsistence in the Woman the Gatherer thesis had its own antecedents in James Frazer's argument in *The Golden Bough* that women invented agriculture (the "Mother of Agriculture" thesis). See Rude-

beck, *Tilling*, 129–30 and 135. The most famous mid-century study of contemporary hunter-gatherers to understand early human history is probably
the Harvard Kalahari Project, a long-term study of the !Kung San (1963–
80), directed by Richard Lee and Irven DeVore. See discussion later in this
chapter and citations in n. 25.

22. The distinction between farmers and non-farmers or farmers and hunter-
gatherers remains essential for formulating research questions across disciplines because it provides the theoretical foundation for many forms of
"origins" research. These ideas about the origins of our humanity range in
quality from sophisticated to ridiculous, but they prove the power of the association between subsistence and difference. For example, current research in the fields of economics and biology explore similarities between
the gathering work and group organization of primates and hunter-gatherers
in the contemporary world, who, we must suppose, represent once again the
very earliest, very first attempts of our more distant ancestors in becoming
human, in distinguishing themselves (unsuccessfully, this research would
suggest) from their beastly neighbors. See Yengoyan, "Anthropological History," 61. In a new twist on the relationship between subsistence and human
origins, some scholars are now claiming that it was the shift to agriculture
that produced the first culturally modern humans, recalling the antique juxtaposition of the civilized farmer and the barbaric non-farmer. This is a
sophisticated field of study. But we would do well to recall the powerful
role of subsistence as a marker of identity in reading such studies. Compare: Cauvin, *Birth of the Gods;* Hodder, *Domestication of Europe;* Renfrew,
Prehistory; Watkins, "Neolithic Revolution," 84–88.

23. Kenneth Oakely and Sherwood Washburn voiced persistent opposition to
Dart's Killer Ape theory, with the latter proposing the first model of the Man
the Hunter hypothesis. In 1970, Bob Brain advanced the idea that hominids
were actually more often prey than predator. Lewis Binford supported Brain's
hypothesis and, from the early 1980s, helped to establish a new paradigm in
paleoanthropological studies of the relationship between hominids and other
animals. Binford, *Bones;* Brain, *Hunters or the Hunted?;* Oakely, "Dating of
Australopithecinae"; Washburn, "Australopithecines." This debate continues; see Hard and Sussman, *Man the Hunted.* For the classic volume on
complex hunter-gatherers, see Price and Brown, eds., *Prehistoric Hunter-
Gatherers.* For an influential summary of scholarship in North America, see
Sassaman, "Complex Hunter-Gatherers." In addition to citations above, rep-
resentative examples of scholarship on the variety of subsistence economies

developed by hunter-gatherers also include Kelley, *Foraging Spectrum,* and Kent, ed., *Cultural Diversity.*

24. For example, comments to this effect frame the introductions to three influential edited volumes on African archaeology and precolonial history: McIntosh, ed., *Beyond Chiefdoms;* Shaw et al., eds., *Archaeology of Africa;* Stahl, ed., *African Archaeology.*

25. On the Kalahari debate, see Wilmsen, *Land Filled with Flies;* Wilmsen and Denbow, "Paradigmatic History." For a bibliography, see Barnard, *Kalahari Debate.* For an historical approach to hunter-gatherer communities in equatorial Africa, see Klieman, *"Pygmies."*

26. On mosaics in African archaeology, see Stahl, "Political Economic Mosaics." For an early example of this integrated regional approach to subsistence, see Ambrose, "Hunter-Gatherer Adaptations." See also McIntosh, *Ancient Middle Niger;* Kusimba, Kusimba, and Wright, "Development and Collapse."

27. My thanks to Jeffrey Fleisher for framing the problem of mosaics as a shift from chronology to geography as a marker of difference in comments on a presentation of parts of this chapter to colleagues in the Anthropology Department at Rice University, March 14, 2012.

28. Kent, *Cultural Diversity.*

29. Vansina, "Slow Revolution."

30. Klieman, *"Pygmies."*

31. McIntosh, ed., *Beyond Chiefdoms.* Historians have used this idea to change how they write the histories of famous states. Consider, for example, the use of heterarchy in scholarship on the kingdom of Buganda: Hanson, *Landed Obligation;* Kodesh, *Beyond the Royal Gaze.*

32. Vansina contributed a chapter to McIntosh's *Beyond Chiefdoms* volume. See Vansina, "Pathways."

33. The root is *-kúmú, identified by Ehret as the ritual leader of a small kinship group and by Vansina as a Big Man. See chapter 1 for a discussion of this root. Ehert, *Classical,* 146–49; Vansina, *Paths,* 73–74.

34. Guyer and Belinga "Wealth in People"; Vansina, *Paths.*

35. This is a common observation about the relationship between hierarchy and heterarchy in the literature. Quote from Monroe, "Power and Agency," 4. Compare to Jan Vansina's "two contradictory ideological principles": the "supernatural powers of leaders" and the "equality of all people" in "Pathways," 166.

36. Quote from Vansina, "Pathways," 168.

37. This line of inquiry dates as far back as the interest in the forms of sovereignty associated with divine kingship but was revitalized in African Studies with the publication of Arens and Karp, eds., *Creativity of Power.* Many of the works cited in this section, including McIntosh, ed., *Beyond Chiefdoms* and Schoenbrun, "Intellectual History of Power," developed from engaging with Arens's and Karp's volume. See also Fleisher and Wynne-Jones, "Authorisation and the Process of Power."

38. Herbert, *Iron, Gender, and Power.* See also Klieman's use of the concept "transformative power" in *"Pygmies."*

39. Schoenbrun, *Green Place*, 13; Schoenbrun, "Intellectual History of Power."

40. On creative power, consider Schoenbrun, *Green Place;* Kodesh, *Beyond the Royal Gaze.* On spirits' agency, see Gordon, *Invisible Agents.* On leaders' and followers' honor, see de Luna, "Affect and Society." Victor Turner observed long ago the relationship between transcendent affective experiences and group making during rituals in his notion of *communitas*, outlined in *Ritual Process.* On the existential status of objects and people, consider scholarship on *minkisi:* MacGaffey, "Personhood of Ritual Objects"; MacGaffey, "Complexity, Astonishment, and Power." See the discussion in de Luna, "Affect and Society."

41. Iliffe, *Honour in African History.*

Chapter 1. The Sources and Settings of Botatwe History

1. Colin Graham Trapnell produced the most extensive ecological survey of south central Africa in Northern Rhodesia (now Zambia) in the 1930s and 1940s, covering thousands of miles on foot, by boat, and by truck. Smith, *Ecological Survey.*

2. Most Botatwe settlements in the Caprivi area date to the eighteenth and nineteenth centuries. Fisch, *Caprivi Strip.*

3. Phillipson, "First South African Pastoralists."

4. Herskovits, "Cattle Complex."

5. Roberts, "Pre-colonial Trade in Zambia," 737.

6. Smith and Dale, *Ila-Speaking.*

7. Vansina, *How Societies*, 17–21.

8. Livingstone, "22,000 Year Pollen Record"; Tomlinson, *Imayanga Area.*

9. Guy, *"Andansonia Digitata"*; Hall, "Dendrochronology"; Kalk, McLachlan, and Howard-Williams, *Lake Chilwa;* Shaw, "Lake Chilwa." For further sources, see citations in de Luna, "Collecting Food," ch. 3.

10. Cooke, "Landform Evolution"; Cooke and Verstappen, "Landforms of the Western Makgadigadi"; Crossley et al., "Lake Level Fluctuations"; Heine, "Main Stages"; Nugent, "Zambezi River"; Robbins and Murphy, "Archaeology, Palaeoenvironment and Chronology"; Shaw, "Fluctuations"; Shaw, "Late Quaternary Landforms." For further sources, see de Luna, "Collecting Food," ch. 3.

11. Data from Lake Ngami evince high levels, peaking at 0 CE as a result of high rainfalls in the Okavango cachement. Shaw et al., "Holocene Fluctuations," 33-34. Similarly, warmer, wetter conditions reach the southern Kalahari and northern portions of South Africa c. 0-400 CE. Thomas and Shaw, "Late Quaternary," 794.

12. Again, these peaks are somewhat later in the data nearest to the Botatwe region. The Northern Kalahari peaks around 600 CE. Thomas and Shaw, "Late Quaternary," 794.

13. Shaw et al., *Archaeology of Africa*. See also Trigger, *History of Archaeological Thought*.

14. The most famous synthesis remains Oliver, "Problem of the Bantu Expansion." For a review of approaches to the Bantu Expansion through the 1970s, see Vansina, "Bantu in the Crystal Ball." See also de Luna, "Bantu Expansion."

15. The publications of Joseph Vogel are exceptions to this generalization. Francis Musonda's work is an example of the shift toward in situ processes. See citations in n. 16, below.

16. Musonda, "Significance of Pottery"; Musonda, "Cultural and Social Patterning"; Robertson, "Early Iron Age," 179.

17. Phillipson, "First South African Pastoralists"; Robertson, "Early Iron Age."

18. Robertson, "Early Iron Age," 177-78.

19. On possible population increase in south central Africa c. 1000 CE, see Vansina, "Slow Revolution," 25-26.

20. Generally, this distinction is discussed in the context of continental syntheses like textbooks. Compare Birmingham and Martin, *History of Central Africa*, ch. 1; Curtin et al., *African History*, ch. 8; Phillipson, *African Archaeology*, 261.

21. Derricourt, *Man on the Kafue*.

22. Vogel, "Subsistence Settlement Systems."

23. For a more detailed discussion of archaeologists' sometimes conflicting typologies of regional pottery, see de Luna, "Surveying the Boundaries," 222-29 and cites therein.

24. Bostoen, *Mots et des Pots;* Ehret, *Classical;* Fields-Black, *Deep Roots;* Gonzales, *Societies, Religion, and History;* Klieman, *"Pygmies";* Nurse and Spear, *Swahili;* Saidi, *Women's Authority;* Schoenbrun, *Green Place;* Shetler, *Imagining Serengeti;* Stephens, *African Motherhood;* Vansina, *Paths;* Vansina, *How Societies.*

25. Schoenbrun, *Green Place, Good Place,* 263.

26. For two excellent introductions to the value of the comparative method for African history, see Ehret, *History and the Testimony of Language;* Nurse, "Contributions of Linguistics."

27. Convergence is another process that shaped the pacing and character of language change. Linguists have debated the relative impact of divergence and convergence on language change, best known in the debate between traditionalists and neo-grammarians over the tree and wave models. On the wave model in Bantu linguistics, see Vansina, "New Linguistic Evidence." See also Bastin, Coupez, and Mann, *Continuity and Divergence.*

28. An assessment of earlier classifications of Botatwe languages and technical evidence supporting this classification are discussed in de Luna, "Classifying Botatwe."

29. In the African context, compare the positions of Christopher Ehret and Jan Vansina: Ehret, "Testing the Expectations"; Vansina, *How Societies,* 279–83. The two positions may not be irreconcilable: de Luna, "Surveying the Boundaries," 245–46. On the debate more generally, compare: Embleton, *Statistics in Historical Linguistics;* Morris, "Myth of Rapid Language Change." I thank Jan Vansina for bringing Morris's work to my attention.

30. Robertson and Bradley, "New Paradigm."

31. Vansina, *How Societies.* Detailed arguments for the direct associations I use to connect Botatwe speech communities and particular archaeological sites or material cultural traditions are elaborated in de Luna, "Surveying the Boundaries."

32. The establishment of a diachronic phonology is central to the reconstruction of words, but it is a little understood (and sometimes under-practiced) aspect of the methodology. Ehret, "Linguistic Archaeology."

33. For example, consider David Schoenbrun's uncertainly about the protolanguage to which *-lubaale may be reconstructed: Schoenbrun, *Historical Reconstruction,* 213.

34. On the region as a linguistic crossroads: Bastin, Coupez, and Mann, *Continuity and Divergence;* Bostoen, "Bantu Plant Names"; Ehret, *Classical;* Ehret, "Subclassifying Bantu"; Vansina, *How Societies.*

35. The next two paragraphs draw extensively from a more detailed discussion of the history and ethnography of *mfumu* in de Luna, "Affect and Society."

36. We might consider the nineteenth-century history of the Bemba chiefdoms as an example. Roberts, *History of the Bemba.*

37. Vansina, *Paths,* 73, 274–75.

38. Ehret, *Classical,* 147–48, 249–50.

39. Næss, *Prototypical Transitivity.*

40. Sapir, "Time Perspective in Aboriginal American Culture"; Schoenbrun, *Green Place,* 52–55, 265–69. See also de Luna, Fleisher, and McIntosh, "Thinking across the African Past"; Schoenbrun, "Mixing, Moving, Making, Meaning," esp. 294–300.

41. Similarly, proto-Falls innovated no definitive sound changes.

42. But see Bostoen, "Bantu Plant Names."

43. The next four paragraphs draw extensively on de Luna, "Classifying Botatwe" and de Luna, "Surveying the Boundaries," summarizing findings in those two works as well as: Bastin, Coupez, and Mann, *Continuity and Divergence;* Bostoen, "Shanjo and Fwe"; Bostoen, "Bantu Plant Names"; Ehret, *Classical;* Ehret, "Subclassifying Bantu"; Saidi, *Women's Authority.*

44. Most linguistic evidence for contact between western Botatwe (particularly Fwe) and Khwe languages, which are so closely associated with hunter-gatherer lifestyles, is of recent (post-fifteenth century) origin because it exists most intensely in Fwe. This contact can be explained with equal validity through: first, an indirect influence of Khoisan vocabulary and phonemes mediated by another Bantu language, such as Yeyi; second, a limited borrowing of words with clicks and, subsequently, a further internal elaboration as non-click consonants are replaced with clicks; or, third, direct contact between Fwe and speakers of Khoisan languages after the divergence of proto-Zambezi Hook around the mid-fifteenth century. See Bostoen and Sands, "Clicks in South-western Bantu," 4–14 and cites therein. Genetic research suggests some mixing between the ancestors of populations who now speak Fwe and Shanjo and the ancestors of populations who now speak Khoisan languages, but the shared genetic material may have been exchanged through an intermediate population. See Barbieri et al., "Genetic Perspectives," 434–36. The most widespread evidence of the influence of Khwe languages on western Botatwe languages is the loanword *-gʊ, "sheep," which Christopher Ehret argues was actually an Eastern Sahelian loanword borrowed into proto-Khwe. Ehret also argues that the word was borrowed into southeastern Bantu languages from pastoral Khoikhoi societies, whose lan-

guage belonged to the Khwe group. Therefore, the widespread use of *ngu* for "sheep" in western Botatwe languages may well be a result of the influence of SiLozi, a Sotho language in the southwest Bantu group, after the 1830s. See Ehret, *Classical*, 216–18, 228–29.

45. Musonda, "Significance of Pottery"; Musonda, "Cultural and Social Patterning."

46. The method of direct association and its application to protolanguages in the Botatwe group are elaborated in de Luna, "Surveying."

47. de Luna, "Collecting," root numbers 418, 423, 425, 427, and 428. Many of these terms indicate multiple instances of borrowing from eastern Bantu languages into different sub-branches of Botatwe.

48. Denbow, "Congo to Kalahari."

49. Bostoen, "Plant Names"; de Luna, "Classifying"; de Luna, "Surveying"; Ehret, *Classical*; Ehret, "Subclassifying."

50. Possible correlations are assessed in de Luna, "Surveying." See also Derricourt, *Man on the Kafue;* Fagan, *Iron Age Cultures;* Fagan, "Gundu and Nonde"; Fagan and Phillipson, "Sebanzi"; Fagan, Phillipson, and Daniels, *Iron Age Cultures in Zambia;* Huffman, *Iron Age Migrations;* Vogel, "Subsistence Settlement"; Vogel, "Iron Age Farmers"; Vogel, "Savanna Farmers."

51. These disagreements are discussed in de Luna, "Surveying."

52. Flint, "State-Building"; Kangumu, *Contesting Caprivi;* Mainga, *Bulozi under the Luyana Kings;* Prins, *Hidden Hippopotamus.*

Chapter 2. Planting Settlements, Forging the Savanna

1. Vansina, "Slow Revolution."

2. Bastin, Coupez, and Mann, *Continuity and Divergence;* Ehret, *Classical;* de Luna, "Surveying"; Saidi, *Women's Authority.*

3. The distribution of *mwene* in Botatwe is problematic because it is solid in the west, suggesting recent borrowing, and relict in east, suggesting antiquity. The phonology within Botatwe contributes little to our understanding of its antiquity.

4. Colson, *Tonga Religious Life*, 41; see also the discussion of *sikatongo* in ch. 5.

5. Kairn Klieman argues for the great antiquity of the concept of "first-comer" and the relationship between authority and control of both ancestral and territorial spirits and of followers. Klieman, *"Pygmies."*

6. Vansina, *Paths*, 297.

7. Ehret, *Classical;* Ehret, "Subclassifying."

8. Vansina, "Slow Revolution." For an ethnographic treatment of overlaps between farming and food collection in the Botatwe region in recent times, see Scudder, *Ecology*.

9. Vansina, *Paths*, 90.

10. Ehret, *Classical*, 309.

11. For reconstructions of yam vocabulary, see Ehret, *Classical*, 309; Maniacky, "Quelques thèmes pour 'igname' en bantu"; Philippson and Bahuchet, "Cultivated Crops." Consider attestations in Ila, *cilungu* and *impama*, in Fowler, *Dictionary of Ila*, 839.

12. Ehret, *Classical*, 312. Botatwe attestations show great antiquity.

13. Ehret, *Classical*, 105, 305, 309–10; Vansina, *How Societies*, passim. It is more difficult to discern the antiquity of sheep in Botatwe history. Attestations in western Botatwe languages follow *-gʊ, a loanword from Khoe speakers that Ehret argues originated in Eastern Sahelian languages. Ehret, *Classical*, 228–29. In eastern Botatwe languages, speakers use *-belele. This divide is one example in a common pattern whereby the eastern and western groups were oriented toward communities in opposite geographical directions.

14. This verb root also provides the name for the technology used when fishing in this manner: *-lóbò-, "fishhook." Angling is the earliest form of fishing we can reconstruct for Bantu languages. It seems likely that fishing with nets and traps were innovations that date to later millennia.

15. See citations in ch. 1.

16. Cooke claims about a 200 percent increase over modern rainfall averages. Cooke, "Paleoclimatic Significance," 443.

17. This idea can be traced to Childe's influential volume, *Man Makes Himself*, though he is indebted to a range of eighteenth- and nineteenth-century thinkers, some of whom are referenced in the introduction.

18. Ehret, *Classical*, 132, 269–71, 274. Koen Bostoen argues for two introductions of pearl millet to Bantu-speaking communities and reconstructs *-cángó as a root for "pearl millet" that may date as early as proto-Western Bantu or even proto-Bantu. Bostoen, "Pearl Millet"; see also Vansina, *How Societies*, 75–76. On the emerging case for the antiquity of pearl millet in the Bantu region and in West Africa, see Kahlheber, Bostoen, and Neumann, "Early Plant Cultivation"; Manning et al., "4500-Year Old," 312–22, esp. 318–21.

19. Ehret, *Classical*, 132, 269–71, 274. Koen Bostoen reconstructs *-bèdé as an early eastern Bantu root, perhaps even a proto-Eastern Bantu root borrowed from western Nilotic speakers, probably with the meaning "pearl millet." He argues that pearl millet was borrowed far earlier than sorghum based on

the phonological regularity of the root (which, arguably, carries little room for the phonological variations that allow us to identify instances of inheritance and borrowing) and its wide distribution. If the root was such an early borrowing, its distribution resulted from the spread of pearl millet farmers speaking eastern Bantu languages. Bostoen also argues for a later introduction of sorghum to Bantu-speaking communities on the basis of its higher lexical heterogeneity. Bostoen, "Pearl Millet," 189–93; see also Philippson and Bahuchet, "Cultivated Crops."

20. Denbow, "Congo to Kalahari"; Fagan, *Iron Age Cultures;* Robertson, "Early Iron Age."

21. Fagan, *Iron Age Cultures.* Oliver and Fagan, *Africa in the Iron Age,* 99.

22. Although specialists continue to debate evidence for the relative likelihood of independent or external, single or multiple origins for metallurgy on the continent, we know more about the paths of diffusion after the adoption of ironworking in the eastern Bantu-speaking world. See Alpern, "Did They or Didn't They"; Killick, "Cairo to Cape."

23. Like iron smelting, the evidence for copper smelting dates to the first centuries of the Common Era. Cooper smelting was far more rare because most copper ore in south central Africa is constricted to the Lufilian arc, an 800-kilometer belt stretching from Kolwezi in the west to the Lubumbashi cluster of deposits in the east. Evidence for copper smelting at Naviundu springs near Lubumbashi dates to the fourth century, and slag and a crucible were recovered at Kansanshi to the southwest and dated to the fifth century. Copper is discussed in greater detail in chapter 5. For an overview, see Bission, "Precolonial Copper Metallurgy"; de Maret, "New Survey."

24. Christopher Ehret makes this argument on the basis of two widespread loans that, in their earliest proto-Eastern Bantu usage, referred to small valuables for personal decoration. Ehret, "Establishment of Iron-Working," 128–30. Jan Vansina argues that these reconstructions are far more recent in "Linguistic Evidence," 353–54.

25. On iron hoes: Fagan, *Iron Age Cultures;* Robertson, "Early Iron Age"; Vogel, *Kumadzulo.* On digging stick weights: Fagan, *Iron Age Cultures;* Derricourt, *Man on the Kafue.* Among abundant regional evidence for stone tool use during the Iron Age, consider the fifty-seven pieces of flaked stone recovered at Kumadzulo, dated between the late sixth and mid-seventh century and the eighty-three specimens of flaked stone from Simbusenga, with an occupation in the eighth century and another between tenth and sixteenth centuries. Vogel, *Kumadzulo,* 41–44; Vogel, *Simbusenga,* 26, 40–41, 80–87.

26. Compare Ehret, "Establishment of Iron-Working," and Vansina, "Linguistic Evidence." See also de Maret and Nsuka, "History of Bantu Metallurgy"; Klein-Arendt, *Traditionellen Eisenbandwerke.*

27. The earliest slag was recovered from M'teteshi in the Mulungushi Valley. Quantities remain low through the mid-tenth century. Robertson, "Early Iron Age."

28. Phillipson, "Kapwirimbwe, Lusaka."

29. Bisson, "Prehistoric Coppermines of Zambia"; Fagan, *Iron Age Cultures,* 88–91; Fagan, Phillipson, and Daniels, *Iron Age Cultures,* 43; Inskeep, "Some Iron Age Sites," 152–53, 155–56; Inskeep, "An Iron-Smelting Furnace," 113–17; Killick, "Technology in Its Social Setting," 76–77; Vogel, *Kumadzulo,* 39–40; Vogel, *Kamangoza,* 39; Vogel, *Simbusenga,* 66.

30. Philip de Barros suggests a shift to smelting outside the village c. 1200. de Barros, "Iron Metallurgy," 190. See the discussion of this shift in chapter 3.

31. Fagan, *Iron Age Cultures,* 90–91; Childs and Herbert, "Metallugy and Its Consequences," 285.

32. For south central Africa, the clearest statement is Vansina, "Slow Revolution."

33. Vansina, "Slow Revolution," 20.

34. Robertson, "Early Iron Age," 154; Fagan, "Gundu and Ndonde."

35. The earliest known archaeological evidence for a cereal, in this case carbonized sorghum seeds from M'teteshi dated to the first century, were recovered not as burnt remains on the inside of an ancient pot, but from a soil sample adjacent to the carbonized remains of tree roots, probably burned in the process of field clearing. The lead archaeologist, John Robertson, hypothesizes that the seeds were planted shortly after the fire, such that the tree roots were still smoldering under the ground and burned the newly sown sorghum seeds. Robertson, "Early Iron Age," 153–54. See also Derricourt, *Man on the Kafue,* 125.

36. Generation estimates follow those in Vansina, *How Societies.*

37. Vansina's distinction between the initial phase of farming and the formative phase may be usefully applied, with the sixth century marking the beginning of the formative phase. Vansina, "Slow Revolution." See also Robertson's comparison of M'teteshi to subsequent settlements in the Mulungushi Valley in "Early Iron Age."

38. The changing labor regimes (and the changing social relationships that underpinned them) have been described by many scholars of precolonial history. Compare Ehret, *Classical;* Schoenbrun, *Green Place;* Vansina, *Paths;*

Vansina, *How Societies*. For an eloquent history of such shifts in the colonial period, see Moore and Vaughan, *Cutting Down Trees*. The labor regimes associated with agriculture were a particular concern to anthropologists and ecologists in the twentieth century. Consider, for example, Allan, *African Husbandman;* Richards, *Land, Labor, and Diet;* Scudder, *Ecology*.

39. Robertson, "Early Iron Age," 152–53 and cites therein.

40. Robertson, "Disease and Culture Change," 165–73.

41. Robertson, "Early Iron Age," 177.

42. Fagan, "Gundu and Ndonde."

43. The regional history of copper working is considered in greater detail in chapter 5.

44. Ehret, "Establishment of Iron-Working," 139; Vansina, "Linguistic Evidence," 340–43.

45. Vansina argues that the semantic innovation "iron ore" was first developed on the eastern or southeastern border of the rainforests and that a second semantic shift to "iron bloom" developed later, in the corridor region. Ehret reconstructs the semantic innovation to proto-Mashariki with the meaning "iron ore." Ehret, "Establishment of Iron-Working," 131–32; Vansina, "Linguistic Evidence," 336–40.

46. Ehret, "Establishment of Iron-Working," 138–40; Ehret, *Classical*, 230; Vansina, "Linguistic Evidence," 350–53.

47. This modest proto-Greater Eastern Botatwe investment in cattle keeping contrasts with the intensive pastoralism associated with the seventeenth century. Linguistic and archaeological evidence for the history of regional pastoralism is discussed in de Luna, "Surveying."

48. A directly dated horn core from the KN2005/041 site in Namaqualand in South Africa pushes back the earliest date for the arrival of cattle (*Bos taurus*) in southern Africa by about three hundred years, from the eighth to the fifth or sixth century. Orton et al., "Early Date for Cattle."

49. Ehret, *Classical;* Turner, "Herders"; Turner, "Hunters"; Wilmsen, *Land*. See also Vansina, *How Societies*, ch. 2.

50. Botatwe attestations of these roots carry the phonology and distribution of proto-Botatwe forms. See also Ehret, *Classical*, 133–36, 271–73 and Vansina, *How Societies*, 81.

51. Christopher Ehret notes that "the complete lack of nouns for milk in soured form until much later times, after Bantu communities spread out across eastern and southern Africa, suggests that milk and milk fat were products more often obtained from or known among neighboring peoples than produced

and processed in the Bantu communities themselves." That may be true, but soured milk would seem a more likely trade item than fresh milk or cream, given the natural tendency of raw milk to sour after a few days of storage. Ehret, *Classical*, 134–35.

52. Ehret, *Classical*, 235, 242.

53. Ehret, *Classical*, 133–36; Vansina, *How Societies*, 81.

54. For the Tonga, consider Nkolola-Wakumelo, "Names of Cattle."

55. Fagan, "Gundu and Ndonde."

56. Gifford-Gonzalez, "Animal Disease Challenges."

57. de Luna, "Surveying."

58. Ehret, *Classical*.

59. Christopher Ehret and Christine Saidi have made the most significant contributions to the early history of Botatwe communities using linguistic evidence, so it is worth considering their argument in detail. They agree that the earliest communities of Botatwe speakers inherited from proto-Eastern Savanna, an ancestral speech community of the early first millennium BCE, both the institution of *-àmí ritual leaders and the wider groupings of matrilineages that constituted the clans, *-gàndá, over which such *-àmí held authority. Based on new research in western Botatwe languages—information that was not available at the time Ehret and Saidi were writing—I respectfully disagree with this assessment. Ehret has explained that the link he proposes between *-àmí and ritual control over clans can be found in the ethnographic record of languages of the Luhya branch of Great Lakes Bantu (pers. comm. June 23, 2014). But unless it can be found widely dispersed among other Bantu communities using the root *-àmí, this link between *-àmí and clan leadership is more likely an innovation in just the Luhya group. The argument then turns on the distribution of *-àmí and the parallel occurrence of clans in communities speaking languages that use the root *-àmí to talk about different kinds of leaders: kings and ritual clan leaders in the Great Lakes languages and "chiefs" in glosses from Botatwe languages. It bears stating explicitly that *-àmí are not connected to clans in Botatwe languages, that clans in most Botatwe communities do not have leaders, and that Botatwe speakers do not use an attestation of the root *-gàndá to speak of clans. Ehret, *Classical*, ch. 5, and pers. comm., June 23, 2014. Saidi agrees with Ehret's position in *Women's Authority*. For more detail on the history of clans in Botatwe history, see chapter 4.

60. Bastin and Schadeberg, "Bantu Lexical Reconstructions 3," ID 3183; Ehret, *Classical*, ch. 5; Saidi, *Women's Authority*.

61. Bastin and Schadeberg, "Bantu Lexical Reconstructions 3," ID 3183, 3173–75, 3177–78; David Schoenbrun, *Historical Reconstruction*, 173–74. See also citations below to individual attestations in Ila and Tonga.

62. Bastin and Schadeberg, "Bantu Lexical Reconstructions 3," ID 3178, 3177, 3173, der. 3175, der. 3174, and der. 8202.

63. Mukanzubo, *Chitonga-English*, 674. The verb combined with the separative verbal extension creates the verb *kuyaamika*, meaning "to lean a thing against; to adjourn, give up, leave off; to place in position." This Tonga verb echoes David Schoenbrun's reconstructed interlake areal in Great Lakes Bantu languages: *-yamuka, "disappear, cease raining," with further semantic ranges in individual attestations connecting to this verb the idea that speech activates medicines and leadership. Schoenbrun *Historical Reconstruction*, 173–74.

64. Schoenbrun, *Historical Reconstruction*, 173.

65. Vansina marks this as a Great Lakes root shared in some forest languages: *Paths*, 356, n. 61; Schoenbrun suggests the root was available to Great Lakes Bantu speakers. See his discussion of the etymology of *-yamuka: *Historical Reconstruction*, 173–74.

66. Schoenbrun, *Historical Reconstruction*, 173.

67. Ehret, *Classical*, 146–49, 155; Saidi, *Women's Authority*; Schoenbrun, *Historical Reconstruction*, 172–74; Schoenbrun, *Green Place*, 102–6, 146–48; Vansina, *Paths*, 177–91.

68. All attestations in this paragraph may be found in Fowler, *Dictionary of Ila*, 74, 500, 502; Mukanzubo, *Chitonga-English*, 783, 1210, 1211–12. Consider also the Tonga attestation *mwaamu*, "a sexually unbridled person," in Mukanzubo, *Chitonga-English*, 1210. On mwami as a locally respected person, see also Colson, *Marriage and Family*, 30–31.

69. For a more detailed regional discussion of the entwined histories of sexuality, gender, and authority beyond Botatwe communities, see Saidi, *Women's Authority*.

70. Vansina, "Slow Revolution."

71. This shift also occurred in the Zambezi and Mulungushi Valleys: see Robertson, "Early Iron Age"; Vansina, "Slow Revolution"; and Vogel, *Kumadzulo*.

Chapter 3. Fame in the Kafue

1. Derricourt, *Man on the Kafue*.

2. I summarize here the attributes of the middle Kafue Middle Iron Age culture sequence reconstructed by Derricourt, *Man on the Kafue*. On the direct

associations underpinning the middle Kafue homeland of the proto-Central Eastern Botatwe speech community, see de Luna, "Surveying."

3. The southward spread of the strategy of settlement across microenvironments is discussed in chapter 1 as well as de Luna, "Surveying." For the expansion of Botatwe speech communities beyond the middle Kafue, see chapter 4.

4. Robertson, "Early Iron Age."

5. For other animal words attesting to knowledge of new environments, see chapter 1.

6. Mitchell, "Bush Fires," cited in Fagan, *Iron Age Cultures*, 74. In a pilot field season in 2014, archaeologist Matthew Pawlowicz recovered charcoal in nearly every test pit dug along transects through the higher elevated woodlands around which Basanga and Mwanamaipma and other grassland Iron Age mound sites were built south of the Kafue hook. The charcoal was distributed across the stratigraphy of the test pits and was more common in woodland test pits than those dug in the floodplain or grassland regions. Pers. comm. August 27, 2014. According to Derricourt, the woodlands north of the hook were only exploited regularly beginning in the Middle Iron Age, the period that corresponds to proto-Central Eastern Botatwe settlement. Derricourt, *Man on the Kafue*.

7. This shift also occurred in the Zambezi and Mulungushi Valleys. Robertson, "Early Iron Age"; Vansina, "Slow Revolution"; Vogel, "Micro-Environments."

8. The shift in the meaning of *-dùb- also seems to have occurred in Kaskazi languages, where the term came to refer (perhaps exclusively) to fishing with a net. In the Sabi languages spoken to the east of Botatwe communities, the root was used to talk about fishing with a trap. To the west, the same root referred to fishing with a basket or a net.

9. A distribution in Botatwe, Sabi, and Mashariki languages could attest to a proto-Eastern Savanna origin for the fishing verb. Regardless of its antiquity, eastern Botatwe societies' innovation was to broaden the semantic domain of the root; they used it to talk about a far wider range of fishing methods than were employed by neighbors using the same root.

10. These are common roots; their phonology does not determine their antiquity, but their distributions suggest a proto-Central Eastern Botatwe provenance for *buyeelo* and a proto-Kafue provenance for *buyali*. Both innovations drew on a set of older, related Botatwe verbs, *-yeela, "to fence," and *-yala, "to encircle," that derive from an old Bantu transitive verb, *-jàd-, "to spread."

Bastin and Schadeberg, "Bantu Lexical Reconstructions 3," ID main 3147.

11. Ehret suggests that this trap, *-gònò, was developed by Kaskazi speakers and borrowed into Luba-Kasai and Botatwe. It is widespread in eastern and western Botatwe in a form that indicates inheritance. An attestation in Shanjo with *g in the position of the first consonant would have indicated that it was inherited by proto-Botatwe speakers while Ø would indicate a loan, but I was not able to solicit an attestation in Shanjo. Ehret, *Classical*, 313; de Luna, "Collecting Food," root 503.

12. Scudder, "Fishermen."

13. A few western Sabi languages have borrowed this word from Botatwe languages.

14. Although *masiko* is used by some eastern Botatwe speakers to refer to a trolling basket, the innovation of *iʒubo* by proto-Kafue speakers and glosses of masiko as a scooping basket suggest that it either originally or by the proto-Kafue era referred to a scoop basket.

15. Bantu languages do not mark gender. Rarely, the feminine or masculine possessive prefix may enter a reconstruction, but such morphology is difficult to reconstruct into the deep past. Unless particular tools are consistently interred with human remains with an identifiable sex, we have no direct evidence of the gendering of particular forms of labor from archaeology.

16. Colson, "Plateau Tonga of Northern Rhodesia," 103–7; Reynolds, *Material Culture;* Scudder, "Fishermen"; Scudder, *Ecology;* Smith and Dale, *Ila-Speaking*, vol. 1.

17. Reynolds, *Material Culture*, 41–55; Scudder, "Fishermen," 41–49; Scudder, *Ecology*, 190. See also Smith and Dale, *Ila-Speaking*, vol. 1, 160–67. Interestingly, among Tonga speakers today, only men may make izubo baskets.

18. These observations are frequent and will be considered in greater detail below. For cross-cultural studies developed by Africanists, see comments in Herbert, *Iron, Gender, and Power,* 165; Kent, *Farmers as Hunters.* The evidence for specialist status is slim until the development of specialized regional hunting guilds in the nineteenth century. For hunting guilds, see de Luna, "Hunting Reputations," 291–96. For fishing, consider that *museli,* the agentive noun form of *kuʒela,* does not gloss as specialist fisher, though ethnographers have long identified some Tonga or Ila fishers as more skilled than others. Consider Reynolds, *Material Culture,* 41.

19. The roots of this gendered understanding of subsistence lie, in part, in feminist reactions to the Man the Hunter thesis. Scholars sought to prove the

essential contributions of women as gatherers, a contribution that was starkly contrasted with men's meager and unpredictable contributions as hunters. Consider the review of this literature in Dahlberg's introduction to *Woman the Gatherer*. The idea that agriculture supports specialization has an equally long history that can be traced back to V. Gordon Childe, if not to the eighteenth- and nineteenth-century thinkers who influenced him. See, for example, Childe, *Man Makes Himself*.

20. The following four paragraphs draw extensively or verbatim from de Luna, "Hunting Reputations," 280–81, 285–88. Regional classics include: Douglas, *Lele of Kasai;* Marks, *Large Mammals;* Turner, *Forest of Symbols;* White, "Role of Hunting and Fishing." See also Bird and Kendall, "Mande Hero"; Kent, *Farmers as Hunters*.

21. Among many, consider: de Heusch, *Roi Ivre;* Hoover, "Seduction of Ruwej"; Reefe, *Rainbow and the Kings;* Yoder, *Kanyok of Zaire*. In East Africa, see Feierman, *Shambaa Kingdom*.

22. Schecter, "*A propos* the Drunken King," 117.

23. Sound changes (*d > /l/ and *p > Ø) and distribution support the reconstruction of this root to proto-Central Eastern Botatwe. Vowel lengthening is a common feature of Bantu languages in the context of a glide created through the fusion of two vowels across morphemic boundaries. Here, the noun class prefix mu- and the initial vowel of the root itself after the loss of /p/ combine to produce the extant Botatwe form, *mwaalu*. For individual attestations discussed in this paragraph, see Doke, *English-Lamba Vocabulary*, 81; Isaacman and Isaacman, *Slavery and Beyond*, 102, 338; Matthews, "Portuguese, Chikunda"; Marks, *Large Mammals*, 67; Nash, *Ruwund Vocabularies*, 47; White Fathers, *Bemba-English Dictionary*, 479, 584. On Ruund, see also Hoover, "Seduction," 487–89; Papstein, "Upper Zambezi," 70–71. The retention of /p/ and distribution in Chikunda and two Botatwe societies that absorbed Chikunda speakers in the nineteenth century suggests that Chikunda borrowed the root from Sabi speakers and carried it west, probably during the Chikunda warlord Kanyemba's expansion along the middle Zambezi in the late nineteenth century.

24. Schadeberg, "Derivation," 77, 85; Schadeberg, "Extensive Extension in Bantu." In Botatwe grammars, the suffix is -*aula*, which suggests that *-pàdó is borrowed, though vowel assimilation can account for /a/ > /u/. Carter, *Outline of ChiTonga Grammar*, 50; Madan, *Lenje Handbook*, 48; Smith, *Handbook*, 131–32.

25. The antiquity of this meaning for the extensive affix is uncertain in Botatwe due to the paucity of descriptive grammars, but it does exist in each of the three best documented Central Eastern Botatwe languages (ChiTonga, Ila, and Lenje) and is widely documented in southern Bantu languages. Carter, *Outline;* Madan, *Lenje;* Smith, *Handbook.*

26. Smith, *Handbook,* 131–32.

27. Schadeburg, "Derivation," 81.

28. Tonga speakers also use *bwaalu* to refer to a communal hunt in an explicit link to *-pàdó's huntsmanship. Scudder, *Ecology,* 195; Siamwiza, "Famine and Hunger," 251.

29. This is a correction of the reconstruction published as *-weja in de Luna, "Hunting Reputations."

30. The root is also found in Soli and proto-Western Botatwe, but with phonology that indicates borrowing.

31. See attestations in Kati languages, such as -wéèja, "to hunt," in the Elwana dialect of Swahili. Nurse and Hinnebusch, *Swahili and Sabaki,* 614.

32. Fielder notes, "The Ila themselves describe a man's economic struggle, his seeking for wealth and power, as his *buwezhi,* his hunting (*kuweza*—to hunt, pursue)." Fielder, "Economic Spheres," 624. For glosses mentioned in this paragraph, see Fowler, *Dictionary of Ila,* 493, 761. The verb in the phrase kuwesa lubono was glossed as a form of prostitution by early missionaries; the practice is discussed in further detail in de Luna, "Affect and Society." See also Tuden, "Political System," 33.

33. The following paragraph draws extensively or verbatim from de Luna, "Hunting Reputations."

34. Phillipson, "Kapwirimbwe"; Vogel, *Kumadzulo;* Vogel, *Kamangoza;* Vogel, *Simbusenga.* For a study of the collaboration between smiths and hunters in the more recent history of west central Africa, see Kriger, *Pride of Men,* 129–34.

35. Derricourt, *Man on the Kafue,* 66, 72.

36. The root *lusákò follows the expected phonology and distribution for proto-Kafue making it a more certain reconstruction. The attestation in Lundwe is borrowed.

37. The word *mukana* refers to hunters' medicines in Falls languages, Totela, Sala, and Soli. Totela is adjacent to Falls languages while Soli the frontiers of Sala and Soli speech communities come near to one another west of Lusaka. The Totela form matches Falls languages whereas Soli attestations

follow Sala speakers' reduplicated form; these forms and distributions suggest that Soli speakers borrowed the term from Sala-speaking hunters and Totela speakers from Falls hunters. Speakers of Falls languages and Sala are nonadjacent, however, and the presence of a term for this kind of fast-changing technology in their languages is best explained as an inherited form from their shared ancestry in proto-Central Eastern Botatwe.

38. The next two paragraphs draw on de Luna, "Surveying"; Derricourt, *Man on the Kafue*, 208–15; Fagan, *Iron Age Cultures*, 70–82; Fagan, Phillipson, and Daniels, *Iron Age Cultures*.

39. Fagan, *Iron Age Cultures*, 78.

40. The following four paragraphs draw extensively or verbatim from de Luna, "Hunting Reputations."

41. Guyer and Belinga, "Wealth in People as Wealth in Knowledge."

42. Apter, *Black Kings and Critics;* Hanson, *Landed Obligation;* Kodesh, "Networks of Knowledge; McIntosh, ed., *Beyond Chiefdoms;* Schoenbrun, *Green Place;* Vansina, *Paths.* More recently, see Dueppen, *Egalitarian Revolution.*

43. Reconstructable Botatwe terms for formal political titles and institutions are rare, demonstrating the persistence of autonomy as a political ideal and the ephemeral nature of power to the fourteenth century. Kinship vocabulary may contribute more to our understanding of political life in the earliest periods of Botatwe history. For a lively debate about the antiquity of decentralized Botatwe politics, see contributions to Lancaster and Vickery, eds., *Tonga-Speaking Peoples.*

44. Guyer, "Wealth in People and Self-Realization"; Guyer, "Traditions of Invention."

45. I appreciatively build on John Iliffe's recent insights into householder honor. Yet honor is a particular outcome of reputation and its study as an "enforceable right" masks the other reasons (negative) reputations were acquired and used. Iliffe, *Honour in African History.*

46. On affect in precolonial Africa, see de Luna, "Affect and Society"; Hanson, *Landed Obligation;* Iliffe, *Honour in African History;* Schoenbrun, "Violence, Marginaltiy, Scorn and Honour."

47. Parts of this and the following two paragraphs draw extensively or verbatim from de Luna, "Affect and Society."

48. Colson, *Plateau Tonga*, 12–13. See also Colson, "Life among the Cattle-Owning Plateau Tonga," 15–16; Colson, *Social Organization of the Gwembe Tonga*, 145–46; Colson, *Tonga Religious Life*, 46, 134–35, 165–67; Reynolds,

Material Culture, 91–92; Reynolds and Cousins, *Lwaano Lwanyika*, 107–9; Smith and Dale, *Ila-Speaking*, vol. 1, p. 180, 203, 219–21.

49. Colson, *Plateau Tonga*, 12.

50. It is the widespread distribution of the practice by which technicians inherit their skills from ancestors that suggests its antiquity. However, I've not been able to reconstruct a name for this practice that might date it. The broadest collection of comparative ethnographic evidence can be found in Herbert, *Iron, Gender, and Power*, but the belief is found throughout Bantu-speaking Africa and parts of West Africa.

51. Kriger, *Pride of Men*, chs. 1 and 2. The cultural value of iron was obvious in south central Africa as early as the eighth-century burials at Chundu where Early Iron Age vessels contain hoards of iron and copper objects, including axes, hoes, bangles (both iron and copper), and lumps of iron bloom alongside cowries. Vogel, "Early Iron Age Burial."

52. There is some disagreement about the antiquity of the underlying root, but we can be surer of the antiquity of the semantic innovation.

53. As discussed in chapter 5, in Plateau Tonga, the term came to mean domestic animal when used in noun class 3/4, probably as cattle keeping intensified after the sixteenth century. Tonga speakers also used a verb form of the root to talk about owning slaves, an innovation that probably dates to the second half of the nineteenth century. Collins, *Tonga Grammar*, 156; Holy, *Strategies and Norms*, 67–69, 75–76; Nkazi, *Citonga Note Book*.

54. For a deeper discussion of the investment of women in men's hunting, see de Luna, "Marksmen and the Bush."

55. Mavhunga, *Transient Workspaces*. Mavhunga builds on Tim Ingold's influential concept "wayfaring," which stresses the entwined relationship between mobility and knowing. Ingold, *Lines*, ch. 3.

56. On the danger of animals catching the scent of a hunter on the wind, see Isaacman and Isaacman, *Slavery and Beyond*, 108.

57. This builds on Webb Keane's application of Peirce's theory of semiotics to the changing material world. See Keane, "Signs Are Not the Garb of Meaning." The process by which hunters and smelters worked creatively with overlaps in the material and kinesthetic qualities of their crafts is further developed in de Luna, "Marksmen and the Bush."

58. For the most widespread collection of references to ethnographic evidence, see Herbert, *Iron, Gender, and Power*. See also individual citations in n. 59.

59. This pattern was observed by Bisson, "Prehistoric Coppermines of Zambia"; Fagan, *Iron Age Cultures*, 88–91; Fagan et al., *Iron Age Cultures*, 43; Inskeep,

"Some Iron Age Sites," 152–53, 155–56; Inskeep, "Iron-Smelting Furnace," 113–17; Killick, "Technology in Its Social Setting," 76–77; Robertson, "South African Early Iron Age in Zambia," 262; Vogel, *Kumadzulo*, 39–40; Vogel, *Kamangoza*, 39; Vogel, *Simbusenga*, 66. Earlier Zambezi Valley smelting sites like Kumadzulo and Kabondo Kumbo built furnaces in or very near the site, albeit in special occupational zones: Vogel, "Kabondo Kumbo," 69.

See also Saidi, *Women's Authority*, 138–39. Saidi attributes the shifting geography of smelting to the arrival of Central Savanna Bantu, Botatwe, and Sabi speech and culture in east central Africa in the second half of the first millennium. Further work is needed on the chronology and the geography of the shift; evidence at the northern site of Kansanshi, for example, suggests that smelting was undertaken in the village until the ninth century, which is quite late in light of Saidi's dating for the proposed southward spread of Central Savanna Bantu, Botatwe, and Sabi languages and cultures. From the available evidence, the change seems to result from a wider, regional shift in smelting culture adopted across the region, rather than a change attributable to a narrower or single point of origin. However, in localized instances, such as the much later adoption of smelting beyond the village in the Zambezi Valley, we can identify the origins of the practice with greater confidence.

Schmidt's research in Buhaya reminds us that the changing geography of smelting does not always imply secrecy, for the spaces beyond village boundaries indicate separation from village doings, not necessarily remoteness and isolation. Schmidt, *Iron Technology*, 191. However, Schmidt's smelters may well have associated their efforts with the forces of the bush because they invoked the symbols and responsibilities of the ritual specialist associated with Irungu, which is the spirit of the wilderness in most Lakes Bantu societies. See Schoenbrun, *Good Place*, 215, n. 105; 216, n. 115. Farther south, archaeologists have identified many sites, such as Swart Village south of the Zambezi River and sites in KwaZulu-Natal, where smelts continued to be done in the village. See Fredriksen and Chirikure, "Beyond Static Models," 12.

60. Quotes in this paragraph are taken from Colson, *Tonga Religious Life*, 107, 92, 104, 92, 107, and 93, respectively. These observations accord with my own fieldwork experiences studying wild resource use among Botatwe communities as well as observations throughout Reynolds, *Material Culture;*

Reynolds and Cousins, *Lwaano Lwanyika;* Scudder, *Ecology;* Smith and Dale, *Ila-Speaking.*

61. Herbert, *Iron, Gender, and Power,* 172.

62. Eugenia Herbert's cross-cultural study demonstrates the geographical range of these associations in Africa while Victor Turner's work on the Lunda Ndembu is perhaps the most famous ethnography of "the bush." Herbert, *Iron, Gender, and Power;* Turner, *Forest of Symbols.* See also citations to scholarship on hunter-founder figures in nn. 21, 22, and 71.

63. Kreike, *Recreating Eden;* Mavhunga, *Transient Workspaces.* Further afield, consider Per Ditlef Fredricksen's interpretations of settlements, stone walls and the construction of gendered landscapes and understandings of wealth in the Magaliesberg region and on the Mpumalanga Escarpment in South Africa. Fredricksen, *Material Knowledges,* 105–9 cited in Fredricksen and Chirikure, "Beyond Static Models," 8–9.

64. Kent, *Farmers as Hunters;* Colson also follows this dichotomized view in Colson, *Tonga Religious Life.*

65. Herbert, *Iron, Gender, and Power.*

66. It is difficult to determine whether this word was innovated in proto-Central Eastern Botatwe or proto-Kafue. The lenition of the initial consonant in Lundwe is unexpected, which suggests a proto-Kafue origin, but the very short duration of the proto-Central Eastern Botatwe speech community reminds us that the history of the two linguistic periods bleed into one another in a matter of a few short generations. Consider the related term *cisoko,* "a bush, a hiding-place, refuge; the usual way; the origin or nature of a thing" in Fowler, *Dictionary of Ila,* 129.

67. Fowler, *Dictionary of Ila,* 652–53. *Kusokoma* seems to include the positional (stative) suffix *-am-,* but with an assimilation to the first vowel of the root.

68. Kairn Klieman, *"Pygmies";* Turnbull, *Forest People.* See also Herbert, *Iron, Gender, and Power.*

69. Herbert, *Iron, Gender, and Power,* ch. 7.

70. Star and Griesemer, "Institutional Ecology."

71. Bird and Kendall, "Mande Hero"; Turner, *Forest of Symbols.*

72. For a more complete exploration of the relationship between the affective and the material and the benefits of studying their relationships in African Studies, see de Luna, "Affect and Society."

73. The association between men's hunting and childbirth is common in central Africa. Herbert, *Iron, Gender, and Power,* ch. 7. On women's access to

motherhood as a source of status and wealth, see Stephens, *African Mother-hood;* Stephens, "Birthing Wealth." On women's status and potting, see also Saidi, *Women's Authority.*

74. Packard, *Chiefship and Cosmology,* 3–4, 26–28.
75. de Luna, "Marksmen and the Bush."
76. Fielder, *Dictionary of Ila,* 129–30.
77. Herbert, *Iron, Gender, and Power.*
78. de Luna, "Marksmen and the Bush."

Chapter 4. Of Kith and Kin

1. For evidence of previous Bantu settlement in the region, see Bostoen, "Bantu Plant Names"; Ehret, *Classical Age;* Ehret, "Subclassifying Bantu"; Saidi, *Women's Authority.*
2. Matthew Pawlowicz documented the pattern by which mounded villages, including Basanga and Mwanamaipma discussed further below, were established along the elevation line marking the transition between grassland and woodland environments in the greater Basanga area. Pers. comm. Aug. 20, 2014. The descriptions of such mounded sites in the following paragraphs refer to the second occupations of Basanga and Mwanamaipma, which have been dated; the seven additional mounds identified and mapped by Pawlowicz have not yet been dated. A wildfire in Sycamore Canyon in Santa Barbara destroyed Fagan's field notes of the excavations at Basanga and Mwanamaimpa. Preliminary reports were published by Fagan in *Archaeologia Zambiana* in 1968 and 1969 and summarized in *Azania* a decade later. Fagan, "Gundu and Nonde." The next several paragraphs summarize Fagan's published findings.
3. Fagan notes that domesticates more generally were "remarkably rare" at both sites at all levels and that goats and cattle were only identified in lower, Early Iron Age levels. "Gundu and Nonde," 133. It should be noted, however, that it is difficult to distinguish between goats and sheep, so early communities may have (also) kept sheep. See also the discussion of cattle in chapter 2.
4. Fragments of the grain were recovered even without floatation at Basanga and Mwanamaimpa.
5. For a description of this relationship in recent times, see Scudder, *Ecology.* For a historical example in equatorial Africa, see Vansina, *Paths,* 83.
6. The use of the verb *-kód-, "to take, to touch," may have described the light touch needed to ensnare smaller, sure-footed field pests. Proto-Kafue and

Kaskazi speakers independently made the same minor semantic leap, applying an inherited root for bark string, *-ooye from *-gòdí, to the noose trap made with that material. What may have been new about the trap developed from the *-ooye bark string was the quality of the bark fibers themselves. Perhaps Kafue trappers or their Kaskazi-speaking neighbors to the east discovered a new species of tree that could produce bark string with different qualities than familiar species. Or, perhaps the bark string was stronger, frictionless, or more pliable and, therefore, more adaptable to the particular application of a spring noose trap.

7. The Central Eastern Botatwe innovation *-nkólı remained the word for warthog in proto-Kafue languages, while *-ngılı and the common form -nyemba were both used to designate feral swine, with the latter also serving to refer to wild boars. See chapter 3.

8. de Luna, "Surveying," 235–37, table 4.

9. Huffman, *Iron Age Migrations*. See also a discussion of regional pottery studies in de Luna, "Surveying," 222–29.

10. Fagan, *Iron Age Cultures;* Fagan and Phillipson, "Sebanzı"; Fagan, Phillipson, and Daniels, *Iron Age Cultures*.

11. This process and the archaeological evidence supporting it are described in chapter 1, where the archaeological and linguistic frameworks for the broader narrative of subsistence are outlined.

12. While Smith and Dale suggest that Ila-speaking societies were already patrilineal in the early twentieth century, Cutshall and Tuden describe the situational use of family on the father's and mother's side, including breaking such kinship ties. Cutshall goes so far as to call Ila kinship "ambilateral." Ladislov Holy's ethnography of the Toka documents a transition from matrilineal to patrilineal forms of inheritance. Similarly, Lisa Cligget's recent work on Tonga communities of the Gwembe exposes the different experience men and women have of the kinship institutions of *mukowa,* a clan relationship reckoned through the mother, and *lutundu,* a "patrilineal nuclear unit" in times of shortage and famine. Cligget, *Grains from Grass;* Cutshall, Disputing for Power," ch. 3; Holy, *Strategies and Norms;* Smith and Dale, *Ila-Speaking;* Tuden, "Political System," ch. 2.

13. This is a vast literature. For recent interventions in these debates, see Kodesh, "Networks of Knowledge"; MacGaffey, "Changing Representations"; MacGaffey, "A Note"; Stephens, "Lineage and Society." For different perspectives on the antiquity of matrilineality among scholars working with Bantu language evidence, see Ehret, *Classical,* 149–55; Hage and Marck,

"Proto-Bantu Descent Groups"; Marck and Bostoen, "Proto-East Bantu Society"; Saidi, *Women's Authority;* Vansina, *Paths,* 113–14, 123–26, 152–55; Vansina, *How Societies,* 88–98.

14. Ehret, *Classical,* ch. 5; Saidi, *Women's Authority.* See the discussion of this root in chapter 2.

15. MacGaffey, "Changing Representations"; MacGaffey, "A Note"; Vansina, *Paths;* Vansina, *How Societies.*

16. Much of this disagreement is an outcome of the Bantu classification used and the weight the scholar gives to a comparative reading of the ethnographic record compared to the derivational process. Compare, for example, Ehret's and Vansina's reconstructions of *-gàndá, "clan": Ehret, *Classical,* 151–55; Vansina, *How Societies,* 90, n. 59. See also MacGaffey, "Changing Representations," 200.

17. Though he does not trace out the history of each term, Vansina provides examples of such renovation in the institutions and practices of matrilineality in the variety and distributions of the terms he collects from across the matrilineal belt. Vansina, *How Societies,* 88–98.

18. According to Vansina, the only languages that do not attest the semantic shift from "skin" to "navel cord" belong to the Umbundu and Middle Kwilu groups. Vansina, *How Societies,* 94.

19. On the wider region, see Vansina, *How Societies,* 94–96.

20. People use the word *mukowa* throughout the Botatwe area but the inherited form would take the shape *mukoβa* in Soli and Lenje and *mukoba* and *mukova* in most other Botatwe languages.

21. The leveled results of Bantu spirantization in eastern Botatwe languages make it difficult to determine whether the reconstruction should derive from a root with the form *-kɪtia, *-kɪpia, or *-kɪkia. If the Soli attestation is not borrowed from Lenje, the root could be proto-Greater Eastern Botatwe and date to the middle of the first millennium. However, attestations of the term are skewed in Lundwe and Toka, which represent the other two branches of proto-Greater Eastern Botatwe. In addition, Soli and Lenje have a long history of contact and borrowing. Regardless, the root is certainly consistent within proto-Kafue both in terms of meaning and phonology. We can conclude that the term certainly existed in proto-Kafue with a small possibility that is it might be as old as proto-Greater Eastern Botatwe.

22. de Luna "Surveying"; Denbow, "Congo to Kalahari"; Denbow, *Archaeology and Ethnography,* 164–66; Ehret, *Classical,* 271–73; Vansina, *How Societies,* 81–87.

23. Tuden, for example, discusses mukowa as one of the social ties that might be used for cattle loans among Ila communities. Matrikin certainly did inherit cattle, among other things, from relatives. I don't reject the link between cattle and clans, but I don't think the intensification of cattle keeping was the catalyst for the adoption of mukowa in the case of eastern Botatwe communities. Tuden, "Political System," ch. 2.

24. Madan, *Lenje Handbook*, 99.

25. The Ila dictionary entry reads: "Mukowa n.2—a clan, family, generation. *Ukulwila bamukowa takuzimwa* (p) One must not hesitate to fight for one's clan. *Inkondo ilamana; njamukowa, telambilwa mulambo* (p) The fighting is finished; since it was a clan affair, it was not necessary to be smeared with white clay." Fowler, *Dictionary of Ila*, 446. Jaspan even suggests that the term is used to describe "a kind of covenanted friendship" between clansmen. Jaspan, *Ila-Tonga*, 31–32, citing Smith and Dale, *Ila-Speaking*, vol. 1, 294–96, 384. See also Cutshall, "Disputing for Power," ch. 3; Tuden, "Political Systems," ch. 2.

26. For quotes, see Colson, *Marriage and Family*, 15–16. On the noncorporate nature of Botatwe mukowa in most contexts, see also Colson, "Clans and Joking-Relationship," 45–60; Cutshall, "Disputing for Power," ch. 3; Holy, *Strategies*; Tuden, "Political System," ch. 2. Vansina makes the same observation that matriclans in ancient west central African societies were not corporate bodies in *How Societies*, 88–98. Matrilineal groups may even break apart based on personal differences. Colson, *Marriage and Family*, 20. In fact, Tonga speakers on the Batoka Plateau might use any of a number of terms to talk about the ideas of the kind of relatedness Colson defines as the "matrilineal group": *citiba, cilongo, cibuwa, mukwaasi, cikoto, cikombo, iciinga, luzubo,* and *cipani*. On examples of Ila speakers making and breaking clans ties, see Cutshall, "Disputing for Power," 88.

27. Consider the Soli gloss of "family" in Mwewa, *Meeting the Soli People*, 14. Ladislav Holy describes two meanings for mukowa among Toka communities. On the one hand, a mukowa is a vague group with "members . . . scattered all over Toka territory. . . . The clans have no recognised heads, they do not claim any common property and common clan membership is not a principle of recruitment into any group." But mukowa can also refer to a "subdivision of the clan" that "comprises the matrilineal descendants of one recognised ancestress" and has "a genealogical depth of five or six generations." Holy, *Strategies*, 20–21.

28. I borrow this adjective from Cutshall, who offers rich evidence of the situational nature of kinship ties: "Disputing for Power."

29. Kodesh, *Beyond the Royal Gaze*, chs. 2 and 3.

30. Wyatt MacGaffey offers a valuable critique of such one-to-one matches between reconstructed terms and particular relatives. He argues that kinship was more fluid than such correspondences suggest because people can choose the scale on which they reckon (and name) kin—either individually (as relationships to Ego) or at the level of the clan in MacGaffey's Kongo example. People had many options for labeling their kin, some of which could create distance and others that might imply a closer relationship and more significant obligations. MacGaffey, "A Note," 274–76. See also Colson, *Plateau Tonga;* Colson, *Marriage and the Family;* Colson, *Social Organization;* Cutshall, "Disputing for Power"; Holy, *Strategies;* Tuden, "Political Systems."

31. Ila speakers use *bakwesu* to reference one's brother or sister, including all the children of one's father, parallel cousins, and, with the phrase muka mukwesu, one's brother's wife. Similarly, Lenje speakers use bakwesu to refer to parallel cousins and all one's mother's daughters. A Sala man in 2010 described bakwesu as his father's family. They were paternal cousins without distinguishing between parallel and cross-cousins: "one's father's sister's son" and "one's father's brother's son and daughters." Among Plateau Tonga speakers in the 1950s, however, bakwesu was a generic term for fellow clan members or a child of one's father's clan and often translated by Tonga speakers as "brother," though the term was never applied to siblings. For Ila, see Jaspan, *Ila-Tonga*, 32, 52; Smith and Dale, *Ila-Speaking* vol. 1, 316–18, 321, 368. For Tonga, see Colson, *Marriage and the Family*, 16, 349; Jaspan, *Ila-Tonga*, 52.

32. Colson, *Marriage and Family;* Colson, *Social Organization*.

33. Bastin and Schadeberg, "Bantu Lexical Reconstructions 3," ID main 7240 and 7241–42, 7247–50; Schoenbrun, *Historical Reconstruction*, 94–95; Stephens, *African Motherhood*, 41; Vansina, *Paths*, 283–85.

34. This interpretation was inspired by James Pritchett's historical and anthropological study of cohorts in central Africa. Pritchett, *Friends for Life*.

35. This word could be as old as proto-Greater Eastern Botatwe, but it is borrowed into Lundwe and the Soli attestation also follows Kafue sound shifts. The phonology supports its reconstruction to proto-Kafue, though it is distributed south of the Kafue across the Batoka and into Soli lands. This distribution suggests a very old areal form conforming to Kafue sound correspondences. In Colson's words, such marriages among Tonga in the twentieth century created "basic ties between married men each married to women of the same generation." Colson, *Marriage and the Family*,

59. The additional /a/ in Colson's ethnography is likely an intensifying infix. On *mukwashi* as a residential group of Ila male matrikin who render mutual aid, see Cutshall, "Disputing for Power," 90; Tuden, "Political System," 96. "Mukwashi" has come to refer exclusively to one's patrilineal relatives in Soli and Ila. This emphasis on patrilineal relatives rather than in-laws and matrilineal cross-cousins is probably an outcome of more recent shifts to patrilineal inheritance combined with a long history of virilocal residence.

36. Fowler, *Dictionary of Ila*, 324.

37. Colson, *Marriage and Family*. Among the Plateau Tonga, the mukwashi is both an ephemeral residential unit as well as a group of nonmembers for which the lineage feels responsible, including the wives, children, and dependents of the lineage's sons. Fathers forming a mukwashi might, in turn, administer to the lineages of their wives and children, performing work at funerals and initiations. Colson, *Tonga Religious*, 124, quoting Machila, "History of the Malende," xi. On mukwashi as Ila groups rendering mutual aid, see Cutshall, "Disputing for Power," 90; Tuden, "Political System," 96.

38. Among Tonga communities in the twentieth century, mukwashi captured an important organizational principal of Tonga society, the pairing of alternate generations, because it also referred to one's spouse's grandparent or one's grandchild's spouse. Colson, *Marriage and the Family*. See also Tuden, "Political System."

39. This innovation dovetails with Christine Saidi's argument about the importance of sororal groups in the precolonial history of east central Africa, although Saidi emphasizes the authority of older generations of women over the social status of younger women and the men who sought to marry them. Saidi associates such groups with the root *-bumba, which named a group of "adult sisters and their mother, with their mother's sisters and their adult daughters as further potential members." The reconstructions presented here emphasize the lateral ties of cohorts of classificatory siblings and classificatory cross-cousins. My dating for the significance of sibling and cross-cousin cohorts is far later than Saidi's reconstruction of *-bumba, but this is because our linguistic classifications differ. I reconstruct to Kafue, Central Eastern, or Greater Eastern Botatwe terms that are proto-Botatwe innovations in Saidi's research because Saidi had no time to incorporate western Botatwe languages into her much larger study of central African Bantu languages. Unfortunately, I have not been able to elicit during fieldwork or find in any published records attestations of this root in Botatwe languages with the

meaning sororal group (instead, the root is connected to potting). Regardless of the uncertain status of Saidi's reconstruction of *-bumba in Botatwe languages, our research shows that groups of women and the groups of men they married were significant in regional social history because they were the social units around which marriage and residence were organized. Saidi, *Women's Authority*, quote from p. 75.

40. The paragraphs in this section draw heavily from or were previously published in de Luna, "Affect and Society," 145–48.

41. Smith and Dale, *Ila-Speaking*, vol. 1, 308–9; Fowler, *Dictionary of Ila*, 457. Tuden describes the application of this term to friends who share wives and lovers through such relationships: "Political System," 30–31, 36.

42. Compare Colson, *Marriage and the Family*, 45–47; Colson, *Social Organization*, 46–49; Colson, *Tonga Religious*, 8, 137.

43. Fowler, *Dictionary of Ila*, quotes on pp. 457, 112, 357–58, respectively. See also the Tonga glosses as "to bless" and "eternal." Mukanzubo, *Chitonga-English*, 312, 831.

44. Though this meaning could have spread between neighboring languages after the breakup of proto-Kafue, the relict distribution of the term with this meaning within Kafue languages and its lack of association with the gloss "friend" outside the Kafue languages suggests that the attribution of the meaning "friend" to the root *mulòngó dates to the proto-Kafue period.

45. Ehret, *Classical*, 150.

46. Bastin and Schadeberg, "Bantu Lexical Reconstructions 3," ID main 1120.

47. Consider the IciBemba attestation *mulongo*: "a line of people, a file in march." White Fathers, *Bemba-English Dictionary*, 464.

48. Tuden, "Political Systems," 30–31, 36. See a similar argument in MacGaffey, "Changing Representations."

49. See also Kodesh's discussion of clans developed as networks of knowledge ensuring public health but couched in the idiom of kinship. Kodesh, *Beyond the Royal Gaze*.

50. Mukanzubo, *Chitonga-English*, 831.

51. The argument about the negotiation between the status of *-lòngó and *-kwàshı is encapsulated in Tuden's attestation of the root *-lòngó with the meaning "male cross-cousin" and term of address between a male grandfather and his son's and daughter's son. See "Disputing for Power," 30–31.

52. For a similar argument about cattle herds in west central Africa, see Vansina, *How Societies*, 126–27.

53. The following four paragraphs draw heavily from de Luna, "Hunting Reputations," 288–91; de Luna, "Surveying," 231–38.

54. See chapter 3 and cites therein.

55. My reconstruction of proto-Kafue *chila* is a composite of field observations and descriptions in Ansell, "Declining Red Lechwe," 15–18; Boyle, "Secretary's African Tour," 216–69; Colson, *Marriage and the Family*, 32; Colson, "Plateau Tonga of Northern Rhodesia," 106; Colson, *Tonga Religious*, 104–5; Haller, *Contested Floodplain*, 342–57; Livingstone and Livingstone, *Narrative of an Expedition*, 311; Rennie, "Traditional Society," 35–46; Reynolds, *Material Culture*, 19, 57–58; Scudder, *Ecology*, 198–99; Siamwiza, "Famine and Hunger," 153–55.

56. Phonology can't resolve the antiquity of *ibalo*, though its distribution may indicate an older areal form.

57. de Luna, "Surveying"; Derricourt, *Man*, 208–15; Fagan, *Iron Age Cultures*, 70–82; Fagan, Phillipson, and Daniels, *Iron Age Cultures*, 254–55.

58. Colson, *Tonga Religious*, 105.

59. Kairn Klieman presents a wonderful study of a similar process in the equatorial region in *"Pgymies,"* esp. chapter 3.

60. On this loan, see chapter 1. For evidence supporting the homeland of the proto-Kafue speech community, see de Luna, "Surveying."

61. When Lozi speakers raided the Batoka and Kafue areas in the mid to late nineteenth century, they borrowed the root, adding the ka- prefix to create *kabololo* with the meaning "successful hunt." Literally, this word glossed as "great, big, mighty kudu." The semantic connection in Lozi between the Botatwe word for kudu and successful hunting may tell us something of why Kafue speakers invented a new word for this animal—kudu was a prized quarry!

62. Also -NyeNye created by reduplication of the first syllable. The term's distribution is limited to Kafue languages and in the exact Lenje form in Bemba, probably resulting from the heavy contact between Lenje and the Sabi languages to which Bemba belongs.

63. Colson, *Social Organization*, 20, 110–11; Smith and Dale, *Ila-Speaking*, vol. 1, 96, 155.

64. Eugenia Herbert analyzes the association of antelopes with smithing, hunting, medicines, and fertility in her comparative study. She argues that antelopes represent animals that blur the boundary between the village and the bush or forest. Herbert, *Iron, Gender and Power*, 180–84.

65. Fagan, *Iron Age*, Isamu Pati burial 1; Derricourt, *Man on the Kafue*, burial 1; Styen and Nienaber, "Human Skeletal"; Vogel, "Early Iron Age Burial";

Vogel, "Early Iron Age Funerary"; Vogel, *Simbusenga*, burial 4; Vogel, *Kamangoza*, Nansanzu burials 3, 4, 5.

66. For a more detailed argument about the relationship between hunting and sex, see de Luna, "Marksmen and the Bush."

67. Colson, *Tonga Religious*, ch. 2, esp. 28–29, 32–33.

68. New historical approaches to mobility in the eighteenth and nineteenth centuries are complicating this critique, but they generally focus on those who are moving through, rather than the host communities. Rockel, *Carriers of Culture;* von Oppen, *Terms of Trade.*

Chapter 5. Life on the Central Frontier

1. Kopytoff, "Internal African Frontier"; Vansina, *How Societies*, 182–86. James Scott traces the history of a central frontier he names Zomia, which encompasses communities in the central Asian massif and juxtaposes their political culture with that of lowlands societies. For Scott, like Vansina, zomia is a refuge area exhibiting a fascinating history in which residents actively avoided the often quite violent attempts of lowland states to incorporate them. But Scott's story is more state-centric; here I'm interested in the history of politics both within the frontier and between its peoples and those beyond the central frontier. Scott, *Art of Not Being Governed.*

2. Mavhunga, *Transient Workspaces.*

3. For maps, see Ehret, *Classical*, 266, 274; Vansina, *How Societies*, 106. For arguments about this contact zone from linguists and archaeologists, consider Bostoen, "Bantu Plant Names"; Denbow, *Archaeology and Ethnography*, ch. 8.

4. Specularite was mined in the Tsodilo Hills long before copper bangles were fashioned, but it is difficult to trace its consumption.

5. Fagan, Phillipson, and Daniels, *Iron Age Cultures*, 39; Herbert, *Red Gold*, 80; Inskeep, "Some Iron Age Sites," 151; Mills and Filmer, "Chondwe," 135; Phillipson, "Twickenham Road"; Phillipson, "Zambian Copperbelt"; Vogel, "Early Iron Age Tools"; Vogel, "Kabondo Kumbo"; Vogel, *Kumadzulo;* Vogel, *Kamangoza;* Vogel, *Simbusenga.*

6. Bisson, "Precolonial Copper Metallurgy"; Miller, *Tsodilo Jewelry;* Styen and Nienaber, "Iron Age Human Skeletal Remains." On copper bangles as payments, see Bisson, "Copper Currency," 279–81; Herbert, *Red Gold*, 80–81, 104. See also Fagan, "Early Trade."

7. Two more bars were found at Kamusongolwa Kopje near Kasempa and Luano Main Site in the greater Copperbelt region but date to slight later

centuries, between the ninth and twelfth centuries. Bisson, "Precolonial Copper," 115–18.

8. Vogel, *Kumadʒulo;* Vogel, *Kamangoʒa;* Vogel, *Simbusenga.* Archaeologists found copper strip worked into beads at the early to mid-twelfth-century site of Chondwe in the Copperbelt. Mills and Filmer, "Chondwe."

9. One exception might be the oval form recovered on the Batoka Plateau, which seems to match fifteenth- and sixteenth-century Urungwe forms. Fagan, *Iron Age Cultures,* 122; Garlake, "Urungwe District."

10. Fagan doesn't clarify whether this measurement applies to the internal or external diameter. Even as an external measurement, it is much larger than other bangles. The original measurement was given as 4.5 inches and was converted to millimeters to facilitate comparison with other bangles' reported diameters. Fagan, *Iron Age,* 120.

11. Smith and Dale, *Ila-Speaking,* 180–83.

12. de Maret, *Fouilles,* 131–32, 165, 180, 184, 213, 220, 243–44; Hiernaux, da Longrée, and de Buyst, *Fouilles Archaeologiques* vol. 1, 18–21, 41.

13. Fagan, Phillipson, and Daniels, *Iron Age Cultures,* 138, 143. See also Fagan, *Iron Age Cultures,* 22.

14. The Gwembe Valley in particular was famed for its elephant herds as early as the seventeenth century. Axelson, *Portuguese in South-East Africa,* 190, as cited in Fagan, Phillipson, and Daniels, *Iron Age Cultures,* 57. For patterns of loanwords for terms glossing as "professional ivory hunter," see de Luna, "Hunting Reputations."

15. Denbow, Klehm, and Dussubieux, "Glass Beads of Kaitshàa"; Wilmsen et al., "Social Geography"; Wood, Dussubieux, and Robertshaw, "Glass of Chibuene"; and cites below.

16. For an introduction to the archaeology of the region, see Campbell, Robbins, and Taylor, *Tsodilo Hills;* Denbow, "Dialectics of Identity"; Denbow, "Excavations at Divuyu"; Miller, *Tsodilo Jewelry;* Wilmsen, "Nqoma."

17. Denbow, Klehm, and Dussubieux, "Glass Beads of Kaitshàa"; Wilmsen et al., "Social Geography."

18. Denbow, Klehm, and Dussubieux, "Glass Beads of Kaitshàa"; Robertshaw et al., "Southern African Glass Beads"; Sinclair, Ekblom, and Wood, "Trade and Society"; Wood, *Interconnections;* Wood, Dussubieux, and Robertshaw, "Glass of Chibuene."

19. Denbow, Klehm, and Dussubieux, "Glass Beads of Kaitshàa"; Wilmsen et al., "Social Geography."

20. In addition to citations in nn. 15–19, above, see also Pwiti, *Continuity and Change*.

21. Archaeologists are rapidly rewriting the early history of the Zimbabwe culture. It would be interesting to learn more about the possible historical relationship between this early northern route and emerging evidence for a polycentric approach to the development of the Zimbabwe culture because the polycentric approach argues for the significance of many walled and terraced centers north of the Shashe-Limpopo region. For an introduction to some of the revisionist prehistories of Zimbabwe culture, see Chirikure et al., "New Pathways"; Chirikure et al., "Zimbabwe Culture"; Chirikure et al., "Bayesian"; Chirikure and Pikirayi, "Inside and Outside." See also Huffman, "Social Complexity."

22. Miller, *Tsodilo Jewelry*.

23. Ibid., 89.

24. In addition to the aforementioned references in nn. 15–23, see Denbow et al., "Archaeological Excavations at Bosutswe"; Denbow and Miller, "Metal Working at Bosutswe."

25. Denbow, Klehm, and Dussubieux, "Kaitshàa"; Denbow et al., "Archaeological Excavations at Bosutswe"; Reid and Segobye, "Politics, Society, and Trade"; Sinclair, Ekblom, and Wood, "Trade and Society"; Wood, *Interconnections*. For a synthesis of the historical development of Zimbabwe culture, see Pikirayi, *Zimbabwe Culture;* Pikirayi, *Archaeological Identity*. See also Kusimba, *Rise and Fall of Swahili States* and consider revisionists' arguments cited in n. 21.

26. Vogel, *Kumadzulo*, 38. Wood, Dussubieux, and Robertshaw note the absence of any glass shards in the interior in "Glass of Chibuene," esp. 68–70. The presence of glass shards at Chibuene peaks between the mid-ninth and mid-tenth century.

27. Jeffrey Fleisher shared these impressions about the frequency of ostrich eggshell beads from the preliminary results of the 2014 season at Basanga, pers. comm. October 23, 2014. Ostrich eggshell beads were also recovered in the Zambezi Valley. Only two were found on the Batoka Plateau, both at Isamu Pati. Fagan, *Iron Age Cultures;* Vogel, "Early Iron Age Tools," 764–65; Vogel, "Early Iron Age Funerary Practice," 583–86; Vogel, "Early Iron Age Burial"; Vogel, *Simbusenga*.

28. Denbow, "Dialectics of Identity."

29. Bisson, "Continuity and Discontinuity," 46.

30. Ibid., 44.

31. Robertson, "New Early Iron Age."

32. The adoption of the "prestigious" Kansanshi guilloche designs in the ninth century is discussed by Vansina in *How Societies*, 213–14, n. 20; 245, n. 120 citing Robertson, "New Early Iron Age," and Ervedose, *Arqueología*, 244–53.

33. This section summarizes and amplifies Vansina, *How Societies*, 206–34.

34. Quotes in this paragraph from Vansina, *How Societies*, 211. See also pp. 211–12, n. 13.

35. See chapter 3.

36. Although examples from Lunda, Luba, Chokwe, Bemba and others are well known, consider the use of metaphors in the transformation of governance in Nkoya history, which is represented as a shift from the female Mwene Shilayi Mashiku leader to the father-hunter Wene figure. van Binsbergen, *Tears of Rain*, esp. 177, 191–92.

37. Significantly, this historical moment of experimentation around the status of hunters coincides with the development of "forest specialists" and new ideas about chiefly status and wealth between the eighth and tenth centuries further north and west. See Klieman, *"Pygmies,"* ch. 4 and, for timing, 171–72.

38. Colson, "Trade and Wealth"; Miracle, "Plateau Tonga Entrepreneurs."

39. Fagan, "Early Trade."

40. Colleen Kriger makes this argument about precolonial smiths in the later precolonial centuries in west central Africa in *Pride of Men*.

41. Kriger, *Pride of Men*.

42. Ibid.

43. See chapter 3.

44. Bastin and Schadeberg, "Bantu Lexical Reconstructions 3," ID 6877. Consider the significance of fishing and control over the creation and maintenance of fishing pools to the founding of the Luba kingdom in Reefe, *Rainbow and the Kings*.

45. For the copper sources of Nqoma jewelry, see Miller, *Tsodilo Jewelry*. For a discussion of ostrich eggshell in Sanga, see de Maret, *Fouilles Archeologiques*, vol. 2, 165; Nenquin, *Excavations*. See also Hiernaux, de Longrée, and De Buyst, *Fouilles Archeologiques*, vol. 1, 21. Sanga was located about halfway between the distribution zones of ostrich in southern and eastern Africa, but evidence for trade links to the south are stronger.

46. This is a fairly standard narrative in many of the sources cited in this chapter, but its ubiquity is perhaps best demonstrated by its adoption into textbooks. Consider, for example, Curtin et al., *African History*, ch. 8.

47. Consider as one example, the debates about the role of trade in the development of centralized authority in Great Zimbabwe and related communities as described in Pikirayi, *Zimbabwe Culture.*
48. de Luna, "Surveying."
49. Fagan et al., *Iron Age Cultures;* Kusimba, *Swahili States;* Lancaster and Pohorilenko, "Ingombe Ilede"; Phillipson and Fagan, "Date of the Ingombe Ilede Burials"; Pikirayi, *Zimbabwe Culture.*
50. Bisson, "Copper Currency," 280–86; Garlake, "Urungwe."
51. Fagan et al., *Iron Age Cultures.*
52. Bisson, "Copper Currency," 280–86.
53. Only one among the many copper bangles recovered from the modest villages of the Batoka, middle Kafue, Lusaka area, and Zambezi Valley was identified as belonging to the Ingombe Ilede style. This bangle was recovered from burial 10 at Isamu Pati, a grave of a forty- to sixty-year-old woman dated to thirteenth or fourteenth century. The bangle suggests the fourteenth century date is more likely. Fagan, *Iron Age Cultures.*
54. Derricourt, *Man on the Kafue.*
55. Bisson, "Precolonial Copper."
56. de Maret, *Fouilles.*
57. Sutherland-Harris, "Zambian Trade."
58. Beach, *Shona and Their Neighbors;* Garlake, "Dambarare"; Pikirayi, *Zimbabwe Culture,* ch. 6.
59. Lancaster and Pohorilenko, "Ingombe Ilede."
60. I have found Jeremy Prestholdt's work on consumption and the "traveling culture" of nineteenth-century Zanzibaris to be particularly inspiring in thinking about life on the central frontier. Part of the construction of this sentence plays on concepts in *Domesticating the World,* esp. 97–105.
61. Vogel, *Simbusenga.*
62. The source of this estimate is a 1696 document by A. da Conceição. Cited in Lancaster and Pohorilenko, "Ingombe Ilede," 11–12.
63. See the description of burial 1 in Derricourt, *Man on the Kafue,* 65. For the new ivory bangle see, p. 76, and fig. 3.6a–b on p. 77.
64. On the practice of women taking lovers to improve their economic and social standing (and that of their husband if they were married) in the very late precolonial period, see the discussion of the Ila practice of *kuweza lubono* in de Luna, "Affect and Society."
65. Colson, *Social Organization,* 63–64.
66. Lancaster and Pohorilenko, "Ingombe Ilede."

67. Collins, *Tonga Grammar,* 156.
68. Nkazi, *Citonga Note Book.*

Epilogue

1. Colson, *Nampeyo.* Chief Chona and the residents of Nampeyo worried that the history of their area would be forgotten, a particularly acute concern as the political dominance of UNIP, with its tight alliances with ethnic groups living in Northern Province, grew stronger. Colson, "Bantu Botatwe"; Macola, *Liberal Nationalism.*
2. Colson, *Nampeyo,* 8–9.
3. Ibid., 12–14.
4. Ibid., 13. Material in parentheses was in the original. I added material in brackets for clarity.
5. Ibid., 14, 21, 24.
6. Colson, "Rain-Shrines," 280. Consider similar comments about the Valley Tonga in Colson, *Social Organization.*
7. Colson, "Spirit Possession."
8. Colson, "Modern Political Organization," 91–98.
9. Colson, *Tonga Religious Life,* ch. 2, esp. pp. 28–29, 32–33.
10. Colson, "Rain-Shrines," 280; Colson, "Continuing Dialog," 129.
11. Colson, *Tonga Religious,* 351.
12. Colson, "Biases: Place, Time, Stance."
13. An edited volume contains both sides of the debate: Lancaster and Vickery, eds. *Tonga-Speaking Peoples.* Among many publications by each of the following scholars, consider also Lancaster, "Ethnic Identity"; Matthews, "Historical Traditions"; Matthews, "Portuguese, Chikunda"; O'Brien, "Chiefs of Rain"; van Binsbergen, *Religious Change.*
14. van Binsbergen, *Religious Change,* 130. See also contributions by Lancaster, O'Brien, and Matthews to Lancaster and Vickery, eds., *Tonga-Speaking.*
15. McIntosh, ed., *Beyond Chiefdoms.* Research on the history of Buganda over the last fifteen years provides a particularly robust engagement with these ideas: Hanson, *Landed Obligation;* Kodesh, *Beyond the Royal Gaze;* Stephens, *African Motherhood.*
16. Colson herself remarked on the misunderstanding of scale. See "Biases."
17. In order: "The Hunters" in Fell, *Folk Tales,* 189–91; Fowler, *Ila Speaking,* 174; "The Chief of the Fishes" in Fell, *Folk Tales,* 197–99.
18. Colson, *Nampeyo,* 21.

19. Derek Peterson, for example, considers larger scale affiliation outside the rubric of the nation-state in twentieth-century East Africa in *Ethnic Patriotism*.
20. Landau, *Popular Politics*.

Appendix

1. Bastin and Schadeberg, eds., "Bantu Lexical Reconstructions 3"; Guthrie, *Comparative Bantu*.
2. de Luna, "Collecting Food," 367–70.
3. de Luna, "Affect and Society," 133–40; Ehret, *Classical*, 147–48, 249–50; Schoenbrun, *Historical Reconstruction*, 139, 203–4; Schoenbrun, *Green Place*, 108–11; Vansina, *Paths*, 73, 274–75.
4. de Luna, "Collecting," 483–84; Ehret, *Classical*, 42, 234, 300; Meeussen, *Bantu Lexical*, 23.
5. de Luna, "Collecting," 498–99; Ehret, *Classical*, 42, 301.
6. de Luna, "Collecting," 481–82; Ehret, *Classical*, 42, 301.
7. de Luna, "Collecting," 482–83; Ehret, *Classical*, 42, 300.
8. Vansina, *Paths*, 274.
9. Vansina, *How Societies*, 46.
10. de Luna, "Collecting," 461–62.
11. Vansina, *Paths*, 297.
12. de Luna, "Collecting," 507–8, 583–84; Vansina, *Paths*, 283.
13. de Luna, "Collecting," 537–39, 565–66; Vansina, *Paths*, 283.
14. de Luna, "Collecting," 508–9; Ehret, *Classical*, 312; Vansina, *Paths*, 282–83.
15. de Luna, "Collecting," 509–10; Ehret, *Classical*, 313. For *-bànjí, see Ehret, *Classical*, 313; Vansina, *Paths*, 287.
16. de Luna, "Collecting," 513–15; Ehret, *Classical*, 307; Ehret, "Subclassifying Bantu," 66.
17. de Luna, "Collecting," 510–11; Ehret, *Classical*, 313; Meeussen, *Bantu Lexical*, 26, 33.
18. de Luna, "Collecting," 511–13.
19. de Luna, "Collecting," 515–16; Ehret, *Classical*, 312; Vansina, *Paths*, 287.
20. de Luna, "Collecting," 516–17.
21. Ibid., 517–18.
22. Ibid.; Ehret, *Classical*, 313.
23. Ehret, *Classical*, 309; Vansina, *Paths*, 289.
24. Ehret, *Classical*, 309; Vansina, *Paths*, 289.
25. Ehret, *Classical*, 309.

26. Ibid., 309.

27. Bostoen, "Bantu Plant Names," 23–24.

28. Ehret, *Classical*, 105.

29. Ibid., 104–5.

30. de Luna, "Collecting," 502–3; Ehret, *Classical*, 124, 312; Vansina, *Paths*, 288.

31. de Luna, "Collecting," 503–4, 526–27; Ehret, *Classical*, 313; Vansina, *Paths*, 288.

32. de Luna, "Collecting," 519–20, 554–55; Ehret, *Classical*, 313; Vansina, *Paths*, 290.

33. de Luna, "Collecting," 520–21.

34. Ibid., 521–22.

35. Ibid. For *-púlá, see Ehret, *Classical*, 314.

36. de Luna, "Collecting," 523–24.

37. Ehret, *Classical*, 310.

38. Ibid.

39. Ibid.

40. Bostoen, "Plant Names," 20–21; Ehret, *Classical*, 315; Philippson and Bahuchet, "Cultivated Crops."

41. Bostoen, "Pearl Millet"; Philippson and Bahuchet, "Cultivated Crops."

42. For roots 41–50, consider more detailed discussions and debates in de Maret and Nsuka, "History of Bantu Metallurgy"; Ehret, "Establishment of Iron-Working"; Klein-Arendt, *Traditionellen Eisenbandwerke;* Vansina, "Linguistic Evidence."

43. For roots numbered 51–57, see Ehret, *Classical*, 133–36, 212, 224–25, 228–29, 234–37, 271–72; Vansina, *How Societies*, 81–87.

44. de Luna, "Collecting," 478–79.

45. Ibid., 472–73.

46. Ibid., 527–28.

47. Ibid., 529–30; Ehret, *Classical*, 124.

48. de Luna, "Collecting," 535–37; see also attestations of *-bìng in Kati languages, such as -wééja, "to hunt," in the Elwana dialect of Swahili: Nurse and Hinnebusch, *Swahili and Sabaki*, 614.

49. de Luna, "Collecting," 532–33.

50. Ibid., 528–29.

51. Ibid., 528.

52. Ibid., 533–35; Christopher Ehret reconstructs the root for the instrument as *-palʊ, "long, stabbing blade," to proto-Bantu; the distribution he lists for the blade includes eastern Bantu and Bobangi. The blade likely predates the

application of the root to its wielder in class 1/2, but the Bobangi attestation may actually result from later contact and trade in central Africa rather than the proto-Bantu status of the reconstruction for the tool proposed by Ehret. Ehret, *Classical*, 113.

53. de Luna, "Collecting," 543–44.

54. Ibid., 541–42; Ehret, *Classical*, 299.

55. de Luna, "Collecting," 545–46.

56. Ibid., 544–45; Ehret, "Subclassifying Bantu," 96; Ehret, "Establishment of Iron-working," 153. On the parallels between the function of the adze and the point named after this older tool, see Smith and Dale, *Ila-Speaking*, vol. 1, 216.

57. Colson, *Tonga Religious Life*, 50; Fowler, *Dictionary of Ila*, 206, 436, 492, 381; Mukanzubo Kalinda Institute, *Chitonga-English Dictionary*, 1118.

58. de Luna, "Affect and Society," 144–45; Ehret, "Establishment of Iron-Working"; Vansina, "Linguistic Evidence."

59. de Luna, "Collecting," 478; Fowler, *Dictionary of Ila*, 242; Mukanzubo, *Chitonga-English Dictionary*, 970, see also 861 for *cisokwe*. Consider also the related term *cisoko*, "a bush, a hiding-place, refuge; the usual way; the origin or nature of a thing," in Fowler, *Dictionary of Ila*, 129.

60. de Luna, "Collecting," 474. Ehret reconstructs the term as proto-Mashariki (narrow eastern Bantu), but the distribution in Botatwe, Sabi, and southwest Bantu suggests that is it older. Ehret, *Classical*, 299.

61. de Luna, "Collecting," 552–53.

62. Ibid., 553–54.

63. Vansina, *How Societies*, 88–98.

64. Schoenbrun, *Historical Reconstruction*, 91–93; Stephens, *African Motherhood*, 188; Vansina, *Paths*, 284.

65. Schoenbrun, *Historical Reconstruction*, 94–95; Stephens, *African Motherhood*, 188; Vansina, *Paths*, 283–85.

66. Schoenbrun, *Historical Reconstruction*, 949–5; Stephens, *African Motherhood*, 188; Vansina, *Paths*, 284–85.

67. de Luna, "Affect and Society," 145–48. Christopher Ehret, however, argues that this root must be distinct because of its odd tonal pattern and the fact that it has a meaning that doesn't connect well, in Ehret's opinion, with his reconstructed meaning for *-lòngò, "patrilineage." Therefore, Ehret argues that the root is either distinct or derives from a more general term for social affiliation, *-lòngò. If this is so, the shift in the second vowel may be easier to account for, but the shift in the first vowel is far more difficult to explain. Ehret, *Classical*, 169 nn. 10, 11, 13 and pers. comm. November 17–19, 2011.

68. de Luna, "Collecting," 548–50; Vansina, *Paths*, 287; Vansina, "Do Pygmies," 431–35.

69. de Luna, "Collecting," 550–51.

70. Ibid., 551–52.

71. Ibid., 584–85.

72. Ibid., 469–70.

73. Ibid., 484–85; Ehret, *Classical*, 42, 300.

74. de Luna, "Collecting," 485–86.

75. Ibid., 468–89.

Bibliography

Archives and Private Collections

Belgium

MUSÉE ROYAL DE L'AFRIQUE CENTRALE
Bantu Files, Linguistics Section, Research Institute

Botswana

SPECIAL COLLECTIONS, UNIVERSITY OF BOTSWANA LIBRARY
Schapera Papers, Special Collections

United States

THERA CRANE PERSONAL COLLECTION
Crane, Thera. "Field Notes and Recordings." Berkeley, CA

DAVID LEE SCHOENBRUN PERSONAL COLLECTION
Schoenbrun, David. "Field Notes." Evanston, IL

YALE DIVINITY LIBRARY
Methodist Missionary Society Archives, Special Series, Biographical: Central Africa. Microfiche

Zambia

JESUIT ARCHIVES, LUWISHA HOUSE
Father Kovanda Papers
Father Torrend Papers

SPECIAL COLLECTIONS, UNIVERSITY OF ZAMBIA LIBRARY
Lehmann Papers.

Other Works Cited

Allan, William. *The African Husbandman*. New York: Barnes and Noble, 1965.

Alpern, Stanley. "Did They or Didn't They Invent It? Iron in Sub-Saharan Africa." *History in Africa* 32 (2005): 41–94.

Alpers, Edward. *Ivory and Slaves: Changing Patterns of International Trade in East Central Africa to the Later Nineteenth Century*. Berkeley: University of California Press, 1975.

Ambrose, Stanley. "Hunter-Gatherer Adaptations to Non-Marginal Environments: An Ecological and Archaeological Assessment of the Dorobo Model." *Sprache und Geschichte in Afrika* 7, no. 2 (1986): 11–42.

Ansell, H. "The Declining Red Lechwe." *Oryx: The International Journal of Conservation* 3, no. 1 (1955): 15–18.

Apter, Andrew. *Black Kings and Critics: The Hermeneutics of Power in Yoruba Society*. Chicago: University of Chicago Press, 1992.

Arens, W., and Ivan Karp, eds. *Creativity of Power*. Washington, DC: Smithsonian Institution Press, 1989.

Axelson, Eric. *Portuguese in South-East Africa, 1600–1700*. Johannesburg: Witwatersrand University Press, 1960.

Baloglou, Christos. "The Tradition of Economic Thought in the Mediterranean World from the Ancient Classical Times through the Hellenistic Times until the Byzantine Times and Arab-Islamic World." In *Handbook of the History of Economic Thought: Insights on the Founders of Modern Economics*, ed. Jürgen Georg Backhaus, 7–91. New York: Springer, 2012.

Barbieri, Chiara, Anne Butthof, Koen Bostoen, and Brigitte Pakendorf. "Genetic Perspectives on the Origins of Clicks in Bantu Languages from Southwestern Zambia." *European Journal of Human Genetics* 21 (2013): 430–36.

Barnard, Alan. "Hunting-and-Gathering Society: An Eighteenth Century Scottish Invention." In *Hunter-Gatherers in History, Archaeology and Anthropology*, ed. Alan Barnard, 31–43. New York: Berg, 2004.

———. "Images of Hunters and Gatherers in European Social Thought." In *The Cambridge Encyclopedia of Hunters and Gatherers*, ed. R. Lee and R. Daly, 375–83. Cambridge: Cambridge University Press, 1999.

———. *The Kalahari Debate: A Bibliographic Essay*. Edinburgh: Edinburgh University Press, 1992.

————. "Through Radcliffe-Brown's Spectacles: Reflections on the History of Anthropology." *History of the Human Sciences* 5 (1992): 1–20.

Bastin, Yvonne, André Coupez, and Michael Mann. *Continuity and Divergence in the Bantu Languages: Perspectives from a Lexicostatistic Study.* Annales Sciences Humaines, no. 162. Tervuren, Belgium: Musée Royal de l'Afrique Centrale, 1999.

Bastin, Yvonne, and Thilo Schadeberg, eds. "Bantu Lexical Reconstructions 3." Tervuren, Belgium: Musée Royale de l'Afrique Centrale. http://www .metafro.be/blr (accessed October 2006 through July 2015).

Beach, David. *The Shona and Their Neighbors.* Oxford: Blackwell Publishers, 1994.

Binford, Lewis. *Bones: Ancient Man and Modern Myths.* New York: Academic Press, 1981.

Bird, C. S., and M. B. Kendall, "The Mande Hero." In *Explorations in African Systems of Thought,* ed. I. Karp and C. S. Bird, 13–26. Bloomington: Indiana University Press, 1980.

Birmingham, David, and Phyllis Martin, eds. *History of Central Africa,* vol. 1. New York: Longman, 1983.

Bisson, Michael. "Precolonial Copper Metallurgy: Sociopolitical Context." In *Ancient African Metallurgy,* ed. Joseph O. Vogel, 83–145. Walnut Creek, CA: AltaMira Press, 2000.

————. "Continuity and Discontinuity in Copperbelt and North-Western Province Ceramic Sequences." *Nyame Akuma* 31 (1989): 43–46.

————. "The Prehistoric Coppermines of Zambia." PhD diss., University of California, Santa Barbara, 1976.

————. "Copper Currency in Central Africa: The Archaeological Evidence." *World Archaeology* 6, no. 3 (1975): 276–92.

Bostoen, Koen. "Shanjo and Fwe as Part of Bantu Botatwe: A Diachronic Phonological Approach." In *Selected Proceedings of the 39th Annual Conference on African Linguistics,* ed. Akinloye Ojo and Lioba Moshi, 110–30. Somerville, MA: Cascadilla Proceedings Project, 2009.

————. "Bantu Plant Names as Indicators of Linguistic Stratigraphy in the Western Province of Zambia." In *Selected Proceedings of the 37th Annual Conference on African Linguistics,* ed. Doris L. Payne and Jaime Peña, 16–29. Somerville, MA: Cascadilla Proceedings Project, 2007.

————. "Pearl Millet in Early Bantu Communities in Central Africa: A Reconsideration of the Lexical Evidence." *Afrika und Übersee* 89 (2006/2007): 183–213.

———. *Des Mots et des Pots en Bantou: Une Approche Linguistique de l'Histoire de la Céramique en Afrique*. Frankfurt am Main: Peter Lang Verlag, 2005.

Bostoen, Koen, and Bonny Sands. "Clicks in South-western Bantu Languages: Contact-Induced vs. Language-Internal Lexical Change." In *Proceedings of the 6th World Congress of African Linguistics*, ed. M. Brenzinger, 129–40. Cologne: Rüdiger Köppe Verlag, 2012.

Boyle, C. L. "The Secretary's African tour: An Account by the Secretary of His Visit with His Wife to East and Central Africa between June and October 1957." *Oryx: The International Journal of Conservation* 4, no. 4 (1958): 216–69.

Brain, Charles. *The Hunters or the Hunted? An Introduction to African Cave Taphonomy*. Chicago: University of Chicago Press, 1981.

Campbell, Alec, Larry Robbins, and Michael Taylor. *Tsodilo Hills: Copper Bracelet of the Kalahari*. East Lansing: Michigan State University Press, 2010.

Carter, Hazel. *An Outline of Chitonga Grammar*. Lusaka: Bookworld, 2002.

Cartmill, Matt. *A View to a Death in the Morning: Hunting and Nature through History*. Cambridge, MA: Harvard University Press, 1993.

Cauvin, Jacques. *The Birth of the Gods and the Origins of Agriculture*. Cambridge: Cambridge University Press, 2000.

Cavalli-Sforza, L. L., P. Menozzi, and A. Piazza, eds. *The History and Geography of Human Genes*. Princeton: Princeton University Press, 1994.

Childe, V. Gordon. *Man Makes Himself*. London: Watts, 1936.

Childs, S. Terry, and Eugenia W. Herbert. "Metallugy and Its Consequences." In *African Archaeology*, ed. Ann B. Stahl, 276–300. Malden, MA: Blackwell Publishers, 2005.

Chirikure, Shadreck, Munyaradzi Manyanga, Innocent Pikirayi, and Mark Pollard. "New Pathways to Sociopolitical Complexity in Southern Africa." *African Archaeological Review* 30 (2013): 339–66.

Chirikure, Shadreck, Munyaradzi Manyanga, A. Mark Pollard, Foreman Bandama, Godfrey Mahachi, and Innocent Pikirayi. "Zimbabwe Culture before Mapungubwe: New Evidence from Mapela Hill, South-Western Zimbabwe." *PLoS ONE* 9, no. 10 (2014): e111224. doi:10.1371/journal.pone.0111224.

Chirikure, Shadreck, and Innocent Pikirayi. "Inside and Outside the Dry Stone Walls: Revisiting the Material Culture of Great Zimbabwe." *Antiquity* 82 (2008): 976–93.

Chirikure, Shadreck, Mark Pollard, and Foreman Bandama. "A Bayesian Chronology for Great Zimbabwe: Re-threading the Sequence of a Vandalized Monument." *Antiquity* 87 (2013): 854–72.

Cligget, Lisa. *Grains from Grass: Aging, Gender and Famine in Rural Africa.* Ithaca: Cornell University Press, 2005.

Collins, B. *Tonga Grammar.* London: Longmans, Green, 1962.

Colson, Elizabeth. "Biases: Place, Time, Stance." In *The Tonga-Speaking Peoples of Zambia and Zimbabwe,* ed. Chet Lancaster and Kenneth Vickery, 345–79. New York: University Press of America, 2007.

———. *Tonga Religious Life in the Twentieth Century.* Lusaka, Zambia: Bookworld Publishers, 2006.

———. "The Bantu Botatwe: Changing Political Definitions in Southern Zambia." In *The Politics of Cultural Performance,* ed. David Parkin, Lionel Caplan, and Humphry Fisher, 61–80. Providence, RI: Berghahn Books, 1996.

———. *The History of Nampeyo.* Lusaka: Kenneth Kaunda Foundation, 1991.

———. "In Good Years and in Bad: Food Strategies of Self-Reliant Societies." *Journal of Anthropological Research* 35, no. 1 (1979): 18–29.

———. "A Continuing Dialog: Prophets and Local Shrines among the Tonga in Zambia." In *Regional Cults,* ed. R. P. Werbner, 119–39. London: Academic Press, 1977.

———. "Heroism, Martyrdom, and Courage: An Essay on Tonga Ethics." In *The Translation of Culture,* ed. T. O. Beidelman, 19–35. London: Tavistock Publications, 1971.

———. "Assimilation of Aliens among the Zambian Tonga." In *Tribe to Nation: Processes of Political Incorporation in Africa,* ed. J. Middleton and R. Cohen, 35–54. San Francisco: Chandler Press, 1970.

———. "Spirit Possession among the Tonga of Zambia." In *Spirit Mediumship and Society in Africa,* ed. J. Middleton and J. H. M. Beattie, 69–103. London: Routledge and Kegan Paul, 1969.

———. "The Alien Diviner and Local Politics among the Tonga of Zambia." In *Political Anthropology,* ed. M. Swartz, A. Tuden and V. Turner, 121–28. Chicago: Aldine Press, 1966.

———. *The Plateau Tonga of Northern Rhodesia.* Manchester: Manchester University Press, 1962.

———. "The Plateau Tonga." In *Matrilineal Kinship,* ed. D. Scheneider and K. Gough, 36–95. Berkeley: University of California Press, 1961.

———. *The Social Organization of the Gwembe Tonga.* Manchester: Manchester University Press, for the Rhodes-Livingstone Institute, 1960.

————. *Marriage and the Family among the Plateau Tonga of Northern Rhodesia.* Manchester: Manchester University Press, for the Rhodes-Livingstone Institute, 1958.

————. "Plateau Tonga Diet" *Rhodes-Livingstone Journal* (1958): 51–67.

————. "Ancestral Spirits and Social Structure among the Plateau Tonga." *Internationales Archiv für Ethnographie / International Archives of Ethnography* 47, no. 1/2 (1954): 21–68.

————. "Clans and the Joking-Relationship among the Plateau Tonga of Northern Rhodesia." *Kroeber Anthropological Society Papers* 8, no. 9 (1953): 45–60.

————. "Social Control and Vengeance in Plateau Tonga Society." *Africa* 23 (1953): 199–212.

————. "The Plateau Tonga of Northern Rhodesia." In *Seven Tribes of Central Africa,* ed. E. Colson and M. Gluckman, 94–162. London: Oxford University Press, 1951.

————. "Residence and Village Stability among the Plateau Tonga." *Rhodes-Livingstone Journal* 12 (1951): 41–67.

————. "The Role of Cattle among the Plateau Tonga of Mazabuka District." *Rhodes-Livingstone Journal* 12 (1951): 10–46.

————. "Life among the Cattle-Owning Plateau Tonga." *Occasional Papers of the Rhodes-Livingstone Institute,* no. 6 (1949): 3–40.

————. "Modern Political Organization of the Plateau Tonga." *African Studies* 7, no. 2/3 (1948): 85–98.

————. "Rainshrines of the Plateau Tonga of Northern Rhodesia" *Africa* 18, no. 4 (1948): 272–83.

Cooke, H. J. "Landform Evolution in the Context of Climatic Change and Neotectonism in the Middle Kalahari of North-Central Botswana." *Transactions Institute of British Geographers,* n.s., 5 (1980): 80–90.

————. "The Paleoclimatic Significance of Caves and Adjacent Landforms in Western Ngamiland, Bostwana." *Geographical Journal* 141 (1975): 430–44.

Cooke, H. J., and H. T. Verstappen. "The Landforms of the Western Makgadigadi Basin in Northern Botswana, with a Consideration of the Chronology of the Evolution of Lake Paleo-Makgadigadi." *Zeitschrift für Geomorphologie* 28 (1984): 1–19.

Crossley, R., S. Davison-Hirschmann, R. B. Owen, and P. Shaw. "Lake Level Fluctuations during the Last 2000 years in Malawi." In *Late Cainozoic Paleoclimates of the Southern Hemisphere,* ed. J. C. Vogel, 305–16. Rotterdam: A. A. Balkema, 1984.

Curtin, Philip, Steven Feierman, Leonard Thompson, and Jan Vansina, *African History: From Earliest Times to Independence*. New York: Longman, 1995.

Cutshall, Charles R. "Disputing for Power: Elites and the Law among the Ila of Zambia." PhD diss., Boston University, 1980.

Dahlberg, Frances. "Introduction." In *Woman the Gatherer*, ed. Frances Dahlberg, 1–33. New Haven: Yale University Press, 1981.

Dart, Raymond. "Australopithecus Africanus: The Man-Ape of South Africa." *Nature* 115 (1925): 195–99.

de Barros, Philip. "Iron Metallurgy: Sociocultural Context." In *Ancient African Metallurgy: The Sociocultural Context*, ed. Joseph O. Vogel, 147–98. Walnut Creek: AltaMira Press, 2000.

de Heusch, Luc. *Le Roi Ivre ou L'origine de l'État*. Paris: Gallimard, 1972.

de Luna, Kathryn M. "Marksmen and the Bush: the Affective Micro-Politics of Landscape, Sex, and Technology in Precolonial South Central Africa." *Kronos: Southern African Histories* 41 (2015): 21–44.

———. "Bantu Expansion." In Oxford Bibliographies in "African Studies," ed. Thomas Spear. New York: Oxford University Press, November 25, 2014. doi: 10.1093/OBO/9780199846733-0165.

———. "Affect and Society in Precolonial Africa." *International Journal of African Historical Studies* 46, no. 1 (March/April 2013): 123–50.

———. "Hunting Reputations: Talent, Individuals, and Community in Precolonial South Central Africa." *Journal of African History* 53, no. 3 (2012): 279–99.

———. "Surveying the Boundaries of History and Archaeology: Early Botatwe Settlement in South Central Africa and the 'Sibling Disciplines' Debate." *African Archaeological Review* 29, no. 2/3 (September 2012): 209–51.

———. "Classifying Botatwe: M.60 and K.40 Languages and the Settlement Chronology of South Central Africa." *Africana Linguistica* 16 (2010): 65–96.

———. "Collecting Food, Cultivating Persons: Wild Resource Use in Central African Political Culture, c. 1000 BCE to c. 1900 CE." PhD diss., Northwestern University, 2008.

de Luna, Kathryn M., Jeffrey Fleisher, and Susan K. McIntosh. "Thinking across the African Past: Interdisciplinarity and Early History." *African Archaeological Review* 29, no. 2/3 (September 2012): 75–94.

de Maret, Pierre. *Fouilles Archaeologiques dans la Vallée du Haut-Lualaba, Zaire*. vols. 2 and 3. Tervuren: Musée Royal de l'Afrique Centrale, 1985.

————. "New Survey of Archaeological Research and Dates for West-Central and North Central Africa." *Journal of African History* 23 (1982): 1–15.

————. "Luba Roots: The First Complete Iron Age Sequence in Zaire." *Current Anthropology* 20, no. 1 (1979): 233–35.

————. "Sanga: New Excavations, More Data and Some Related Problems." *Journal of African History* 18 (1977): 321–37.

de Maret, Pierre, and F. Nsuka. "History of Bantu Metallurgy: Some Linguistic Aspects." *History in Africa* 4 (1977): 43–65.

Denbow, James. *The Archaeology and Ethnography of Central Africa*. Cambridge: Cambridge University Press, 2013.

————. "Excavataions at Divuyu, Tsodilo Hills." *Botswana Notes & Records* 43 (2011): 76–94.

————. "Material Culture and the Dialectics of Identity in the Kalahari: AD 700–1700." In *Beyond Chiefdoms: Pathways to Complexity in Africa*, ed. Susan McIntosh, 110–23. Cambridge: Cambridge University Press, 1999.

————. "Congo to Kalahari: Data and Hypotheses about the Political Economy of the Western Stream of the Early Iron Age." *African Archaeological Review* 8 (1990): 139–76.

————. "A New Look at the Later Prehistory of the Kalahari." *Journal of African History* 27 (1986): 3–29.

Denbow, James, Carla Klehm, and Laure Dussubieux. "The Glass Beads of Kaitshàa and Early Indian Ocean Trade into the Far Interior of Southern Africa." *Antiquity* 89 (2015): 361–77.

Denbow, James, and Duncan Miller. "Metal Working at Bosutswe, Botswana." *Journal of African Archaeology* 5 (2007): 271–313.

Denbow, James, Jeannette Smith, Nonofho Mathibidi Ndobochani, Kirsten Atwood, and Duncan Miller. "Archaeological Excavations at Bosutswe, Botswana: Cultural Chronology, Paleo-Ecology, and Economy." *Journal of Archaeological Science* 35 (2008): 459–80.

Denbow, James, and Edwin N. Wilmsen. "Advent and Course of Pastoralism in the Kalahari." *Science*, n.s., 234, no. 4783 (December 19, 1986): 1509–15.

Derricourt, Robin. *Man on the Kafue: The Archaeology and History of the Itezhi-itezhi Area of Zambia*. New York: Lilian Berber Press, 1985.

Douglas, Mary. *The Lele of Kasai*. London: Oxford University Press for the International African Institute, 1963.

Doke, Clement. *English-Lamba Vocabulary*. 2nd ed. Johannesburg: University of Witwatersrand Press, 1963.

Dueppens, Stephen. *Egalitarian Revolution in the Savanna: The Origins of a West African Political System.* Sheffield, UK: Equinox, 2012.

Dueppens, Stephen, and Cameron Gokee. "Hunting on the Margins of Medieval West African States: A Preliminary Study of the Zooarchaeological Record of Diouboye, Senegal." *Azania* 49, no. 3 (2014): 354–85.

Ehret, Christopher. "Linguistic Archaeology." *African Archaeological Review* 29, no. 2/3 (2012): 109–30.

———. *History and the Testimony of Language.* Berkeley: University of California Press, 2011.

———. "Bantu Expansions: Re-envisioning a Central Problem of Early African History." *International Journal of African Historical Studies* 34, no. 1 (2001): 5–41.

———. "The Establishment of Iron-Working in Eastern, Central, and Southern Africa: Linguistic Inferences on Technological History." *Sprache und Geschichte in Afrika* 16/17 (2000): 125–76.

———. "Testing the Expectations of Glottochronology against the Correlations of Language and Archaeology in Africa." In *Time Depth in Historical Linguistics,* ed. Colin Renfrew, April McMahon, and Larry Trask, 373–99. Cambridge: MacDonald Institute for Archaeological Research, 2000.

———. "Subclassifying Bantu: The Evidence of Stem Morpheme Innovations." In *Bantu Historical Linguistics: Theoretical and Empirical Perspectives,* ed. Jean-Marie Hombert and Larry M. Hyman, 43–163. Stanford, CA: Center for the Study of Language and Information Publications, 1999.

———. *An African Classical Age: Eastern and Southern Africa in World History, 1000 B.C. to A.D. 400.* Charlottesville: University of Virginia Press, 1998.

———. "Agricultural History in Central and Southern Africa, c. 1000 B.C. to A.D. 500." *Transafrican Journal of History* 4 (1974): 1–25.

Ehret, Christopher, and Merrick Posnansky, eds., *The Archaeological and Linguistic Reconstruction of African History.* Berkeley: University of California Press, 1982.

Ellingson, Ter. *The Myth of the Noble Savage.* Berkeley: University of California Press, 2001.

Embleton, Sheila. *Statistics in Historical Linguistics.* Bochum: Brockmeyer, 1986.

Fagan, Brian M. "Gundu and Nonde, Basanga and Mwanamaimpa." *Azania* 13 (1978): 127–34.

———. "Early Trade and Raw Materials in South Central Africa." *Journal of African History* 10, no. 1 (1969): 1–13.

————. *Iron Age Cultures in Zambia*, vol. 1. London: Chatto and Windus, 1967.

————. *Southern Africa in the Iron Age*. London and New York: Thames and Hudson, 1965.

————. "Pre-European Ironworking in Central Africa, with special reference to Northern Rhodesia." *Journal of African History* 2, no. 2 (1961): 199–210.

Fagan, Brian M., and D. W. Phillipson. "Sebanzi: The Iron Age Sequence at Lochnivar, and the Tonga." *Journal of the Royal Anthropological Institute of Great Britain and Ireland* 95, no. 2 (1965): 253–94.

Fagan, Brian M., D. W. Phillipson, and S. Daniels. *Iron Age Cultures in Zambia*, vol. 2. London: Chatto and Windus, 1969.

Feierman, Stephen. *Peasant Intellectuals: Anthropology and History in Tanzania*. Madison: University of Wisconsin Press, 1990.

————. *The Shambaa Kingdom: A History*. Madison: University of Wisconsin Press, 1974.

Fell, J. R. *Folk Tales of the BaTonga and Other Sayings*. London: Holborn Publishing House, 1930.

Ferguson, Arthur. *Utter Antiquity: Perceptions of Prehistory in Renaissance England*. Durham: Duke University Press, 1992.

Fielder, Robin. "Economic Spheres in Pre-colonial Ila Society." *African Social Research* 28 (December 1979): 617–41.

Fields-Black, Edda. *Deep Roots: Rice Farmers in West Africa and the African Diaspora*. Bloomington: Indiana University Press, 2008.

Finlayson, Bill and Graeme Warren. *Changing Natures: Hunter-Gatherers, First Farmers and the Modern World*. London: Duckworth, 2010.

Fisch, Maria. *The Caprivi Strip during the German Colonial Period, 1890–1914*. Windhoek, Namibia: Out of Africa Publishers, 1999.

Fleisher, Jeffrey, and Stephanie Wynne-Jones. "Authorisation and the Process of Power: The View from African Archaeology." *Journal of World Prehistory* 23 (2010): 177–93.

Flint, Lawrence. "State-Building in Central Southern Africa: Citizenship and Subjectivity in Barotseland and Caprivi." *International Journal of African Historical Studies* 36, no. 2 (2003): 393–428.

Fowler, Dennis. *The Ila Speaking: Records of a Lost World*. Hamburg: Lit, 2002.

————. *A Dictionary of Ila Usage, 1860–1960*. Hamburg: Lit, 2000.

Fredriksen, Per Ditlef, and Shadreck Chirikure. "Beyond Static Models: An Evaluation of Present Status and Future Prospects for Iron Age Research in Southern Africa." *Cambridge Archaeological Journal*, available on CJO 2015. doi:10.1017/S0959774314001115.

Garlake, Peter. "Iron Age Sites in the Urungwe District of Rhodesia." *South African Archaeological Bulletin* 25, no. 97 (1970): 25–44.

———. "Ecavations at the Seventeenth-Century Portuguese Site of Dambarare." *Proceedings and Transactions of the Rhodesia Scientific Association* 54, no. 1 (1969): 23–61.

Gifford-Gonzalez, Diane. "Animal Disease Challenges to the Emergence of Pastoralism in sub-Saharan Africa." *African Archaeological Review* 17, no. 3 (2000): 95–139.

Gonzales, Rhonda. *Societies, Religion, and History: Central-East Tanzanians and the World They Created, c. 200 B.C.E. to 1800 C.E.* New York: Columbia University Press, 2009.

Gordon, David. *Invisible Agents: Spirits in a Central African History.* Athens: Ohio University Press, 2012.

Guthrie, Malcolm. *Comparative Bantu,* 4 vols. Farnborough, Eng.: Gregg, 1967–71.

Guy, G. L. "*Andansonia Digitata* and Its Rate of Growth in Relation to Rainfall in South Central Africa." *Proceedings and Transactions of the Rhodesia Scientific Association* 54 (1969): 68–84.

Guyer, Jane. "Traditions of Invention in Equatorial Africa." *African Studies Review* 39, no. 3 (1996): 1–28.

———. "Wealth in People and Self-Realization in Equatorial Africa." *Man,* n.s., 28, no. 2 (1993): 243–65.

Guyer, Jane, and Samuel Eno Belinga. "Wealth in People as Wealth in Knowledge: Accumulation and Composition in Equatorial Africa." *Journal of African History* 36, no. 1 (1995): 91–120.

Hage, Per, and Jeff Marck. "Proto-Bantu Descent Groups." In *Kinship, Language and Prehistory: Per Hage and the Renaissance in Kinship Studies,* ed. Doug Jones and Bojka Milicic, 75–78. Salt Lake City: University of Utah Press, 2011.

Hall, Martin. *Farmers, Kings, and Traders: The People of Southern Africa, 200–1860.* Chicago: University of Chicago Press, 1990.

———. "Dendrochronology, Rainfall and Human Adaptation in the Later Iron Age of Natal and Zululand." *Annals of the Natal Museum* 22 (1976): 693–703.

Haller, T. "The Contested Floodplain: Institutional Change of Common Pool Resource Management and Conflicts among the Ila, Tonga, and Batwa, Kafue Flats (Southern Province), Zambia." Habilitation, University of Zurich, 2007.

Hanson, Holly. *Landed Obligation: The Practice of Power in Buganda*. Portsmouth, NH: Heinemann, 2003.

Hard, Donna, and Robert Sussman. *Man the Hunted: Primates, Predators, and Human Evolution*. Boulder: Westview Press, 2005.

Harlan, J. "Agricultural Origins: Centers and Noncenters." *Science*, n.s., 174 (1971): 468–74.

Heine, K. "The Main Stages of the Late Quaternary Evolution of the Kalahari Region, Southern Africa." *Palaeoecology of Africa* 15 (1982): 53–76.

Herbert, Eugenia. *Iron, Gender and Power: Rituals of Transformation in African Societies*. Bloomington: Indiana University Press, 1993.

———. *Red Gold of Africa: Copper in Precolonial History and Culture*. Madison: University of Wisconsin Press, 1984.

Hermitte, Eugene. "An Economic History of Barotseland, 1800–1940." PhD diss., Northwestern University, 1974.

Herskovtis, Melville J. "The Cattle Complex in East Africa." *American Anthropologist*, n.s., 28, nos. 1–4 (1926): 230–72; 361–88; 494–528; 633–64.

Hiernaux, Jean, Emona Longrée, and Josse de Buyst. *Fouilles Archéologique dans la Vallée du Haute Lualaba, I. Sanga, 1958*. Tervuren: Musée Royal de l'Afrique Centrale, 1971.

Hodder, Ian. *The Domestication of Europe: Structure and Contingency in Neolithic Societies*. Oxford: Blackwell, 1990.

Holy, Ladislav. *Strategies and Norms in a Changing Matrilineal Society: Descent, Succession and Inheritance among the Toka of Zambia*. Cambridge: Cambridge University Press, 1986.

Homewood, Katherine. *Ecology of African Pastoralist Societies*. Athens: Ohio University Press, 2008.

Hoover, J. Jeffery. "The Seduction of Ruwej: Reconstructing Ruund History (The Nuclear Lunda; Zaire, Angola, Zambia)," 2 vols. PhD diss., Yale University, 1978.

Huffman, Thomas. "Social Complexity in Southern Africa." *African Archaeological Review* 32 (2015): 71–91.

———. *Iron Age Migrations: The Ceramic Sequence in Southern Zambia*. Johannesburg: Witwatersrand University Press, 1989.

Iliffe, John. *Honour in African History*. New York: University of Cambridge Press, 2005.

Ingold, Tim. *Lines: A Brief History*. New York: Routledge, 2007.

Inskeep, Ray. "An Iron-Smelting Furnace in Southern Zambia." *South African Archaeological Bulletin* 33 (1978): 113–17

———. "Some Iron Age Sites from Northern Rhodesia." *South African Archae-ological Bulletin* 14 (1962): 91–96.

Isaacman, Allen F., and Barbara S. Isaacman. *Slavery and Beyond: The Making of Men and Chikunda Ethnic Identities in the Unstable World of South-Central Africa, 1750–1920*. Portsmouth, NH: Heinemann, 2004.

Jalla, A. *Silozi-English Dictionary*. 3rd ed. Lusaka: National Educational Co. of Zambia, 1982.

Janko, Jan. "Two Concepts of the World in Greek and Roman Thought: Cyclicity and Degeneration." In *Nature and Society in Historical Context*, ed. Mikuláš Teich, Roy Porter, and Bo Gustafsson, 18–36. Cambridge: Cambridge University Press, 1997.

Jaspan, M. A. *The Ila-Tonga Peoples of North-western Rhodesia*. London: International African Institute, 1953.

Kahlheber, Stefanie, Koen Bostoen, and Katharina Neumann. "Early Plant Cultivation in the Central African Rain Forest: First Millennium BC Pearl Millet from South Cameroon." *Journal of African Archaeology* 7, no. 2 (2009): 253–72.

Kalk, Margaret, A. J. McLachlan, and C. Howard-Williams, eds. *Lake Chilwa: Studies of Change in a Tropical Ecosystem*. The Hague: W. Junk, 1979.

Kangumu, Bennett. *Contesting Caprivi: A History of Colonial Isolation and Regional Nationalism in Namibia*. Basel: Basler Afrika Bibliographien, 2011.

Katanekwa, Nicholas. "Some Early Iron Age Sites from the Machili Valley of South Western Zambia." *Azania* 13 (1978): 135–66.

Keane, Webb. "Signs Are Not the Garb of Meaning: On the Social Analysis of Material Things." In *Materiality*, ed. Daniel Miller, 182–205. Durham: Duke University Press, 2006.

Kelly, Robert. *The Foraging Spectrum: Diversity in Hunter-Gatherer Lifeways*. Washington, DC: Smithsonian Institution Press, 1995.

Kent, Susan, ed. *Cultural Diversity among Twentieth-Century Foragers: An African Perspective*. Cambridge: Cambridge University Press, 1996.

Kent, Susan. *Farmers as Hunters: The Implications of Sedentism*. Cambridge: Cambridge University Press, 1989.

Killick, David. "Cairo to Cape: The Spread of Metallurgy through Eastern and Southern Africa." *Journal of World Prehistory* 22 (2009): 399–414.

———. "Technology in its Social Setting: Bloomery Iron-Smelting at Kasungu, Malawi, 1860–1940." PhD diss., Yale University, 1990.

Kingsley, Judith. "Pre-colonial Society and Economy in a Bisa Chiefdom of Northern Zambia." PhD diss., University of Michigan, 1980.

Klein-Arendt, Reinhard. *Die traditionellen Eisenbandwerke der Savannen-Bantu: Eine sprachhistorische Rekonstruktion auf lexicalischer Grundlage*. Frankfurt: Peter Lang, 2004.

Klieman, Kairn. *"The Pygmies Were Our Compass": Bantu and Batwa in the History of West Central Africa, Early Times to c. 1900 C.E.* Portsmouth, NH: Heinemann, 2003.

Kodesh, Neil. *Beyond the Royal Gaze: Clanship and Public Healing in Buganda*. Charlottesville: University of Virginia Press, 2010.

———. "Networks of Knowledge: Clanship and Collective Well-Being in Buganda." *Journal of African History* 49 (2008): 197–216.

Kopytoff, Igor. "The Internal African Frontier: The Making of African Political Culture." In *The African Frontier*, ed. Igor Kopytoff, 3–84. Bloomington: Indiana University Press, 1987.

Kreike, Emmanuel. *Re-creating Eden: Land Use, Environment, and Society in Southern Angola and Northern Namibia*. Portsmouth, NH: Heinemann, 2004.

Kriger, Colleen. *Pride of Men: Ironworking in 19th Century West Central Africa*. Portsmouth, NH: Heinemann, 1999.

Kuper, Adam. *The Invention of Primitive Society: Transformations of an Illusion*. New York: Routledge, 1988.

———. "Lineage Theory: A Critical Retrospect." *Annual Review of Anthropology* 11 (1982): 71–95.

Kusimba, Chapurukha. *The Rise and Fall of Swahili States*. Walnut Creek, CA: AltaMira, 1999.

Kusimba, Chapurukha, Sibel Kusimba, and David Wright. "The Development and Collapse of Precolonial Ethnic Mosaics in Tsavo, Kenya." *Journal of African Archaeology* 3, no. 2 (2005): 243–65.

Lancaster, Chet. "Ethnic Identity, History and the 'Tribe; in the Middle Zambezi Valley." *American Ethnologist* 1 (1974): 707–30.

Lancaster, Chet, and A. Pohorilenko. "Ingombe Ilede and the Zimbabwe Culture." *International Journal of African Historical Studies* 10, no. 1 (1977): 1–30.

Lancaster, Chet, and Kenneth Vickery, eds. *The Tonga-Speaking Peoples of Zambia and Zimbabwe*. New York: University Press of America, 2007.

Landau, Paul. *Popular Politics in the History of South Africa, 1400–1948*. Cambridge: Cambridge University Press, 2010.

Langworthy, Harry. *Zambia before 1890: Aspects of Pre-colonial History*. London: Longman, 1972.

Lee, Richard B., and Irven DeVore, eds. *Man the Hunter*. Chicago: Aldine, 1968.

Lehmann, Dorothy. "Languages of the Kafue Basin: Introductory Notes." In *Language in Zambia*, ed. Sirarpi Ohannessian and Mubanga Kashoki, 101–20. London: International African Institute, 1979.

Liengme, C. "Plants Used by the Tonga People of Gazankulu." *Bothalia* 13 (1981): 501–18.

Livingstone, David A. "A 22,000 Year Pollen Record from the Plateau of Zambia." *Limnology and Oceanography* 16 (1971): 349–56.

Livingstone, D., and C. Livingstone. *Narrative of an Expedition to the Zambesi and Its Tributaries: And of the Discovery of the Lakes Shirwa and Nyassa, 1858–1864*. London: John Murray, 1865.

Machila, Emmerson L. M. C. M. "A History of the Malende among the Tonga of Southern Province of Zambia: A Case Study of Chief Hanjalika's Area, 1890–1986." Master's thesis, University of Zambia, 1987.

MacGaffey, Wyatt. "A Note on Vansina's Invention of Matrilinearity," *Journal of African History* 54, no. 2 (2013): 269 80.

———. "Changing Representations in Central African History." *Journal of African History* 46 (2005): 189–207.

———. "Personhood of Ritual Objects: Kongo 'Minkisi.' " *Etnofoor* 3, no. 1 (1991): 45–61.

———. "Complexity, Astonishment, and Power: The Visual Vocabulary of Kongo Minkisi." *Journal of Southern African Studies* 14 (1988): 188–203.

MacLaren, P. *The Fishing Devices of Central and Southern Africa*. Rhodes-Livingstone Museum Occasional Paper No. 12. Manchester: Manchester University Press, 1958.

Macola, Giacomo. *Liberal Nationalism in Central Africa: A Biography of Harry Mwaanga Nkumbula*. New York: Palgrave Macmillan, 2010.

———. *The Kingdom of Kazembe: History and Politics in North-Eastern Zambia and Katanga to 1950*. Munster: Lit Verlag, 2002.

Madan, A. C. *Lenje Handbook*. Oxford: Clarendon Press, 1908.

Mainga, Mutumba. *Bulozi under the Luyana Kings: Political Evolution and State Formation in Pre-colonial Zambia*. London: Longmans, 1973.

Manchishi, P. C., and E. T. Musona. *The People of Zambia: A Short History of the Soli from 1500 to 1900*. Lusaka: Multimedia Publication, n.d.

Maniacky, Jacky. "Quelques thèmes pour 'igname' en bantu." In *Studies in African Comparative Linguistics*, ed. Koen Bostoen and Jacky Maniacky, 165–87. Tervuren, Belgium: Royal Museum for Central Africa, 2005.

Manning, Katie, Ruth Pelling, Tom Higham, Jean-Luc Schwenniger, and Dorian Q. Fuller. "4500-Year Old Domesticated Pear Millet (Pennisetum glaucum) from the Tilemsi Valley, Mali: New Insights into an Alternative Cereal Domestication Pathway." *Journal of Archaeological Science* 38 (2011): 312–22.

Marck, Jeff, and Koen Bostoen. "Proto-Oceanic Society (Austronesian) and Proto-East Bantu Society (Niger-Congo) Residence, Descent, and Kin Terms, ca. 1000 BC." In *Kinship, Language and Prehistory: Per Hage and the Renaissance in Kinship Studies,* ed. Doug Jones and Bojka Milicic, 83–91. Salt Lake City: University of Utah Press, 2011.

Marks, Stuart. *Large Mammals and a Brave People: Subsistence Hunters in Zambia.* Seattle: University of Washington Press, 1976.

Matthews, Timothy. "Portuguese, Chikunda, and the People of the Lower Gwembe Valley: The Impact of the Lower Zambezi Complex on Southern Zambia." *Journal of African History* 22 (1981): 23–41.

———. "The Historical Tradition of the People of the Gwembe Valley, Middle Zambezi." PhD diss., School for Oriental and African Studies, 1976.

Mavhunga, Clapperton. *Transient Workspaces: Technologies of Everyday Innovation in Zimbabwe.* Cambridge, MA: MIT Press, 2014.

McGregor, Joann. *Crossing the Zambezi: The Politics of Landscape on a Central African Frontier.* Oxford: James Currey, 2009.

McIntosh, Roderick. *Ancient Middle Niger: Urbanism and the Self-Organizing Landscape.* Cambridge: Cambridge University Press, 2005.

McIntosh, Susan K., ed, *Beyond Chiefdoms: Pathways to Complexity in Africa.* Cambridge: Cambridge University Press, 1999.

Medeiros, Eduardo, and José Capela. "Processes of Identity Building in the Zambesi Valley: Ethnic Solidarity and the Zambesian Ethos." In *Ethnicity and the Long-Term Perspective: The African Experience,* ed. Alexander Keese, 35–65. Bern: Peter Lang, 2010.

Meek, R. L. *Social Science and the Ignoble Savage.* Cambridge: Cambridge University Press, 1976.

Meeussen, A. E. *Bantu Lexical Reconstructions.* Tervuren, Belgium: Musée Royal de l'Afrique Centrale, 1980.

Miller, Duncan. *The Tsodilo Jewelry: Metal Work from Northern Botswana.* Cape Town: University of Cape Town Press, 1996.

Miller, Joseph. *Way of Death: Merchant Capitalism and the Angolan Slave Trade, 1730–1830.* Madison: University of Wisconsin Press, 1988.

————. *Kings and Kinsmen: Early Mbundu States in Angola*. Oxford: Clarendon Press, 1976.

————. *Cokwe Expansion, 1850–1900*. Occasional Papers of the University of
Wisconsin African Studies Program, no. 1. Madison: University of Wisconsin Press, 1967.

Mills, E. A., and N. T. Filmer. "Chondwe Iron Age Site, Ndola, Zambia." *Azania* 7 (1972): 129–45.

Miracle, Marvin. "Plateau Tonga Entrepreneurs in Historical Inter-regional
Trade." *Rhodes-Livingstone Journal* 26 (1959): 34–50.

Monroe, J. Cameron. "Power and Agency in Precolonial African States." *Annual Review of Anthropology* 42 (2013): 17–35.

Moore, Henrietta, and Megan Vaughan. *Cutting Down Trees: Gender, Nutrition,
and Agricultural Change in the Northern Province of Zambia, 1890–1990*.
Portsmouth, NH: Heinemann, 1993.

Morris, Jonathan Sherman. "The Myth of Rapid Language Change," parts 1–4.
Mother Tongue 13 (2008): 41–61; 14 (2009): 51–72; 15 (2010): 79–100; 16
(2011): 137–98.

Mukanzubo Kalinda Institute. *Chitonga-English Dictionary*. Monze, Zambia:
Mukanzubo Kalinda Institute, 2011.

Musonda, Francis. "Cultural and Social Patterning in Economic Activities and
Their Implications for Archaeological Interpretation: A Case Study from
the Kafue Basin, Zambia." *African Studies* 48 (1989): 55–69.

————. "The Significance of Pottery in Zambian Later Stone Age Contexts."
African Archaeological Review 5, no. 1 (1987): 147–58.

Mwewa, Stephen Kapita. *Meeting the Soli People in their Cultural Environment*.
Lusaka: Stephen Kapita Mwewa Publication, 2010.

Nash, Jay. *Ruwund Vocabularies*. Occasional Papers Series, no. 3. Urbana: Center for African Studies, University of Illinios at Urbana-Champaign, 1991.

Næss, Åshild. *Prototypical Transitivity*. Amsterdam: J. Benjamins, 2007.

Nenquin, J. *Excavations at Sanga, 1957*. Tervuren, Belgium: Musée Royal de
l'Afrique Centrale, 1963.

Newitt, Malyn. "Kinship, Religion, Language and Political Control: Ethnic
Identity among the Peoples of the Zambesi Valley." In *Ethnicity and the
Long-Term Perspective: The African Experience*, ed. Alexander Keese, 67–
92. Bern: Peter Lang, 2010.

————. *History of Portuguese Overseas Expansion, 1400–1668*. London: Routledge, 2005.

Nkazi, L. *Citonga Note Book*. London: Longman, 1957.

Nkolola-Wakumelo, Mildred. "Names of Cattle and the Cattle-Naming System among the Tonga of Zambia." In *Tonga Timeline: Appraising Sixty Years of Multidisciplinary Research in Zambia and Zimbabwe*, ed. Lisa Cliggett and Virginia Bond, 81–108. Lusaka: Lembani Trust, 2013.

Nugent, Christopher. "The Zambezi River: Tectonism, Climate Change and Drainage Evolution." *Palaeogeography, Palaeoclimatology, Palaeoecology* 78, no. 1/2 (May 1990): 55–69.

Nurse, Derek. "Towards a Historical Classification of East African Bantu Languages." In *Bantu Historical Linguistics: Theoretical and Empirical Perspectives*, ed. Jean- Marie Hombert and Larry M. Hyman, 1–43. Stanford, CA: CSLI, 1999.

———. "The Contributions of Linguistics to the Study of History in Africa." *Journal of African History* 38, no. 3 (1997): 359–91.

Nurse, Derek, and Thomas Hinnebusch. *Swahili and Sabaki: A Linguistic History*. Berkeley: University of California Press, 1993.

Nurse, Derek and Thomas Spear. *The Swahili: Reconstructing the History and Language of an African Society, 800–1500*. Philadelphia: University of Pennsylvania Press, 1985.

Oakely, Kenneth. "The Dating of Australopithecinae of Africa." *American Journal of Physical Anthropology* 12 (1954): 9–28.

O'Brien, Daniel. "Chiefs of Rain—Chiefs of Ruling: A Reinterpretation of Precolonial Tonga (Zambian) Social and Political Structures." *Africa* 53, no. 4 (1983): 21–41.

Oliver, Roland. "The Problem of the Bantu Expansion." *Journal of African History* 7, no. 3 (1966): 361–376.

Oliver, Roland, and Brian Fagan. *Africa in the Iron Age*. Cambridge: Cambridge University Press, 1975.

Orton, Jayson, Peter Mitchell, Richard Klein, Teresa Steele, and K. Ann Horsburgh. "An Early Date for Cattle from Namaqualand, South Africa: Implications for the Origins of Herding in Southern Africa." *Antiquity* 87 (2013): 108–20.

Packard, Randall. *Chiefship and Cosmology: An Historical Study of Political Competition*. Bloomington: Indiana University Press, 1981.

Papstein, Robert Joseph. "The Upper Zambezi: A History of the Luvale People, 1000–1900." PhD diss., University of California, Los Angeles, 1978.

Peterson, Derek. *Ethnic Patriotism and the East African Revival: A History of Dissent*. Cambridge: Cambridge University Press, 2012.

Pfouts, Anita. "Economy and Society in Northern Namibia 500 B.C.E. to 1800 C.E.: A Linguistic Approach." PhD diss., University of California, Los Angeles, 2003.

Philippson, Gérard, and S. Bahuchet. "Cultivated Crops and Bantu Migrations in Central and Eastern Africa: A Linguistic Approach." *Azania* 29/30 (1994/1995): 103–20.

Phillipson, D. W. *African Archaeology.* 3rd ed. Cambridge: Cambridge University Press, 2005.

———. "The First South African Pastoralists and the Early Iron Age." *Nsi* 6 (1989): 127–34.

———. *Later Prehistory of Eastern and Southern Africa.* New York: Africana Publishing Company, 1977.

———. "Early Iron Age Sites on the Zambian Copperbelt." *Azania* 7 (1972): 93–128.

———. "Excavations at Twickenham Road, Lusaka." *Azania* 5 (1970): 77–118.

———. "The Early Iron Age Site at Kapwirimbwe, Lusaka." *Azania* 3 (1968): 87 105.

Phillipson, David W., and Brian Fagan. "The Date of the Ingombe Ilede Burials." *Journal of African History* 10, no. 2 (1969), 199–204.

Phiri, Kings M. "Chewa History in Central Malawi and the Use of Oral Traditions, 1600–1920." PhD diss., University of Wisconsin, 1975.

Pikirayi, Innocent. *The Zimbabwe Culture: Origins and Decline of Southern Zambezian States.* Walnut Creek, CA: AltaMira Press, 2001.

———. *The Archaeological Identity of the Mutapa State: Towards an Historical Archaeology of Northern Zimbabwe.* Uppsala: Societas Archaeologica Upsaliensis, 1993.

Pluciennik, M. "The Meaning of 'Hunter-Gatherers' and Modes of Subsistence: A Comparative Historical Perspective." In *Hunter-Gatherers in History, Archaeology and Anthropology,* ed. Alan Barnard, 17–29. Oxford: Berg, 2004.

———. "The Invention of Hunter-Gatherers in Seventeenth-Century Europe." *Archaeological Dialogues* 9 (2002): 98–151.

———. "Archaeology, Anthropology, and Subsistence." *Journal of the Royal Anthropological Institute,* n.s., 7 (2001): 741–58.

Prestholdt, Jeremy. *Domesticating the World: African Consumerism and the Genealogies of Globalization.* Berkeley: University of California Press, 2008.

Price, Douglas, and James Brown, eds., *Prehistoric Hunter-Gatherers: The Emergence of Cultural Complexity.* New York: Academic Press, 1985.

Prins, Gwyn. *The Hidden Hippopotamus, Reappraisal in African History: The Early Colonial Experience in Western Zambia.* Cambridge: Cambridge University Press, 1980.

Pritchett, James. *Friends for Life, Friends for Death: Cohorts and Consciousness among the Lunda-Ndembu.* Charlottesville: University of Virginia Press, 2007.

Pwiti, Gilbert. *Continuity and Change: An Archaeological Study of Farming Communities in Northern Zimbabwe, AD 500–1700.* Uppsala: Department of Archaeology, 1996.

Reefe, Thomas Q. *Rainbow and the Kings: A History of the Luba Empire to 1891.* Berkeley: University of California Press, 1981.

Reid, Andrew, and Alinah Segobye. "Politics, Society, and Trade on the Eastern Margins of the Kalahari." *Goodwin Series* 8 (2000): 58–68.

Renfrew, Colin. *Prehistory: The Making of the Human Mind.* London: Weidenfeld and Nicolson, 2007.

Rennie, J. K. "Traditional Society and Modern Ddevelopments in Namwala District." In *Proceedings of the National Seminar on Environment and Change: The Consequences of Hydroelectric Power Development on the Utilization of the Kafue Flats, Lusaka, April 1978,* ed. G. W. Howard and G. J. Williams, 35–46. Lusaka: Kafue Basin Research Committee of the University of Zambia, 1982.

Reynolds, Barrie. *The Material Culture of the Peoples of the Gwembe Valley.* Manchester: Manchester University Press, 1968.

Reynolds, Pamela, and C. C. Cousins. *Lwaano Lwanyika: Tonga Book of the Earth.* London: Panos Publications, 1989.

Richards, Audrey. *Land, Labor, and Diet in Northern Rhodesia: An Economic Study on the Bemba Tribe.* Oxford: Oxford University Press, 1939.

Robbins, Lawrence, and M. L. Murphy. "Archaeology, Palaeoenvironment and Chronology of the Tsodilo Hills White Paintings Rock Shelter, Northwest Kalahari Desert, Botswana." *Journal of Archaeological Science* 27, no. 11 (2000): 1086–1111.

Robbins, Lawrence, Michael L. Murphy, Alec C. Cambell, and George A. Brook. "Intensive Mining of Specular Hematite in the Kalahari, A.D. 800–1000." *Current Anthropology* 39 (1998): 144–50.

Roberts, Andrew. *A History of Zambia.* New York: Africana, 1976.

———. *A History of the Bemba: Political Change in North-eastern Zambia before 1900.* Madison: University of Wisconsin Press, 1973.

————. "Pre-colonial Trade in Zambia." *African Social Research* 10 (1970): 715–46.

Roberts, Mary Nooter, and Allen F. Roberts. *Memory: Luba Art and the Making of History.* New York: Museum for African Art, 1996.

Robertshaw, Peter, Marilee Wood, Erik Mechiorre, Rachel Popelka-Filcoff, and Michael Glascock. "Southern African Glass Beads: Chemistry, Glass Sources, and Patterns of Trade." *Journal of Archaeological Science* 17 (2010): 1898–1912.

Robertson, John. "South African Early Iron Age in Zambia." In *Encyclopedia of Prehistory,* vol. 1: *Africa,* ed. Peter Peregrine and Melvin Ember, 260–71. New York: Springer, 2001.

————. "Early Iron Age Archaeology in Central Zambia." *Azania* 35 (2000): 147–82.

————. "Disease and Culture Change in South Central Africa." In *Culture and Environment: A Fragile Coexistance,* ed. Ross Jamieson, Sylvia Abonyi, and Neil Mirau, 165–73. Calgary: University of Calgary, 1993.

. "Origin and Development of the Early Iron Age in South Central Africa." PhD diss., Union Institute, 1991.

————. "A New Early Iron Age Pottery Tradition from South-Central Africa." *Nyame Akuma* 32 (1989): 59–64.

Robertson, John, and Rebecca Bradley. "A New Paradigm: The African Early Iron Age without the Bantu Migrations." *History in Africa* 27 (2000): 287–323.

Rockel, Stephen J. *Carriers of Culture: Labor on the Road in Nineteenth-Century East Africa.* Portsmouth, NH: Heinemann, 2006.

Rudebeck, E. *Tilling Nature, Harvesting Culture: Exploring Images of the Human Being in the Transition to Agriculture.* Stockholm: Almqvist and Wiksell International, 2000.

Sadr, Karim. "The Neolithic of Southern Africa." *Journal of African History* 44 (2003): 195–209.

Sahlins, Marshall. *Stone Age Economics.* Chicago: Aldine, 1972.

————. "Notes on the Original Affluent Society." In *Man the Hunter,* ed. Richard Lee and Irven DeVore, 85–89. Chicago: Aldine, 1968.

Saidi, Christine. *Women's Authority and Society in Early East-Central Africa.* Rochester: University of Rochester Press, 2010.

Sapir, Edward. "Time Perspective in Aboriginal American Culture: A Study in Method." In *Selected Writings of Edward Sapir in Language, Culture, and*

Personality, ed. David Mandelbaum, 389–467. Berkeley: University of California Press, 1985.

Sassaman, Kenneth. "Complex Hunter-Gatherers in Evolution and History: A North American Perspective." *Journal of Archaeological Research* 12, no. 3 (2004): 227–80.

Schadeberg, Thilo. "Derivation." In *The Bantu Languages,* ed. Derek Nurse and Gérard Philippson, 71–89. New York: Routledge, 2003.

———. "Die extensive Extension im Bantu." In *Sprachen und Sprachzeugnisse in Afrika,* ed. T. Geider and R. Kastenholz, 357–66. Cologne: Rüdiger Köppe, 1994.

Schecter, Robert. "*A Propos* the Drunken King: Cosmology and History." In *The African Past Speaks: Essays on Oral Tradition and History,* ed. Joseph Miller, 108–25. Kent: Archon, 1980.

Schmidt, Peter. *Iron Technology in East Africa: Symbolism, Science, and Archaeology.* Bloomington: Indiana University Press, 1997.

Schoenbrun, David L. "Mixing, Moving, Making, Meaning: Possible Futures for the Distant Past." *African Archaeological Review* 29, no. 2/3 (2012): 293–317.

———. "Violence, Marginaltiy, Scorn and Honour: Language Evidence of Slavery to the Eighteenth Century." In *Slavery in the Great Lakes Region of East Africa,* ed. Herni Médard and Shane Doyle, 38–75. Athens: Ohio University Press, 2007.

———. *A Green Place, a Good Place: Agrarian Change, Gender, and Social Identity in the Great Lakes Region to the 15th Century.* Portsmouth, NH: Heinemann, 1998.

———. *Historical Reconstruction of Great Lakes Cultural Vocabulary: Etymologies and Distributions.* Cologne: Rüdiger Köppe, 1997.

———. "An Intellectual History of Power: Usable Pasts from the Great Lakes Region." In *Aspects of African Archaeology,* ed. Gilbert Pwiti and Robert Soper, 693–702. Harare: University of Zimbabwe Press, 1996.

Scott, James. *The Art of Not Being Governed: An Anarchist History of Upland Southeast Asia.* New Haven: Yale University Press, 2009.

Scudder, Thayer. *Gathering among African Woodland Savannah Cultivators.* Zambian Papers, no. 5. Manchester: Manchester University Press, 1971.

———. *The Ecology of the Gwembe Tonga.* Manchester: Manchester University Press, 1962.

———. "Fishermen of the Zambezi." *Rhodes-Livingstone Journal* 27 (1960): 41–49.

Shaw, Paul A. "Late Quaternary Landforms and Environmental Change in North-west Botswana: The Evidence of Lake Ngami and the Mabebe Depression." *Transactions of the Institute of British Geographers* 10 (1985): 333–46.

———. "Lake Chilwa and the Iron Age." *Palaeoecology of Africa* 16 (1984).

———. "Fluctuations in the Level of Lake Ngami: The Historical Evidence." *Botswana Notes and Records* 15 (1983): 79–84.

Shaw, Paul, Mark Bateman, David Thomas, and Frances Davies. "Holocene Fluctuations of Lake Ngami, Middle Kalahari: Chronology and Responses to Climate Change." *Quaternary International* 111 (2003): 23–35.

Shaw, T., P. Sinclair, B. Andah, and A. Okpoko, eds. *The Archaeology of Africa: Food, Metals, and Towns.* London: Routledge, 1993.

Shetler, Jan. *Imagining Serengeti: A History of Landscape Memory in Tanzania from Earliest Times to the Present.* Athens: Ohio University Press, 2007.

Siamwiza, Bennett. "Famine and Hunger in the History of the Gwembe Valley, Zambia, c. 1850–1958." In *The Tonga-Speaking Peoples of Zambia and Zimbabwe*, ed. Chet Lancaster and Kenneth P. Vickery, 237–61. Lanham, MD: University Press of America, 2007.

Sinclair, Paul, Anneli Ekblom, and Marilee Wood. "Trade and Society on the South-East African Coast in the Later First Millennium AD: The Case of Chibuene." *Antiquity* 86 (2012): 723–37.

Smith, Edwin W. *A Handbook of the Ila Language.* London: Oxford University Press, 1907.

Smith, Edwin W., and Andrew M. Dale. *The Ila-Speaking Peoples of Northern Rhodesia.* 2 vols. London: Macmillan, 1920.

Smith, Paul, ed. *Ecological Survey of Zambia: The Traverse Records of C. G. Trapnell.* 3 vols. Kew: The Board of Trustees of the Royal Botanic Gardens, 2001.

Sollas, William. *Ancient Hunters and their Modern Representatives.* London: Macmillan, 1911.

Stahl, Ann. "Political Economic Mosaics: Archaeology of the Last Two Millennia in Tropical Sub-Saharan Africa." *Annual Review of Anthropology* 33 (2004): 145–72.

———., ed. *African Archaeology.* Malden, MA: Blackwell, 2005.

Star, Susan Leigh, and James Griesemer. "Institutional Ecology: 'Translations' and Boundary Objects: Amateurs and Professionals in Berkeley's Museum of Vertebrate Zoology, 1907–39." *Social Studies of Science* 19, no. 3 (1989): 387–420.

Steinhart, Edward. *Black Poachers, White Hunters: A Social History of Hunting in Colonial Kenya.* Oxford: James Currey, 2006.

————. "Elephant Hunting in Nineteenth-Century Kenya: Kamba Society and Ecology in Transformation." *International Journal of African Historical Studies* 33, no. 2 (2000): 335–49.

Stephens, Rhiannon. *A History of African Motherhood: The Case of Uganda, 700–1900.* Cambridge: Cambridge University Press, 2013.

————. "Birthing Wealth? Motherhood and Poverty in East-Central Uganda, c. 700–1900." *Past and Present* 215 (2012): 235–68.

————. "Lineage and Society in Precolonial Uganda." *Journal of African History* 50, no. 2 (2009): 203–21.

Stocking, George. *Race, Culture, and Evolution: Essays in the History of Anthropology.* Chicago: University of Chicago Press, 1968.

Styen, Maryna, and Willem Nienaber. "Iron Age Human Skeletal Remains from the Limpopo Valley and Soutpansberg Area." *Goodwin Series* 8 (2000): 112–16.

Sutherland-Harris, Nicola. "Zambian Trade with Zumbo in the Eighteenth Century." In *Pre-colonial African Trade,* ed. Richard Gray and David Birmingham, 231–42. London: Oxford University Press, 1970.

Thomas, David, and Paul Shaw. "Late Quaternary Environmental Change in Central Southern Africa: New Data, Synthesis, Issues and Prospects." *Quaternary Science Reviews* 21 (2002): 783–97.

Tlou, Thomas. *A History of Ngamiland, 1750–1906: The Formation of an African State.* Gaborone, Botswana: Macmillan Botswana, 1985.

Tomlinson, R. W. *The Imayanga Area: An Essay in Regional Biogeography.* Harare: University of Rhodesia Occasional Papers, 1973.

Torrend, Julius. *An English-Vernacular Dictionary of the Bantu-Botatwe Dialects of Northern Rhodesia.* Natal: Mariannhill, 1931.

Trigger, Bruce. *A History of Archaeological Thought.* 2nd ed. Cambridge: Cambridge University Press, 2006.

Tuden, Arthur. "The Political System of the Ba-Ila: An Analysis of Change and Stability in the Patterns of Authority." PhD diss., Northwestern University, 1962.

Turnbull, Colin. *The Forest People.* New York: Simon and Schuster, 1961.

Turner, G. "Early Iron Age Herders in Northwestern Botswana: The Faunal Evidence." *Botswana Notes & Records* 19 (1987): 7–23.

————. "Hunters and Herders of the Okavango Delta, Northern Botswana." *Botswana Notes & Records* 19 (1987): 25–40.

Turner, Victor. *The Ritual Process: Structure and Anti-Structure.* Chicago: Aldine, 1969.

————. *The Forest of Symbols: Aspects of Ndembu Ritual.* Ithaca: Cornell University Press, 1967.

Tyson, P. D., and J. A. Lindesay. "The Climate of the Last 2000 Years in Southern Africa." *Holocene* 2 (1992): 271–78.

van Binsbergen, Wim. " 'Then Give Him to the Crocodiles': Violence, State Formation, and Cultural Discontinuity in West Central Zambia, 1600–2000." In *The Dynamics of Power and the Rule of Law,* ed. Wim van Binsbergen and Riekje Pelgrim, 197–219. Munster: Lit, 2003.

————. *Tears of Rain: Ethnicity and History in Central Western Zambia.* London: Kegan Paul International, 1992.

————. *Religious Change in Zambia: Exploratory Studies.* London: Kegan Paul, 1981.

Vansina, Jan. "Linguistic Evidence for the Introduction of Ironworking in Bantu Speaking Africa." *History in Africa* 33 (2006): 321–63.

————. *How Societies Are Born: Governance in West Central Africa before 1600.* Charlottesville: University of Virginia Press, 2004.

————. "Pathways of Political Development in Equatorial Africa and Neo Evolutionary Theory." In *Beyond Chiefdoms: Pathways to Complexity in Africa,* ed. Susan McIntosh, 166–72. Cambridge: Cambridge University Press, 1999.

————. "Government in Kasai before the Lunda." *International Journal of African Historical Studies* 31, no. 1 (1998): 1–22.

————. "New Linguistic Evidence and 'the Bantu Expansion.' " *Journal of African History* 36, no. 2 (1995): 173–95.

————. "A Slow Revolution." *Azania* 29/30 (1994/1995): 15–26.

————. *Paths in the Rainforests: Toward a History of Political Tradition in Equatorial Africa.* Madison: University of Wisconsin Press, 1990.

————. "Do Pygmies Have a History?" *Sprache und Geschtichte in Afrika* 7, no. 1 (1986): 5–34.

————. "Bantu in the Crystal Ball," 2 parts. *History in Africa* 6 (1979): 287–333; 7 (1980): 293–325.

————. *Kingdoms of the Savanna.* Madison: University of Wisconsin Press, 1966.

Vencl, Slavomil. "The Problem of Disappearance of Hunter-Gatherer Societies in Prehistory: Archaeological Evidence and Testimonies of Classical Authors." *Listy Filologické* 111 (1988): 129–43.

Vickery, Kenneth. *Black and White in Southern Zambia: The Tonga Plateau Economy and British Imperialism, 1890–1939.* Westport, CT: Greenwood Press, 1986.

Vogel, Joseph O. "Savanna Farmers on the Sandveldt: Patterns of Land-Use and Organizational Behavior of Some Shifting Cultivators in South-Central Africa." *Azania* 24 (1989): 38–50.

———. "Iron Age Farmers in Southwestern Zambia: Some Aspects of Spatial-organization." *African Archaeological Review* 5 (1987): 159–70.

———. "Microenvrionments, Swidden and the Early Iron Age Settlement of South Western Zambia." *Azania* 21 (1986): 85–97.

———. "Subsistence Settlement Systems in the Prehistory of South-Western Zambia." *Human Ecology* 14 (1986): 397–414.

———. "An Early Iron Age Settlement System in Southern Zambia." *Azania* 19 (1984): 61–78.

———. "An Early Iron Age Burial from Chundu Farm, Zambia." *Zambia Museums Journal* 6 (1982): 118–25.

———. "Iron Age Pottery from the Victoria Falls Region." *Zambia Museums Journal* 5 (1980): 41–77.

———. "The Early Iron Age (A.D. 500–1100) in the Victoria Falls Region, Zambia." *Current Anthropology* 17, no. 4 (1976): 764–65.

———. "Kabondo Kumbo and the Early Iron Age in the Victoria Falls Region." *Azania* 10 (1975): 49–75.

———. *Simbusenga: The Archaeology of the Intermediate Period in Southern Zambia.* London: Oxford University Press for the National Museums of Zambia, 1975.

———. "The Early Iron Age Site at Sioma Mission, Western Zambia." *Zambia Museums Journal* 4 (1973): 153–69.

———. "The Mosioatunya Sequence: The Iron Age Cultures in the Victoria Falls Region of Zambia." *Zambia Museums Journal* 4 (1973): 105–52.

———. "Some Iron Age Sites in Southern and Western Zambia." *Azania* 8 (1973): 25–54.

———. "On Early Iron Age Funerary Practice in Southern Zambia." *Current Anthropology* 13 (1972): 583–86.

———. *Kamangoza: An Introduction to the Iron Age Cultures of the Victoria Falls Region.* Nairobi: Oxford University Press for the National Museums of Zambia, 1971.

———. *Kumadzulo: An Early Iron Age Village Site in Southern Zambia.* Lusaka: Oxford University Press for the National Museums of Zambia, 1971.

———. "Early Iron Age Tools from Chundu Farm, Zambia." *Azania* 6 (1970): 173–78.

von Oppen, Achim. *Terms of Trade and Terms of Trust: The History and Contexts of Pre-colonial Market Production around the Upper Zambezi and Kasai.* Munster: Lit, 1993.

Washburn, Sherwood. "Australopithecines: The Hunters or the Hunted?" *American Anthropologist* 9 (1957): 612–14.

Washburn, Sherwood, and Chet Lancaster. "The Evolution of Hunting." In *Man the Hunter,* ed. Richard Lee and Irven DeVore, 293–303. Chicago: Aldine, 1968.

Watkins, Trevor. "The Neolithic Revolution and the Emergence of Humanity: A Cognitive Approach to the First Comprehensive World View." In *Archaeological Perspectives on the Transmission and Transformation of Culture in the Eastern Mediterranean,* ed. J. Clarke, 84–88. Oxford: CBRL and Oxbow, 2005.

White, C. M. N. "The Role of Hunting and Fishing in Luvale Society." *African Studies* 15, no. 2 (1956): 75–86.

White Fathers. *Bemba-English Dictionary.* Rev. ed. Cape Town: Longmans, Green, 1954.

Wilmsen, Edwin. "Nqoma." *Botswana Notes & Records* 43 (2011): 95–114.

———. *Land Filled with Flies: A Political Economy of the Kalahari.* Chicago: University of Chicago Press, 1989.

Wilmsen, Edwin, and James Denbow. "Paradigmatic History of San-Speaking Peoples and Current Attempts at Revision." *Current Anthropology* 31, no. 5 (1990): 489–524.

Wilmsen, Edwin, David Killick, Dana Drake Rosenstein, Phenyo Thebe, and James Denbow. "The Social Geography of Pottery in Botswana as Reconstructed by Optical Petrography." *Journal of African Archaeology* 7 (2009): 3–39.

Wood, Marilee. *Interconnections: Glass Beads and Trade in Southern and Eastern Africa and the Indian Ocean, 7th to 16th Centuries AD.* Uppsala: Department of Archaeology, 2012.

Wood, Marilee, Laure Dussubieux, and Peter Robertshaw. "The Glass of Chibuene, Mozambique: New Insights into Early Indian Ocean Trade." *South African Archaeological Bulletin* 67, no. 195 (2012): 59–74.

Yengoyan, Aram. "Anthropological History and the Study of Hunters and Gatherers: Cultural and Non-Cultural." In *Hunter-Gatherers in History, Archaeology, and Anthropology,* ed. A. Barnard, 57–66. Oxford: Berg, 2004.

Yoder, J. C. *The Kanyok of Zaire: An Institutional and Ideological History to 1895.* Cambridge: Cambridge University Press, 1992.

Young, W. J. *The Quiet, Wise Spirit, Edwin W. Smith (1876–1957) and Africa.* London: Epworth Press, 2002.

Zvelebil, Marek. "The Invention of Hunter-Gatherers in Seventeenth Century Europe? A Comment on Mark Pluciennik." *Archaeological Dialogues* 9, no. 2 (2002): 123–29.

Index

Acephalous societies, 3, 17–18, 146, 223–24, 227–28

Affluent society theory, 12–13

Agriculture. *See* Cereal agriculture; Farming

-àmí. See Mwami

Ancestral spirits. *See* Spirits

Antelope, 27, 159–60, 165–68, 170, 189, 191

Bakwashi. See Mukwashi

Bakwesu. See Mukwesu

Bantu languages: Bantu Expansion, 35, 52; *chila* and, 162; Kaskazi, 52, 56, 85, 90, 109; Kusi, 52, 56–57, 90, 133, 139, 143–44, 153, 191; map, *53*; Savanna, 52, 66–68, 80, 88, 155, 166; in wooded grasslands, 66, 123–24, 177. *See also* Botatwe languages/societies

Basanga village, 82, 85, 134–39, 272n6, 280n2

Batoka Plateau, 22, 56; blended settlements on, 139, 146–47, 162; butchery patterns, 112, 163; cattle keeping, 84, 143–44, 193, 209; ceramic traditions, 40, 57, 137–39; mound sites, 36, 76, 134, 137, 138, 153, 178, 180, 183; railway towns, 28; trade, 183, 184, 210, 214

Belinga, Samuel Martin Eno, 114

Bellows-worker. *See Muvubi*

Big Man, authority of, 17–18, 20, 171, 198, 226–29

Bisson, Michael, 195

Bond friendship. *See Mulongo*

Borrowed words, 44–46, 50, 51, 55–57, 63, 73–75, 82–87, 89, 109, 142, 170–71, 177, 191, 200, 211–19, 216

Bosutswe, 188–89, 191

Botatwe languages/societies, 2; archaeological evidence, 34–41, *37–38*; borrowed words, 44–46, 50, 51, 55–57, 63, 73–75, 82–87, 89, 109, 142, 170–71, 177, 191, 200, 211–19, 216; central frontier, overview, 172–76; central frontier borderlands, 206–9, 211–19; central frontier networks, 178–83, 202–6, 217–18; centralized power, 207–8; classification of languages, 43–44; cognation rates, 42–43, 52; comparative linguistics, 41–51; as decentralized, 115; historical framework, 52–60; integrated subsistence system, 61; linguistic content, 44–49; linguistic framework, 42–44; linguistic uncertainties, 49–51; maps, *26, 54, 59, 174*; marginalization, 23; narrative framework, 52–60; north of Zambezi River, 190–93; as oral, 24; political culture, 3, 5, 15–16, 17, 20, 175, 218–19, 227–28; proto-Botatwe languages/speakers, 3–4, 21, 50, 52–55, 58, 60, 61–62, 63–79, 84, 87, 89, 91, 97, 141, 202; proto-Western Botatwe languages, 50, 55, 58, 74, 79; savannas, history, 24; settlements, 52–60, 78–80, *174*; social world, 63–66; south of Zambezi River, 177–78, 183–90; subsistence terminology, 5; subsistence theory/practice, 4–7; success and, 87–92; trade networks, 3–4, 177, 186–90, 192–94, 208, 211–14; along Zambezi River, 27. *See also* Bushcraft, Botatwe; *specific languages and protolanguages*